£5-00
(45)

The Five Books Of Machabees In English With Notes And Illustrations

You are holding a reproduction of an original work that is in the public domain in the United States of America, and possibly other countries. You may freely copy and distribute this work as no entity (individual or corporate) has a copyright on the body of the work. This book may contain prior copyright references, and library stamps (as most of these works were scanned from library copies). These have been scanned and retained as part of the historical artifact.

This book may have occasional imperfections such as missing or blurred pages, poor pictures, errant marks, etc. that were either part of the original artifact, or were introduced by the scanning process. We believe this work is culturally important, and despite the imperfections, have elected to bring it back into print as part of our continuing commitment to the preservation of printed works worldwide. We appreciate your understanding of the imperfections in the preservation process, and hope you enjoy this valuable book.

THE FIVE BOOKS

OF

MACCABEES

IN ENGLISH.

WITH NOTES AND ILLUSTRATIONS,

BY

HENRY COTTON, D.C.L.
ARCHDEACON OF CASHEL, AND LATE STUDENT OF CHRIST
CHURCH, OXFORD.

OXFORD,
AT THE UNIVERSITY PRESS.
MDCCCXXXII.

ANDOVER-HARVARD
THEOLOGICAL LIBRARY
CAMBRIDGE, MASS.

H65.810

March 14, 1942

BS
1823
.C6
1832

TO

THE PROVOST, FELLOWS, AND SCHOLARS,

OF

TRINITY COLLEGE, DUBLIN,

TO WHOSE VALUABLE LIBRARY

I HAVE HAD MOST LIBERAL ACCESS,

THE PRESENT PUBLICATION IS INSCRIBED,

IN TESTIMONY

OF RESPECT AND REGARD.

CONTENTS.

PREFACE	P. vii
Introduction	xi
The Greek text of Eleazar's prayer	xxxix
Genealogy of the Maccabees	xliii
———— of the family of Herod	xliv
Chronological table	xlv
Book I.	1
—— II.	43
—— III.	147
—— IV.	219
—— V.	277
Index	447

PREFACE.

IT is well known, that the history of the period intervening between the days of Nehemiah, where the accounts of the Old Testament close, and the birth of Jesus Christ, is very insufficiently attended to by the greater part of our students in theology.

For this defect there is indeed some show of reason: for the history of these times is scanty and incomplete; the narratives themselves being few in number, and moreover lying detached and dispersed in various places, with the single exception of the writings of Josephus.

With a view of removing one cause of this deficiency, I have collected together the writings of some ancient Jewish authors which refer to this period, translating some, and correcting the current versions of the rest: and have endeavoured to illustrate or confirm their statements, by noticing accounts of the same transactions, which are to be found in the works of Greek and Roman historians.

Of the five books presented in this volume, only two are familiar to the generality of readers, as being found in the editions of our English Bible. As for the others, scarcely one student in a hundred has heard their names; and perhaps not one in a thousand may have read a line of their contents. Yet, since they all contain interesting and valuable matter, I have here brought them together in an English dress, arranged in such a form as to be consulted or perused with the greatest ease and best prospect of advantage.

The history of each book, and of my labours upon it, will be found detailed in the Introduction. I have merely to add *here* a few words, on the *occasion* which has caused their appearance.

Driven from my parish, by the violence of that storm which has suddenly burst upon the heads of the Irish clergy,—at once reducing to the verge of ruin a body of men who were peaceably pursuing the duties of their holy calling, under the presumed sanction and protection of the laws, —men, against whom, be it remembered, *no charge has been produced, either of moral or ministerial delinquency;*—and thus compelled to seek temporary shelter at a distance from my home:—I judged it right to employ some portion of the leisure thus thrown upon my hands, in an occupation, which, while it was not unsuitable to my profession, might also hereafter have its use.

Doubtless the present work is susceptible of numerous improvements: and even in the same hands its execution might have been less faulty, under more favourable circumstances. Whatever literary aids this city could furnish, I have sought out, and have endeavoured to make available: but we cannot hope to find in every place all the works requisite for pursuing inquiries into points of ancient literature, nor every where to command the ample resources of

PREFACE.

the Bodleian Library or the British Museum.

For the omissions and imperfections, arising from this and other causes, I have to entreat the reader's kind forbearance: and to hope that, even in its present state, this publication may not be wholly unsuccessful, in calling the attention, more especially of students in divinity, to an important supplement to the inspired records of Holy Writ;—to a very instructive portion of Jewish history;—to those transactions, in which the Maccabæan family, " according " to the prophecies which went before" concerning them, took for some time so distinguished and influential a part, on behalf of the favoured country, the peculiar people of God.

H. C.

Dublin, 26th April, 1832.

INTRODUCTION.

THE portion of Jewish history, which is comprised between the return from Babylon and the birth of Jesus Christ, commends itself to our consideration on a variety of grounds.

Restored to their liberty and home by Cyrus, and furnished, both by him and several of his successors, with liberal supplies of all things necessary for their purpose, the Jews commenced and brought to a happy conclusion, the building of their "Second House." (B. C. 515.) Some few years afterwards, under the guidance of Nehemiah, they repaired the walls and private dwellings of Jerusalem; and, both there and throughout the other cities of Judæa, once more established the name and semblance of a people, and employed themselves, as heretofore, in the ordinary occupations of civil life.

But their condition was not such as it had been in the former golden days of their prosperity: their numbers were diminished, their resources were impaired, their limits circumscribed, their authority restricted; since now they were no longer governed by independent princes of their own, but were subjected to the uncertain and arbitrary controul of governors appointed by the kings of Persia.

We thus see them already placed in a new position: they are also entering on a new career of action; as being now brought into immediate contact with other nations; and about to bear their part in the fulfilment of those prophecies of Daniel, which speak of the rise and progress of the Grecian empire in Asia, and of the treatment which the religion and fortunes of the Jews should experience at the hands of the successors of Alexander.

Unable, by their numbers and position, to maintain their independence as a state, we find them falling alternately under the sway of Syria or of Egypt; and suffering perpetual annoyance from the mutual quarrels which arose between these states, in addition to the positive persecutions, on *religious* grounds, which they underwent from Ptolemy Philopator, (B. C. 217.) and from Antiochus Epiphanes.

One short bright space in their history succeeds, when resistance to religious tyranny procured for them civil freedom also: when under the leadership of the Asmonæan princes they obtained, not merely independence, but some portion of renown and splendour.

This light, however, was soon quenched through the bane of internal dissensions; and by the growing influence of the Romans, who now began to appear on the Eastern stage, and to take an active part in the politics of Asia and Egypt, they were consigned to the hands and dominion of a half-stranger in the person of Herod the Great; who wielded a sceptre, which he had obtained through rivers of blood, *really* at the will and beck of a Roman commander, though *nominally* retaining the name and diadem of a sovereign; because the Word of God had announced that "the sceptre " should not depart from Judah," till the Shiloh, the Messiah, should appear.

Mixed up as we have seen the Jews to have been during the above-named period, with the affairs, not only of Asia, but also of Greece and Rome, we might reasonably expect to find ample notices concerning them in the several Greek and Roman historians. To a certain extent this expectation has been realized: we still possess various and valuable information on Jewish matters, in the works of classic authors which are yet remaining; and there is ground for believing that much more of the same stamp and value has been lost to us, through that common misfortune which has deprived these later ages of so large a portion of the literary treasures bequeathed by the learned of former days.

Polybius, of Megalopolis in Arcadia, who flourished during the times of the Maccabees, and is known and valued for the extent and accuracy of his observations, had particular reasons for directing his attention to the Jewish affairs of his day; inasmuch as he was not only acquainted with the general outline of their proceedings, but enjoyed the personal and close friendship of Demetrius the Second, whose escape from Rome he certainly was privy to, and perhaps had originally advised. Polybius left behind him a history in forty books: of these, no more than five entire, with fragments of twelve others, have been preserved to the present time: but from these small remains we learn to estimate the extent of our loss: and, judging from that portion of Jewish history which we find in these fragments, we might have expected from his unmutilated works very considerable accessions of important information.

Diodorus Siculus lived during the reigns of Hyrcanus and Herod: he wrote a history of Roman affairs in forty books; of which only fifteen are now remaining, with extracts from some few of the rest. We collect that Diodorus had given particular attention to Jewish matters: in his 34th book he speaks of the bad character which that nation bore amongst foreigners, and relates several of the acts of Antiochus Epiphanes. Again, in a fragment of the fortieth book, there is evidence that he had written a narrative of Pompey's expedition against Jerusalem; as he begins with the words Ἡμεῖς δὲ μέλλοντες ἀναγράφειν τὸν πρὸς Ἰουδαίους πόλεμον, &c.: but all which now remains of this, whatever it might have been, is merely the introductory part, relating to the early history and habits of the Jews, such as they were believed by Diodorus to be. For the preservation of even this short fragment we are indebted to the most learned and diligent Photius, patriarch of Constantinople.

Another historian, who was contemporary with Herod the Great, is *Dionysius* of *Halicarnassus*:

but, as the plan of his work did not embrace the period of time with which these books are concerned, we are not to expect from him any thing either of corroborative or corrective information.

Strabo, the eminent Greek geographer, likewise, flourished before the death of Herod. He is said to have written some historical books; but these unfortunately are lost. This author is very frequently quoted by Josephus; and there is good ground for supposing that if his works had survived, they would have contained much valuable matter connected with this period of Jewish history.

Livy, who was alive during the time of Herod and Augustus, is well known to have related every thing belonging to Roman history with considerable minuteness of detail: but a very large portion of his great work has perished through lapse of time, and especially that part which contained the transactions belonging to the period of the Maccabees: had these survived, there is little doubt that, from the close connexion at this time existing between the affairs of Syria and Rome, ample notice and information upon various points of this our history would have been found in the pages of Livy.

Besides these writers, most of whom were living during the times of which the five books of Maccabees treat; and all of whom wrote their accounts or histories before Josephus published his great work on Jewish history, and therefore could not have been either biassed or informed at secondhand by him:—we find others, of high name and great celebrity, who have taken more or less pains in transmitting to posterity some memorials of the Jews and their affairs.

Tacitus, who lived at a time when the Jewish name and nation was either odious or utterly despised at Rome, after the final overthrow of Jerusalem,—has left to us, in the fifth book of his Histories, a short account of the origin and customs of the Jews; defective indeed and distorted, as rather through prejudice than ignorance. He relates the expedition of Pompey against Jerusalem; and probably in the latter part of that book, which unhappily has perished, had given a fuller detail of the part which the Romans took in the concerns of Judæa, from the commencement of Augustus' reign till the destruction of the Holy City by Titus.

Plutarch, who flourished about thirty years after the destruction of Jerusalem, has incidental notices of the Jews and their affairs.

Appian, about twenty or twenty-five years later, composed, among other works, a History of Syria: in which he relates the transactions of Antiochus the Great and his successors on the Syrian throne; likewise the deeds of Pompey in Judæa, and his putting an end to the dynasty of the Seleucidæ.

Athenæus is said to have written a history of Syria; but not a vestige of it is now remaining. He flourished at the close of the second century after Christ.

Besides the above named, *Dion Cassius* and some other authors are known to have touched

INTRODUCTION. xvii

more or less on points of Jewish history; but from none of them have we obtained, or at least do we now possess, any thing like a continuous or comprehensive work upon the subject.

It is manifest that all these united, interesting as they certainly are, and affording valuable confirmation of accounts derived from another quarter, are very far from supplying us with any thing like a complete history of the times, or furnishing that accurate or continuous information concerning the Jews and their transactions during this period, which we should greatly have desired to possess.

We turn therefore, not more naturally than necessarily, to the Jewish historians themselves; and enquire what amount of information we can gather thence, checked, and (if need be) corrected, by the concurrent testimonies of the writers of other nations. I say *checked* and *corrected:* for it is remembered that for all *this portion* of Jewish history we lack the infallible direction of inspired guides. The *historical* books of the Holy Scripture reach no lower in point of time than to Nehemiah (B. C. 434.): and from the *Prophets* who lived after the captivity, Haggai, Zachariah, and Malachi, we gather little or nothing of historical relation; and even Malachi, the last of these, wrote at a period nearly four hundred years antecedent to the birth of Christ.

We are dependant therefore upon such accounts as are transmitted to us by Josephus, who lived and wrote subsequently to the destruction of Je-

b

rusalem by Titus; and by certain other writers, whose relations, less known than his, or, at least, less studied, though some of them are prior in point of time, and perhaps superior in accuracy on many points, are here collected and exhibited in attempted order, as separate yet not useless links of a much to be desired chain.

Although the entire five treatises bear the same name, that of "*Books of Maccabees*," it is to be borne in mind that this connection between them is more nominal than real. Composed, perhaps at different times, by different authors, in different languages, on different subjects, they may derive importance and usefulness from juxta-position and a common name: but at the same time it is necessary that the reader should be furnished with a separate account of each; more especially, since I have felt it right to invert the order of some of them which are more familiar to common readers, with the view of making a chronological arrangement subservient to the purposes of general information.

BOOK I.

The *first* book, commonly known as the *third*, contains the history of not more than eight or nine years. It opens with the battle of Raphia, which was fought between Antiochus the Great, king of Syria, and Ptolemy Philopator, king of Egypt; in the third year of the 140th Olympiad,—of Rome 537,—of the Seleucidæ 96,—before Christ 217. The principal event recorded in it is the attempted punishment and extraordinary deliverance of the

INTRODUCTION. xix

Jews at Alexandria. This transaction, as we learn from chap. ii. took place during the high-priesthood of Simon, son of Onias, who succeeded to that office in the year B. C. 211.

This book in time is prior to both the second and the third, and in authority is considered superior to the latter[a]: although Philostorgius, a writer of the fourth century, declares it "mon-"strous" and full of improbabilities. Its author is unknown: he is supposed to have been a Jew of Alexandria; indeed some, as Franciscus Junius, attribute both this and the Book of *Wisdom* to Philo: and the work is thought by Dr. Allix ("Judgment of the Jewish Church") to have been written during the reign of Ptolemy Philopator, or a little after the Book of *Ecclesiasticus*, about two hundred years before Christ.

The Greek text is considered to be the Original. There is a Syriac version of it, to be seen in the Polyglott Bibles of Paris and London, and a literal Latin *from this Syriac* is given in the Bible of P. de la Haye. There is no *ancient Latin*; but a *modern* one, by Nobilius, is in the Polyglotts. Calmet observes, that the Latins, so far as he knew, had never quoted this book: nor does it appear in their earlier printed Bibles; the first edition in which he had found it was one printed by Froben, of the year 1538. The book also appears in the *German* Bibles, in a version made by Jo.

[a] Mr. Milman, in his History of the Jews, flippantly calls the Third (First) Book a "romantic story," and "a "legend." But ancient writers of sound learning speak of it with respect: and Grotius disdained not to comment on it, as well as on the other two books.

xx   INTRODUCTION.

Circemberger, first printed at Wittemburg in 1554. It was translated into French by Calmet, and is found in the third volume of his " Literal " Commentary on the Bible."

Although it was reckoned Canonical by some of the Fathers, and is contained in most manuscripts of the Septuagint; yet, as it never found its way into the Vulgate translation, nor was received by the western church, our authorized English Bibles have not usually contained it. Yet an English version of it was put forth by Walter Lynne[b], in a small volume, in 1550; which in the next year, with some few alterations, and many corrections of the spelling, was appended to a folio Bible printed by John Daye.—About 170 years afterwards, a new translation of it was published by Whiston, in his " Authentic Documents," 2 vols. 8vo. 1719 and 1727. And a third version, made by Clement Crutwell, was added to his edition of the Bible with bishop Wilson's notes, 3 vols. 4to. Bath, 1785. Having compared each of these with the Greek text, I think Whiston's version to be the most faithful of the three; but have not at all considered myself as bound to retain it, wherever an examination of the Original suggested an alteration as advisable.

---

[b] Lynne dedicates his book to lady Anne, duchess of Somerset: and assigns as his reason for the publication, that the work was often quoted in the Table, or Concordance, compiled by Bullinger and others of the church of Zurich, which he had translated, and was publishing in the same volume; and that it was to be found in no English Bible except one which John Daye was then printing. This edition of Lynne was reprinted in 12mo, in 1563.

The book, in reality, does not belong to the history of the Maccabees; since it relates events which took place fifty years before their time. But it has been remarked, that the expression "Maccabee" was adopted by the Jews to designate any one who had suffered persecution for religion; in honourable remembrance of that family, which so nobly fought and fell, in the sacred cause of their country and their God.

The events of this book are not found in the historical works of Josephus: but in the *Latin* portion (where the Greek is wanting) of his second book *against Apion*, a somewhat similar transaction is related as having occurred; not indeed under Ptolemy Philopator, but fifty or sixty years later, during the reign of Ptolemy Physcon. There is good reason for believing that Josephus is here in error.

BOOK II.

The *second* book, or the *first* of our English Bibles, contains a clear and succinct account of events which befell the Jews during the space of forty years; namely, from the accession of Antiochus Epiphanes, to the death of Simon Maccabæus, in the 135th year before Christ.

Its author is unknown; and its original language has been greatly controverted. Origen and St. Jerome assert, that they had seen the original *in Hebrew*; but this is considered to have been lost. Yet it is to be observed, that Dr. Kennicott, in his "Dissertatio Generalis," cites two MSS., one of which, No. 474, is preserved at Rome, "Libr.

"Maccab. Chaldaice," written early in the 13th century: a second, No. 613, existing at Hamburg, "Libr. Maccab. Hebraice," written in the year 1448. Archbishop Ussher, following St. Jerome, says, "it is a book exactly translated out of the "Hebrew, and containeth every where the brevity "and Hebraisms of it." Annals of the World. Michaelis, in "Biblioth. Oriental. part. XII." (as quoted by Harles in his edition of Fabricius,) asserts that Josephus took his account of these transactions from the *Hebrew* book of Maccabees, and did not consult the Greek version. Theodotion has by some writers been considered as its translator into Greek: and the book is thought to have been compiled partly from the memoirs collected by Judas Maccabæus, and partly from those of John Hyrcanus, whose leadership began at the period where this book leaves off, and who moreover himself has been regarded by some persons as its author. Others again, as Beveridge, in his "Codex Canonum Vindicatus," contend that both books were originally written in Greek.

There is in bishop Walton's Polyglott Bible a *Syriac* version of this book, made from the Greek: also an *ancient Latin* one; respecting which, see Sabatier in the Prolegomena to his edition of the Hebrew Bible: there is likewise a *modern Latin* translation, by Nobilius.

It deserves to be noticed, that a short history of king Antiochus, *in Hebrew*, but differing in many points from the account given in this book of Maccabees, is printed, accompanied by a Latin version, by Bartoloccius in his "Bibliotheca Rab-

INTRODUCTION. xxiii

" binica," (tom. I. p. 383, &c.) who states it to be found in the Ritual of the Spanish Jews. Fabricius, in his "Codex Pseudepigraphus Veteris Tes-"tamenti," (tom. I. p. 1165,) has reprinted the Latin version of Bartoloccius, but without his long and learned notes; in which he maintains that the author of the work is unknown, but that beyond doubt it was compiled from the Talmud.

Christopher Wagenseil reports that he had discovered a manuscript of the same work, in *Chaldee*, in the dirty study of a Jew at Nicolasburg in Moravia. Wagenseil translated this into Latin, and his version is said to be remaining in the public library at Leipsic.

In Archbishop Marsh's library at Dublin is a small Hebrew roll on parchment, without points, containing this history of Antiochus and of "John "the son of Mattathias;" of which the beginning (and probably the whole) agrees with that which has been published by Bartoloccius.

BOOK III.

The *third* book, or *second* of our Bibles, contains, under the form of an abridgment, some account of the transactions of about fifteen years, commencing with a period ten or twelve years earlier than the preceding book. Jason, one of the Jews who were living at Cyrene in Africa, appears to have described, in five books, the principal transactions of the Jews during the reigns of Seleucus IV, Antiochus Epiphanes, and Antiochus Eupator. His work was abridged, by order of the Sanhedrim of Jerusalem, (as is asserted by

Sixtus Senensis,) by some unknown writer; who has also added to the book, as we now possess it, the acts and death of Nicanor, derived from some other source. It is observable, that the two epistles occurring at the beginning of the work belong to a later period; and these, in the opinion of Grotius, may have been taken from the records of the Jewish synagogue at Alexandria. By the style, and also by the manner of computation, which differs from that of the preceding book, the abridger at least, if not the author, appears to have been a Hellenistic Jew.

The work exists in *Greek*, but is not known in *Hebrew*. It has been attributed to Philo, and to Josephus; and by Leo Allatius, to Simon Maccabæus. It is thought to be the Μακκαβαϊκῶν Ἐπιτομή mentioned in the "Stromata" of Clemens Alexandrinus. In point of authority and historic value it is considered far inferior to the former book, from which it differs in several particulars. There is a *Syriac* version of it in the London Polyglott. A *German* translation was published in 1786, by Jo. G. Hasse, accompanied by several critical disquisitions; the author of which is of opinion that it was written about B.C. 150, by some Egyptian Jew, namely, the same person who composed the book of *Wisdom*, attributed to Solomon.

The *English* version of the second and third books, which appears in the present volume, is that of our authorized Bible; but corrected in very many places by aid of the various readings from Greek manuscripts, furnished in the folio Oxford Septuagint, edited by Holmes and Parsons.

As these two have generally accompanied the Bibles throughout the western church, they have, much more than all the others, engaged the attention both of critics and commentators. A *Harmony* of them was composed and printed, though never published, by a French author, named Nicolas Toinard, who died in 1706. There seems great reason to regret the non-appearance of this work, from the high character which is bestowed on its author by cardinal Noris, in his " Epochæ " Syro-Macedonum," 4to. 1696. At p. 78, Noris thus expresses himself: " Spero fore ut hunc no- " bis nodum solvat Nicolaus Toinardus Aurelia- " nensis, in Harmonia libri utriusque Maccabæo- " rum. Nam cum in sacra æque ac profana his- " toria sit versatissimus, idemque peregrinarum " linguarum peritissimus, simulque veterum num- " morum Regum Syriæ aliorumque curiosus per- " scrutator et interpres doctissimus, in laudato " opere typis quidem impresso sed nondum pub- " lici juris facto, historiam Maccabæorum ac re- " rum ab iis gestarum tempora summa eruditione " explicabit." Again, at p. 244 : " Idem etiam " qui totam hanc messem metet, longe probabilio- " rem eorundem interpretationem exhibebit, quam " et ipse veluti ab oraculo emissam cum plausu " excipiam."

A short *ordo temporum* accompanies Houbigant's preface to these books, in his edition of the Hebrew Bible, 4 vols. folio, 1753. Information illustrative of the Maccabæan history from *coins* may be found in "Vaillant's Historia Regum Syriæ," fol. 1732.

A *Latin* version, or rather *Harmony*, is said (by Harles, "Introductio ad Ling. Græc." tom. II. part. 2. p. 54.) to have been commenced by Jo. Melchior Faber of Anspach, in a dissertation entitled, " Harmonia Maccabæorum," Onoldini, 1794. This treatise I have not seen.

BOOK IV.

The *fourth* book, such as we now possess it, contains the history of the martyrdom of Eleazar and the seven brethren, under Antiochus Epiphanes; together with mention of Heliodorus' attempt to plunder the temple at Jerusalem.

It exists in *Greek*, in the Alexandrian manuscript of the Septuagint; and from thence was printed by Dr. Grabe, about 125 years ago, and was reprinted at Oxford in 1817, 8vo., and again in the folio Septuagint by Parsons. (In fact it had appeared in Greek Bibles at least so long ago as the year 1545.) From the various readings of this last edition I have been enabled to correct the text of 1817, which is extremely faulty.

The author of this fourth book is not known for a certainty; but it has been generally attributed to Josephus; with whose treatise *De Maccabæis*, or *De imperio rationis*, it certainly agrees very much; yet not entirely, as may be readily seen upon a close comparison.

Its character as a composition is highly spoken of both by Augustin and Jerome: the former of whom thus expresses himself in his *Sermo de Maccabæis:* " Quorum mirabiles passiones cum " legerentur non solim audivimus, sed etiam vidi-

"mus et spectavimus." Augustin. Oper. tom. V. p. 850. And Jerome, at greater length, and with still warmer admiration, thus writes on the subject: " Quid memorem insignes Macchabæorum "victorias? qui ne illicitis carnibus vescerentur, "et communes tangerent cibos, corpora obtulere "cruciatibus; totiusque orbis in ecclesiis Christi "laudibus prædicantur, fortiores poenis, ardentio- "res quibus comburebantur ignibus. Victa sunt "in eis omnia crudelitatis ingenia, et quicquid ira "persecutoris invenerat, patientium fortitudo su- "peravit. Inter poenas magis paternæ legis quam "dolorum memores: lacerantur viscera, tabo et "sanie artus diffluebant, et tamen sententia per- "severabat immobilis: liber erat animus, et mala "præsentia futurorum spe despiciebat. Lassa- "bantur tortores, et non lassabatur fides: frange- "bantur ossa, et volubili rota omnis compago "nervorum atque artuum solvebatur, et in im- "mensum spirantia mortem incendia consurge- "bant: plenæ erant ferventis olei sartagines, et "ad frigenda sanctorum corpora terrore incredi- "bili personabant: et tamen inter hæc omnia pa- "radisum animo deambulantes, non sentiebant "quod patiebantur sed quod videre cupiebant. "Mens enim Dei timore vallata flammas superat; "varios tormentorum spernit dolores. Cumque "semel virtuti se tradiderit, quicquid adversi eve- "nerit calcat et despicit." Hieron. Epist. 100. Oper. tom. I. p. 613. edit. Vallarsii.

In fact, this is the treatise which, by Athanasius and other ancient writers, is understood by "the fourth book of Maccabees:" yet Sixtus Senensis, in his *Bibliotheca Sancta*, asserts that he had seen in the library of Sanctes Pagninus, a learned friar, a manuscript calling itself *the fourth book*, but very different from the above, and containing the acts of John Hyrcanus: [thus following the series of history of our *second* book.] This manuscript was never published, and the library of Sanctes Pagninus, at Lyons in France, was destroyed by fire: I shall therefore subjoin a translation of the whole account, as given by Sixtus.

"The fourth book of Maccabees, which the
" synopsis of Athanasius classes among the apo-
" cryphal books, contains the history of thirty-one
" years; that is, the acts of John Maccabæus,
" who, from having conquered Hyrcanus, took
" that surname. After the treacherous murder of
" his father Simon by Ptolemy, John succeeded
" both to the high-priesthood and the chieftaincy;
" and instantly led out an army against his fa-
" ther's murderer. He afterwards entered into
" a treaty with Antiochus king of Syria, upon
" whose death he took by force of arms many
" cities of Syria. He was the first Jewish leader
" who employed hired soldiers. He dug up three
" thousand talents which were buried in the tomb
" of David. He renewed the treaty which his
" father had entered into with the Romans. He
" conquered and put to flight Antiochus Cyzice-
" nus king of Syria. After a siege of a year, he
" levelled with the ground the rival city of Sa-
" maria; and, by bringing the course of some
" streams over the spot, utterly erased all traces

"of the vanquished city. He renewed the walls
of Jerusalem, which had fallen down through
age.

"After these successful achievements, he dies
in the thirty-first year of his authority, (being
a man illustrious in three distinct characters, as
a priest, a general, and a prophet,) in the
hundredth year before Christ; at which period
the fourth and last book of the Maccabees ends.
The commencement of which book is thus, as it
is found in a Greek manuscript which I have
read in the library of that very learned preacher
Sanctus Pagninus: Καὶ μετὰ τὸ ἀπεκτανθῆναι τὸν
Σίμωνα ἐγενήθη Ἰωάννης υἱὸς αὐτοῦ ἀρχιερεὺς ἀντ' αὐτοῦ.
The series of the history, and the narrative, are
almost the same with those which are in the
thirteenth book of Antiquities of Josephus;
but the style abounds with Hebrew idioms, and
is very unlike his. It is most probable that
this work was translated, by some unknown
hand, from 'the Book of Days' (Chronicles) of
the priesthood of John, of whom it is written at
the end of the first book of Maccabees, 'The
rest of the sayings of John, &c. &c.'

"From the above, it clearly appears that those
persons are mistaken, who think that the fourth
book of Maccabees is that in which Josephus
has described the martyrdom of the Maccabæan
mother and her seven sons; which book also is
found in some Greek Bibles, with the title,
Ἰοσίππου εἰς τοὺς Μακκαβαίους." Sixti Senensis
Biblioth. lib. i. sect. 3.

But Calmet, in his "Dictionary of the Bible,"

under the article "Maccabees," supposes that Sixtus was mistaken in his opinion of this being the true fourth book: and that probably what he saw was that work which in Arabic has been printed in the Paris and London Polyglotts, [namely my *fifth* book:] this latter however contains much more than Sixtus takes notice of, and reaches down to the birth of Jesus Christ.

In his "Literal Comment on Scripture," Calmet has given *our* fourth book both in Latin and French.

I do not believe that it has ever yet appeared in *English;* except in a very loose paraphrase, in L'Estrange's translation of Josephus, folio, London, 1702: but Whiston, a subsequent translator of that author, does not consider it as the production of Josephus, and therefore has wholly passed it by, for reasons which may be seen at the end of his version of the treatise against Apion. I have endeavoured to suit the style and language to those of the preceding books, as closely as was consistent with a careful adherence to the Original.

BOOK V.

The *fifth* book, although Calmet supposes that it was originally written in *Hebrew*, and from thence was translated into *Greek*, is not now known to exist in either of those languages. We have it in *Arabic*, and also in *Syriac*. It is a kind of Chronicle of Jewish affairs, commencing with the attempt on the treasury at Jerusalem made by Heliodorus, (with an interpolation of the history of the Septuagint version composed by desire of Ptolemy,) and reaching down to the birth of Jesus Christ: or, speaking accurately, to that particular point of time, at which Herod, almost glutted with the noblest blood of the Jews, turned his murderous hands upon the members of his own family; and completed the sad tragedy of the Asmonæan princes, by the slaughter of his own wife Mariamne, her mother, and his own two sons.

The *Arabic* of this book, with a Latin version of it by Gabriel Sionita, first appeared in the Paris Polyglott Bible of Le Jay, with no other notice than the following preface. "Liber hic a "cap. 1 usque ad 16 inclusive inscribitur 'II. "*Machabæorum ex Hebræorum translatione,*' uti "in calce ejusdem cap. 16 videre est. Reliquus "vero liber simpliciter notatur 'II. *Machabæo-* "*rum*,' continuata tamen cum antecedentibus ca- "pitum serie. At cum neque textui Syriaco, qui "præcipuæ inter Orientales auctoritatis est, neque "Græco, neque Vulgatæ editioni consonet, (quan- "quam in omnibus ferme Orientalium extet codi- "cibus,) illum in calce horum Bibliorum reposui- "mus, et quidem destitutum apicibus suis: tum "ne cuiquam inter cæteros Canonicos libros recen- "seri a nobis videatur: tum quia secundus Macha- "bæorum, qui pro Canonico habetur, ex integro "nobis extat, quanquam sub nomine primi. Habes "tamen in hoc quædam ex primo et secundo; "quædam vero alia hactenus forte in lucem non "edia quæ tibi non injucunda fore speramus: "quandoquidem liber totus est quædam historiæ

" continuatio, ab ipsis Machabæis deducta usque
" ad regnum Herodis et præfecturam Pilati [c], et
" consequenter Christi Domini tempora. Tandem
" hoc unum scias velimus, nos ea bona fide textum
" expressisse, ut ne ea quidem quæ facile emendari
" poterant mutaverimus."

The appearance of this book in the Paris Polyglott, without any account of the Manuscript from which it had been taken, or any farther particulars connected with its publication, is thought to have arisen from the quarrels which were continually taking place between two of the editors of the Oriental department of that Bible, Gabriel Sionita and Abraham Ecchellensis. From the Paris edition it was copied into the London Polyglott of Bishop Walton.

Its author is wholly unknown. He may have been contemporary with Josephus, but was not Josephus himself; as may be proved by many differences from that historian, and some contradictions of him, collected instances of which may be seen in Calmet. That he lived after the capture of Jerusalem by Titus may be evidenced by the expression occurring at chap. ix. "till after " the third captivity:" and again, in chap. xxi. " till the destruction of the second House." It has been supposed to have been compiled from the Acts of each successive high priest. In three places, chap. xxv. 5, lv. 25, and lix. 96, mention is made of " the author of this book;" but *who* is

---

[c] This appears to be a mistake, as will be perceived on referring to the note on chap. lix. verse 25.

the person designated by this expression, it is not perhaps easy to say.

The book contains some remarkable peculiarities of language; such as "The House of God," and "The Holy House," for *the Temple*:—"the "land of the Holy House," for *Judæa*:—"the "city of the Holy House," for *Jerusalem*:—the exclamations, "to whom be peace!" and "God be "merciful to them," used in speaking of the dead: —"the men of the west:"—the "great and good "God," (answering to the "Deus Optimus Maxi- "mus" of Roman authors;) and the same expression is found in the Samaritan Chronicle:—"the "land of the sanctuary:" in the Samaritan Chronicle Jerusalem is called "the sanctuary," and its king, "the king of the sanctuary."

I may here remark, in passing, that this *Samaritan Chronicle* exists in an Arabic translation, made from the Hebrew, but in the ancient Samaritan characters, in a manuscript which formerly belonged to the learned Joseph Scaliger, and is now preserved in the public library at Leyden. It begins from the death of Moses, (whence it obtained the title of "the book of Joshua,") and ends with the emperor Antonine. I am not aware that it has ever been published; but Hottinger has given an epitome of it in his "Exercitationes "Anti-morinianæ," 4to. 1644; and several extracts in his "Smegma Orientale," 4to. 1658: it is also briefly mentioned by Basnage, in his "His- "tory of the Jews," II. i. 2.

The learned Dr. Huntington, who about a hundred and thirty years ago travelled into the East,

xxxiv INTRODUCTION.

and visited the town of *Sichem*, where he found only small and miserable remains of the Samaritans, saw there a "Samaritan Chronicle" different from that which is mentioned by Scaliger, and less copious, but still embracing the period from the Creation to the time of Mahomet. This book he brought over with him to England, and it is now deposited among the Huntington MSS. in the Bodleian library. A chronological abstract of it appears in the "Acta Eruditorum" for 1691: where it seems to have been continued by some unknown hand down to the year of Christ 1492.

In the "Biblia Maxima" by Jo. de la Haye, 19 tom. folio, Paris, 1660, the *Latin* version of Le Jay's Polyglott is reprinted, but with the omission of the first nineteen chapters.

A *French* translation of this *fifth* book, from the Arabic, appears, with other apocryphal writings, in the Appendix to De Sacy's Bible: and Calmet has given a version of a portion of it, viz. of chapters xx to xxvi; being so much as contains the acts of John Hyrcanus, namely, that part only which Sixtus Senensis had seen, and had considered to be the legitimate fourth book. He adds, that the entire book had been recently published in French by M. Baubrun, in the third volume of Le Maitre's Bible, fol. Paris. This I have not seen.

I do not know that it has hitherto appeared in *English*. I have rendered it from the Latin version of the Arabic text printed in the Polyglotts; taking care to adhere as closely as possible to my copy, lest a translation of a translation

INTRODUCTION.

should be found to have wholly lost sight of the Original, if too much liberty were allowed; only endeavouring, as before stated, that the English should bear some resemblance to that of the other Maccabaic books.

In the several notes and illustrations from heathen authors subjoined to the text, I have thrown upon various parts of it whatever light I was able to procure. But at the same time I have been unwilling to quote at length the corresponding passages of those authors, lest the volume should be swelled to a bulk disproportionate to its worth.

On the Canonical authority sought to be affixed to two of these books.

It is well known to the learned, that of these five books, those which are commonly called the *first* and *second* have been usually attached to copies of the Bible throughout the western church; and by the adherents to the see of Rome they are, even at this day, deemed to be of Canonical authority. The ground for this may perhaps be sought, and found, in an overstrained interpretation of those approving terms in which several of the early Fathers spoke of these books, either as faithful or edifying narratives.

But, on the question of their having been considered *as the work of inspiration,* and in such a character admitted either into the Jewish or early Christian canon, I shall beg permission to adduce one single testimony from each of these two churches; which, as it is that of a writer of high character, and is direct and unambiguous, I trust may be thought decisive of the question, according to the maxim of Aristotle, εἷς πιστὸς μάρτυς ἱκανός.

For the *Jewish* canon, hear Josephus, in his first book against Apion, sect. 8. Ἀπὸ δὲ Ἀρταξέρξου μέχρι τοῦ καθ᾽ ἡμᾶς χρόνου γέγραπται μὲν ἕκαστα· πίστεως δ᾽ οὐχ ὁμοίας ἠξίωται τοῖς πρὸ αὐτῶν, διὰ τὸ μὴ γενέσθαι τὴν τῶν προφητῶν ἀκριβῆ διαδοχήν. "But from "Artaxerxes down to our own times all events "are indeed recorded: but they are not consi- "dered equally worthy of belief with those which "preceded them, because there was not an exact "succession of prophets *as before*."

And for the *Christian* church, no less an authority than St. Jerome distinctly affirms, "Macha- "bæorum libros legit quidem ecclesia, SED EOS "INTER CANONICAS SCRIPTURAS NON RECI- "PIT." Præfat. in Proverb. Salomonis.

One might have thought, that this solemn assertion, coming from so high a quarter, would have been decisive: that a Roman catholic at least would have bowed with implicit deference to the recorded judgment of this learned Father, to whom he owns himself indebted for *his* Bible. And so indeed he did, during earlier and better times. But Rome found troubles come upon her: doubts arose, and objections were made, and must be met at all events: and the third book of Maccabees offered too fair a field, of dreams, and visions, and miraculous appearances, and a (fancied) recommendation of prayers for the dead, to be neglected by that church. The council of Trent boldly pronounced the two books Canonical; and as such they are professedly received by all the adherents of the Roman see.

It is sad however, to see some of her learned followers betraying their distrust of the grounds upon which they are bidden to stand; and such men as P. de la Haye, and Calmet after him, driven to the miserable shift of attempting to find reasons for the propriety of their being deemed Canonical, from the mere fact of St. Paul's having used, in his Epistle to the Hebrews, ch. xii. 35, where he is speaking of the martyrs, the expression, ἄλλοι δ᾽ ἐτυμπανίσθησαν—" which torture," say they, " Eleazar suffered !" as if *therefore* it necessarily followed, that the particular book which details these his sufferings must be, not only that one which the Apostle had in view, but moreover must have been written by divine inspiration, and consequently be Canonical!

The reader, who desires to see this point treated in detail, is referred to " Jo. Rainoldi censura li-" brorum apocryphorum Veteris Testamenti, ad-" versum Pontificios," 2 tom. 4to. Oppenheimii 1591: and to Archbishop Ussher's "Summary of " Christian Religion."

I may also take leave to mention, that the question of the Canonical character of these books was warmly debated in Germany, about the middle of the last century, by Frœlich and the two Wernsdorfs; the former of whom denied, and the latter maintained, their title to that high distinction. The contest began by some observations made in a publication of Frœlich, entitled " Annales Re-" gum Syriæ," 4to. 1744. To these E. Wernsdorf replied, in " Prolusio de Fontibus Historiæ " Syriæ in Libris Maccabæorum," 4to. Lipsiæ, 1746. Frœlich rejoined, in " Prolusio in Examen " vocata," 4to. 1746. G. Wernsdorf then entered the field, with a " Commentatio de Fide Histo- " rica Librorum Maccabæorum," 4to. 1747; and was supported by an anonymous Jesuit, who published a treatise entitled, " Authoritas Libro- " rum Maccabæorum canonico-historica adserta," 4to. Viennæ, 1749. In 1754, Frœlich republished his " Annales," and probably replied to all the arguments of his opponents: for in the Preface he states, " post ultimum anno 1749, pro li- " bris Maccabæorum finitum certamen, silentium " et pax."

What may be the character or merits of these last-named publications, I am unable to judge or pronounce; as not a single one of them was to be procured in any public or private library in Dublin.—Nor have I been able to meet with " Mi- " chaelis on the Maccabees," 4to. 1774: nor " Charles Wilson's Version of the apocryphal " books, with critical and historical Observations," 8vo. 1801: nor the dissertations said to be contained in the " Bibliotheca Historica" of Meuselius: nor the " Harmony" by J. M. Faber, 8vo. 1794, &c. &c.: a perusal of which treatises, together with many others illustrating the same subject, might perhaps have considerably diminished the imperfections of the present work.

*The Prayer of Eleazar, occurring in
Book I. Chapter* vi.

It will be at once perceived and allowed, that both the imagery and language of this prayer are highly poetical, although the words themselves have never yet been submitted to the strict rules of a metrical arrangement.

Βασιλεῦ μεγαλοκράτωρ, ὕψιστε, παντοκράτωρ Θεὲ, τὴν πᾶσαν διακυβερνῶν ἐν οἰκτιρμοῖς κτίσιν, ἔπιδε ἐπὶ Ἀβραὰμ σπέρμα ἐπὶ ἡγιασμένου τεκνα Ἰακὼβ, μερίδος ἡγιασμένης σοῦ λαὸν ἐν ξένῃ γῇ ἀδίκως ἀπολλύμενον, πατέρ.

Σὺ Φαραὼ πληθύνοντα ἅρμασι, τοπρὶν Αἰγύπτου ταύτης δυναστὴν, ἐπαρθέντα ἀνόμῳ θράσει καὶ γλώσσῃ μεγαλορρήμονι, σὺν τῇ ὑπερηφάνῳ στρατιᾷ παντοβρόχους ἀπώλεσας, φέγγος ἐπιφάνας ἐλέους Ἰσραὴλ γένει.

Σὺ τὸν ἀναριθμήτοις δυνάμεσι γαυρωθέντα, Σενναχηρεὶμ βαθὺν Ἀσσυρίων βασιλέα, δοράτι τὴν πάσαν ὑποχείριον ἤδη λαβόντα γῆν, καὶ μετεωρισθέντα ἐπὶ τὴν ἁγίαν σοῦ πόλιν, βαρέα λαλοῦντα κόμπῳ καὶ θράσει σὺ δέσποτα ἔθραυσας, ἔκδηλον δεικνὺς ἔθνεσι πολλοῖς τὸ σὸν κράτος.

Σὺ τοὺς κατὰ τὴν Βαβυλωνίαν τρεῖς ἑταίρους, πυρὶ τὴν ψυχὴν αὐθαιρέτως δεδωκότας, εἰς τὸ μὴ λατρεῦσαι τοῖς κενοῖς, διάπυρον δροσίσας κάμινον, ἐρρύσω μέχρι τριχὸς ἀπημάντους, φλόγα πᾶσιν ἐπιπέμψας τοῖς ὑπεναντίοις.

Σὺ τὸν διαβολαῖς φθόνου λέουσι κατὰ γῆς ριφέντα θηρσὶ βορὰν Δανιὴλ εἰς φῶς ἀνήγαγες ἀσινῆ.

Τόν τε βυθοτρεφοῦς ἐν γαστρὶ κήτους Ἰωνᾶν τηκόμενον ἀφειδῶς, ἀπήμαντον πᾶσιν οἰκείοις ἀνέδειξας, πατέρ.

Καὶ νῦν μισύβρι, πολυέλεε, τῶν ὅλων σκεπαστὰ, τὸ τάχος ἐπιφάνηθι τοῖς ἀπὸ Ἰσραὴλ γένους, ὑπὸ δὲ ἐβδελυγμένων ἀνόμων ἐθνῶν ὑβριζομένοις.

xl THE PRAYER OF ELEAZAR.

Εἰ δὲ ἀσεβείαις κατὰ τὴν ἀποικίαν ὁ βίος ἡμῶν ἐνέσχηται, ῥυσάμενος ἡμᾶς ἀπὸ ἐχθρῶν χειρὸς, ὡς προαίρῃ δέσποτα ἀπόλεσον ἡμᾶς μόρῳ.

Μὴ τοῖς ματαίοις οἱ ματαιόφρονες εὐλογησάτωσαν ἐπὶ τῇ τῶν ἠγαπημένων σοῦ ἀπωλείᾳ, λέγοντες, οὐδὲ ὁ Θεὸς αὐτῶν ἐρρύσατο αὐτούς.

Σὺ δὲ, ὁ πᾶσαν ἀλκὴν καὶ δυναστείαν ἔχων ἅπασαν, Αἰώνιε, νῦν ἔπιδε, ἐλέησον ἡμᾶς τοὺς καθ᾽ ὕβριν ἀνόμων ἀλόγιστον ἐκ τοῦ ζῆν μεθισταμένους ἐν ἐπιβούλων τρόπῳ.

Πτηξάτω δὲ ἔθνη σὴν δύναμιν ἀνίκητον σήμερον, ἔντιμε, δύναμιν ἔχων, ἐπὶ σωτηρίᾳ Ἰακὼβ γένους.

Ἱκετεύει σε τὸ πᾶν πλῆθος τῶν νηπίων, καὶ οἱ τούτων γονεῖς μετὰ δακρύων.

Δειχθήτω πᾶσιν ἔθνεσιν ὅτι μεθ᾽ ἡμῶν εἶ Κύριε, καὶ οὐκ ἀπέστρεψας τὸ πρόσωπον σοῦ ἀφ᾽ ἡμῶν· ἀλλὰ καθὼς εἶπας, ὅτι οὐδ᾽ ἐν τῇ γῇ τῶν ἐχθρῶν αὐτῶν ὄντων ὑπερεῖδες αὐτοὺς, οὕτως ἐπιτέλεσον, Κύριε.

The words of the foregoing prayer fall almost naturally into English blank verse; the following translation being, *for the most part,* no more than a mere verbal rendering of the Greek, as it stands at present.

Monarch most powerful! highest, mightiest GOD!
Whose mercies all creation ever guide—
Lo! Abraham's seed—lo! Jacob's sacred race—
Thy sanctified inheritance—thy lot—
What wrongs we suffer in a stranger-land.
  Thou—when stern Pharaoh, Egypt's mighty lord,
Spread forth his chariot-band in proud array,
And with high-swelling boasts defied thy power;
Him and his host, beneath the boiling wave
Of his own sea didst whelm; while with mild ray
O'er Israel's rescued sons thy mercy shone.

THE PRAYER OF ELEAZAR.

Thou—when Sennacherib, Assyria's chief,
The self-styled conqueror of a little world,
Proud of his countless troops, his battles won,
His cities sack't, and idol-gods o'erthrown—
Could not restrain his bursting insolence,
But rashly dar'd thy holy land to invade;—
Thou, to the world displaying thy vast might,
The empty threatenings of his idle tongue
Didst in one moment, and for ever, quell.

When the three Hebrew youths in Babel's court
Sustain'd the trial; whom nor threats could force,
Nor soft persuasion charm, to bow the knee
In idol-worship;—firm in faith they stood,
Unmov'd, unflinching; while beneath their glance
The courtiers wither'd, and the baffled king
Champ't at his favours spurn'd, his power defied.
He ask'd their *conscience*—and they gave their *lives*.

But when his angry furnace flam'd on high
With seven-fold fury charg'd, from its huge mouth
Gaping as if for prey, whole sheets of fire
Burst forth beyond controul, and with blind rage
The helpless ministers for victims slew.

Into this lake, of fire and seeming death,
Bound hand and foot, they sank.—But quickly rose,
And walked, unharm'd, and free.—For THOU wert
    there!
At thy command, above, below, around,
The laughing flames played harmless; and a dew
Heaven-sent, breathed such cool freshness o'er the place,
The tyrant's Hell became God's Paradise.—

Thou from the Assyrian lions' hungry jaws
Didst rescue Daniel, foully doom'd to die.
And Jonah, in the huge sea-monster's maw
Immur'd, beyond all hope of human aid,
To his despairing friends didst safe restore.

And now, most merciful, all-seeing GOD,
Hater of insolence, thyself display
A swift avenger of thy people's wrongs,
Whom odious heathens lawlessly oppress.

And, for those sins, which idly we have wrought
Against thy name in this sad pilgrimage,
We dare not ask forgiveness:—Yet, at least
Save us, we pray, from *man's* rude tyranny;
Into *Thy* hands, O LORD, content we fall.
    Let not vain Gentiles with mistaken joy
Thank their false idols for our overthrow;
Nor ask exulting, "Where lies Israel now?
"Where is their promis'd aid, their boasted GOD?"
    But THOU, who hast all majesty and might,
Eternal One! look down, behold thy sons
Smarting beneath oppression's iron rod,
And to a traitor's abject fate consign'd.
    Thou honour'd mighty One! this very morn
Let heathens own thy power, o'er Israel sav'd.
Our elders pray Thee, and our infant babes
In untaught eloquence of tears implore.
    Prove to the world that Thou art with us still,
Thy face still on us sheds its favouring light:
And for thy promise, never to desert
E'en in captivity thy once-lov'd race,
That gracious promise, LORD, this day fulfil.

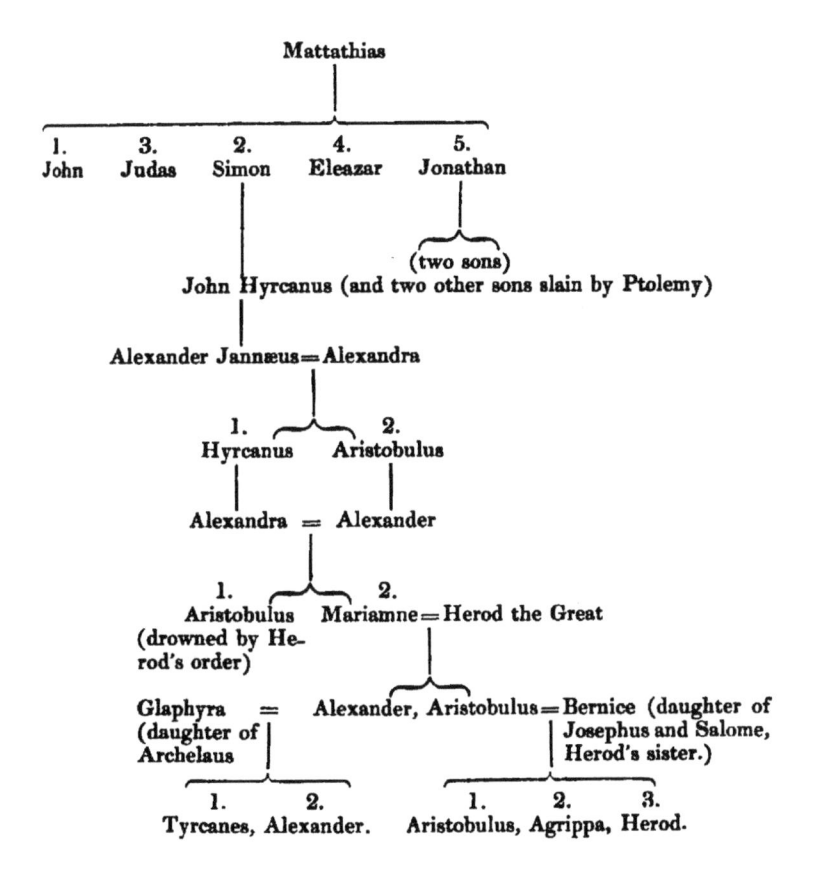

The Genealogy of the Maccabæan Family, so far as it is mentioned in these Five Books.

```
                           Mattathias
                               |
   ┌─────────┬─────────┬─────────┬─────────┐
   1.        3.        2.        4.        5.
  John     Judas     Simon    Eleazar   Jonathan
                       |                   |
                       |              (two sons)
           John Hyrcanus (and two other sons slain by Ptolemy)
                       |
           Alexander Jannæus = Alexandra
                       |
                  ┌────┴────┐
                  1.        2.
               Hyrcanus  Aristobulus
                  |          |
             Alexandra  =  Alexander
                       |
                  ┌────┴────┐
                  1.        2.
             Aristobulus  Mariamne = Herod the Great
          (drowned by He-              |
          rod's order)
                                                        
   Glaphyra    =   Alexander, Aristobulus = Bernice (daughter of
   (daughter of |                         | Josephus and Salome,
   Archelaus    |                         | Herod's sister.)
          ┌────┴────┐            ┌────────┼────────┐
          1.       2.            1.       2.       3.
     Tyrcanes, Alexander.   Aristobulus, Agrippa, Herod.
```

The Genealogy of Herod the Great, so far as it relates to these Five Books.

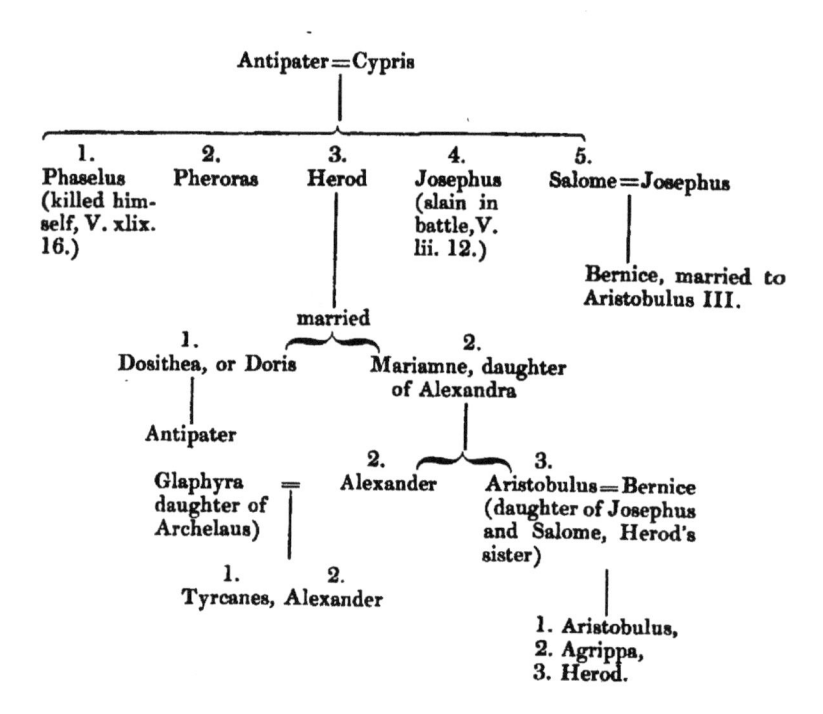

Antipater=Cypris

1. Phaselus (killed himself, V. xlix. 16.)
2. Pheroras
3. Herod
4. Josephus (slain in battle, V. lii. 12.)
5. Salome=Josephus

Bernice, married to Aristobulus III.

Herod married:
1. Dosithea, or Doris
2. Mariamne, daughter of Alexandra

Antipater (son of Doris)

From Mariamne:
2. Alexander
3. Aristobulus=Bernice (daughter of Josephus and Salome, Herod's sister)

Glaphyra (daughter of Archelaus) = Alexander

1. Tyrcanes, 2. Alexander

Children of Aristobulus and Bernice:
1. Aristobulus,
2. Agrippa,
3. Herod.

'S TABLES.

PARTHIA.	MEMORABLE EVENTS.
323	324 Alexander the Great dies.
284 :s.	312 The Æra of the Seleucidæ begins.
246 ius.	277 Translation of the Bible into Greek.
221 tius.	217 The battle of Raphia in Egypt.
	Ptolemy orders the Jews to be destroyed by his elephants.
204 s.	
180 s II.	176 Heliodorus sent to rob the temple at Jerusalem.
	167 The "abomination of desolation," or statue of Jupiter set up in the temple, by Antiochus Epiphanes.
169 us II.	
ates II.	
	The martyrdom of Eleazar, and the seven brethren.
145 res.	
116 kes.	166 Judas Maccabæus begins his exploits.
s III.	164 Judas purifies the temple.
ates III.	157 Judas is slain. Jonathan succeeds him.
106 ·	144 Jonathan treacherously slain by Tryphon.
s IV. (who	143 Simon acknowledged for an independent prince. He coins money.
88 —ed till four after the	142 Simon is created high priest, governor, and captain, by the Jews.
81 —of Christ.)	130 Hyrcanus shakes off the Syrian yoke.
nus the last	126 Hyrcanus takes the title of king.
80 —was killed,	80 (about) Antipater, Herod's father, comes to dwell at Jerusalem.
226; with	63 Pompey reduces Judæa, enters the temple, and puts an end to the kingdom of Syria.
65 — ended the	
ian empire,	54 Crassus plunders the temple.
51 —	49 The battle of Pharsalia. Pompey defeated.
3 existed	40 Herod declared king of Judæa by the Romans.
46 Cle ears.]	
	37 The Asmonæan dynasty extinguished, by Herod putting to death Antigonus.
43 Cle	31 The battle of Actium: Antony defeated.
30 Au	30 The kingdom of Egypt ended, by the death of Cleopatra.
	28 Herod murders his wife Mariamne.
	19 Herod undertakes to rebuild the temple.
	6 Herod puts to death his two sons.
	3 Herod slays his son Antipater, and dies.

THE

FIRST BOOK

OF

MACCABEES:

CONTAINING

OCCURRENCES WHICH TOOK PLACE AT JERUSALEM AND ALEXANDRIA, DURING PART OF THE REIGN OF PTOLEMY PHILOPATOR, KING OF EGYPT, BETWEEN THE YEARS 217 AND 209 BEFORE CHRIST.

CHAPTER I.

Ptolemy defeats Antiochus. He visits Jerusalem; and attempts to enter the Temple.

1 NOW[a] when Philopator[b] learned from those who returned, that Antiochus[c] had taken away the places[d] which had been under his dominion, he gave orders to all his forces, both 2 foot and horse, to march: and taking with him his sister Arsinoe, he proceeded as far as the parts about Raphia[e], where Antiochus and his army had pitched their camp.

B.C. 217.

[a] Grotius has remarked, that this book opens abruptly, as though it were part of some larger work; and this idea appears to be confirmed by an expression occurring at ch. ii. 25.

[b] Ptolemy Philopator, king of Egypt, the fourth of that family and name.

[c] Antiochus the Great, king of Syria, the son of Seleucus Callinicus.

[d] Namely, Tyre, Seleucia, Ptolemais, Abila, Gadara, Scythopolis, and other towns; as related by Polybius, lib. V.

[e] A town on the southern border of the Holy Land; ἡ κεῖται μετὰ 'Ρινοκόλουρα πρώτη τῶν κατὰ Κοίλην Συρίαν πόλεων ὡς πρὸς τὴν Αἴγυπτον. (Polybius.) Coins struck here are still extant.

But one Theodotus[f], intending to complete a treacherous design which he had, took the best of the arms which Ptolemy had formerly intrusted to him, and approached by night to Ptolemy's tent, as *intending* himself alone to kill him, and thereby to put an end to the war. But Dositheus, called *the son* of Drimylus, by birth a Jew, but one who afterwards forsook his religion and estranged himself from the ordinances of his forefathers, taking *Ptolemy* out of the way, caused a certain obscure person[g] to lodge there in his stead; who accordingly received that punishment which was intended for the other.

Now when a sharp battle took place, and success seemed rather to favour Antiochus[h], Arsinoe[i] went frequently up and down among the troops; and exhorted them with lamentation and tears, having her hair in disorder, to fight manfully for themselves and for their children and wives; promising to give to every one, if they conquered, two

---

[f] This individual, who here is so lightly spoken of, appears, from Polybius's account, to have been a person of considerable importance. He was by birth an Ætolian, was high in the confidence of Ptolemy, by whom he was advanced to posts of the utmost consequence, and at length was made governor of Cœlosyria. Having from some cause incurred the king's ill graces, and suspecting that his life was in danger, he took the resolution of separating himself from his former master, and thenceforth espoused the interests of king Antiochus. See Polybius, V. 40, and 61.

[g] Polybius relates in detail this attempt of Theodotus; adding, that he wounded two persons, and slew the king's physician, who probably is the person here alluded to. Polyb. V. 81.

[h] In fact Ptolemy's left wing had been vanquished and put to flight; so that Antiochus, young and inexperienced in the field, was fully persuaded that the victory was his own: nor was he undeceived till it was too late to repair the disaster.

[i] This princess is also mentioned by Polybius, as zealously assisting Ptolemy in the battle.

6 minæ [k] of gold *as a reward*. By which means it came to pass that their enemies were destroyed [l] in the battle [m], and many of them were taken pri-
7 soners also. *Ptolemy* therefore, having overcome this treachery, determined to go and encourage the neighbouring cities [n]; by doing which, and by making presents to their temples, he made his subjects to be full of courage. B.C. 216.
8 But when the Jews had sent to him some of their council [o] and elders, to salute him and to bring with them presents, and to congratulate with him on past events; it came to pass that he felt a stronger desire to take a journey to them with all speed.
9 Now when he was come to Jerusalem, he offered a sacrifice to the Most High God, and returned thanks, and did what was then proper in B.C. 214.
10 that place [p]. Moreover, when he was on the spot, he was astonished at the diligence and decency there observed. And wondering at the good order

---

[k] There is the Hebrew, the Attic, the Roman, and the Egyptian mina; each differing from the others in value. If the last be the one here meant, as is most probable, it is equivalent to thirty-two Hebrew shekels (or eight ounces) of gold: so that two such minæ would be worth, in our present money, about sixty guineas.

[l] The particulars of this battle of Raphia are well and minutely given by Polybius, lib. V.

[m] Gr. ἐν χειρονομίαις διαφθαρῆναι. The reading has been questioned, but surely without reason. Every one remembers that διαφθείρεσθαι ἐν χειρῶν νόμῳ is a classical expression, used by Polybius and other Greek writers. Of the same class is εἰς χεῖρας βιάζεσθαι, *to resist hand to hand*, which we find in Diodorus Siculus.

[n] Polybius is severe upon the fickle readiness with which these cities received and hailed the victor.

[o] Gr. Γερουσία, a word which usually denotes the Roman senate, but is used to express the Jewish Sanhedrim or Great Council, in these books, also in that of Judith, and by Josephus.

[p] Namely, in the court of the Gentiles.

about the holy place, he took a design to manage matters so, that he might enter into the temple itself^q. But when they said that this could not be done, because it was not lawful for even persons of their own nation to enter into that place; no, not for all the priests themselves, but only for the superior of them all, the high priest, and even for him but once in a year:—he would by no means be dissuaded. And when the law[r] *to this effect* was read in his presence, he would by no means cease offering himself: but said that he must go in; and "even if they are deprived of that ho-"nour, I must not be so deprived." He asked also *this question*—why none of those who attended any other temples hindered him from entering into them? And when a certain person inadvertently said, that this was an unlucky fiction[s] *of his:* he answered, " Now that this has been done, from " whatever cause it may, why shall I not enter at " all events, whether you will or no?"

Then the priests fell down in their holy garments, and prayed the Most High God to assist them in the present distress, and to avert the violence of him who was making this wicked attempt

---

q Here is meant the inmost recess, the Holy of Holies.

r And besides these ordinances of the Law of Moses, Antiochus the Great, in his benevolence towards the Jews, had issued a public decree that no foreigner should enter into the temple without their will and permission. Joseph. Ant. XII. 3.

s Gr. κακῶς αὐτὸ τοῦτο τεραπεύεσθαι. The sense appears somewhat doubtful. Grotius would read ἱερατεύεσθαι for τεραπεύεσθαι. Crutwell translates the passage, " that it was " monstrously wicked." The sense seems to be, that " this " very thing," viz. his entering into other temples, " was im-" properly done," (qu. πράττεσθαι?) Or, " that they mind-" ed their business badly in " thus allowing him to go in."

upon them: and they filled the temple with cries
17 and tears. And they which were left in the city
were troubled, and came running, as thinking the
affair to be something new and wholly unexpected.
18 The virgins also, who were shut up[t] in private chambers, together with their mothers, rushed out; and
sprinkling ashes and dust upon their heads, filled
19 the streets with groans and lamentations. And
those who lately were adorned *in wedding garments*, leaving their marriage-chambers[u], and that
decent modesty which belonged to them, ran
20 about the city together in disorder. And as for
the young children, both their mothers and nurses
who had charge of them, left these, one in one
place, one in another; some in their houses, others
in the streets, without any regard: and went in
21 troops together to the most high temple. And
various was the prayer of the whole company on
22 account of this his unhallowed attempt. Together
with these were the bolder citizens, who would
not bear his persevering in the business, and his
23 resolution to effect his purpose. And crying out,
that they must arm themselves for this onset, and
courageously die for the Law of their fathers, they
occasioned no small stir[x] in the place: and having
with difficulty been dissuaded by the seniors[y] and
elders, at last these also retired to the same station
of prayer.
24 As for the multitude, they continued as before,
25 in the same manner, praying. While the elders

[t] Gr. κατάκλειστοι, called by Philo, πάρθενοι θαλαμευόμεναι. Compare 2 Macc. iii. 19.

[u] Gr. τοὺς πρὸς ἀπάντησιν διατεταγμένους παστούς.

[x] Or, confusion. Gr. τραχύτητα: as in Homer, τετρήχει δ' ἀγορή. Il. B. 95.

[y] Gr. γηραιοί; whom Grotius conceives to be the members of the council or Sanhedrim.

who were about the king tried in many ways to divert his proud mind from his intended purpose. But he, in a haughty manner, and disdaining[z] all their persuasions, began now to make an advance; as thinking to accomplish his declared design. Which, when his attendants perceived, even they turned to join with our people in calling upon Him who has all power, to give help in the present distress, and not to overlook this lawless and proud behaviour.

Now from the reiterated and vehement cry of the multitude united together there was an inconceivable sort of noise[a]: for one might suppose that not the men alone, but the very walls and the ground echoed again; as if the whole multitude at that time chose to die rather than that place should be profaned.

CHAPTER II.

The prayer of Simon. Ptolemy is baffled. His cruel edicts.

[b] THEREUPON the high priest Simon[c], bowing his knees before the holy place, and spreading out his hands in reverent form,

B.C. 211.

---

[z] Or, "sending them all aside:" or, "dismissing all other considerations:" Gr. πάντα παραπέμψας, (or πάντας).

[a] Gr. ἀνείκαστός τις ἦν βοή. Homer uses a similar expression, βοὴ δ' ἄσβεστος ὀρώρει.

[b] There is some uncertainty respecting the exact time at which the transactions mentioned in this book took place. Archbishop Ussher, in his "Annals of the World," places Ptolemy's ill-usage of the Jews under the year B.C. 216; and Vaillant, in his "Historia Ptolemæorum," assigns it to the eighth year of that king's reign, viz. B. C. 212. But, if we support the reading in the text of ver. 1 of this chapter, that "the high priest *Simon* prayed for the people," we must carry the occurrence a few years onward; as it is allowed that Simon did not succeed to that office until B. C. 211.

[c] The son of Onias II. and father of Onias III.: he suc-

2 made the following prayer: "O Lord, Lord, king
"of heaven, and ruler of all creation, Holy in the
"holies[d], the only Governor, the Almighty;—
"give ear unto us who are afflicted by this wicked
"and profane man, puffed up with insolence and
3 "strength. For thou, who hast created all things,
"and rulest all things, *thou* art the righteous Go-
"vernor, and judgest those who do any thing in
4 "insolence and pride. Thou didst destroy them
"who in former times worked wickedness, among
"whom were the giants[e], trusting in their
"strength and courage, by bringing upon them
5 "an immense mass of water. Thou didst burn
"up with fire and brimstone the Sodomites, work-
"ers of wickedness, who were infamous for their
"iniquities; and madest them an example[f] to
6 "those who *should* come afterward. Thou shew-
"edst thy dominion by trying the vaunting bold
"Pharaoh, (who had enslaved thy people the holy
"Israel,) with many and various kinds of punish-
"ment, whereby thou madest known thy great
7 "strength. And when he pursued *them* with his
"chariots and the multitude of his troops, thou
"didst drown him in the depth of the sea: and
"didst carry through unhurt those who trusted
8 "on thee, the Lord of the whole creation. Who
"also, after they had experienced the works of
9 "thy hands, praised thee[g], the Almighty. Thou,

---

ceeded to the high priesthood in the year B.C. 211. He is thought to have been the person of whom that eulogy is pronounced in the book of Ecclesiasticus, chap. l.

[d] Gr. Ἅγιε ἐν ἁγίοις.

[e] So in the book of Wis-dom, xiv. 6, "the proud giants" are mentioned, in allusion to Genesis vi. 4. See also Ecclesiasticus, xvi. 7.

[f] Compare 2 Peter ii. 6; and Jude, ver. 7.

[g] See the fine song of Moses, on the deliverance of the Is-

"O King, when thou hadst created the boundless
"and immeasurable earth, didst chuse this city,
"and sanctify this place for thy name[g], who
"standest in need of nothing[h]: and hast glorified
"it by thy magnificent presence, and compacted
"it for the glory of thy great and honourable
"name. And out of love to the house of Israel, 10
"thou promisedst[i] truly that if we should fall off
"from thee, and distress[j] should overtake us, and
"we should come to this place and pray; thou
"wouldest hear our supplication. And indeed 11
"thou art faithful and true.

"And since, when our fathers were often in 12
"affliction, thou hast afforded them assistance in
"their low estate, and hast delivered them out of
"great dangers:—Lo now, O holy King, we are 13
"afflicted on account of our many and great sins:
"we are also become subject to our enemies, and
"are fainting in our infirmities. Now in our 14
"calamity[k] this insolent and profane man endea-
"vours to dishonour this holy place, which has
"been set apart upon earth for thy glorious
"name. Thy habitation indeed is the heaven of 15
"heaven[l], unapproachable[m] by men. But because 16
"thou hast been pleased *to place* thy glory
"among thy people Israel, thou hast sanctified

raelites, at Exodus xv. 1—19.

[g] See 1 Kings xiv. 21; 2 Chron. vii. 15. xii. 13; Ezra vi. 12; Nehemiah i. 9, &c.

[h] τῷ τῶν ἀπάντων ἀπροσδεεῖ. So at 3 Macc. xiv. 35, God is said to be τῶν ὅλων ἀπροσδεής. Compare Acts xvii. 25.

[i] See 1 Kings viii. and ix. and 2 Chron. vi. and vii.

[j] See Deuteron. iv. 30.

[k] Literally, "our fall," (or *prostration*,) Gr. καταπτώσει.

[l] See 1 Kings viii. 27; 2 Chron. ii. 6; vi. 18.

[m] So at 1 Tim. vi. 16, Christ is said to dwell "in the light "which no man can approach "unto."

17 " this place. Do not thou take vengeance[n] on us
" by the pollution of these men: neither do thou
18 " punish us by their profanation: that the trans-
" gressors may not glory[o] in their fury, nor re-
" joice in the pride of their tongue; saying, 'We
" have trodden down[p] the house of sanctification,
" as the houses of abominations[q] are trodden
19 " down.' Blot out our sins, and disperse our
" errors, and send the light of thy mercy *upon*
20 " *us* at this hour. Let thy mercies prevent us[r]
" quickly: and put praises into the mouth of us
" who are fallen down and become contrite in our
" souls, by giving us peace."
21 Here the all-seeing God, who is before all things, Holy in the holies, heard our righteous supplication; and chastised him who was greatly
22 exalted with insolence and boldness: shaking him this way and that way, as a reed *is shaken* by the wind; so that he lay upon the floor without the power[s] of exertion, and paralysed in his limbs, and not even able to speak, being overtaken with
23 a just judgment. Whereupon his friends and body-guards, when they saw that speedy and sharp punishment which had overtaken him, being afraid lest he should even die; struck with overwhelming fear they quickly drew him out of the place.

[n] See the same sentiment expressed at 3 Macc. x. 4; and also below, chap. vi. 10, of this book.

[o] See Psalm xxv. 2.

[p] Compare Isaiah lxiii. 18; Daniel viii. 13.

[q] Literally " stumbling-blocks," Gr. προσοχθισμάτων, a word of frequent occurrence in the Septuagint version, denoting *idols*.

[r] See precisely the same words at Psalm lxxix. 8.

[s] Gr. ἄπρακτον, a word frequently used by Polybius in this sense.

But when after some time he had recovered him- 24
self, his punishment did not bring him to repent-
ance: but he departed with bitter threatenings. So
that when he came into Egypt, he both grew 25
worse in wickedness, and upon conversing
with his drinking companions and such friends as
were estranged from all which was good, of whom
we have already spoken[t]; he not only persevered 26
in countless instances of debauchery[u], but proceeded farther to that degree of insolence, that he
raised reproaches against us in those places; and
that many of our friends, carefully watching the
king's purpose, did themselves also follow his will.

Now he proposed to bring forward publicly an 27
accusation against our nation: and raising up a
pillar at the door of his court, he engraved on it
an inscription: "That none who did not sacrifice 28
" in their temples should enter; and that all the
" Jews should be brought to the *lowest* registry[x],
" and to the condition of slaves: and that those
" who refuse to comply should be seized upon by
" force and put to death. That those also who 29
" are registered shall have a mark imprinted by
" fire upon their body, namely, an ivy-leaf[y], the

---

[t] This does not appear in any previous part of the book, such as we now possess it; it therefore furnishes an additional reason for our thinking, with Grotius, that that which remains is only a portion of a larger work. See the note on chap. i. 1.

[u] Historians, as Polybius, Justin, and Strabo, speak of the systematic luxury and licentiousness of this monarch, especially at this period.

[x] Gr. εἰς λαογραφίαν, which Grotius translates "relatio in " plebem." See his note.—Compare chap. vii. 22.

[y] Compare 3 Maccabees, vi. 7. From the horror with which the Jews appear to regard this threat, may be judged the falsehood of the story, which is mentioned by Plutarch and alluded to by Tacitus, (Histor. V. 5.) that they were supposed by some writers to be worshippers of Bacchus.

"emblem of Bacchus: and that those thus mark-
"ed² shall be inscribed in a separate register with
"inferior and diminished rights." But, that he
might not appear an enemy to them all, he wrote
underneath thus: "that if any of them chuse to
"be joined with those who are initiated into our
"mysteries, *and* to live accordingly, they shall
"have equal privileges ª with the citizens of Alex-
"andria ᵇ."

Then indeed a few of those who dwelt in the city, who hated the advances ᶜ of the religion of the city, easily resigned themselves *to his will:* as expecting to be made partakers of some great glory, from the familiarity which they would have with the king. But the greatest part persevered with a generous spirit, and did not depart from their religion: and redeeming their lives with money, did fearlessly endeavour to escape from the registries, and stood in good hope of obtain-

---

ᶻ Gr. οἷς καὶ καταχωρίσαι εἰς τὴν προσυνεσταλμένην αὐθεντίαν. Crutwell wholly omits this clause. See Grotius's note on the place.

ª Precisely the same thing had been granted to their ancestors by Ptolemy Lagus. See Josephus, Ant. XII. 1. And at a still earlier period Seleucus Nicator had honoured them in a similar manner, by creating them citizens of Antioch. Joseph. Ant. XII. 3.

ᵇ That is, with the Macedonians who had been planted at Alexandria by Alexander and his successors.

ᶜ Gr. τὰς τῆς πόλεως εὐσεβείας ἐπιβάθρας στυγοῦντες. The sense of the word ἐπιβάθρα appears from a passage in Josephus, Ant. XI. 8. Ἡγοῦντο γὰρ τὸν τούτου γάμον ἐπιβάθραν τοῖς παρανομεῖν—βουλησομένοις γενέσθαι: where it signifies, "they considered that "his marriage would become "a *step* (or stepping-stone) to "those who wished to trans- "gress the laws." Ἐπιβάθρα was the name of an engine of war used in sieges; as may be seen in Vitruvius, who translates it "Accessus, seu "ascendens machina." See Vitruv. de Architect. X. 19. and the note of Philander on the passage. It is also used by Polybius, and by Diodorus Siculus.

ing assistance. They also abhorred those of themselves who had apostatized; and deemed them the enemies of their nation; and excluded them from common intercourse and the advantages of social life.

CHAPTER III.

Ptolemy's persecuting edict against the Jews.

Now as soon as this wicked man was informed of these things, he was so enraged as not only to be very angry with those Jews who dwelt at Alexandria, but also he became a more grievous adversary to those who dwelt in the country[a]: and commanded to make haste and gather them all together[b], and put them to death in the most cruel manner.

While these things were in agitation, a malignant report went forth against our nation, from those men who were consenting to this wicked project; a handle being given for this their design, *upon the complaint of those apostates* that we forbade them to communicate with us in our ordinances. But the Jews continued to preserve unchangeable their good will and fidelity to their kings. But, as they worshipped God, and ordered their conversation according to his law, they made a separation in some points, and rejections[c] of some

---

[a] Namely, in the country parts of Egypt.
[b] Viz. to Alexandria.
[c] The Greek text has καταστροφάς: but Grotius pronounces that by all means we must read ἀποστροφὰς, rejections. Several of these national peculiarities are brought forward, in disparagement of the Jews, by the historian Diodorus Siculus: Eclog. lib. XXXIV. and XL.: others are mentioned (as erroneously) by Dio Cassius: and Tacitus has left on record some curious particulars, exhibiting the imperfect knowledge and

others: on which account to some persons they
5 appeared odious. Yet by adorning their conversation[d] with the works of the righteous, they had
6 become well approved by all men. But those foreigners[e] paid no regard to that character for good deeds of the nation everywhere so much
7 spoken of: but made a great noise about the separation which they made from others, in their ways of worship and sorts of food: and said, that these men were not sociable either with the king or with his armies; but that they were disaffected[f], and greatly opposed to the success of their affairs: so that they covered them with no small
8 blame. Now those Greeks, who were in the city, and were in no wise injured *by them*, observing the unexpected disturbance which was raised, and unforeseen concourses of people about these men, were indeed unable to help them, for the consti-
9 tution[g] of the government was tyrannical: yet

loose notions which even the polished Romans then had, respecting a people lately subdued by their own generals. Hist. V. 2, &c.

[d] Doing that which St. Paul recommends to the Christian converts, at Coloss. iv. 5, and 1 Thess. iv. 12, "Walk honestly" [in wisdom] "towards them that are without."

[e] Namely, the Macedonians, settled at Alexandria.

[f] It is remembered that the same charge was made by Haman, the Agagite, when he persuaded king Ahasuerus to issue an edict for a general massacre of the Jews throughout his dominions: "There is a certain people, scattered abroad and dispersed among the people in all the provinces of thy kingdom: and their laws are diverse from all people, neither keep they the king's laws: therefore it is not for the king's profit to suffer them." Esther, iii. 8. See also the Apocryphal additions, xiii. 5. See likewise Josephus's justification of his nation in these particulars, in his Antiquities, XVI. 10.

[g] Gr. διάθεσις: which Schleusner contends to mean here no more than a simple edict.

they used exhortations *in their favour*, and were very sorry for them, and thought these things would have a change; for that so vast a body of men who had done no harm through ignorance[h] would not be thus overlooked *by their God*. And besides, certain of their neighbours and friends and partisans called some of them together privately, and plighted their faith to protect them, and to use every endeavour for their assistance.

Ptolemy then, as exulting in his present prosperity; and having no regard to the power of the Most High God; but supposing that he should continue always in the same design, wrote this epistle against them: " King Ptolemy Philopator " to his commanders and soldiers in Egypt and " elsewhere, joy and health. I myself am in health, " and our affairs also *are prosperous*. Since our " last expedition into Asia, as you yourselves " know, has, through the unforeseen[i] assistance " of the gods to us, and by our own fortitude, " justly been brought to a happy conclusion; we " determined to treat the nations which inhabit " Cœlosyria and Phœnice, not with force of arms, " but to nurse them with kindness and great ten- " derness, and willingly to do them good. And " having bestowed great revenues on the temples " of the several cities, we proceeded as far as " Jerusalem: and went up with an intention to " honour the temple of these wretches, who will " never leave off their madness. Now those men

---

[h] Gr. μηδὲν ἠγνοηκός. Compare 3 Macc. xi. 31.

[i] The Greek text reads ἀπροπτώτῳ: but the interpreters unanimously translate the word as if it had been ἀπροόπ_τῳ. See Schleusner's Lexicon Vet. Test.

B.C. 210.   CHAP. III.   15

"in word took our coming thither kindly, but in
"their behaviour insincerely[k]: for, when we in-
"tended to go into their holy place, and to ho-
"nour it[l] with excellent and most noble gifts:
18 "they, carried away with their ancient pride, pro-
"hibited our entrance, not having experienced[m]
"our power by reason of that kindness which we
19 "shew to all mankind. And making manifest
"their ill-will towards us, and being the only na-
"tion in the world which is insolent towards
"kings and towards its own benefactors, they are
"not willing to bear anything kindly[n].
20 "Now we, being moved by the madness of these
"men, though we had returned home with vic-
"tory, and had come back into Egypt with the
"testimony of having met all nations with kind-
"ness, have done that which was fit for us to do.
21 "And in the midst of these things we have de-
"clared to all men our forgiveness of their na-
"tion; and on account of their assistance in war
"and the innumerable affairs with which from
"the beginning we innocently intrusted them[o],
"we earnestly endeavoured to change them, and
"were willing to bestow on them the privileges
"of citizens of Alexandria, and to make them

[k] Gr. νόθως.
[l] As several kings had done before, according to the account given by Josephus, Ant. XII. 3.
[m] Gr. ἀπολειπόμενοι τῆς ἡμετέρας ἀλκῆς.
[n] Gr. οὐδὲν γνήσιον βούλονται φέρειν. or, the sense may be, "will not behave themselves "kindly:" or, "will not bear "any thing which is fair and "equitable." γνήσιον appears to be opposed to νόθως (insincerely) above in ver. 17. See the same word occurring again at ver. 23.
[o] Josephus relates that Ptolemy Lagus intrusted several of his garrisons to the keeping of the Jews. See also ch. vi. 25, of this book.

"companions of our priests[p] for the time being.
"But they, taking this offer in a contrary light,
"and by that wicked habit which is natural to
"them[q], rejecting the good and inclining per-
"petually to that which is evil; did not only
"turn away from that inestimable privilege, but
"abhorred both publicly and privately[r] those few
"amongst themselves who were favourably dis-
"posed towards us: ever expecting that by their
"infamous course of procedure we should speedily
"change our just measures.

"Wherefore, we both being well assured by
"certain signs that these men do in every way
"bear us ill-will; and providing lest, upon any
"sudden trouble which may come upon us here-
"after, we should have these wicked wretches be-
"hind our backs as traitors and barbarous ene-
"mies: have given order, that as soon as this
"epistle is brought to you, the same hour you
"seize on these people who are dwelling among
"you, together with their wives and children[s],
"with insult and vexation; and send them to us
"every way secured in iron bonds, that they may
"suffer an inevitable and ignominious death, such

---

[p] Gr. τῶν ἀεὶ ἱερέων. Grotius proposes a preferable reading, ἱερῶν, "the ancient" (or perpetual) "rites of our religion."

[q] It is too notorious that the Jews universally bore a bad name among surrounding nations: and the strange notions which even the learned and polished Romans could allow themselves to entertain respecting their origin and customs, may be seen in Tacitus, Histor. V. 2, 4, and 5.

[r] Gr. λόγῳ τε καὶ σιγῇ.

[s] There is a remarkable similarity between this epistle of Ptolemy and that of Artaxerxes, written at the suggestion of Haman, which is mentioned at Esther, iii. 13; and is given at length in the apocryphal part of that book, xiii. 4—7.

26 " as is suitable to the disaffected. For when once
" all these have been brought to punishment to-
" gether, we suppose that during the rest of our
" time our affairs will be perfectly established, in
27 " security and the best condition. And whoso-
" ever shall conceal any individual of the Jews,
" from an old man to an infant and the very suck-
" lings, he and all his family shall be racked to
28 " death with the severest tortures. But whoso-
" ever is willing to discover any of them, he shall
" thereby obtain the substance[t] of him who fell
" under punishment, and two thousand drachmæ
" of silver[u] besides out of the royal treasury. He
" shall also be made free, and shall be crowned.
29 " And every place where a concealed Jew shall
" be by any means caught, let it be made impas-
" sable[x] and be burned with fire: and it shall be
" rendered wholly useless to every mortal being
" for all time to come."
30   The form, then, of that epistle was to this effect.

[t] This custom, which has more or less obtained among both ancient and modern nations, appears to be recognised in the Old Testament, 2 Sam. xvi. 3, 4: where David confiscates the property of Mephibosheth, and gives it to his accuser Ziba.

[u] Assuming the Hebrew drachma to be equal to the Roman, namely, one eighth of an ounce, this weight of silver will amount to about fifty-seven pounds sterling.

[x] Gr. ἄβατος καὶ πυριφλεγὴς γινέσθω. So in the letter of Artaxerxes recorded in the apocryphal part of the book of Esther, it is commanded that every place which disobeys the king's command be made οὐ μόνον ἀνθρώποις ἄβατος, ἀλλὰ καὶ θηρίοις καὶ πετεινοῖς εἰς τὸν ἅπαντα χρόνον ἔχθιστος. The expression ἄβατος (in the sense of *unentered, unprofaned*) is applied to the temple of Jerusalem by Josephus, Antiq. XIV. 8. Compare the note on ch. v. 43, of this book.

CHAPTER IV.

The king's edict is executed with great severity.

Now wheresoever this decree came to hand, there was made a general festival among the heathen, with shouting and joy: that hatred, which had been hardened over [a] in their mind of old, now shewing itself outwardly in open discourse. But among the Jews there was intolerable lamentation, and a most doleful cry with tears; as if their hearts were set on fire on every side with their groans: while they bewailed that unexpected destruction which was suddenly decreed against them.

What district[b] or city, or indeed what habitable place or what streets were there, which were not filled with lamentations and mourning over them? For they were sent away unanimously with such bitter and merciless feeling by the commanders in every city, that at their extraordinary[c] punishment some of their very enemies, having common pity before their eyes, and considering the uncertain catàstrophe of human life, wept at their most miserable expulsion.

For there was led along a multitude of aged men decked with hoary heads, stooping by reason

---

[a] Gr. προκατεσκιρρωμένης, literally signifying, "covered by a callus."

[b] Gr. νόμος, the proper appellation of the præfectures or districts of Egypt.

[c] Gr. ἐξάλλοις τιμωρίαις. So in the Septuagint version of 2 Sam. vi. 14, David is said to be ἐνδεδυκὼς στολὴν ἔξαλλον, though our English translators do not thus render the Hebrew. Compare chap. vii. 3, and 3 Macc. ix. 6. Thucydides also, in book III. chap. 82, uses a similar expression, ἀτοπία τῶν τιμωριῶν.

of the slowness of their feet[d], through old age and the hurry of a forcible removal, obliged, without any *regard to* shame, to walk at a quick pace.

6 Nay, the young women, who had lately entered into the marriage-chamber in order to *enjoy* matrimonial society, were made to partake of groans instead of pleasure; and being defiled with dust sprinkled on their hair, which was moist with ointment, *and* led along unveiled, with one accord they sang lamentations instead of wedding-songs, as being torn to pieces with vexations unknown[e] 7 in the country. And, *like* public captives[f], they were dragged by force to an embarkation on board ship.

8 Their husbands also, wearing halters, instead of garlands, about their necks, in their flourishing and youthful vigour, instead of feasting and juvenile relaxation, passed the rest of their nuptial days in lamentations, as seeing the grave lying 9 *open* immediately beneath their feet. And they were conveyed like beasts, led in the confinement of iron bonds: some of them fastened by the neck to the benches of the ships; others having their 10 feet made fast in indissoluble fetters. And besides all this, they were shut out from the light by the thick planks[g] which lay above them; that their

---

[d] Or, "While they (viz. the "king's officers and soldiers) "forced the sluggishness of "their crippled feet to a quick "pace, without any regard to "shame, through the hurry of "a forcible removal." The Greek text is somewhat obscure.

[e] Gr. σκυλμοῖς ἀλλοεθνέσι, a kindred phrase to that which appears above, at ver. 4, ἐξ- άλλοις τιμωρίαις.

[f] Or, "like captives they "were publicly dragged."

[g] It appears that they were thrust down into the lowest part (the hold) of the vessel;

20   BOOK I.   B.C. 210.

eyes might be wholly in the dark; and that they might receive the treatment of traitors during their whole voyage.

When these men therefore had been carried 11 thus unto the *port called* Schedia^h, and the journey by water was ended, according to the king's former decree; he gave further orders to put them into the Hippodromeⁱ, which was before the city, a place of vast circuit, and very fit for exposing them to the view of all who entered into the city, or who went out thence into the country to sojourn: that they might hold no communication with his forces, nor might have the favour of walls^j to enclose them.

But as soon as this was done, the king, hearing 12 that those of their nation who lived in the city went out privately and frequently to bewail that opprobrious misery of their brethren,—fell into a 13 passion; and gave command to treat those also exactly in the same way as the others; and not at all to abate to them the punishment which the others suffered. And that the entire race should 14 be enrolled by name: not now with a view of forcing them to that painful way of worship which we briefly explained before^k: but in order to have them tortured miserably according to his edict, and at last to destroy them utterly in the space of

so as to be deprived as much as possible both of light and fresh air.

^h A place in Lower Egypt, possessing a harbour, distant about thirty miles from Alexandria.

ⁱ See a description of this building in Strabo, b. XVII.

^j That is, " might not be " honoured so far as to be " admitted within the city " walls."

^k Namely, at ch. ii. 29.

B.C. 210.   CHAP. IV.   21

15 one day. The registering of them therefore was made with bitter diligence and zealous perseverance from sun-rising to sun-setting, not being
16 completely ended[1] for forty days. But the king *was* greatly and continually filled with joy; ordaining festivals *in the temples* of all his idols; with a mind far erring from the truth, and a profane mouth, praising such *gods* as were deaf, and could neither speak to nor assist them; and uttering unbecoming expressions against the Most High God.

17 Now after the aforesaid space of time, the scribes addressed themselves to the king, *informing* him that they could no longer make the enrolment of the Jews by reason of their immense number;
18 there being still a great number throughout the country, some of them abiding quietly at home, others being scattered here and there; so that the business was impracticable, *even* for all the com-
19 manders in Egypt. But after he had threatened them severely as having been bribed in order to procure their escape, it turned out that he became
20 fully satisfied on that point: when they said, and proved, that both the paper[m] and pens which they used had failed them. This was the powerful operation of that invincible Providence which gave help to the Jews from heaven.

---

[1] The sense appears to be, that the registering continued during forty days, and even then was not finished. See vv. 18, 19.

[m] The Greek word here used is χαρτηρία, manifestly adopted from the Latin tongue; several instances of which usage we have in the New Testament, familiar to every scholar.

CHAPTER V.

The Jews ordered to be destroyed by elephants. The king's irresolution.

THEN calling to him Hermo, who had the care of the elephants, being full of fierce anger, and totally unchangeable through rage; he commanded that against the next day they should dose all the elephants, in number five hundred[a], with large handfuls of frankincense[b] and a great quantity of undiluted wine; and when they had been maddened by the copious supply of this drink, they should then introduce them to meet and destroy[c] the Jews. He then, having given this command, returned to his banquet, having collected round him those of his friends and of his army who were the greatest enemies to the Jews. But Hermo, the commander of the elephants, performed exactly what had been ordered. And the servants, who were appointed to that business, going out in the evening, bound the hands of the poor wretches, and took all other care necessary to secure them; supposing that *the whole* tribe would together, that very night[d], receive their final destruction.

---

[a] Bochart suspects some error in this number; as Ptolemy had only seventy-three elephants at the battle of Raphia, and several of these were lost there. (Hierozoicon, tom. I. p. 260.)

[b] The stimulating effects of this drug were early known, and are mentioned by Dioscorides and Pliny.

[c] Gr. πρὸς συνάντησιν τοῦ μόρου τῶν Ἰουδαίων, "that the "Jews by them might meet "their death."

[d] It may seem strange that the servants should have imagined this, seeing that the elephants were ordered to be ready for *the next morning*. Grotius therefore would alter the punctuation, and by join-

6 Now the Jews, who seemed to the heathen to be destitute of all protection, by reason of the confinement in chains which environed them on all
7 sides, did all with an unceasing cry and with tears call upon the Almighty Lord, the supreme Disposer of all power, their merciful God and Father:
8 beseeching him to change the unholy design against them; and to deliver them, by a glorious manifestation of himself, from that fate which was
9 ready at their feet. So the earnest supplication of these *Jews* ascended up to heaven.
10 But Hermo, having given to the merciless elephants their potion, and filled them with a plentiful supply of wine and crammed them with frankincense, was early at the palace in the morning to
11 inform the king thereof. But He[e], who bestows what He pleases upon all men, had cast upon the king a sleep, a thing which from all eternity has been considered good in the night, but now was
12 sent in the day. And he was detained in a most sweet and deep slumber, through the operation[f] of the Lord of all things: being greatly disappointed of his unlawful purpose, and mightily deceived in
13 his immutable contrivance. But the Jews, having escaped the appointed hour, praised their holy

ing ἔννυχον with ἀσφάλειαν, would render the passage, "the servants took all other "care necessary to secure "them *for that night.*"

[e] The Greek text of this verse is obscure, and possibly corrupt: Τοῦτο δ᾽ ἀπ᾽ αἰῶνος χρόνου κτίσμα καλὸν ἐν νυκτὶ καὶ ἡμέρᾳ ἐπιβαλλόμενον ὑπὸ τοῦ χαριζομένου πᾶσιν, οἷς ἂν αὐτὸς θελήσῃ ὕπνου μέρος ἀπέστειλε πρὸς τὸν βασιλέα. Nor do the various readings resolve the intricacy. Grotius explains the text agreeably to the translation here given.

[f] Nonne lapsus est in hoc loco Schleusnerus, qui voces masculas ἡδίστῳ καὶ βαθεῖ cum v. fœminea ἐνεργείᾳ conjungendas censuerit? Confer Lex. Vet. Test.

God; and prayed again to Him who is easy to be reconciled, that He would shew to the proud heathen the strength of his powerful hand.

And when it was about half way past the ninth hour, he who was appointed to invite the guests, when he saw them in great numbers about him, came and shook the king. And when he had awaked him with great difficulty, he informed him that the time for the feast was passing by, entering into conversation on these matters [g]. Which the king reflecting on, betook himself to his banquet, and commanded that the guests who were come to the feast should sit down in his presence. Which being done, he exhorted them to give up themselves to revelry, and to honour the abundant feast before them, by spending the time in merriment.

And when the interview had lasted long, the king sent for Hermo, and asked him with bitter threatening for what cause the Jews had been suffered to outlive that day. And when he shewed that even over-night he had completely finished that which was enjoined him[h], and his friends also testified to this effect: *the king*, with a barbarity worse than that of Phalaris, said that they might thank his sleep of that day: " but against " the next morning without all excuse do thou " prepare the elephants in like manner for the " annihilation of the wicked Jews." And when

---

[g] Gr. τὸν περὶ τούτων λόγον ποιούμενος: which Grotius interprets, "discoursing about "the quality of the guests "whom he had invited." Whiston rendered it, "adding a few words about the "other design."

[h] Namely, to bind and secure the Jews.

the king had said this, all who were present cheerfully and joyfully commending it with one accord,
22 departed each to his own home. And they did not so much employ the night-time in sleep, as in devising all sorts of indignities[i] against those who seemed to be miserable wretches.

23 Now as soon as the cock had crowed at daybreak, Hermo had armed the elephants, and was exercising them in the great cloistered court[k].
24 And the multitudes in the city crowded together to this most sad spectacle, earnestly waiting for
25 the morning. But the Jews being in suspense[l] for some short time, with weeping supplication in mournful strains, stretching out their hands to heaven, besought the Most High God again to assist them with all speed.

26 The rays of the sun were not yet spread abroad, when, the king waiting to receive his friends, Hermo stood by his side, and called to come forward, shewing that the royal desire was in a way
27 to be speedily fulfilled. But when he received this intelligence, and was astonished at that unusual[m] coming forth *so early*, being overcome with total ignorance, he asked what that matter

---

[i] Similar treatment of the early Christians is described by Tacitus (Annal. lib. XV.) Compare Juvenal, Sat. I. 155.

[k] Gr. Περιστύλῳ, literally "an area enclosed or surrounded by columns." Bochart contends that the place here spoken of must have been some distinct public building; as scarcely any court or part of a palace could have afforded space for the manœuvring of five hundred elephants. He judges it to have been a particular *street* in the city of Alexandria so called, and adduces the grounds of his opinion from Achilles Tatius, book V.

[l] Gr. κατὰ τὸν ἀμερῆ ψυχουλκούμενοι χρόνον: or, "expecting to live only a moment of time."

[m] Gr. τῇ παρανόμῳ ἐξόδῳ.

was for which *all* this had been so diligently done by him.

Now this was the operation of God who disposeth all things, who had planted in his mind an entire forgetfulness of the plans which before he had contrived. 28

But Hermo and all his friends explained *to him* that the beasts and the troops are ready, " according 29 " ing to thine earnest desire, O King." But he, 30 filled with great wrath at their words, (because that through God's providence all his sense about these matters was scattered to nought,) looking steadfastly *on Hermo* with threats, said, " If your 31 " parents ⁿ or children had been here, they should " have furnished a glorious prey for the wild " beasts, instead of these blameless Jews; who " have shewn in a remarkable degree, to me and " to my ancestors, an entire and unshaken fidelity. " And indeed, but for that affection which our 32 " education together and your usefulness ᵒ has " kept up, you should have been put to death in- " stead of these."

So Hermo underwent an unexpected and dangerous threatening; and was cast down in his eyes and countenance. The king's friends also 33 34

ⁿ I do not know that any commentator has noticed this speech of Ptolemy as being in verse: yet it will be seen that the greater portion of it (with the help of some critical emendation) forms tolerable trimeter Iambics:

Εἴ σοι γονεῖς παρῆσαν ἢ παίδων γοναί,

['Η] τήνδε θήρσιν ἀγρίοις ἐσκεύ- ασαν

Δαψιλῆ θοίναν ἀντὶ τῶν ἀνεγκλή- των

Ἐμοὶ [τε] καὶ προγόνοισ' ἐμοῖς δεδειγμένων

Ὁλοσχερῆ βεβαίαν πίστιν ἐξόχως Ἰουδαίων. [The last word is probably a Gloss.] Καί περ εἰ μὴ διὰ τὴν τῆς συντροφίας στοργὴν, καὶ τῆς χρείας, τὸ ζῆν ἀντὶ τούτων ἐστερήθης.

ᵒ Or, " office which you " hold:" Gr. τῆς χρείας.

coming out secretly P one by one with a sad countenance, sent away the assembled multitudes each
35 to his own private affairs. And when the Jews had heard what the king had said, they praised the glorious God and King of kings, having obtained from Him this *second* assistance also.
36 But the king after the very same manner appointed another banquet, and invited *his friends*
37 to turn their minds to mirth. And calling for Hermo, he said to him with threats, " How often, " O thou wretch, must I give fresh orders to thee
38 " about these same people? Arm the elephants " once again for to-morrow, for the annihilation " of the Jews."
39 But his kinsmen who were seated with him at the banquet, wondering at his unstable mind, said
40 thus: " O king, how long wilt thou trifle with us, " as though we were irrational brutes? command-" ing us now this third time to destroy these men; " and then, when the business was begun 9, repent-
41 " ing and rescinding thy *former* orders: by rea-" son of which the city is disturbed through ex-" pectation; and, being filled with assembled " groups of people, has been in frequent danger " of being pillaged in various ways."
42 Upon this the king, exactly like *another* Phalaris, filled with absurdity, and counting for nothing those changes of mind which had been wrought in him respecting the visitation r of the

---

P Gr. ὑπεκρέων, "gradually "stealing away, as if ashamed." Compare 2 Sam. xix. 3, " The " people gat them by stealth " into the city, as people be-" ing ashamed steal away " when they flee in battle."
q Gr. ἐπὶ τῶν πραγμάτων.
r Gr. ἐπισκοπὴν, which may signify either " punishment"

Jews; swore vehemently a most impious oath[s], determining that without delay he would send these people into the other world, foully trampled *to death* by the knees[t] and feet of the elephants. And that he would send an army into Judæa and quickly level it with the ground by fire and sword; and speedily would destroy with fire that "temple "of theirs, which (said he) we are not allowed to "enter[u]," and would make it destitute of those who offer sacrifice for all time to come.

Then his friends and kinsmen departing, overjoyed and with belief in him, disposed the troops in the most proper parts of the city for securing it. But the governor of the elephants, having driven the animals, as I may say, into a state of

or "deliverance." See the word occurring at Luke xix. 44, also in chap. iii. of the Wisdom of Solomon, ver. 20. (where by the way it is very incorrectly translated) and in several other parts of the same book.

[s] Gr. ἀτελέστατον ἐβεβαίωσεν ὅρκον, an oath which was not likely to be fulfilled.

[t] Gr. ἐν γόνασι καὶ ποσί. Whiston takes no notice of the word *knees*, and Grotius pronounces the phrase a Hebraism. But there is reason to think that each word has an intended and distinct meaning; and that the author was acquainted with the habits of the animals which he is describing. Bochart, (Hierozoic. I. p. 261, &c.) commenting on this passage, mentions that it was customary with elephants trained for war to use both their knees and feet for treading down and crushing their enemies; and refers to Ælian's History of Animals for confirmation of his remark. Ælian observes, πατουμένων δὲ τῶν ἁλισκομένων, καὶ ἀλοωμένων τοῖς γόνασι, ἄραβος πολὺς τῶν ὀστέων συντριβομένων ἀκούεται καὶ πόρρωθεν: which fully bears out Bochart in his assertion. Æl. Hist. Anim. VIII. 10. And Hirtius, de Bello Africano, sect. 72, relating the bravery of a soldier when attacked by an elephant, uses the following words: "Quum elephantus vulnere "ictus—in lixam inermem "impetum fecisset, eumque "sub pede subditum, *deinde* "*genu innixus* pondere suo "—premeret et enecaret."

[u] Gr. τὸν ἄβατον αὐτῶν ἡμῖν ναόν.

madness by highly-scented potions of wine mixed with frankincense, they being decked out in fearful array [x] :—about daybreak, the city being already filled with countless multitudes about the Hippodrome [y], he entered into the court, and called out the king to the business before him. Then he, having his wicked mind filled with fierce anger, rushed forth with all his retinue [z] and with the beasts: resolving to behold, with an untouched heart and with his own eyes, the painful and miserable destruction of the aforementioned *Jews*.

But the Jews, when they saw the dust raised by the elephants going out of the gate, and by the armed force which followed, and by the march of the multitude; and heard the tumultuous noise: thinking that moment to be the last of their lives, the conclusion of their most woeful expectation, they betook themselves to lamentations and wailings; they kissed one another, embracing their relatives and falling about their necks, fathers on their sons, and mothers upon young girls, and other women who had new-born babes at their breasts drawing their last milk.

Nevertheless, having regard to those former assistances which they had received from heaven, throwing themselves flat down with one accord, and removing the infants from their breasts, they cried out with an exceeding great cry, beseeching the Lord of all power to shew pity on them, by

---

[x] Gr. φοβεραῖς κατεσκευασμένα σκευαῖς. Thus Diodorus Siculus (lib. XVII.) speaks of elephants, καταπληκτικῶς κεκοσμημένους.

[y] See above, chap. iv. 11.

[z] Gr. βάρει: or the word may signify " in all his might, " in all the weight of his an-" ger," τῆς ὀργῆς βαρείας.

the manifestation *of his presence*, who were now at the gates of the other world.

CHAPTER VI.

Eleazar's prayer. The Jews are wonderfully delivered.

Now one Eleazar, a man eminent among the priests of the country, a man already stricken in age, and adorned through life with every kind of virtue, bidding the elders who were about him to call upon the holy God, offered up the following prayer:

"O King[a], most powerful, most high, almighty "God, who governest the whole creation in mer-"cies: Look, O Father, upon the seed of Abra-"ham, upon the children of Jacob sanctified *to* "*thee*, the people of thy sanctified portion, strang-"ers in a strange land, *and* perishing unjustly. "Thou didst destroy with all his host, by drown-"ing, Pharaoh the former ruler of this Egypt, "when he abounded with chariots and was elated "with lawless confidence, and with a tongue speak-"ing great things; having caused the light of "thy mercy to shine upon Israel's race. Thou, "Lord, didst break in pieces Sennacherim, the "cruel king of Assyria, who was puffed up with "his innumerable armies; who had already sub-"dued the whole earth with his spear[b], and being

---

[a] Undoubtedly the language of this prayer is poetry, as will appear to any one who inspects the original, which is printed at the end of the introduction; although it is neither divided nor stopped in the proper manner, and the commentators are silent on the point: both the sentiments and language are very fine.

[b] Gr. δόρατι τὴν πᾶσαν ὑποχείριον ἤδη λαβόντα γῆν. The expression is common among the classic authors; in whom

B.C. 210.   CHAP. VI.   31

" lifted up with pride against thy holy city, spake
" harsh things in insolence and boasting; making
6 " thy power conspicuous to many nations. Thou
" didst deliver, unhurt even to a hair of their
" head, the three companions in the land of Baby-
" lon, who voluntarily exposed their lives to the
" fire that they might not worship vain *gods*, by
" shedding a dew [c] throughout the fiery furnace,
" whilst thou sentest the flame [d] upon all their ad-
" versaries.
7   " Thou didst restore to the light *of day*, unhurt,
" Daniel, who through spiteful calumnies had been
" cast for a prey to the fierce lions under ground.
8 " Thou, Father, didst shew again to all his house-
" hold unharmed [e], Jonas, who was pining away [f]

we meet with δορυάλωτος, δο-
ριθήρατος, δορίκτητος, δορίληπτος,
&c.

[c] Gr. διάπυρον δροσίσας κάμινον. Can any idea, or any
expression, be more beautiful?
In the prayer of Azarias (in
the apocryphal additions to
the third chapter of Daniel,
ver. 25, 26,) we read, ὁ δὲ
ἄγγελος Κυρίου—— ἐποίησε τὸ
μέσον τῆς καμίνου ὡς πνεῦμα
δρόσου διασυρίζον.

[d] " Because the king's com-
" mandment was urgent, and
" the furnace exceeding hot,
" the flame of the fire slew
" those men that took up
" Shadrach, Meshach, and A-
" bednego." Daniel iii. 22.

[e] In the apocryphal epistle
of St. Paul to the Corinthians,
which is preserved in the Armenian church, and was translated into English from that
language by lord Byron, is
the following apposite and expressive phrase upon this subject of Jonah's complete preservation: " Neither was any
" part of his body corrupted;
" *neither was his eyebrow*
" *bent down.*"

[f] Gr. τηκόμενον: namely in
mind, not in body. The reader will readily call to mind
the expressions of the prophet, as recorded in his second chapter: " Then Jonah
" prayed unto the Lord his
" God, out of the fish's belly,
" and said; ' I cried by rea-
" son of my affliction unto
" the Lord:—the waters com-
" passed me about, even to
" the soul: the depth closed
" me round about, the weeds
" were wrapped about my
" head.—When my soul faint-
" ed within me, thou heardest
" me,' " &c.

" unpitied[g] in the belly of the whale bred in the
" depths of the sea.

" And now, O thou who hatest insolence, plen- 9
" teous in mercy, Protector of the Universe, shew
" thyself quickly to them of the race of Israel, who
" now are injuriously treated by abominable, law-
" less heathens. And if our life has been guilty 10
" of impieties during our captivity, deliver us
" from the hand of our enemies, and do thou, O
" Lord, destroy us[h] by whatever death[i] thou dost
" chuse. Let not these followers of vanity bless 11
" their vain *idols* over the destruction of thy be-
" loved, saying, 'Even their God has not delivered
" them[k].' But do thou, O eternal One, who hast 12
" all might and all dominion, now look upon us;
" pity us, who through the causeless insolence of
" wicked men are to be deprived of life like trai-
" tors. O God, whom we honour, who hast all 13
" power, let the heathens dread thy invincible
" might this day, on the deliverance of the race of
" Jacob. The whole multitude of infants and 14
" their parents supplicate to thee with tears. Let 15
" it be shewn to all nations that thou, O Lord, art
" with us, and hast not turned away thy face from
" us: but even, as thou hast said[l] that not even
" when they were in the land of their enemies
" thou wouldest overlook them, so bring it to pass,
" O Lord."

[g] Gr. ἀφειδῶς. There is a various reading, ἀφιδών.

[h] Compare David's prayer, at 2 Samuel xxiv. 14. and see above, ch. ii. 17.

[i] Gr. μόρῳ, which more particularly denotes, in Scripture, death *by pestilence*.

[k] See the words of Rabshakeh, the general of Sennacherib, to this effect, in 2 Kings xviii. and Isaiah xxxvi. Also Psalm lxxix. 10.

[l] Compare Levit. xxvi. 42. Deuteron. xxx. 3, 9, 10.

16 Now as soon as Eleazar had ceased praying, the king with the beasts and the whole marching array[m] of his army arrived at the Hippodrome.

17 And the Jews beholding it cried aloud to heaven; insomuch that even the adjoining valleys, echoing back the sound, created an uncontrollable wailing throughout the whole army.

18 Then the most glorious, almighty, and true God, manifesting his holy countenance, opened the doors of heaven; from whence two glorious and terrific angels descended, visible to all except

19 the Jews: and stood against them, and filled the enemies' army with confusion and fear, and bound

20 them in bonds which could not be loosed. The king's own person also became horror struck[n], and oblivion seized on his violent and angry boldness.

21 And they turned back the elephants[o] upon the

---

[m] Gr. φρυάγματι, expressing the noise and bustle necessarily attendant on such movements.

[n] Gr. ὑπόφρικον τὸ σῶμα τοῦ βασιλέως ἐγενήθη.

[o] Josephus relates a similar act of violence attempted against the Jews, with similar success and several corresponding circumstances, in his second book against Apion. But this is said to have occurred under the reign of Ptolemy Physcon, sixty or seventy years later than the event described in our text. Yet from the general similarity appearing in the two accounts, it has been judged, not unreasonably, that in reality the thing occurred only once, but has been differently related by historians. The Greek of Josephus, in this passage, is lost: the Latin version runs thus: "Physcon "Ptolemæus cum adversum "exercitum quidem Oniæ pug- "nare præsumeret, omnes ve- "ro Judæos in civitate posi- "tos cum filiis et uxoribus "capiens nudos atque vinctos "elephantis subjecisset, ut ab "eis conculcati deficerent; et "ad hoc etiam bestias ipsas "inebriasset, in contrarium "quæ præparaverat evenere. "Elephanti enim relinquentes "sibi appositos Judæos, im- "petu facto super amicos "ejus, multos ex ipsis intere- "mere. Et post hæc Ptole- "mæus quidem aspectum ter- "ribilem contemplatus est, "prohibentem se ut illis no- "ceret hominibus." Joseph. c. Apion. II. 5.

armed troops which were following, and they trampled upon them and destroyed them.

And the king's anger was turned into pity and tears, on account of what he formerly had devised. For when he heard the cry, and saw them all prostrate *ready* for destruction, shedding tears, he angrily threatened his friends, saying: " You " abuse^p the royal authority, and have outdone " tyrants in barbarity; and even me your bene-" factor you are now endeavouring to remove both " from my authority and my life, by secretly de-" vising measures disadvantageous to my king-" dom. Who has brought away, each from his " home, and absurdly collected together here, " these men who were faithfully guarding the " fortresses ^q of our country? Who has encom-" passed with such lawless indignities these men " who from the beginning have in all things sur-

---

P Gr. παραβασιλεύετε, a very expressive word: "you assume a power to which you have no claim." Grotius well observes, that the Greeks often use the preposition παρά in this sense in compound words, such as παρασοφίζω, παρασυνάγω, &c.; also that an equivalent expression occurs in Terence, "quandoquidem solus regnas."

q Josephus, c. Apion. lib. II. says, Ὅμοια δὲ Ἀλεξάνδρου καὶ Πτολεμαῖος ὁ Λάγου περὶ τῶν ἐν Ἀλεξανδρείᾳ κατοικούντων ἐφρόνησεν· καὶ γὰρ τὰ κατὰ τὴν Αἴγυπτον αὐτοῖς ἐνεχείρισε φρούρια, πιστῶς ἁμὰ καὶ γενναίως φυλάξειν ὑπολαμβάνων. The same is asserted by him, in similar terms, in the twelfth book of his Antiquities, ch. 1, and 3. where he states that Ptolemy Lagus, finding that the inhabitants of Jerusalem were especially to be depended on for honourable keeping of their oaths and engagements, intrusted many of his fortresses to their hands, and bestowed on several of them the freedom of Alexandria, so that they were placed on a par with his Macedonians; exacting from them an oath that they would continue faithful to his descendants for his sake. And well indeed they appear to have fulfilled the trust reposed in them. Compare ch. iii. 21, *supra*.

"passed all nations in good-will towards us, and
"frequently have undertaken the greatest dangers
27 "of all men *for our sake?* Loose, loose utterly,
"the unjust bonds: send them away in peace to
"their own homes, having asked their forgiveness
28 "of what has been already done. Set free the
"sons of the almighty, heavenly, living God, who
"from the days of our ancestors until this pre-
"sent time has vouchsafed to our affairs an unin-
"terrupted prosperous stability."

29   Thus he spake; and the Jews being released in
a moment blessed the holy God their deliverer,
30 having that instant escaped from death. Then
the king returning to the city called for him who
was over his revenues, and commanded him to
supply the Jews with wines and other things requisite for a feast during seven days: resolving
that in the place wherein they had expected to
meet destruction, in that they should keep a festival of deliverance with all joyfulness.

31   Then those who before were reviled and were
near to death, or rather were entering into it; instead of a bitter and most lamentable fate, formed
together a festive party[r] to celebrate their preservation; and parted the place[s], which had been pre-

---

[r] Gr. κώθωνα σωτήριον, which strictly may denote "the cup "of salvation," equivalent to the expression ποτήριον σωτηρίον, in Psalm cxvi. 13; and to πότον σωτήριον occurring below, ch. vii. 18. The verb κωθωνίζομαι, "to drink or feast," occurs in Polybius, and is also used by the seventy interpreters.

[s] Gr. τόπον κλισίαις κατεμέρισαν, they fixed up tents in various places, in imitation of the feast of tabernacles. The old translation of 1550 renders the passage, "they point-"ed out with their stoles the "place where they were ap-"pointed to be slain." But see Luke ix. 14; where the expression κατακλίνατε αὐτοὺς κλισίας ἀνὰ πεντήκοντα, is rendered in our version, "make

pared for their fall and funeral, into several tents, (*or companies*,) being filled with gladness. And 32 leaving off their doleful strain of lamentation, they again took up the hymn[t] of their fathers, praising the Saviour and wonder-working God: and having put away from them all groaning and wailing, they formed themselves into dances as a sign of peaceful joy. In like manner also the king made 33 a great feast on this occasion, and without ceasing made acknowledgments to Heaven in a magnificent way, on account of the unexpected deliverance which had befallen them.

And they, who before gave them up as lost and 34 about to be devoured by birds[u], and had joyfully registered them; now groaned for that they had clothed themselves in shame, and their fire-breathing[x] boldness was ingloriously quenched.

But the Jews, as we have said already, having 35 formed the aforementioned dance, passed the time in feasting, with joyful thanksgivings and psalms. And made a common decree on this occasion 36 through all the dwellings of their pilgrimage[y] for after generations; and appointed to celebrate the above-named days as days of gladness: not for the sake of drinking and gluttony[z], but by reason of

"them sit down by fifties in "a company."

[t] Probably, as Grotius remarks, the 136th Psalm; which, we learn from 1 Chronicles xvi. 41, 2 Chron. v. 13, vii. 3, Ezra iii. 11, &c., was their usual hymn of thanksgiving.

[u] Compare 3 Macc. ix. 15. See also Genesis xl. 19; Ezech. xxxix. 4, and other passages of Scripture.

[x] Gr. καὶ τὴν πυριπνοῦν τόλμαν ἀκλεῶς ἐσβεσμένοι. Πυρίπνους, πύρπνοος, and πυρπνέουσα, are expressions occurring in the classic authors.

[y] Gr. ἐπὶ πᾶσαν τὴν παροικίαν αὐτῶν. Compare chap. vii. 19; or the words may mean, "for all the time of their "sojourning."

[z] The old translation of

that deliverance which they had received through
37 God. And they addressed themselves to the king, desiring their dismissal to their own homes.

38 Now they *had* registered them from the five and twentieth day of Pachon[a], to the fourth day of Epiphi, during forty days: and they determined their destruction from the fifth day of Epi-
39 phi[b] until the seventh, for three days. In which the Lord of the universe did most gloriously manifest his mercy, and delivered them all together without hurt.

40 And they feasted, being supplied with all things by the king, until the fourteenth day, wherein
41 they made address for their dismissal. And when the king had acceded to[c] their request, he wrote for them to his commanders in every city the subjoined epistle, to the following generous purport[d].

CHAPTER VII.

Ptolemy's letter in favour of the Jews. Their happy return home.

1 " KING Ptolemy Philopator to the commanders " in Egypt, and all who are set over our affairs,
2 " joy and health. We ourselves are well, as also

1550 renders it, "not to bib " and bowl in, for gluttony;" thus incidentally illustrating the English habits and games of the age of king Edward VI.

[a] This Egyptian month answers nearly to our April and May.

[b] Answering nearly to our June and July, and to the Macedonian Panemus. Archbishop Ussher reckons these forty days of registering to have included from the 20th of May to the 29th of June.

[c] Or, " had commanded " them:" Gr. συναινέσας αὐτούς. Compare ch. vii. 12.

[d] Gr. μεγαλοψύχως τὴν ἐκτενίαν ἔχουσαν. Josephus, on a similar occasion, uses the phrase, προσθεῖναι γράμματα ὑπίσχετο μεγαλοπρεπῶς ἔχοντα. Antiq. xii. c. 2.

"are our children, the great God having directed
"our affairs according as we wish.

"Certain of our friends, out of ill-nature, did
"frequently press hard upon us, and persuade us
"to collect in a body the Jews who were in our
"kingdom, and to punish them with the strange
"punishments[a] of traitors. Alleging that our af-
"fairs would never be firmly settled, by reason of
"that disaffection[b] which these men have towards
"all other nations, until this were done. Who also,
"having brought them in bonds with vexation, as
"slaves, or rather as traitors, attempted to put
"them to death without any examination or in-
"quiry, having cloked themselves[c] in a more than
"Scythian barbarity. But we upon this most
"severely threatened them, out of that equity
"which we bear towards all men, and with diffi-
"culty granted them their lives; and acknow-
"ledging that God of heaven, who has protected
"the Jews in safety; and constantly has fought
"for them as a father for his children: and call-
"ing to mind that firm, friendly affection, which
"they have had for us and our ancestors;——
"we have in justice released them from all blame,
"on any account whatsoever. And have enjoined
"them every one to return to their own homes,
"no person in any place doing them harm, or re-
"proaching them with the things which have
"been done to them without all reason. For
"know ye, that if we shall maliciously devise evil

[a] Compare chapter iv. 4, and the note there: also 3 Macc. ix. 6.
[b] See, above, the note on chapter iii. 7.
[c] Gr. νόμου Σκυθῶν ἀγριοτέραν ἐμπεπορπημένοι ὠμότητα. The expression is remarkable, signifying literally "fastening "around them as a cloak."

"against these men, or at all grieve them, we shall
"ever inevitably have not man, but the Most High
"God, the Lord of all power, opposed to us, for
"the avenging of such deeds. Fare ye well."

10 But the Jews having received this epistle, did not immediately hasten to begin their journey: but petitioned the king that those of the Jewish race who had voluntarily transgressed against the holy God and the law of God, might meet through them such punishment as they had deserved[d].

11 Alleging that they who had transgressed the Divine commands for their belly's sake, would never be well affected[e] even to the king's affairs.

12 He then, admitting what they said to be true, and approving it, gave them full liberty to destroy those who had transgressed the law of God, in every place within his kingdom: and this with all freedom, without any *further* authority or inspec-
13 tion[f] from the king. Hereupon, having paid him

---

[d] See Deuteron. xiii. 6—10. In subsequent times the Jews were compelled to ask permission from their foreign rulers to execute this law: as at Esther vi. 8—11, and here. So likewise the Jews hypocritically reply to Pontius Pilate, "It is not lawful for "us to put any man to "death." John xviii. 31.

[e] Grotius, in a note on this passage, cites the act of Constantius Chlorus, father of the emperor Constantine; who, wishing to put to a proof the fidelity and principle of his officers, threatened all of them with the loss of their dignities unless they renounced Christianity. And when some surrendered their religious belief, and others still held it under every prospect of disadvantage, Constantius retained the latter in his service, and dismissed all the former; remarking, that those men were never likely to be faithful to the king, who so readily had consented to renounce their God. By precisely similar reasoning, Antiochus the Great assured himself of the Jews' fidelity towards him: πέπεισμαι γὰρ εὔνους αὐτοὺς ἔσεσθαι τῶν ἡμετέρων φύλακας, διὰ τὴν πρὸς τὸν Θεὸν αὐτῶν εὐσέβειαν. Joseph. Antiq. xii. 3.

[f] Gr. ἄνευ πάσης βασιλικῆς ἐξουσίας ἢ ἐπισκέψεως.

their acknowledgments as was fit, their priests and all the multitude, singing aloud the halleluia, departed with joy. And whenever they met with 14 any one of their countrymen who had been polluted, they punished him upon the spot, and slew him with marks of public ignominy. And on that 15 very day they slew above three hundred men; and passed it as a festival with joy, having mastered and punished the profane. But they 16 themselves, who had adhered to God unto death, having had full enjoyment of their deliverance, departed from the city crowned with garlands of all sorts of most fragrant flowers, with joy and shouting; giving thanks in praises and most melodious hymns to the eternal God of their fathers, the Saviour of Israel.

And having reached Ptolemais[g], which, on account of the peculiar product of the place, is called " the rose-bearing," where the fleet waited for them according to their common decree, seven days; there they made a feast of deliverance[h], the 18 king having generously supplied them with all things which each might want for his journey even to his own home.

And having arrived in peace with becoming 19 thanksgivings, they resolved to celebrate there also these days as days of joy for the time[i] of

[g] A city of Egypt, which Calmet, not without reason, supposes to be *Rosetta;* which is situate on the coast, between Alexandria and Damietta. Some commentators differ; but the situation on the sea, and the modern name expressing the produce of the soil, plead very forcibly in favour of the opinion which Calmet has advanced.

[h] Gr. πότον σωτήριον, which compare with the note above, at ch. vi. 31.

[i] Gr. ἐπὶ τὸν χρόνον, " in " remembrance of the time." Compare ch. vi. 36.

B. C. 209.   CHAP. VII.   41

20 their sojourning. Which also having consecrated *to that use* by setting up a pillar and an oratory[k] in the place of their festive solemnity, they departed unhurt, free, overflowing with joy, secured by the king's command from all harm by land,
21 sea, or river, each to his own home. And having now greater authority than before among their enemies, with glory and fear; not being despoiled of their goods by any one throughout the journey.
22 And all of them recovered all their goods according to the registry[1]; so that those who held any thing *belonging to them*, restored it to them with the utmost fear[m], the Most High God having worked wonders throughout for their deliverance.
23   Blessed be the Deliverer of Israel, for endless ages. Amen.

[k] Gr. προσευχή, (the same as οἶκος προσευχῆς) a word well known both from the New Testament and Josephus.

[1] Or, "inventory," Gr. ἀπογραφῆς; which, in the old translation of 1550, is rendered by, "bill of attainder."

[m] Compare the departure of the Israelites from Egypt, in Exodus, chap. xii.; also Psalm cv. 38.

END OF BOOK I.

THE SECOND BOOK OF MACCABEES:

CONTAINING

THE HISTORY OF ABOUT FORTY YEARS, VIZ. FROM 175 TO 135 BEFORE CHRIST.

CHAPTER I.

The cruelties of Antiochus Epiphanes to the Jews.

1 AND it happened, after that Alexander, *son* of Philip the Macedonian, who came out of the land of Chittim[a], had smitten[b] Darius king of the Persians and Medes, that he reigned in his 2 stead, the first over Greece[c]: and made many wars, and won many strong holds, and slew the kings 3 of the earth: and went through to the ends of the earth, and took spoils of many nations, insomuch that the earth was quiet before him; whereupon

B. C. 323.

[a] "Wherever the 'land of Chittim' or 'the isles of Chittim' are mentioned in scripture, there are evidently meant some countries or islands in the Mediterranean." Bishop Newton on the Prophecies, I. 5. Here Macedonia seems to be the country particularly pointed out. See Numbers xxiv. 24; Isaiah xxiii. 1. 12; Jer. ii. 10; Ezek. xxvii. 6; Dan. xi. 29, 30.

[b] Namely, at the decisive battle of Arbela in Persia, fought in the year 331 B. C.

[c] Meaning Syria and Egypt, which were so called by the Jews.

44   BOOK II.   B. C. 323.

he was exalted, and his heart was lifted up. And 4 he gathered a mighty strong host, and ruled over countries, and nations, and kings[d], and they became tributaries unto him. And after these things he fell 5 sick, and perceived that he should die. Wherefore he 6 called his servants; such as were honourable, and had been brought up with him from his youth, and parted his kingdom among them, while he was yet alive[e]. So Alexander reigned twelve 7 years, and *then* died. And his servants bear rule 8 every one in his place. And after his death, they 9 all put crowns upon themselves; so did their sons after them many years: and they multiplied evils[f] in the earth.

And there came out of them a wicked root[g], 10

[d] Or "kingdoms;" for the Alexandrian manuscript reads τυραννιῶν, not τυράννων.

[e] The generality of historians give a different account. See Justin, ch. 13, and Quintus Curtius, book X. ch. 5 and 10. Quintus, however, admits the prevalence of a report that Alexander during his lifetime had arranged the succession to his dominions, but he gives no credit to the story: "Credidere quidam "testamento Alexandri dis_ "tributas esse provincias; sed "famam ejus rei, quanquam "ab auctoribus tradita est, "vanam fuisse comperimus." I may here observe, once for all, that this and other deviations of our author from commonly received accounts, are discussed and partly explained by Albericus Gentilis, in a Dissertation appended to the First Book of Maccabees, which is printed in the fifth volume of the "Critici Sa- "cri."

[f] Josephus explains this, by saying of these successors, στασιαζόντων δὲ τούτων, καὶ πρὸς ἀλλήλους φιλοτιμουμένων, ὑπὲρ τῆς ἰδίας ἀρχῆς, πολέμους τε συνεχεῖς καὶ μακροὺς συνέβαινε γίνεσθαι, καὶ τὰς πόλεις κακοπαθεῖν, καὶ πολλοὺς ἐν τοῖς ἀγῶσιν ἀποβάλλειν τῶν οἰκητόρων, ὡς καὶ τὴν Συρίαν ἅπασαν ὑπὸ Πτολεμαίου τοῦ Λάγου, Σωτῆρος τότε χρηματίζοντος, τὰ ἐνάντια παθεῖν αὐτοῦ τῇ ἐπικλήσει. Ant. XII. 1.

[g] The Greek word ῥίζα, which properly signifies a *root*, and metaphorically an *origin*, is also used to denote the *branches*, or *offspring* from that root. Thus Jesus Christ is called *the root of Jesse*, (Isai. i. 10,) *the root of David*: (Apoc. v. 5; xxii. 16):

Antiochus, *surnamed* Epiphanes[h], son of Antiochus the king[i], who had been an hostage at Rome, and he reigned in the hundred and thirty and seventh year[k] of the king-
11 dom of the Greeks. In those days went there out of Israel wicked men[l], who persuaded many, saying, Let us go, and make a covenant with the heathen who are round about us: for since we departed from them, many evils
12 have befallen us. And the word seemed good in
13 their eyes. Then certain of the people were so forward herein, that they went to the king, and he gave them license to do after the ordinances
14 of the heathen: whereupon they built a place of

B. C. 176.

B. C. 175.

B. C. 174.

and such is the signification of the word in the present passage.

[h] Appian relates, that he obtained this name of Epiphanes, (signifying not only *illustrious*, but also *one who appears unexpectedly*,) because, when his brother Seleucus had been dethroned and put to death by Heliodorus, a conspirator, who seized his kingdom, Antiochus then on his way from Rome where he had been detained as a hostage, was generously assisted by Eumenes and Attalus kings of Pergamus, who deposed the usurper, and placed *him* on the throne of Syria, to the joy of his subjects. Appian. de rebus Syriacis, c. 45. But Polybius (cited by Athenæus) calls him *Epimanes* (madman) instead of Epiphanes, from the wildness and inconsistency of his behaviour, several instances of which he gives. Polyb. Fragm. XXVI. 10. Compare Diodorus Siculus, de Virtutibus et Vitiis excerpt. lib. XXVI. and XXXI.

[i] Commonly called, Antiochus the Great.

[k] Viz. of the æra of the Seleucidæ, which began from the capture of Babylon by Seleucus Nicator, B. C. 312. This is the reckoning of time used throughout the books of Maccabees. The Syromacedonian (or Greek) year really commenced in the autumn: but, as the author of the *first* book of Maccabees usually reckons according to the Jewish mode, of beginning the year in the spring, a difference of six months is sometimes observable between the accounts given of the same transaction in the *first* and in the *second* book.

[l] Namely, Menelaus the brother of Jesus (or Jason)

exercise [m] at Jerusalem, according to the customs of the heathen: and made themselves uncircum- 15 cised [n], and forsook the holy covenant, and joined themselves to the heathen, and were sold to do evil [o].

Now when the kingdom was established before 16 Antiochus, he thought to reign over Egypt [p], that he might have the dominion of the two realms. Wherefore he entered into Egypt with 17 a great multitude, with chariots, and elephants, and horsemen, and a great navy [q], and made war 18 against Ptolemy [r] king of Egypt: but Ptolemy was afraid of him, and fled; and many fell down slain. Thus they won the strong cities in the 19 land of Egypt, and he took the spoils of the land of Egypt.

And after that Antiochus had smitten Egypt [s], 20 he returned again in the hundred forty and third year, and went up against Israel and Jerusalem with a great multitude: and entered proudly into 21 the sanctuary, and took away the golden altar,

---

the high priest, and his party; who found the majority of their countrymen adverse to their political views. Joseph. Antiq. XII. 6.

[m] Gr. γυμνάσιον, a Gymnasium.

[n] A thing expressly forbidden by St. Paul. See 1 Cor. vii. 18.

[o] The phrase is Hebrew, and occurs frequently in the Old Testament. The very words of this passage, καὶ ἐπράθησαν τοῦ ποιῆσαι τὸ πονηρὸν, are found at 2 Kings, xvii. 17. (Sept. version.)

[p] See Daniel xi. 25, &c.

[q] Gr. στόλῳ, which indeed may also signify a *land-force*.

[r] Surnamed Philometor, the sixth king of that race.

[s] See Daniel xi. 28. Josephus relates, that although Antiochus met with success in the beginning of his campaign against Egypt, he was compelled to abandon all thoughts of possessing himself of that kingdom, the Romans having sent to him a peremptory message to depart home.

and the candlestick of light, and all the vessels
22 thereof. And the table of the shew-bread, and
the pouring-vessels, and the vials, and the censers
of gold, and the vail, and the crowns [t], and the
golden ornaments which were on the front of the
23 temple, all which he pulled off. He took also the
silver and the gold, and the precious [u] vessels:
also he took the hidden treasures which he found.
24 And when he had taken all away, he went into
his own land, having made a great massacre, and
25 spoken very proudly. Therefore there was great
mourning in Israel, in every place where they
26 were; so that the princes and elders mourned,
the virgins and young men were made feeble, and
27 the beauty of women was changed. Every bridegroom took up lamentation, and she who sat in
28 the marriage-chamber was in heaviness. The
land also was moved for the inhabitants thereof,
and all the house of Jacob was covered with confusion.
29 And after two years fully expired [x], the king
sent his chief collector [y] of tribute unto the
cities of Judah; and he came unto Jerusa-
30 lem with a great multitude, and spake peaceable
words unto them in deceit: and they believed
him, and he fell suddenly upon the city, and smote
it very sore, and destroyed much people of Israel.
31 And when he had taken the spoils of the city, he
set it on fire, and pulled down the houses and

B. C. 168.

---

[t] See Zechariah vi. 14.

[u] Gr. ἐπιθυμητὰ, "vessels of desire:" the same expression occurs at Daniel xi. 8, and Hosea xiii. 15.

[x] Gr. δύο ἔτη ἡμερῶν, "two years of days;" a manifest Hebraism.

[y] Namely, Apollonius, who is mentioned again at 3 Macc. v. 24—27.

walls thereof on every side. But the women and 32
children took they captive, and possessed themselves of the cattle. Then builded they the city 33
of David with a great and strong wall, *and* with
mighty towers, and it became a strong hold [z] for
them. And they put therein a sinful nation [a], 34
wicked men, and they fortified *themselves* therein.
They stored it also with armour and victuals, and 35
when they had gathered together the spoils of Jerusalem, they laid them up there, and so they became a sore snare: for it became a place to lie in 36
wait against the sanctuary, and an evil adversary
to Israel altogether. Thus they shed innocent 37
blood on every side of the sanctuary [b], and defiled
the sanctuary: insomuch that the inhabitants of 38
Jerusalem fled because of them: whereupon *the
city* was made an habitation of strangers, and became strange to those who were born in her, and
her own children left her. Her sanctuary was 39
laid waste like a wilderness, her feasts were turned
into mourning, her sabbaths into reproach, her honour into contempt. As had been her glory, so 40
was her dishonour increased, and her high estate
was turned into mourning.

Moreover, king Antiochus wrote to his whole 41
kingdom, that all should be one people, and every
one should leave his own laws: so all the heathen 42

---

[z] Called *Acra*, or "the "Tower," or citadel.

[a] "He placed therein a "Macedonian garrison." Josephus. It may be well to remark here, once for all, that in these apocryphal books, no less than in those of the New Testament, the words ἁμαρτωλοί, ἄνομοι, ἀσεβεῖς, are used to denote the *Gentiles* as contradistinguished from the *Jews*. Particular instances may be referred to in Schleusner and other writers on the New Testament.

[b] See Psalm lxxix. 1—3.

agreed, according to the commandment of the
43 king. Yea, many also of the Israelites consented
to his religion, and sacrificed unto idols, and pro-
44 faned the sabbath. For the king had sent letters
by the hand of messengers unto Jerusalem, and
the cities of Judah, that they should follow laws
45 strange to the land: and forbid burnt-offerings,
and sacrifice, and drink-offerings in the sanctuary;
and that they should profane the sabbaths and
46 festival days: and pollute the sanctuary and holy
47 people: set up altars, and temples, and chapels
of idols, and sacrifice swine's flesh and unclean [c]
48 beasts: that they should also leave their children
uncircumcised, and make their souls abominable
with all manner of uncleanness and profanation:
49 to the end they might forget the law, and change
50 all the ordinances. And whosoever would not do
according to commandment of the king, *he said*,
51 he should die. According to all these words wrote
he to his whole kingdom, and appointed overseers
over all the people, commmanding the cities of
52 Judah to sacrifice, city by city. Then many of
the people were gathered unto them, to wit, every
one who forsook the law, and so they committed
53 evils in the land: and drove Israel into secret
places, even wheresoever they could flee for succour.

54 Now on the fifteenth day of *the month* Casleu[d],
in the hundred forty and fifth year, they
set up the abomination[e] of desolation upon

B.C. 167.

[c] Gr. κοινὰ, "common," as expressed in St. Peter's vision at Acts x.
[d] The ninth Jewish month, answering to our November and December.
[e] Namely, the statue of Jupiter Olympius. Compare 3 Mac. vi. 2. See also Daniel xi. 31.

E

the altar, and built *idol*-altars throughout the cities of Judah on every side; and burnt incense 55 at the doors of the houses, and in the streets. And when they had rent in pieces the books of 56 the law which they found, they burnt them with fire. And wheresoever was found with any the 57 book of the testament, or if any consented to the law, the king's commandment *was, that they should* put him to death. Thus did they by their 58 might unto Israel every month, to as many as were found in the cities. Now on the five and 59 twentieth day of the month they did sacrifice upon the *idol*-altar, which was upon the altar of burnt-offerings. At which time, according to the com- 60 mandment, they put to death the women who had caused[f] their children to be circumcised. And they 61 hanged the infants about their necks, and rifled their houses, and slew them which had circumcised them. Howbeit, many in Israel were fully 62 resolved and confirmed in themselves, not to eat unclean things. Wherefore they chose rather to 63 die, that they might not be defiled with the meats, and that they might not profane the holy covenant: so then they died. And there was very 64 great wrath upon Israel.

CHAP. II.
The firmness of Mattathias.

IN those days arose Mattathias *the son* of John, 1 *the son* of Simeon[a], a priest of the sons of Joarib, from Jerusalem, and dwelt in Modin[b]. And he 2

---

[f] Gr. τὰς περιτετμηκυίας, "who had circumcised;" for we learn that this operation was sometimes performed by women.

[a] Josephus adds, "*the son* of Asamonæus:" whence this family bore afterwards the title of Asmonæan princes.

[b] Wells, in his Geography

had five sons, Joannan, who was called Caddis: Simon, who was called Thassi: Judas, who was called Maccabæus: Eleazar, who was called Avaran, and Jonathan, who was called Apphus. And when he saw the blasphemies[c] which were committed in Judah and Jerusalem, he said, Wo is me! wherefore was I born to see this overthrow of my people, and of the holy city, and to dwell there when it was delivered into the hand of the enemies, and the sanctuary into the hand of strangers? Her temple is become as a man without glory. Her glorious vessels are carried away into captivity, her infants are slain in the streets, her young men with the sword of the enemy. What nation hath not had a part in *her* kingdom, and gotten of her spoils? All her ornaments are taken away, of a free-woman she is become a bond-slave. And behold, our sanctuary[d], even our beauty and our glory, is laid waste, and the Gentiles have profaned it. To what end therefore shall we live any longer? Then Mattathias and his sons rent their clothes, and put on sackcloth, and mourned very sore.

5 In the mean while the king's officers, such as compelled *the people to* revolt, came into the city

of the Old Testament, states, that "the situation of this "place (where was the se-"pulchre of the Maccabees) "is not well agreed on: some "placing it not very far from "Jerusalem, while others will "have Modin to lie much far-"ther westward, namely, on "the coast, or not far from "the coast, of the Mediter-"ranean sea." He inclines to the latter opinion, which indeed seems to be well supported.

[c] Gr. $\beta\lambda\alpha\sigma\phi\eta\mu\acute{\iota}\alpha s$, which here denotes not merely wicked *words*, but also *deeds*, such as idolatry and the like.

[d] Gr. τὰ ἅγια, literally, *holy things;* the expression used for the sanctuary throughout this book.

Modin, to make them sacrifice. And when many 16
of Israel came unto them, Mattathias also and his
sons came together. Then answered the king's 17
officers, and said to Mattathias on this wise; Thou
art a ruler, and an honourable and great man in
this city, and strengthened with sons and brethren. Now therefore come thou first, and fulfil 18
the king's commandment, like as all the heathen
have done, yea, and the men of Judah also, and
such as remain at Jerusalem: so shalt thou and
thy house be in the number of the king's friends,
and thou and thy children shall be honoured with
silver and gold, and many rewards [e]. Then Mat- 19
tathias answered and spake with a loud voice,
Though all the nations which are under the king's
dominion [f] obey him, to fall away every one from
the religion of their fathers, and give consent to
his commandments: yet will I and my sons and 20
my brethren walk in the covenant of our fathers.
God forbid, that we should forsake the law and 21
the ordinances. We will not hearken to the king's 22
words, to go aside from our religion, either on
the right hand, or the left.

Now when he had left speaking these words, 23
there came one of the Jews in the sight of all, to
sacrifice on the altar which was at Modin, according to the king's commandment. Which thing 24
when Mattathias saw, he was inflamed with zeal,
and his reins trembled, neither could he [g] forbear

---

[e] Gr. ἀποστολαῖς; which Grotius declares to mean properly
*viaticum quo abeuntem prose-
quimur.*

[f] Gr. τὰ ἐν οἴκῳ τῆς βασιλείας
τοῦ βασιλέως.

[g] The rendering is unsatis-
factory; and there is here a
remarkable variety of reading
in the Greek text. The Vatican MS. reads ἀνήνεγκε θυμὸν
κατὰ τὸ κρίμα, which our trans-

to shew his anger according to judgment: where-
25 fore he ran, and slew him upon the altar. Also
the king's commissioner [h], who compelled men to
sacrifice, he killed at that time, and the altar he
26 pulled down. Thus dealt he zealously for the
law of God, like as Phinees [i] did unto Zambri the
27 son of Salom. And Mattathias cried throughout
the city with a loud voice, saying, Whosoever is
zealous of the law, and maintaineth the covenant,
28 let him follow me. So he and his sons fled into
the mountains, and left all which ever they had
29 in the city. Then many who sought after righteousness [k] and judgment, went down into the wil-
30 derness to dwell there: both they and their children, and their wives, and their cattle, because
evils were multiplied upon them.
31 Now when it was told the king's servants, and
the host which was at Jerusalem, in the city of
David, that certain men, who had broken the
king's commandment, were gone down into the
32 secret places in the wilderness: they pursued after
them a great number, and having overtaken them,
they camped against them and made war against
33 them on the sabbath-day. And they said unto
them, Let that which ye have done hitherto suf-

lation appears to follow: but the Alexandrian MS. reads ἀνήνεγκε θυμὸν κατὰ τὴν ῥίνα, "he breathed forth wrath through his nostrils," which seems more accordant with the rest of the imagery. This latter also is approved by Schleusner, (Lex. Vet. Test. III. 384,) who refers to Michaelis on the passage, and to Valckenaer on Theocritus, Idyll. I. 17.

[h] Gr. ἄνδρα.
[i] See Numbers xxv. 7.
[k] Gr. ζητοῦντες δικαιοσύνην, i. e. seeking liberty to observe the law of Moses. So our Saviour, when desiring baptism at the hand of John, alleged, "thus it becometh us to fulfil *all righteousness*." [Schleusner.]

fice; come forth, and do according to the commandment of the king, and ye shall live. But they said, We will not come forth, neither will we do the king's commandment, to profane the sabbath-day. So then they gave them the battle with all speed. Howbeit, they answered them not, neither cast they a stone at them, nor stopped the places where they lay hid; but said, Let us die all in our innocency: heaven and earth shall testify for us, that ye put us to death wrongfully. So they rose up against them in battle on the sabbath, and they died with their wives and children, and their cattle, to the number of a thousand souls[1]. Now when Mattathias and his friends understood hereof, they mourned for them right sore. And one of them said to another, If we all do as our brethren have done, and fight not for our lives and laws against the heathen, they will now quickly root us out of the earth. At that time therefore they decreed, saying, Whosoever shall come to make battle with us on the sabbath-day, we will fight against him; neither will we die all, as our brethren died in the secret places. Then came there unto him a company of Assidæans[m], who were mighty men of Israel, even all such as were voluntarily devoted unto the law. Also all they who fled from persecution, joined

---

[1] Literally, "souls of men," a phrase familiar in scripture: see (in the Hebrew) Numb. xxxi. 35, 1 Chron. v. 21; and in the Apocalypse, chap. xviii. 13, the merchants are said to offer for sale " slaves, and " *souls of men.*"

[m] These appear to have been men who went even beyond the Mosaic Law in the strictness of their observances: as the Rechabites mentioned by Jeremiah did, and as the Pharisees in our Saviour's time boasted to do. See them mentioned again at chap. vii. 13. and 3 Maccab. xiv. 6.

themselves unto them, and were a stay unto them.
44 So they joined their forces, and smote sinful men in their anger and wicked men in their wrath;
45 but the rest fled to the heathen for succour. Then Mattathias and his friends went round about, and
46 pulled down the altars. And what children soever they found within the coast of Israel uncircum-
47 cised, those they circumcised by force[n]. They pursued also after the sons of pride, and the work
48 prospered in their hand. So they recovered the law out of the hand of the Gentiles, and out of the hand of kings, and yielded not the horn[o] *of triumph* to the sinner.

49 Now when the time drew near that Mattathias should die, he said unto his sons, "Now "hath pride and rebuke gotten strength, "and the time of destruction, and the wrath of in-
50 "dignation. Now therefore, my sons, be ye zeal-"ous for the law, and give your lives for the co-
51 "venant of our fathers. Call to remembrance "what acts our fathers did in their generations, "so shall ye receive great honour, and an ever-
52 "lasting name. Was not Abraham found faith-"ful in temptation, and it was imputed unto him
53 "for righteousness[p]? Joseph in the time of his "distress, kept the commandment, and was made
54 "lord of Egypt[q]. Phinees our father, in being "zealous and fervent, obtained the covenant of an
55 "everlasting priesthood[r]. Jesus, for fulfilling the

---

[n] Josephus adds, "and he "drove away those who were "appointed to hinder such "their circumcision." Antiq. XII. 6.

[o] Gr. καὶ οὐκ ἔδωκαν κέρας τῷ ἁμαρτωλῷ. It is a Hebrew phrase, abundantly to be found in Scripture.

[p] See Gen. xxii.
[q] See Gen. xli.
[r] See Numb. xxv.

"word, was made a judge in Israel^s. Caleb, for 56
"bearing witness before the congregation, received
"an heritage of the land^t. David, for being mer- 57
"ciful^u, gained to himself the throne of an ever-
"lasting kingdom^x. Elias, for being zealous and 58
"fervent for the law, was taken up into hea-
"ven^y. Ananias, Azarias, and Misael, by believ- 59
"ing, were saved out of the flame^z. Daniel, for 60
"his innocency, was delivered from the mouth of
"lions^a. And thus consider ye throughout all 61
"generations, that none who put their trust in
"Him, shall fail. Fear not then the words of a 62
"sinful man; for his glory shall be dung and
"worms. To-day he shall be lifted up, and to- 63
"morrow he shall not be found, because he is re-
"turned into his dust^b, and his thought is come to
"nothing. Wherefore, ye my sons, be valiant, and 64
"shew yourselves men in the behalf of the law,
"for by it shall ye obtain glory. And behold, I 65
"know that your brother Simon is a man of coun-
"sel, give ear unto him alway: he shall be a
"father unto you. As for Judas Maccabæus, he 66
"hath been mighty, and strong, even from his
"youth up: let him be your captain, and fight
"the battle of the people. Take also unto you 67
"all those who observe the law, and avenge ye
"the wrong of your people. Recompense fully 68
"the heathen, and take heed to the command-
"ments of the law." So he blessed them, and 69

---

^{s} See Josh. i.
^{t} See Numb. xiv.
^{u} Or, *for his piety:* see Schleusner in v. ἔλεος.
^{x} See 2 Sam. ii.
^{y} See 2 Kings ii.
^{z} See Dan. iii.
^{a} See Dan. vi.
^{b} See Psalm cxlv. 4.

70 was gathered to his fathers. And he died in the hundred forty and sixth year, and his sons buried him in the sepulchres of his fathers, at Modin, and all Israel made great lamentation for him.

CHAPTER III.
The valiant acts of Judas Maccabæus.

1 THEN his son Judas called Maccabæus rose up
2 in his stead. And all his brethren helped him, and so did all they who were joined with his father, and they fought with cheerfulness the battle of Israel.
3 So he gat his people great honour, and put on a breast-plate as a giant, and girt his warlike armour about him, and he fought battles, protecting
4 the host with his sword. In his acts he was like a lion, and like a lion's whelp roaring for his
5 prey. For he pursued the wicked, and sought them out, and burnt up those who vexed his
6 people. Wherefore the wicked shrunk for fear of him, and all the workers of iniquity were confounded together, and deliverance was made to
7 prosper in his hand. He grieved also many kings, and made Jacob glad with his acts, and his me-
8 morial is blessed for ever. Moreover, he went through the cities of Judah, and destroyed the ungodly out of them, and turned away wrath
9 from Israel: so that he was renowned unto the utmost part of the earth, and he received unto him such as were ready to perish.
10 Then Apollonius[a] gathered together the Gentiles, and a great host out of Samaria, to fight
11 against Israel. Which thing when Judas per-

---
[a] The governor of Samaria. See above, chap. ii. 29.

ceived, he went forth to meet him, and so he smote him, and slew him: many also fell down slain, but the rest fled. Wherefore Judas took 12 their spoils, and Apollonius' sword also, and therewith he fought all his life long.

Now when Seron, the captain[b] of the army of 13 Syria, heard say, that Judas had gathered unto him a multitude and company of the faithful to go out with him to war; he said, I will get me a 14 name and will be honoured in the kingdom; for I will go fight with Judas, and them that are with him, who despise the king's commandment. So 15 he made him ready to go up, and there went with him a mighty host of the ungodly to help him, and to be avenged of the children of Israel. And 16 when he came near to the going up of Bethoron[c] Judas went forth to meet him with a small company. Who, when they saw the host coming to 17 meet them, said unto Judas, How shall we be able, being so few, to fight against so great a multitude *and* so strong, seeing we are ready to faint with fasting all this day? Unto whom Judas answered, 18 It is no hard matter for many to be shut up in the hands of a few; and with the God of heaven it is all one to deliver with many[d] or with few; for the victory of battle standeth not in the multi- 19 tude of an host, but strength cometh from heaven. They come to us in the abundance of pride and 20 iniquity, to destroy us and our wives and children, and to spoil us: but we fight for our lives and our 21

---

[b] Gr. ὁ ἄρχων. Josephus calls him governor of Cœlo-syria.

[c] A town lying within the borders of the tribe of Ephraim, north-west from Jerusalem. See Josh. x. 10, 11. 1 Chron. vii. 24.

[d] See 1 Sam. ch. xiv. 6, 2 Chron. xiv. 11.

22 laws. Wherefore *the Lord* himself will overthrow them before our face: and as for you, be ye not
23 afraid of them. Now as soon as he had left off speaking, he leapt suddenly upon them, and so Seron and his host was overthrown[e] before him.
24 And they pursued them in the going down of Bethoron, unto the plain, where were slain about eight hundred men of them; and the residue fled
25 into the land of the Philistines. Then began the fear of Judas and his brethren, and great dread to
26 fall upon the nations round about them; insomuch that his fame came unto the king, and all nations talked of the battles of Judas.
27   Now when king Antiochus heard these things, he was full of indignation: wherefore he sent and gathered together all the forces of his realm, *even*
28 a very strong army. He opened also his treasure[f], and gave his soldiers pay for a year, commanding
29 them to be ready for every need. Nevertheless, when he saw that the money of his treasures failed, and that the tributes[g] in the country were small, because of the dissension, and plague which he had brought upon the land by taking away the
30 laws which had been of old time; he feared that he should not, as in former times, have sufficient for his charges, and for the gifts, which before he had given with a liberal hand: for he had abounded above the kings[h] that were before him.

---

[e] Josephus informs us, that Seron himself was slain in this battle.
[f] See Daniel xi. 24.
[g] Or, "the collectors of "tributes were few:" for the Greek MSS. vary between φόροι and φορολόγοι.
[h] Thus it had been prophesied of him by Daniel, that "he shall do that which his "fathers have not done, nor "his fathers' fathers: he shall "scatter among them the

Wherefore, being greatly perplexed in his mind, he determined to go into Persia, there to take the tributes of the countries, and to gather much money. So he left Lysias, an honourable man, and one of the blood royal, to oversee the affairs of the king, from the river Euphrates, unto the borders of Egypt; and to bring up his son Antiochus, until he came again. Moreover, he delivered unto him the half of his forces, and the elephants, and gave him charge of all things that he would have done, as also concerning them which dwelt in Judæa and Jerusalem: *to wit*, that he should send an army against them, to destroy and root out the strength of Israel and the remnant of Jerusalem, and to take away their memorial from that place; and that he should place strange children in all their quarters, and divide their land by lot. So the king took the half of the forces which remained, and departed from Antioch[i] his royal city, the hundred forty and seventh year; and having passed the river Euphrates, he went through the high countries[j]. 31 32 33 34 35 36 37

Then Lysias chose Ptolemee the *son* of Dorymenes, and Nicanor, and Gorgias, mighty men of the king's friends: and with them he sent forty thousand *foot*-men, and seven thousand horse-men, to go into the land of Judah, and to destroy it, as 38 39

"prey, and spoil, and riches." Dan. xi. 24. Compare Joseph. Antiq. XII. 11.

[i] A celebrated city of Syria, on the river Orontes: near it was the grove called Daphne. See a description of it in the XVIth book of Strabo.

[j] Gr. τὰς ἐπάνω χώρας, i. e. the parts adjoining the Euphrates, and remote from the sea. So Polybius calls the governments of Upper Asia τὰς ἄνω σατραπείας. Lib. III. et V. So also we read in Josephus οἱ ἄνω τόποι—οἱ ἄνω βάρβαροι—ἡ ἄνω χώρα.—and τὰ ἀνωτερικὰ μέρη, in Acts xix. 1.

the king commanded. So they went forth with all their power, and came and pitched by Emmaus[k], in the plain country. And the merchants of the country hearing the fame of them, took silver and gold very much, and servants, and came into the camp to buy the children of Israel for slaves; a power also of Syria, and of the land of the Philistines[l], joined themselves unto them.

Now when Judas and his brethren saw that miseries were multiplied, and that the forces did encamp themselves in their borders, (for they knew how the king had given commandment to destroy the people, and utterly abolish them;) they said one to another, Let us restore the decayed estate of our people, and let us fight for our people, and the sanctuary. Then was the congregation gathered together, that they might be ready for battle, and that they might pray, and ask mercy and compassion. Now Jerusalem was uninhabited as a wilderness, there was none of her children that went in, or out: the sanctuary also was trodden down, and aliens kept the strong hold: the heathen had their habitation in that place, and joy was taken away from Jacob, and

---

[k] A village situate seven miles and a half from Jerusalem, Luke xxiv. 13.

[l] Gr. ἀλλοφύλων. This word in its primary signification denotes any person who is not of the same country with the writer, an alien; and in this sense it is used by Thucydides and other classic authors. To the Greeks all other nations were ἀλλόφυλοι, which was equivalent to βάρβαροι; and to the Romans, on the contrary, the Greeks were ἀλλόφυλοι. Among the Jews the word was used to express all Gentiles generally; but more particularly the race of Philistines.' In both these senses the expression occurs in the books of Maccabees.

the pipe and the harp ceased. Wherefore *the* 46 *Israelites* assembled themselves together, and came to Maspha^m, over against Jerusalem; for in Maspha was the place where they prayed aforetime in Israel. Then they fasted that day, and 47 put on sackcloth, and cast ashes upon their heads, and rent their clothes; and laid open the book of 48 the law, for which the heathen had sought diligently to paint in them the picturesⁿ of their idols. They brought also the priests' garments, 49 and the first-fruits, and the tithes; and the Nazarites° they stirred up^p, who had accomplished their days. Then cried they with a loud voice toward 50 heaven, saying, What shall we do with these, and whither shall we carry them away? For thy 51 sanctuary is trodden down and profaned, and thy priests are in heaviness and brought low. And 52 lo, the heathen are assembled together against us to destroy us: what things they imagine against us, thou knowest. How shall we be able to stand 53 against them, except thou, *O God,* be our help? Then sounded they with trumpets, and cried with 54 a loud voice. And after this, Judas ordained cap- 55 tains over the people, *even* captains over thousands, and over hundreds, and over fifties, and over tens. But as for such as were building 56

---

^m See Judges ch. xx. 1, 1 Sam. vii. 5, 2 Kings xxv.

ⁿ And by these means to render them useless and abominable to the Jews, who by their law were expressly forbidden to use any such representations. See Levit. xxvi. 1, Numb. xxxiii. 52.

° For the particulars of the Nazarites and their vows, consult Numb. vi. 2—21.

^p Gr. ἤγειραν, "put forward," Grotius. Compare Amos ii. 11.

houses, or had betrothed wives, or were planting vineyards, or were fearful[q], those he commanded that they should return every man to his own
57 house, according to the law. So the camp removed, and pitched upon the south side of Em-
58 maus. And Judas said, Arm yourselves, and be valiant men, and see that ye be in readiness against the morning, that ye may fight with these nations which are assembled together against us,
59 to destroy us and our sanctuary. For it is better for us to die in battle, than to behold the calami-
60 ties of our nation and our sanctuary. Nevertheless, as the will *of God* is in heaven, so let him do.

CHAPTER IV.

The wars of Judas. The sanctuary cleansed.

1 THEN took Gorgias five thousand *foot*-men and a thousand chosen horse-men, and the army re-
2 moved by night; to the end that he might rush in upon the camp of the Jews, and smite them suddenly. And the men of the fortress were his
3 guides. Now when Judas heard thereof, he himself removed, and the valiant men with him, that he might smite the king's army which was at
4 Emmaus, while as yet the forces were dispersed
5 from the camp. In the mean season came Gorgias by night into the camp of Judas: and when he found no man there, he sought them in the mountains: for said he, These fellows flee from us.

6 But as soon as it was day, Judas appeared in the plain with three thousand men, who, never-

---

[q] See Deuteron. xx. 5—8. Judges vii. 3.

theless had neither armour[a] nor swords to their minds. And they saw the host of the heathen, that it was strong, and well armed, and the horsemen compassing it round about; and these were expert of war. Then said Judas to the men who were with him, Fear ye not the multitude, neither be ye afraid of their assault. Remember how our fathers were delivered in the Red sea, when Pharaoh pursued them with an army. Now therefore let us cry unto heaven, if peradventure *the Lord* will have mercy upon us, and remember the covenant of our fathers, and destroy this host before our face this day: that so all the heathen may know that there is one, who delivereth and saveth Israel. Then the strangers lifted up their eyes, and saw them coming over against them. Wherefore, they went out of the camp to battle; and they which were with Judas sounded their trumpets.

So they joined battle, and the heathen were discomfited, and fled into the plain. Howbeit, all the hindmost of them were slain with the sword: for they pursued them unto Gazera[b], and unto the plains of Idumæa[c], and Azotus, and Jamnia,

---

[a] Gr. καλύμματα, "body-armour." Compare ch. vi. 2.

[b] Gazara is a town not far from Azotus, or Ashdod, which is a considerable city on the sea-coast. Herodotus speaks of its great size, and mentions the circumstance of its having endured a siege of no less than twenty-nine years, the longest on record in any history. Jamnia also is a town on the coast of the Mediterranean, situate in the tribe of Dan, near to Joppa.

[c] Throughout these books the word Idumæa is to be understood as denoting that southern district of Judæa, which, when unoccupied during the captivity of Judah, was entered upon and possessed by the Edomites, who

so that there were slain of them about three thou-
16 sand men. And Judas and his host returned
17 again from pursuing them: and said to the people, Be not greedy of the spoils, inasmuch as there
18 is a battle before us. And Gorgias and his host are here by us in the mountain: but stand ye now against our enemies, and overcome them, and after
19 this ye shall freely take the spoils. As Judas was yet speaking these words, there appeared a part of
20 them, shewing itself out of the mountain. And they perceived that their host had been put to flight, and that *the Jews* were burning the tents; (for the smoke which was seen declared what was
21 done:) when therefore they perceived these things, they were sore afraid, and seeing also the host of
22 Judas in the plain ready to fight, they fled every
23 one into the land of strangers. Then Judas returned to spoil the tents, where they got much gold and silver, and blue *silk*, and purple of the
24 sea, and great riches. After this they went home, and sung a song of thanksgiving, and praised the Lord in heaven: because it is good, because his
25 mercy *endureth* for ever. Thus Israel had a great deliverance that day.
26 Now as many of the strangers as had escaped, came and told Lysias all which had happened.
27 Who, when he heard thereof, was confounded and discouraged, because neither such things as he would were done unto Israel, nor such things as the king commanded him were come to pass.
28 The next year therefore following, Lysias gathered together threescore thousand choice B.C. 165.

quitted their own land for this purpose. Subsequently, they became almost incorporated with the Jews.

men *of foot*, and five thousand horsemen, that he might subdue them. So they came into Idumæa, 29 and pitched their tents at Bethsura[d], and Judas met them with ten thousand men. And when he 30 saw that mighty army, he prayed, and said, Blessed art thou, O Saviour of Israel, who didst quell the violence of the mighty man by the hand of thy servant David, and gavest the host of Philistines into the hands of Jonathan the son of Saul, and his armour-bearer. Shut up this army 31 in the hand of thy people Israel, and let them be confounded in their power and their horsemen; give to them cowardice, and melt away the bold- 32 ness of their strength, and let them be overwhelmed in their destruction; cast them down 33 with the sword of them which love thee, and let all those who know thy name, praise thee in hymns. So they joined battle; and there were 34 slain of the host of Lysias about five thousand men, even before them were they slain. Now 35 when Lysias saw his army put to flight, and the manliness of Judas' soldiers, and how they were ready either to live or die valiantly, he went to Antiochia, and gathered together a company of strangers, and having made his army greater than it was, he purposed to come again into Judæa.

Then said Judas and his brethren, Behold, our 36 enemies are discomfited: let us go up to cleanse and dedicate the sanctuary. Upon this all the 37

---

[d] This appears to have been the name of a small *district* of Judæa, as well as of its chief town. The fortress of Bethsura was originally built by king Rehoboam, being one of his "cities for defence" towards Idumæa. See 2 Chron. xi. 5, 7. It stood on a high rock (as its name imports) within a short distance from Jerusalem.

host assembled themselves together, and went up
38 into mount Sion. And they saw the sanctuary desolate, and the altar profaned, and the gates burnt down, and shrubs growing in the courts as in a forest, or in one of the mountains, yea, and
39 the priests' chambers pulled down. And they rent their clothes, and made great lamentation, and
40 cast ashes upon their heads, and fell down flat to the ground upon their faces, and blew an alarm with the trumpets, and cried towards heaven.
41 Then Judas appointed certain men to fight against those who were in the fortress, until he had
42 cleansed the sanctuary. So he chose priests of blameless conversation, such as had pleasure in
43 the law: and they cleansed the sanctuary, and bare out the defiled stones into an unclean place.
44 And as they consulted what to do with the altar
45 of burnt-offerings which was profaned; a good counsel came into their minds to pull it down, lest it should be a reproach to them, because the heathen had defiled it; wherefore they pulled it
46 down. And laid up the stones in the mountain of the house in a convenient place, until there should come a prophet to shew what should be done with
47 them. Then they took whole stones according to the law, and built a new altar, according to the
48 former. And built up the sanctuary, and the inner parts of the house, and hallowed the courts.
49 They made also new holy vessels, and into the temple they brought the candlestick, and the
50 altar[e] of incense and the table. And upon the

[e] In our common translation here follow the words, " of burnt offerings and"—; but these are manifestly an interpolation. Judas had already (see ver. 47.) built up

altar they burnt incense, and the lamps which were upon the candlestick they lighted, and they gave light in the temple. Furthermore, they set 5 the loaves upon the table, and spread out the veils[f], and finished all the works which they had begun to make. Now on the five and twentieth 5! day of the ninth month, (which is *called* the month Casleu[g]), in the hundred forty and eighth year, they rose up betimes in the morning. And 5: offered sacrifice according to the law, upon the new altar of burnt-offerings, which they had made. At what time[h], and what day the heathen had pro- 5. faned it, even in that was it dedicated with songs, and citherns, and harps, and cymbals. Then all 5! the people fell upon their faces, worshipping and praising *the God of* heaven, who had given them good success. And so they kept the dedication of 5(the altar eight days, and offered burnt-offerings with gladness, and sacrificed the sacrifice of deliverance and praise. They decked also the fore- 5', front of the temple with crowns of gold, and with small shields; and the gates and the chambers they renewed, and hanged doors upon them. Thus 5{ was there very great gladness among the people, for that the reproach of the heathen was put away. Moreover, Judas and his brethren, with 5{ the whole congregation of Israel, ordained that

---

a new altar of burnt offerings, which was made of stone, and did not stand within the temple itself, but in the court: the altar of incense was of gold, small and portable.— Josephus agrees with this latter statement.

[f] Or "hangings," Gr. καταπετάσματα.
[g] Answering to our November and December.
[h] The profanation of the temple had continued exactly for three years. See chapter i. 59.

the days of the dedication[i] of the altar should be kept in the season from year to year, by the space of eight days, from the five and twentieth day of the month Casleu, with mirth and gladness.

60 At that time also they builded up the mount Sion with high walls and strong towers round about, lest the Gentiles should come and tread
61 it down, as they had done before. And they set there a garrison to keep it: and fortified Bethsura to preserve it, that the people might have a defence against the face of Idumæa.

CHAPTER V.

The wars of Judas. The expedition of Simon.

1 Now it came to pass when the nations round about heard that the altar was built, and the sanctuary renewed as before, they were B.C. 164
2 very wroth. Wherefore they took counsel to destroy the generation of Jacob which was in the midst of them, and thereupon they began to slay
3 and destroy among the people. Then Judas fought against the children of Esau, in Idumæa, at Acrabattine[a], because they besieged Israel; and he gave them a great overthrow, and brought
4 them down, and took their spoils. Also he re-

---

[i] Josephus declares that the observance of this feast continued unto his days. "And "from that time to this we "celebrate this festival, and "call it *lights*. I suppose "the reason was, because this "liberty shone forth to us "beyond our hopes, and that "thence was the name given "to that festival." Antiq. XII. 7.

[a] A district of Idumæa, which in the books of Numbers and Joshua is called Akrabbim.

membered the injury of the children of Bæan[b], who had been a snare and a stumblingblock unto the people, in that they lay in wait for them in the ways. And they were shut up by him in the 5 towers, and he encamped against them, and destroyed[c] them utterly, and burnt the towers of that *place* with fire, with all those who were therein. Afterwards he passed over to the children 6 of Ammon, where he found a mighty power, and much people, with Timotheus their captain. So 7 he fought many battles with them, and they were discomfited before his face; and he smote them. And when he had taken Jazer[d], and the towns[e] 8 belonging thereto, he returned into Judæa. Then 9 the heathen who were in Galaad[f] assembled themselves together against the Israelites who were in their quarters, to destroy them; but they fled to the fortress of Dathema[g]; and sent letters unto 10 Judas and his brethren, "The heathen who are " round about us are assembled together against " us, to destroy us. And they are preparing to 11 " come and take the fortress whereunto we are " fled, Timotheus being captain of their host. " Come now therefore and deliver us from their 12

[b] Bæan, or Baanas, appears from Josephus to have been the name of an Idumæan chief.

[c] Gr. ἀνεθεμάτισεν αὐτούς: which may also mean, " he " took an oath to destroy " them."

[d] A considerable city in the eastern part of the Holy Land, north of Aroer: it is mentioned in the books of Numbers and Joshua.

[e] Gr. τὰς θυγατέρας αὐτῆς: an elegant metaphor. Compare Numbers, ch. xxi. 25; Ezech. xvi. 44—61.

[f] Galaad, or Gilead, is often put for the whole country eastward of the river Jordan.

[g] A fortress in the land of Gilead, the exact situation of which is unknown to us. Possibly it may be the same place with that which is mentioned at Numbers xxxiii. 18, 19.

13 " hands, for many of us are slain. Yea, all our
" brethren who were in the places of Tobie[h], are
" put to death: their wives and their children
" also they have carried away captives, and *borne*
" *away* their stuff, and they have destroyed there
14 " about a thousand men." While these letters
were yet reading, behold, there came other messengers from Galilee, with their clothes rent, who
15 reported according to these words, and said, "They
" of Ptolemais, and of Tyrus, and Sidon, and all
" Galilee of the Gentiles, are assembled together
16 " against us to consume us." Now when Judas
and the people heard these words, there assembled
a great congregation together, to consult what
they should do for their brethren who were in
17 trouble, and assaulted by them. Then said Judas
unto Simon his brother, Chuse thee out men, and
go and deliver thy brethren who are in Galilee;
but I and Jonathan my brother will go into the
18 country of Galaad. So he left Joseph the *son* of
Zacharias and Azarias, captains of the people,
with the remnant of the host in Judæa, to keep it.
19 And he gave them commandment, saying, Take
ye the charge of this people, and make no war
against the heathen, until the time that we come
20 again. Now unto Simon were given three thousand men to go into Galilee, and unto Judas eight
21 thousand men for the country of Galaad. Then
went Simon into Galilee, where he fought many
battles with the heathen, and the heathen were
22 discomfited before his face. And he pursued them
unto the gate of Ptolemais[i]; and there were slain

[h] Compare Judges xi. 3. also 3 Macc. xii. 17.
[i] A seaport town belonging to the Phœnicians, lying

of the heathen about three thousand men, whose spoils he took. And those who were in Galilee, 23 and in Arbatta[j], with their wives and their children, and all which they had, took he away *with him*, and brought them into Judæa with great joy.

Judas Maccabæus also and his brother Jonathan 24 went over Jordan, and travelled three days' journey in the wilderness; where they met with the Naba- 25 thæans[k], who came unto them in peaceable manner, and told them every thing which had happened to their brethren in the land of Galaad: and how 26 that many of them were shut up in Bosora[l], and Bosor[m], and Alema[n], Casphor[o], Maked[p], and Carnaim[q], (all these cities are strong and great:) and 27 that they were shut up in the rest of the cities of the country of Galaad, and that against to-morrow they had appointed to bring their host against the forts, and to take them, and to destroy them all in

to the north of mount Carmel. In ancient times it was called Acca; and now, Acre.

[j] Or Arbattis, a city of Galilee.

[k] These were Arabians, some of the ancient Edomites, descended from Nebaioth, the eldest son of Ishmael; see Genesis xxv. 13. According to Diodorus Siculus, (lib. II. 48,) they possessed the country eastward of the Jordan, as far north as mount Libanus. Their capital city was Petra, concerning which, and the manners and habits of the Nabathæans, see more in Diodorus Siculus, XIX. c. 94 —97.

[l] A city of Idumæa, mentioned by Isaiah, who calls it Bozrah.

[m] A town of the country of Moab, named by Jeremiah at chap. xlviii. 24.

[n] Another town of the Moabites. Grotius judges it to be that which Josephus calls *Malle*.

[o] Or Casphon, as at ver. 36: Calmet thinks it to be the same as Heshbon.

[p] Called Maachathi, or Maacah, in Deuteronomy and 2 Samuel.

[q] A town lying between Abila and Edrai, about eight miles from Maspha.

28 one day. Hereupon Judas and his host turned suddenly by the way of the wilderness unto Bosor; and he won the city, and slew all the males with the edge of the sword, and took all 29 their spoils, and burnt the city with fire. From whence he removed by night, and went till he 30 came to the fortress[r]. And betimes in the morning they lifted up their eyes, and behold, *there was* an innumerable people bearing ladders, and other engines of war to take the fortress, and they 31 assaulted them. When Judas therefore saw that the battle was begun, and that the cry of the city went up to heaven, with trumpets, and a great 32 sound; he said unto his host, Fight this day for 33 your brethren. So he went forth behind them in three companies, who sounded their trumpets, 34 and cried with prayer. Then the host of Timotheus perceived that it was Maccabæus, and fled from his face: wherefore he smote them with a great slaughter; so that there fell of them that 35 day about eight thousand men. This done, *Judas* turned aside to Maspha[s]; and he assaulted it, and took it, and slew all the males therein, and gathered the spoils thereof, and burnt it with 36 fire. From thence went he and took Casphon, Maged, Bosor, and the other cities of the country 37 of Galaad. After these things gathered Timotheus another host, and encamped before Raphon[t] 38 beyond the brook. So Judas sent *men* to espy the host, who brought him word, saying, All the

[r] Namely, of Dathema.
[s] Called Mizpeh in the books of Judges and Samuel. The same with Malle above-named.
[t] Perhaps the town of Syria, called Raphana by Pliny.

heathen which are round about us are assembled unto them, even a very great host. He hath also 39 hired the Arabians to help them, and they have pitched their tents beyond the brook, ready to come and fight against thee. Upon this Judas went to meet them. Then Timotheus said unto 40 the captains of his host, When Judas and his host come near the water-brook, if he pass over first unto us, we shall not be able to withstand him: for he will mightily prevail against us. But if 41 he be afraid, and camp beyond the river, we shall go over unto him, and prevail against him. Now 42 when Judas came near the water-brook, he caused the scribes of the people to remain by the brook: and he charged them all, saying, Suffer no man to pitch his tent, but let all come to the battle. So 43 he went over first unto them, and all the people after him; then all the heathen being discomfited before him, cast away their weapons, and fled unto the temple[u] which was at Carnaim: but they 44 took the city, and burnt the temple, with all who were therein. Thus was Carnaim subdued, neither could they stand any longer before Judas. Then Judas gathered together all the Israelites 45 who were in the country of Galaad, from the least unto the greatest, even their wives and their children, and their stuff, a very great host, to the end they might come into the land of Judah.

Now when they came unto Ephron, (this was 46 a great city in the way as they should go, very well fortified,) they could not turn from it, either on the right hand or the left, but must needs pass

[u] Viz. of the goddess Atargatis. See 3 Macc. xii. 26, and the note there.

47 through the midst of it. Then they of the city shut them out, and stopped up the gates with
48 stones. Whereupon Judas sent unto them with peaceable words, saying, We will pass through your land to go into our own country, and none shall do you any hurt; we will only pass through on foot: howbeit, they would not open unto him.
49 Wherefore Judas commanded a proclamation to be made throughout the host, that every man should pitch his tent in the place where he was.
50 So the soldiers pitched, and assaulted the city all that day and all that night, till at the length the
51 city was delivered into his hands: and he slew all the males with the edge of the sword, and rased the city, and took the spoils thereof, and passed through the city, over them which were slain.
52 And they passed over Jordan, into the great
53 plain before Bethsan[x]. And Judas was gathering together those who were hindmost, and exhorting the people all the way through, till they came
54 into the land of Judah. So they went up to mount Zion with joy and gladness, where they offered burnt offerings, because not one of them were slain until they had returned in peace.
55 Now what time as Judas and Jonathan were in the land of Galaad, and Simon his brother in

---

[x] Or Bethshean, a considerable city, situate in the tribe of Manasseh, about two miles east of Gilboah, in the neighbourhood of the river Jordan: it is often mentioned in the books of Joshua, Judges, and Samuel. The Greeks called it Scythopolis; under which name also it appears in the 3d book of Maccabees, chap. xii. 29. See Josephus, XII. 12: and Herodotus, who in his first book relates that irruption of the Scythians into Egypt and Palestine, from which it is thought by most authors to have derived its name.

Galilee before Ptolemais; Joseph, the *son* of Zacha- 56
rias, and Azarias, captains of the army, heard of
the valiant acts and warlike deeds which they
had done. Wherefore they said, Let us also get 57
us a name, and go fight against the heathen who
are round about us. So when they had given 58
charge unto the army which was with them, they
went towards Jamnia. Then came Gorgias and 59
his men out of the city to meet them in battle.
And so it was that Joseph and Azarias were put 60
to flight, and pursued unto the borders of Judæa:
and there were slain that day of the people of
Israel, about two thousand men. Thus was there 61
a great overthrow among the children of Israel,
because they were not obedient unto Judas and his
brethren, but thought to do some valiant act.
Moreover, these men came not of the seed of those 62
by whose hand deliverance was given unto Israel.
And the man Judas and his brethren were greatly 63
renowned in the sight of all Israel, and of all the
heathen wheresoever their name was heard. In- 64
somuch that the people assembled unto them with
joyful acclamations.

Afterward went Judas forth with his brethren, 65
and fought against the children of Esau in the
land toward the south; where he smote Hebrony,
and the towns thereof, and pulled down the fortress of it, and burnt the towers thereof round
about. From thence he removed to go into the 66
land of the Philistines, and passed through Sama-

---

y This had formerly been one of the towns of Judah: but after that the Idumæans had possessed themselves of the southern portion of Judæa, during the captivity of Babylon, they made Hebron their principal city.

67 ria. At that time certain priests, desirous to shew their valour, were slain in battle, for that
68 they went out to fight unadvisedly. So Judas turned aside to Azotus in the land of the Philistines; and when he had pulled down their altars, and burnt the carved images of their gods with fire, and spoiled their cities, he returned into the land of Judah.

CHAPTER VI.

The death of Antiochus Epiphanes. The wars of Judas. The heroic act of Eleazar.

1 ABOUT *that time*, king Antiochus travelling through the high countries[a], heard say, that Elymais[b] in the country of Persia, was a city greatly
2 renowned for riches, silver and gold: and that the temple[c] which was in it was very rich, wherein were coverings of gold, and breast-plates, and shields, which Alexander *son* of Philip the Macedonian king, who reigned first among the Gre-
3 cians, had left there. Wherefore he came and sought to take the city, and to spoil it; but he was not able, because the design was made known
4 to them of the city. And they rose up against him in battle: so he fled, and departed thence
5 with great heaviness, to return to Babylon. Moreover, there came one who brought him tidings

[a] Namely, on the Euphrates. See the note at chap. iii. 37.

[b] The Greek varies between Ἐλυμαῖς and ἐν Ἐλύμαις; and it is disputed whether this be the name of a region or of a city. In the third book of Maccabees, Persepolis is said to be the city meant. See chap. ix. 1.

[c] Viz. of *Diana*, according to Josephus and Polybius: but Appian alleges that it was of *Venus*. In the third book, chap. i. 13, the Deity is called Nannæa, or Nanea.

into Persia, that the armies which went against the land of Judah were put to flight: and that 6 Lysias, who went forth first with a great power, was driven away by the Jews; and that they were made strong by the armour, and power, and store of spoils, which they had gotten from the armies, whom they had destroyed: also that they had 7 pulled down the abomination which he had set up upon the altar in Jerusalem, and that they had compassed about the sanctuary with high walls as before, and his city Bethsura. And it came 8 to pass when the king heard these words, he was astonished, and sore moved: whereupon he laid him down upon his bed, and fell sick for grief, because it had not befallen him as he looked for. And there he continued many days: 9 for his grief was constantly renewed upon him, and he made account that he should die. Where- 10 fore he called for all his friends, and said unto them, The sleep is gone from mine eyes, and my heart faileth for very care. And I thought with 11 myself, Into what tribulation am I come, and how great a flood *of misery* is it wherein now I am! for I was thought bountiful, and was beloved in my power: but now I remember the evils which 12 I did at Jerusalem, and that I took all the vessels of gold and silver which were therein, and sent to destroy the inhabitants of Judæa without a cause. I perceive therefore that for this cause these 13 troubles are come upon me, and behold I perish through great grief in a strange land. Then 14 called he for Philip, one of his friends, whom he made ruler over all his realm. And gave him the 15 crown, and his robe, and his signet-ring, to the

end he should bring up his son Antiochus, and
16 nourish him up for the kingdom. So king Antiochus died there[d] in the hundred forty and ninth
17 year. Now when Lysias knew that the king was dead, he set up Antiochus his son (whom he had brought up, being young) to reign in his stead, and his name he called Eupator.
18 About this time they which were in the tower, were shutting up the Israelites round about the sanctuary, and seeking always their
19 hurt, and the strengthening of the heathen. Wherefore Judas purposed to destroy them, and called
20 all the people together, to besiege them. So they came together, and besieged them in the hundred and fiftieth year, and he made mounts for shot[e]
21 against them, and *other* engines. Howbeit, certain of them escaped from the siege, and to them some ungodly men of Israel joined themselves.
22 And they went unto the king, and said, How long will it be ere thou execute judgment, and avenge
23 our brethren? We have been willing to serve thy father, and to walk after his decrees, and to obey
24 his commandments; *for which cause* they of our nation besiege the tower, and are alienated from us; moreover, as many of us as were found were put to death, and our inheritances were plundered.
25 Neither have they stretched out their hand against

---

[d] Viz. at Babylon, or near it. Polybius relates that he died at Tabæ, a town of Persia, near to Babylon; and that he shewed symptoms of madness shortly before his death. Polyb. XXXI. 11.

[e] Gr. βελοστάσεις, which is a word used by Polybius in describing the siege of Echinum, and signifies " spots " chosen for planting the Ba-" listæ." His words are, Καὶ τρεῖς ἦσαν βελοστάσεις λιθοβόλοις· ὧν ὁ μὲν εἰς ταλαντιαῖος, οἱ δὲ δύο τριακονταμναίους ἐξέβαλλον λίθους. Lib. IX. 41. See Jeremiah xxxii. 24.

us only, but also against all their borders. And behold, this day are they besieging the tower at Jerusalem, to take it: the sanctuary also, and Bethsura have they fortified. Wherefore, if thou dost not prevent them quickly, they will do greater things than these, neither shalt thou be able to rule them.

Now when the king heard this, he was angry, and gathered together all his friends, and the captains of his army, and those who had charge of the horse. There came also unto him from other kingdoms, and from isles of the sea, bands of hired soldiers. So that the number of his army was an hundred thousand foot-men, and twenty thousand horsemen, and two and thirty elephants exercised in battle. These went through Idumæa, and pitched against Bethsura, which they assaulted many days, making engines of war; but they *of Bethsura* came out and burnt them with fire, and fought valiantly. Upon this Judas removed from the tower, and pitched in Bathzacharias[f], over against the king's camp. Then the king rising very early marched fiercely with his host toward Bathzacharias, where his armies made them ready to battle, and sounded the trumpets. And to the end they might provoke the elephants to fight, they shewed[g] them the blood of grapes and mul-

---

[f] This seems to have been a place of small note, not elsewhere mentioned. Josephus describes it as being seventy stadia distant from Bethsura.

[g] Gr. ἔδειξαν. Schleusner contends, that this liquid was not merely exhibited, but also *given* to the elephants; referring, for the fact, to 3 Macc. v. 10: and he believes that this sense of the verb δεικνύω can be supported by instances drawn from the New Testament. I can scarcely agree with him on the point.

35 berries. Moreover they divided the beasts among the companies; and for every elephant they appointed a thousand men armed with coats of mail, and with helmets of brass on their heads; and for every beast were ordained five hundred horsemen 36 of the best. These were ready at every occasion: wheresoever the beast was they were, and whithersoever the beast went, they went also, neither departed they from him. 37 And upon the beasts there were strong towers of wood, which covered every one of them, and were girt fast unto them with devices: there were also upon every one, two and thirty[h] strong men[i] who fought upon them, besides the Indian who ruled him. 38 As for the remnant of the horsemen, they set them on this side and that side, at the two parts of the host, stirring them up[k] and covering their flanks with them. 39 Now when the sun shone upon the shields of gold and brass, the mountains glittered therewith, and 40 shined like lamps of fire. So part of the king's army was spread upon the high mountains, and part on the valleys below, and they marched on

[h] Bochart (Hierozoicon, tom. I. p. 261, &c.) objects strongly to this number, so much larger than that which approved authors assign to one elephant, namely, two, three, six, rarely ten or twelve. He adduces an ingenious conjectural emendation, viz. that instead of ἄνδρες δυνάμεως δύο καὶ τριάκοντα οἱ πολεμοῦντες ἐπ' αὐτοῖς, we should read ἄνδρες δυνάμεως δύο ἢ τρεῖς ἀκοντίοις πολεμοῦντες. I fear that the MSS. do not confirm this reading. Bochart himself thinks that the author omitted the number altogether, and that the words δύο καὶ τριάκοντα are merely an interpolation from verse 30, where that number of elephants is mentioned. See however Pliny, VIII. 7, as cited by Grotius.

[i] Josephus says, "archers."

[k] The Greek text of the latter portion of this verse is obscure: κατασείοντες καὶ καταφρασσόμενοι ἐν ταῖς φάλαγξι. And there is a various reading, ἐν ταῖς φάραγξι.

safely, and in order. Wherefore all who heard 41
the noise of their multitude, and the marching of
the company, and the rattling of the armour,
were moved: for the army was very great and
mighty.

Then Judas and his host drew near, and entered 42
into battle, and there were slain of the king's
army six hundred men. Eleazar also, *surnamed* 43
Avaran[1], perceived that one of the beasts, armed
with a royal breast-plate, was higher than all the
rest; and supposing that the king was upon him,
he devoted himself, to the end he might de- 44
liver his people, and get him a perpetual name:
wherefore he ran upon him courageously into the 45
midst of the battle, slaying on the right hand and
on the left, so that they were divided from him on
both sides. *Which done*, he crept under the ele- 46
phant, and thrust him under, and slew him:
whereupon the elephant fell down upon him, and
there he died. Howbeit, *the rest of the Jews* see- 47
ing the strength of the king, and the spirit of his
forces, turned away from them.

Then the king's army went up to Jerusalem to 48
meet them, and the king pitched his tents against
Judæa, and against mount Sion. But with them 49
which were in Bethsura he made peace: and they
came out of the city, because they had no victuals
there to endure the siege, it being a year of rest to
the land. So the king took Bethsura, and set a 50
garrison there to keep it. And he encamped 51
against the sanctuary many days: and set there
mounts for shot, and engines, and instruments to

[1] Namely, the son of Mattathias and brother of Judas, mentioned at chapter ii. 5.

cast fire and stones, and scorpions[m] to cast darts,
52 and slings. Whereupon they also made engines against their engines, and held them battle a long
53 season. But *at the last* there were no victuals in the vessels[n], because it was the seventh year, and those who fled from the Gentiles into Judæa to save themselves, had eaten up the residue of the
54 store. And there were but a few left in the sanctuary, because the famine did so prevail against them, that they were scattered, every man to his own place.
55 At that time Lysias heard say, that Philip (whom Antiochus the king, whiles he lived, had appointed[o] to bring up his son Antiochus, that he
56 might be king) was returned out of Persia and Media, and the king's host also which went with him, and that he sought to take unto him the rul-
57 ing of affairs. Wherefore he went in all haste, and said to the king, and the captains of the host, and the company, We decay daily, and our victuals are but small, and the place we lay siege unto is strong, and the affairs of the kingdom lie upon us.
58 Now therefore let us be friends with these men, and make peace with them and with all their nation;
59 and covenant with them, that they shall live after their laws, as *they did* before: for on account of their laws which we abolished, they have been an-
60 gered, and have done all these things. And the say-

[m] Gr. σκορπίδια, for which see Vegetius de Re Militari, IV. 22; also Ammianus Marcellinus, who describes their construction at book XXIII. 5.
[n] Gr. ἀγγείοις. But the Alexandrian manuscript reads Ἁγιοῖς, *the Sanctuary*, which indeed may be thought to derive some countenance from the following verse.
[o] See chapter vi. 15.

ing pleased the king and the princes: wherefore he sent unto them to make peace, and they accepted thereof. Also the king and the princes made an oath unto them: whereupon they went out of the strong hold. Then the king entered into mount Sion: but when he saw the strength of the place, he brake his oath which he had made, and gave commandment to pull down the wall round about. Afterward departed he in all haste, and returned unto Antiochia, where he found Philip to be master of the city: so he fought against him, and took the city by force[p].

CHAPTER VII.

The wars of Judas with Bacchides, Alcimus, and Nicanor. Nicanor's death.

In the hundred and one and fiftieth year, Demetrius[a] *the son* of Seleucus departed[b] from Rome, and came up with a few men unto a city[c] of the sea-coast, and reigned there. And as he entered into the palace[d] of his ancestors, so it

---

[p] Josephus adds, that he took Philip prisoner, and put him to death.

[a] He was son of Seleucus, the elder brother of Antiochus Epiphanes, and therefore rightful owner of the kingdom.

[b] Where he had been detained a hostage, through the policy of the Roman senate. Finding after two applications that his departure never would be permitted, he concerted with some friends the means of escape, and by their assistance was enabled to quit Rome by night, accompanied by Apollonius and a few others. Polybius, the historian, who was his friend and counsellor in this affair, has given us an interesting detail of the particulars, in book XXXI. 19—23.

[c] Namely, Tripolis, as mentioned in 3 Macc. xiv. 1; and Josephus agrees.

[d] Namely, at Antioch ἐπὶ Δάφνης, the regal seat of the kings of Syria: for an account of which city see Strabo, lib. XVI.

was that his forces had taken Antiochus and Ly-
3 sias to bring them unto him. And the thing was
made known to him, and he said, "Shew me not
4 " their faces." So his host slew them: and Demetrius was set upon the throne of his kingdom.
5 And there came unto him all the wicked and ungodly men of Israel, having Alcimus (who was
6 desirous to be high priest) for their captain. And
they accused the people to the king, saying, Judas
and his brethren have slain all thy friends and
7 have driven us out of our own land. Now therefore send some man whom thou trustest, and let
him go and see the entire destruction which he
hath made amongst us, and in the king's land,
and let him punish them and all them who aid
them.
8 Then the king chose Bacchides a friend of the
king, who ruled[e] in the country beyond the river,
and was a great man in the kingdom, and faithful
9 to the king. And him he sent with that wicked
Alcimus, whom he made high priest, and commanded him that he should take vengeance on
10 the children of Israel. So they departed, and
came with a great power into the land of Judah;
and he sent messengers to Judas and his brethren
11 with peaceable words deceitfully. But they gave
no heed to their words; for they saw that they
12 were come with a great power. Then did there
assemble unto Alcimus and Bacchides, a company
13 of scribes to require justice. Now the Assidæans
were the first among the children of Israel who
14 sought peace of them. For said they, One who

[e] Josephus styles him "Governor of Mesopotamia."

is a priest of the seed of Aaron is come with this army, and he will do us no wrong. So he spake 15 unto them peaceably, and sware unto them, saying, We will procure the harm neither of you nor your friends. Whereupon they believed him: 16 howbeit, he took of them threescore men, and slew them in one day, according to the words which he wrote[f], "The flesh of thy saints *have* 17 "*they cast out*, and their blood have they shed "round about Jerusalem, and there was none to "bury them." Wherefore the fear and dread of 18 them fell upon all the people, who said, There is neither truth nor justice in them; for they have broken the covenant and oath which they made. After this removed Bacchides from Jerusalem, 19 and pitched his tents in Bezeth[g], where he sent and took many of the men who had forsaken him, and certain of the people also; and when he had slain them, *he cast them* into the great pit.

Then committed he the country to Alcimus, 20 and left with him a power to aid him: so Bacchides went to the king. And Alcimus contended 21 for the high-priesthood. And unto him resorted 22 all such as troubled the people, who, after they had gotten the land of Judah into their power, did much hurt in Israel. Now when Judas saw 23 all the mischief which Alcimus and his company had done among the Israelites, even above the heathen; he went out into all the coasts of Judæa 24 round about, and took vengeance on those who had deserted from him, so that they were restrained from going forth into the country. But 25

[f] Namely, the author of Psalm lxxix.
[g] Or Bethzetho, a village.

when Alcimus saw that Judas and his company had grown strong, and knew that he was not able to withstand them, he went again to the king, and said all the evil of them that he could.

26 Then the king sent Nicanor[h], one of his honourable princes, a man who bare deadly hate unto Israel, with commandment to destroy the people.
27 So Nicanor came to Jerusalem with a great force; and sent unto Judas and his brethren deceitfully
28 with peaceable words, saying, Let there be no battle between me and you: I will come with a
29 few men that I may see your faces in peace. He came therefore to Judas, and they saluted one another peaceably. Howbeit, the enemies were
30 prepared to take away Judas by violence. Which thing, after it was known to Judas, *to wit*, that he came unto him with deceit, he was sore afraid
31 of him, and would see his face no more. Nicanor also, when he saw that his counsel was discovered, went out to meet Judas in battle beside
32 Capharsalama[i]: where there were slain of Nicanor's side about five thousand men, and *the rest* fled into the city of David.
33 After this went Nicanor up to mount Sion, and there came out of the sanctuary certain of the priests, and certain of the elders of the people, to salute him peaceably, and to shew him the burnt-
34 sacrifice which was offered for the king[k]. But he mocked them, and laughed at them, and abused[l]

[h] Called by Josephus, "his "most intimate and faithful "friend, who had fled from "Rome with him."
[i] A village in the neighbourhood of Jerusalem.
[k] Concerning the sacrifice and prayers customarily offered up for the king by the Jews, see Ezra vi. 10.
[l] Gr. ἐμίανεν, *he defiled;* either by spitting upon them,

them shamefully, and spake proudly: and swore 35
in his wrath, saying, Unless Judas and his host
be now delivered into my hands, if ever I come
again in peace, I will burn up this house: and
with that he went out in a great rage.

Then the priests entered in, and stood before 36
the altar and the temple, weeping, and saying,
Thou, *O Lord*, didst choose[m] this house to be 37
called by thy name, and to be a house of prayer
and petition for thy people: be avenged on this 38
man and his host, and let them fall by the
sword: remember their blasphemies, and suffer
them not to continue any longer. So Nicanor 39
went out of Jerusalem, and pitched his tents in
Beth-horon, where an host out of Syria met him.
But Judas pitched in Adasa[n], with three thousand 40
men, and there he prayed, saying, *O Lord*, when 41
they which were sent from the king of the Assy-
rians[o] blasphemed, thine angel went out and smote
an hundred fourscore and five thousand of them:
even so destroy thou this host before us this day, 42
that the rest may know that he hath spoken wickedly against thy sanctuary, and judge thou him
according to his wickedness.

So the thirteenth day of the month Adar[p] the 43
host joined battle: and Nicanor's host was discomfited, and he himself was first slain in the
battle. Now when Nicanor's host saw that he 44
was slain, they cast away their weapons, and fled.

---

or by using contumelious and blasphemous expressions.

[m] See Deuteron. xii. 5. 11. 14; Isaiah lvi. 7, &c. &c.

[n] A village, which Josephus says is distant thirty stadia from Beth-horon.

[o] See 2 Kings xix, Isaiah xxxvii.

[p] Answering to our February and March.

45 Then they pursued after them a day's journey, from Adasa until thou come to Gazera, sounding
46 an alarm after them with their trumpets. Whereupon, they came forth out of the towns of Judæa, round about, and outflanked them; so that they, turning back upon those who pursued them, were all slain with the sword, and not one of them was
47 left. Afterwards they took the spoils, and the prey, and smote off Nicanor's head, and his right hand, which he stretched out so proudly; and brought them away, and hanged them up towards
48 Jerusalem. For this cause the people rejoiced greatly, and they kept that day a day of great
49 gladness. Moreover, they ordained to keep yearly
50 this day, being the thirteenth of Adar. Thus the land of Judah was in rest a little while.

CHAPTER VIII.

Judas makes a league with the Romans.

1 Now Judas had heard of the fame of the Romans, that they were mighty in power, and such as would lovingly accept all who joined themselves unto them, and make a league of amity
2 with all who came unto them; and that they were men of great valour. It was told him also of their wars and noble acts which they had done among the Galatians[a], and how they had con-

[a] Namely, the Gauls of Asia, or Gallo-græci; who, migrating from Gaul under Brennus and other chiefs, passed over into Asia, and after some time established themselves in the countries on the river Halys. Becoming allies of Antiochus the Great, they incurred the resentment of the Romans, who sent Cneius Manlius to punish them; and from this general they experienced two signal defeats, at Ancyra and at mount Olympus, A.C. 189. See Livy, XXXVIII. 12—26.

quered them, and brought them under tribute. And what they had done in the country of Spain for the winning of the mines of the silver and gold which is there: and that by their policy and patience they had conquered all the place, (though it were very far from them,) and the kings also who came against them from the uttermost part of the earth, till they had discomfited them, and given them a great overthrow, so that the rest did give them tribute every year. Besides this, how they had discomfited in battle Philip, and Perseus king of the Citims[b], with others who lifted up themselves against them, and had overcome them. How also Antiochus[c] the great king of Asia, who came against them in battle, having an hundred and twenty elephants, with horsemen and chariots, and a very great army, was discomfited by them; and how they took him alive, and covenanted that he, and such as reigned after him, should pay a great tribute, and give hostages, and an appointed sum[d]. And the country of India, and Media[e], and Lydia, and of the goodliest coun-

---

[b] Namely, Macedonians. See chapter I. 1. Philip was conquered by the Romans in the first, and Perseus in the second Macedonic war; by the subjugation of whom an end was put to the Macedonian empire.

[c] See the accounts of these transactions given by Polybius and Livy.

[d] Gr. διαστολήν; or, "a di-"vision of his territory."

[e] Grotius takes notice of these two names, (in which, nevertheless, all the MSS. agree,) and suggests, that perhaps we ought to read *Ionia* and *Mysia*, which indeed were given to Eumenes by the Romans; whereas neither of the other two had belonged either to them or to Antiochus. In fact, the precise terms imposed by the Roman senate after the defeat of Antiochus, are furnished to us by Livy, XXXVII. 55. "Ut cis Taurum mon-"tem quæ *intra regni An-*"*tiochi fines* fuissent Eumeni "attribuerentur, præter Ly-

B.C. 161. CHAP. VIII. 91

tries, which they took from him and gave to king
9 Eumenes[f]: moreover, how the Grecians[g] had de-
10 termined to come and destroy them; and that
they, having knowledge thereof, sent against them
a certain captain, and fighting with them slew
many of them, and carried away captives their
wives and their children, and spoiled them, and
took possession of their lands, and pulled down
their strong holds, and brought them to be their
11 servants unto this day. *It was told him* besides,
how they destroyed and brought under their
dominion all other kingdoms and isles, which at
12 any time resisted them: but with their friends
- and such as relied upon them, they kept amity:
and that they had conquered kingdoms both far
and nigh, insomuch that all who heard of their
13 name were afraid of them: also, that whom they
chose to help, and that they should reign, those
reign; and whom again they would, they displace;
14 and that they were greatly exalted: yet for all this,
none of them wore a crown, or was clothed in pur-
15 ple to walk proudly in it: moreover, how they had
made for themselves a senate-house, wherein three
hundred and twenty[h] men sat in council daily,
consulting alway for the people, to the end they

"ciam Cariamque, usque ad
"Mæandrum fluvium." India
and Media therefore are
wholly out of the question.

[f] The son of Attalus, king of Pergamus.

[g] Probably the allusion is to the Ætolians and other Greek allies of Antiochus.

[h] The Roman senate, about this period, consisted *usually* of three hundred members: but the number varied from time to time, so that the author of this book may be correct in his statement. It deserves notice also, that in the Vth book of Maccabees, chap. xii. xiii. xlii., the same precise number is assigned. See the places.

might be well ordered: and that they committed 16
their government to one man[i] every year, who
ruled over all their country; and that all were
obedient to that one, and that there was neither
envy nor emulation amongst them.

And Judas chose Eupolemus the son of John, 17
the son of Accos, and Jason, the son of Eleazar,
and sent them to Rome, to make a league of
amity and confederacy with them; *and to intreat* 18
them, that they would take the yoke from them;
for they saw that the kingdom of the Grecians
did oppress Israel with servitude. They went 19
therefore to Rome, (which was a very great journey,) and came into the senate, where they spake,
and said, "Judas Maccabæus and his brethren, 20
" and the people of the Jews, have sent us unto
" you, to make a confederacy and peace with you,
" and that we might be registered your con-
" federates and friends." So that matter pleased[k] 21
the Romans well.

And this is the copy of the epistle which *the* 22
senate wrote back again, in tables of brass, and
sent to Jerusalem, that there they might have by
them a memorial of peace and confederacy: "Good 23
" success be to the Romans and to the people of
" the Jews, by sea and by land for ever: the
" sword also and the enemy be far from them. If 24

---

[i] Though there were uniformly and invariably *two* consuls, yet, inasmuch as *one* of these had the entire management of military and foreign affairs, he alone was likely to be well-known to the Jewish writer of this history.

[k] The historian Justin has a shrewd remark upon this: " A Demetrio cum descivis- " sent, [Judæi] amicitia Ro- " manorum petita, primi om- " nium ex orientalibus liber- " tatem receperunt, facile " tunc Romanis de alieno lar- " gientibus," lib. XXXVI. 3.

"there come first any war upon the Romans, or
"any of their confederates throughout all their
25 "dominion, the people of the Jews shall help
"them, as the time shall be appointed them, with
26 "all their heart. Neither shall they give any
"thing unto those who make war upon them, or
"aid them with victuals, weapons, money, or ships,
"as it hath seemed good unto the Romans; but
"they shall keep their covenants without taking
27 "any thing therefore. In the same manner also
"if a war come first upon the nation of the Jews,
"the Romans shall help them with all their heart,
"according as the time shall be appointed them.
28 "Neither shall victuals be given to those who
"take part against them, or weapons, or money,
"or ships, as it hath seemed good to the Romans:
"but they shall keep their covenants, and that
29 "without deceit." "According to these articles
"did the Romans make a covenant with the
30 "people of the Jews. Howbeit, if hereafter the
"one party or the other shall think meet to add
"or diminish any thing, they may do it at their
"pleasures; and whatsoever they shall add or
31 "take away, shall be ratified. And as touching
"the evils which Demetrius doeth to the Jews,
"we have written unto him, saying, 'Wherefore
"hast thou made thy yoke heavy upon our friends
32 "and confederates the Jews?' If therefore they
"complain any more against thee, we will do
"them justice, and fight with thee by sea and by
"land."

CHAPTER IX.

The death of Judas. Also, of John. Jonathan is made captain. The death of Alcimus.

FURTHERMORE, when Demetrius heard that 1 Nicanor and his host were slain in battle, he proceeded to send Bacchides and Alcimus into the land of Judah the second time, and with them the chief strength[a] of his host: who went forth 2 by the way which leadeth to Galgala[b], and pitched their tents before Maseloth, which is in Arbela[c], and they won it, and slew much people. Also 3 in the first month of the hundred fifty and second year, they encamped before Jerusalem. From whence they removed and went to 4 Beræa[d], with twenty thousand *foot*-men, and two thousand horse-men.

Now Judas had pitched his tents at Eleasa[e], 5 and three thousand chosen men with him: who 6 seeing the multitude of the other army to be so great, were sore afraid; whereupon many conveyed themselves out of the host, insomuch that there abode of them no more than eight hundred men. When Judas therefore saw that his host slipt 7 away, and that the battle pressed upon him, he was sore troubled in mind, for that he had no

---

[a] Gr. τὸ δεξιὸν κέρας, *the right wing*, which, as the post of honour, usually was occupied by the bravest or most favourite troops.

[b] Or Gilgal, as in Joshua iv. 19. Drusius thinks that we ought to read *Galilee* in this passage.

[c] Perhaps the same as Arbatta, mentioned above, at chap. v. 23. Josephus calls it "a city of Galilee."

[d] Or Berzetho; perhaps the same as Bezeth, mentioned at chap. vii. 19.

[e] There is a variety of reading here. Possibly it may designate Adasa, named above, at chap. vii. 40. Compare book V. chap. 17. 2.

8 time to gather them together. And he was distressed: but nevertheless, unto them which remained, he said, Let us rise and go up against our enemies, if peradventure we may be able to
9 fight with them. But they dehorted him, saying, We shall never be able: let us now rather save our lives, and hereafter we will return with our brethren, and fight against them: for we are but
10 few. Then Judas said, God forbid, that I should do this thing, and flee away from them: if our time be come, let us die manfully for our brethren, and let us not leave behind a stain upon
11 our honour. With that the host *of Bacchides* removed out of their tents, and stood over against them, their horsemen being divided into two troops, and their slingers and archers going before the host, and they which marched in the
12 fore-ward were all mighty men. And Bacchides was in the right wing: so the host drew near on
13 the two parts, and sounded their trumpets. They also of Judas's side, even they sounded their trumpets also, so that the earth shook at the noise of the armies, and the battle was joined from morn-
14 ing till night. And Judas perceived that Bacchides and the strength of his army were on the right-side; and all who were hardy in heart went
15 with him: and the right wing was discomfited by them, and they pursued after them unto the
16 mount Azotus. But when they of the left wing saw that they of the right wing were discomfited, they followed upon Judas and those who were
17 with him, hard at the heels from behind: whereupon there was a sore battle, insomuch that many
18 were slain on both parts. Judas also was killed,

and the remnant fled. Then Jonathan and Simon 19 took Judas their brother, and buried him in the sepulchre of his fathers in Modin. Moreover, 20 they bewailed him, and all Israel made great lamentation for him, and mourned many days, saying, "How is the valiant man fallen, who deli- 21 "vered Israel!" As for the other things [f] con- 22 cerning Judas and his wars, and the noble acts which he did, and his greatness, they are not written: for they were very many.

Now after the death of Judas, the wicked be- 23 gan to lift up their heads in all the coasts of Israel, and there rose up all such as wrought iniquity. In those days also was there a very great famine, 24 *by reason whereof* the country revolted, and went with them. Then Bacchides chose the wicked 25 men, and made them lords of the country. And 26 they made inquiry and search for Judas's friends, and brought them unto Bacchides, who took vengeance on them, and used them despitefully[g]. So 27 there was a great affliction in Israel, the like whereof was not since the time that a prophet [h] was not seen amongst them.

For this cause all Judas's friends came together, 28 and said unto Jonathan, Since thy brother Judas 29 died, we have no man like him to go forth against our enemies and Bacchides, and against them of our nation, which are adversaries to us. Now 30 therefore we have chosen thee this day to be our prince and captain in his stead, that thou mayest

---

[f] Gr. τὰ περισσὰ τῶν λόγων.
[g] Gr. ἐνέπαιζεν αὐτοῖς, literally, "he mocked them."
[h] That is, since the death of the prophet Malachi; a period of more than two hundred years.

31 fight our battles. Upon this, Jonathan took the governance upon him at that time, and rose up
32 instead of his brother Judas. But when Bacchides gat knowledge thereof, he sought to slay
33 him. Then Jonathan and Simon his brother, and all who were with him, perceiving that, fled into the wilderness of Thecoe[i], and pitched their tents
34 by the water of the pool Asphar. Which when Bacchides understood, he came over Jordan with all his host upon the sabbath-day.

35 Now Jonathan had sent his brother *John*, a captain of the people, to pray his friends the Nabathæans[k], that they might leave with them their
36 baggage, which was much. But the children of Jambri came out of Medaba, and took John[l] and all which he had, and went their way with it.
37 After this came word to Jonathan and Simon his brother, that the children of Jambri were making a great marriage, and were bringing the bride from Nadabatha with a great train, as being the daughter of one of the great princes of Chanaan.
38 Therefore they remembered John their brother, and went up and hid themselves under the covert
39 of the mountain. Where they lifted up their eyes and looked, and behold, there was much ado, and great baggage: and the bridegroom came forth, and his friends and brethren, to meet them with drums and instruments of musick, and many wea-
40 pons. Then Jonathan and they which were with him, rose up against them from the place where

---

[i] Or Tekoah, as written at 2 Chron. xx. 20, and Jer. vi. 1. It appears to have been situate at no great distance from Bethlehem, towards the south.
[k] See above, chap. v. 25.
[l] And put him to death; as appears by verse 42.

they lay in ambush, and made a slaughter of them in such sort, that many^m fell down dead, and the remnant fled into the mountain, and they took all their spoils. Thus was the marriage turned into 41 mourning, and the noise of their melody into lamentation. So when they had avenged fully the 42 blood of their brother, they turned again to the marsh of Jordan.

Now when Bacchides heard hereof, he came on 43 the sabbath-day unto the banks of Jordan with a great power. Then Jonathan said to his company, 44 Let us go up now and fight for our lives, for it standeth not with us to-day, as it was yesterday and the day before: for, behold, the battle is be- 45 fore us and behind us, and the water of Jordan on this side and that side, the marsh likewise and wood, neither is there place for us to turn aside. Wherefore cry ye now unto heaven, that ye may 46 be delivered from the hand of your enemies. With 47 that they joined battle; and Jonathan stretched forth his hand to smite Bacchides, but he turned back from him. Then Jonathan and they which 48 were with him leapt into Jordan, and swam over unto the farther bank: howbeit, the other passed not over Jordan unto them. So there were slain 49 of Bacchides' side that day about a thousandⁿ men.

Afterward returned *Bacchides* to Jerusalem, 50 and repaired the strong cities in Judæa, the fort in Jericho, and Emmaus, and Beth-horon, and Beth-el, and Thamnatha Pharathoni, and Taphon, with high walls, with gates, and with

---

^m Josephus reckons them at four hundred. ⁿ Josephus doubles the number.

B.C. 158. CHAP. IX. 99

51 bars. And in them he set a garrison, that they
52 might work malice ᵒ upon Israel. He fortified also the city Bethsura, and Gazara, and the tower, and put forces in them, and provision of victuals.
53 Besides, he took the chief men's sons in the country for hostages, and put them into the tower at Jerusalem to be kept.

54 Moreover, in the hundred fifty and third year, in the second month, Alcimus commanded that the wall of the inner court of the sanctuary should be pulled down ᴾ; he pulled
55 down also the works of the prophets. And as he began to pull down, even at that time was Alcimus plagued, and his enterprises hindered: for his mouth was stopped, and he was taken with a palsy, so that he could no more speak any thing,
56 nor give order concerning his house. So Alcimus died at that time with great torment.

B.C. 160.

57 Now when Bacchides saw that Alcimus was dead, he returned to the king, whereupon the land of Judah was in rest two years.

58 Then all the ungodly men held a council, saying, Behold, Jonathan and his company are at ease, and dwell without care: now therefore we will bring Bacchides hither, who shall
59 take them all in one night. So they went and con-
60 sulted with him. Then removed he, and came with a great host, and sent letters privily to his adherents in Judæa, that they should take Jonathan and those who were with him: howbeit,

B.C. 158.

ᵒ Gr. τοῦ ἐχθραίνειν. it signifies "to do harm, or mischief."

ᴾ So that thenceforward no distinction should be made between Jew and Gentile, but that all should have equal privilege of access to the inner court, which in former times had been open to Jews alone.

H 2

they could not, because their counsel was made known unto them. Wherefore they took of the 61 men of the country who were authors of that mischief, about fifty persons, and slew them. Afterward Jonathan and Simon, and they which were with him, got them away to Bethbasi [q], which is in the wilderness, and they repaired the decays thereof, and made it strong. Which thing when 63 Bacchides knew, he gathered together all his host, and sent word to them which were of Judæa. Then went he and laid siege against Bethbasi; 64 and they fought against it a long season, and made engines of war. But Jonathan left his brother Simon in the city, and went forth himself into the country, and with a certain number went he forth. And he smote Odonarces [r] and his brethren, and the children of Phasiron in their tent. And when he began to smite them, and to advance with his forces, Simon and his company went out of the city, and burnt up the engines of war, and fought against Bacchides, who was discomfited by them, and they afflicted him sore: for his counsel and travail was in vain. Wherefore, 69 he was very wroth at the wicked men who gave him counsel to come into the country, insomuch that he slew many of them, and purposed to return into his own country. Whereof when Jonathan had knowledge, he sent ambassadors unto him, to the end he should make peace with him, and deliver them the prisoners. Which thing he 71

[q] Josephus calls it "Bethalaga, a village in the wilderness."

[r] Or Odoarres, or Odomera. There is great variety of reading, and no less uncertainty about the person designated. Probably he was one of the captains of Bacchides, or some of his allies.

accepted, and did according to his demands, and sware unto him, that he would never devise evil against him all the days of his life. When therefore he had restored unto him the prisoners whom he had taken aforetime out of the land of Judah, he returned and went his way into his own land, neither came he [s] any more into their borders.

73 Thus the sword ceased from Israel: and Jonathan dwelt at Machmas [t], and began to govern the people; and he destroyed the ungodly men out of Israel.

CHAPTER X.

The negociations of Alexander and Demetrius with Jonathan. The death of Demetrius.

1 IN the hundred and sixtieth year, Alexander [a] the *son* of Antiochus *surnamed* Epiphanes, went up and took Ptolemais: for the people had received him, by means whereof he

---

[s] Gr. καὶ οὐ προσέθετο ἔτι ἐλθεῖν; the same phrase occurs at verse 1 of this chapter.

[t] Or Michmash, as at 1 Sam. xiii. 2, &c.; a town situate about nine miles north from Jerusalem.

[a] Namely a younger brother of Antiochus Eupator, whom Demetrius had put to death. (ch. vii. 4.) But it is maintained by authors of credit, that in reality this was no son of Antiochus Epiphanes, but an impostor named Balas, who for purposes merely political, was set up and encouraged in his assumption of the Syrian throne. See Appian; and Justin, XXV. As historians are divided on the subject of Alexander's genuineness, I think that the best evidence on the point is that which is furnished by *himself*. He took the pains to inscribe himself on his coins, Θεοπάτωρ; which looks very much like the act of one who distrusted his own cause. Several of these coins are yet remaining in cabinets. Three of them are figured by Vaillant, in his "Historia Regum " Syriæ," folio, p. 138—140: also in " Frœlichii Annales " Regum Syriæ," fol. 1754. p. 64, &c. and in Gough's " Coins of the Seleucidæ," 4to, Lond. 1803, Tab. xii. p. 79.

reigned there. Now when king Demetrius heard 2 thereof, he gathered together an exceeding great host, and went forth against him to fight. Moreover, Demetrius sent letters unto Jonathan with loving words, so that he magnified him. For said he, Let us first make peace with him, before he join with Alexander against us; else he will remember all the evils which we have done against him, and against his brethren, and his people. Wherefore he gave him authority to gather together an host, and to provide weapons, that he might aid him in battle: he commanded also that the hostages which were in the tower should be delivered to him.

Then came Jonathan to Jerusalem, and read the letters in the audience of all the people, and of them which were in the tower: who were sore afraid, when they heard that the king had given him authority to gather together an host. Whereupon they of the tower delivered their hostages unto Jonathan, and he delivered them unto their parents. And Jonathan settled himself in Jerusalem, and began to build and repair the city. And he commanded the workmen to build the walls, and the mount Sion round about with square stones, for fortification: and they did so. Then the strangers who were in the fortresses which Bacchides had built, fled away: insomuch that every man left his place, and went into his own country. Only at Bethsura certain of those who had forsaken the law and the commandments, remained still: for it was their place of refuge.

Now when king Alexander had heard what promises Demetrius had sent unto Jonathan:

when also it was told him of the battles and noble acts which he and his brethren had done, and of 16 the pains which they had endured, he said, Shall we find such another man? now therefore we will 17 make him our friend and confederate. Upon this he wrote a letter, and sent it unto him, according 18 to these words, saying, "King Alexander to his 19 " brother Jonathan, sendeth greeting: We have " heard of thee, that thou art a man of great 20 " power, and meet to be our friend. Wherefore " now this day we ordain thee to be the high " priest[b] of thy nation, and to be called the king's " friend, (and therewithal he sent him a purple " robe[c], and a crown of gold,) and *require thee* to " take our part, and keep friendship with us." 21 So in the seventh month of the hundred and sixtieth year, at the feast of the tabernacles, Jonathan put on the holy robe, and gathered together forces, and provided much armour.

22 Whereof when Demetrius heard, he was very 23 sorry, and said; What have we done, that Alexander hath anticipated us, in making amity with the 24 Jews to strengthen himself? I also will write unto them words of encouragement, and *promise them* dignities[d] and gifts, that they may be with 25 me to aid me. He sent unto them therefore to this effect: " King Demetrius unto the people of 26 " the Jews, sendeth greeting: Whereas ye have " kept covenants with us, and continued in our

---

[b] This office continued in Jonathan's family until the days of Herod the Great, from which period it became no longer hereditary.

[c] A mark of high dignity, which could not be assumed without permission.

[d] Gr. λόγους ὕψους, which perhaps may signify " words " of commendation."

"friendship, not joining yourselves with our ene-
"mies, we have heard thereof, and are glad.
"Wherefore now continue ye still to be faithful 27
"unto us, and we will well recompense you for
"the things ye do in our behalf; and will grant 28
"you many immunities, and give you rewards.
"And now do I free you, and for your sake I re- 29
"lease all the Jews from tributes, and from the
"customs of salt, and from crown-taxes[e]. And 30
"from that which appertaineth unto me to re-
"ceive for the third part of the grain, and the
"half of the fruit of the trees, I release it from
"this day forth; so that they shall not be taken
"from the land of Judah, nor from the three go-
"vernments which are added thereunto out of the
"country of Samaria, and Galilee[f], from this day
"forth for evermore. Let Jerusalem also be holy 31
"and free, with the borders thereof, both from
"tenths and tributes. I also yield up my autho- 32
"rity over the tower which is in Jerusalem, and
"give it to the high priest, that he may set in it

[e] Gr. στεφάνων, the golden crowns which the Jews were wont to offer every year to the kings, or a sum of money in lieu of them. Compare chap. xi. 35. xiii. 39. The word is used also by Polybius in this sense, XXII. 17. 4. Josephus, speaking of the same impost, as remitted by Antiochus the Great, calls it στεφανίτης φόρος. Antiq. XII. 3.

[f] Here should be inserted the words "and Peræa." The names of these three governments, or "toparchies," as Josephus calls them, appear at ch. xi. 34. In another place (XII. 8.) he speaks of them as belonging to Samaria, Joppe, and Galilee. It is also recorded by Josephus, that a similar immunity had been granted formerly to the Jews by Alexander the Great: τίμα γὰρ ἡμῶν τὸ ἔθνος (sc. ὁ Ἀλέξανδρος) ὥς καὶ φησὶν Ἑκαταῖος περὶ ἡμῶν, ὅτι διὰ τὴν ἐπιείκειαν καὶ πίστιν ἣν αὐτῷ πάρεσχον Ἰουδαῖοι τὴν Σαμαρῖτιν χώραν προσέθηκεν ἔχειν αὐτοῖς ἀφορολόγητον. Joseph. c. Apion. lib. II.

33 " such men as he shall choose to keep it. More-
" over, I freely set at liberty every one of the
" Jews who were carried captives out of the land
" of Judah into any part of my kingdom; and *I*
" *will,* that all my officers remit their tributes,
34 " even of their cattle. Furthermore, *I will,* that
" all the feasts, and sabbaths, and new-moons,
" and solemn days, and the three days before the
" feast, and the three days after the feast, shall
" be all days of immunity and freedom for all the
35 " Jews in my realm. Also no man shall have au-
" thority to meddle *with them,* or to molest any of
36 " them in any matter. *I will* further, that there
" be enrolled amongst the king's forces about
" thirty thousand men of the Jews, unto whom
" pay shall be given, as belongeth to all the king's
37 " forces. And of them *some* shall be placed in the
" king's strong holds, of whom also *some* shall be
" set over the affairs of the kingdom, which are
" of trust: and *I will,* that their overseers and
" governors be of themselves, and that they walk
" after their own laws, even as the king hath com-
38 " manded in the land of Judah. And concerning
" the three governments which are added to Ju-
" dæa from the country of Samaria[g], let them be
" joined with Judæa, that they may be reckoned
" to be under one, and may not obey other au-
39 " thority than the high priest's. As for Ptole-
" mais and the land pertaining thereto, I give it
" as a free gift to the sanctuary at Jerusalem, for
40 " the necessary expences of the sanctuary. More-
" over, I give every year fifteen thousand shekels
" of silver out of the king's accounts, from the

[g] See the note at verse 30, of this chapter.

" places appertaining. And all the overplus, 41
" which the officers payed not in, as in former
" times, from henceforth they shall give towards
" the works of the temple. And besides this, the 42
" five thousand shekels of silver, which they took
" from the uses of the temple out of the accounts
" year by year, even those things are released, be-
" cause they appertain to the priests who minister.
" And whosoever they be which flee unto the 43
" temple at Jerusalem, or be within the liberties
" thereof, being indebted unto the king, or for any
" other matter, let them be at liberty, and all
" which they have in my realm. For the build- 44
" ing also and repairing of the works of the sanc-
" tuary, expences shall be given out of the king's
" accounts : yea, and for the building of the walls 45
" of Jerusalem, and the fortifying thereof round
" about, expences shall be given out of the king's
" accounts, as also for the building of the walls in
" Judæa[h]."

Now when Jonathan and the people heard these 46
words, they gave no credit unto them, nor
received them, because they remembered
the great evil which he had done in Israel ; for he
had afflicted them very sore. But with Alexan- 47
der they were well pleased, because he was the
first who entreated of peaceable words with them,
and they were confederate with him always.

B.C. 152.

Then gathered king Alexander great forces, and 48
camped over against Demetrius. And after 49
the two kings had joined battle, Demetrius's host fled : but Alexander followed after

B.C. 151.

[h] That is, in different cities of Judæa, according as they may require such aid.

50 him, and prevailed against them. And he continued the battle very sore until the sun went down: and that day was Demetrius slain.

51 Afterward Alexander sent ambassadors to Ptolemy[i], king of Egypt, with a message to this ef-
52 fect: "Forasmuch as I am come again to my " realm, and am set on the throne of my fathers, " and have gotten the dominion, and overthrown
53 " Demetrius, and recovered our country: (For " after I had joined battle with him, both he and " his host was discomfited by us, so that we sit in
54 " the throne of his kingdom.) Now therefore let " us make a league of amity together, and give " me now thy daughter to wife: and I will be " thy son-in-law, and will give both thee and her
55 " gifts, according to thy dignity." Then Ptolemy the king gave answer, saying, Happy be the day wherein thou didst return into the land of thy fathers, and sattest in the throne of their king-
56 dom. And now will I do to thee, as thou hast written: meet me therefore at Ptolemais, that we may see one another; and I will marry my
57 daughter to thee, as thou hast said. So Ptolemy went out of Egypt himself and his daughter Cleopatra, and they came unto Ptolemais in the hun-
58 dred threescore and second year: where king Alexander meeting him, he gave unto him his daughter Cleopatra, and celebrated her marriage at Ptolemais with great glory, as the manner of kings is.

59 Now king Alexander had written unto Jona-
60 than, that he should come and meet him. Who thereupon went honourably to Ptolemais, where

[i] Surnamed Philometor, the son of Ptolemy Epiphanes.

he met the two kings, and gave them and their friends silver and gold, and many presents, and found favour in their sight. At that time certain 61 pestilent fellows of Israel, men of a wicked life, assembled themselves against him, to complain of him: but the king did not attend to them. And 62 the king commanded, and they stripped Jonathan of his garments, and put on him a purple robe: and they did so. Also he made him sit near him- 63 self, and said unto his princes, Go with him into the midst of the city, and make proclamation, that no man complain against him of any matter, and that no man trouble him for any manner of cause. Now when those who complained of him saw his 64 glory, according to the proclamation, and himself clothed with a purple robe, they fled all away. So the king honoured him, and wrote him amongst 65 his chief friends, and made him a general, and governor of a province[k]. Afterward Jonathan re- 66 turned to Jerusalem with peace and gladness.

Furthermore, in the hundred threescore and 67 fifth year, came Demetrius[l], son of Demetrius, out of Crete into the land of his fathers. Whereof when king Alexander heard tell, 68 he was right sorry, and returned into Antioch. Then Demetrius made Apollonius[m] the governor 69

B.C. 148.

[k] Gr. μεριδάρχην. Grotius, however, in a note on this passage, and also on 3 Macc. v. 10, contends that μεριδάρχης denotes merely *præpositus mensæ*, a person appointed to sit at the head of a royal table as a post of dignity: but query the correctness of this opinion. See Josephus, Antiq. XII. 7. The substantive μεριδαρχία occurs at 3 Esdras i. 5, 10, where it is used to signify the division of office or dignity among the Levites: also again at ch. v. 4; viii. 28, &c.

[l] Demetrius Nicator, the son of Demetrius Soter. See Justin.

[m] This name is of very frequent occurrence during this

of Cœlosyria his general, who gathered together a great host, and camped in Jamniaⁿ, and sent unto
70 Jonathan the high priest, saying, Thou alone liftest up thyself against us, and I am laughed to scorn for thy sake, and reproached: and why dost thou vaunt thy power against us in the moun-
71 tains? Now therefore, if thou trustest in thine own strength, come down to us into the plain field, and there let us try the matter together: for
72 with me is the power of the cities. Ask, and learn who I am, and the rest who take our part, and they shall tell thee, that thy foot is not able to stand before our face; for thy fathers have been
73 twice^o put to flight in their own land. Wherefore now thou shalt not be able to abide the horsemen, and so great a power in the plain, where is neither
74 stone nor flint^p, nor place to flee unto. So when Jonathan heard these words of Apollonius, he was moved in his mind; and chusing ten thousand men, he went out of Jerusalem, and Simon his brother
75 met him to help him. And he pitched his tents against Joppe: but they of Joppe shut him out of the city, because Apollonius had a garrison there.
76 Then Jonathan laid siege unto it: whereupon they of the city let him in for fear: and so Jonathan

period of Jewish history. Prideaux mentions altogether six persons so called. The one here spoken of is judged to be the son of that Apollonius who also was governor of Cœlosyria at the time when Heliodorus attempted to plunder the temple of Jerusalem, (2 Macc. ii. 5.) and to have been the friend and fellow-fugitive from Rome of Demetrius, who afterwards promoted him to honour.

ⁿ A town on the coast of the Mediterranean, not far from Joppe.

^o See above, ch. v. 60, and ix. 6, 18.

^p This seems to allude to the mode of defence which the Jews had adopted.

won Joppe. Whereof when Apollonius heard, he 77 took three thousand horsemen, with a great host *of footmen*, and went to Azotus as one who was journeying through it; and therewithal marched forth into the plain, because he had a great number of horsemen, in whom he put his trust. Then 78 *Jonathan* followed after him to Azotus, where the armies joined battle. Now Apollonius had left a 79 thousand horsemen in ambush behind them. And 80 Jonathan perceived that there was an ambushment behind him; for they had compassed in his host, and cast darts at the people, from morning till evening. But the people stood still, as Jona- 81 than had commanded them: and so the enemies' horses were tired q. Then brought Simon forth 82 his host, and set them against the footmen r, (for the horsemen were spent;) who were discomfited by him, and fled; the horsemen also, being scat- 83 tered in the field, fled to Azotus, and went into Bethdagon s, their idol's temple, for safety. But 84 Jonathan set fire on Azotus, and the cities t round about it, and took their spoils; and the temple of Dagon, with them which had fled together into it, he burnt with fire. And they which fell by the 85 sword, with those who were burnt, were about eight thousand men. And from thence Jonathan re- 86 moved his host, and camped against Ascalon, where the men of the city came forth, and met him with

q Compare Josephus, Ant. XIII. 8.
r The Greek reading varies between φάλαγγα and φάραγγα, as it did before, in the very same words, at ch. vi. 38.
s Or, "the house of Da-"gon," concerning which see 1 Sam. ch. v.
t Perhaps *villages*, or else *towers*, immediately adjoining to the city.

87 great pomp. After this returned Jonathan and his host unto Jerusalem, having many spoils.

88 Now it came to pass when king Alexander heard these things, he honoured Jonathan yet
89 more; and sent him a buckle^u of gold, as the use is to be given to such as are of the king's blood: he gave him also Accaron^x, and all the borders thereof, in possession.

CHAPTER XI.

The death of Alexander, and of Ptolemy. The exploits of Jonathan.

1 AND the king of Egypt^a gathered together a great host, as the sand which is upon the sea-shore, and many ships, and sought, through deceit, to get Alexander's kingdom, and
2 join it to his own. Whereupon he took his journey into Syria in peaceable manner, so that they of the cities opened unto him, and met him: for king Alexander had commanded them to meet
3 him, because he was his father-in-law. Now as Ptolemy entered into the cities, he set in every
4 one of them a garrison of soldiers to keep it. And when he came near to Azotus, they shewed him the temple of Dagon which was burnt, and Azotus and the suburbs thereof which were destroyed, and the bodies which were cast abroad, and them which he had burnt in the battle; for they had

---

u Gr. πόρπην. See Josephus, Ant. XIII. 4. It was a mark of high distinction among the Persians, Greeks, and Romans.

x Accaron, or Ekron, was the most northern of the five cities belonging to the Philistines.

a Namely, Ptolemy Philometor.

made heaps of them by the way where he should pass. Also they told the king whatsoever Jonathan had done, to the intent he might blame him: but the king held his peace. Then Jonathan met the king with great pomp at Joppe, where they saluted one another, and slept. Afterward Jonathan, when he had gone with the king to the river called Eleutherus[b], returned again to Jerusalem. King Ptolemy therefore, having gotten the dominion of the cities by the sea, unto Seleucia[c] upon the sea-coast, imagined wicked counsels against Alexander. Whereupon he sent ambassadors unto king Demetrius, saying; Come, let us make a league betwixt us, and I will give thee my daughter, whom Alexander hath, and thou shalt reign in thy father's kingdom: for I repent that I gave my daughter unto him, for he sought to slay me. Thus did he slander him, because he was desirous of his kingdom. Wherefore he took his daughter from him, and gave her to Demetrius, and was estranged from Alexander, so that their hatred was openly known.

Then Ptolemy entered into Antioch, where he set two crowns upon his head, the crown of Asia, and of Egypt. In the mean season was king Alexander in Cilicia, because those who dwelt in those parts had revolted from him. But when Alexan-

---

[b] This river runs into the Mediterranean sea, to the north of Tripolis. See Wells's Geography, and the authors there cited.

[c] Situate near the coast, upon the river Orontes. This is accounted by Appian the most celebrated among the numerous cities built by Seleucus, to nine of which he gave the same name (Seleucia). See Appian. de Rebus Syriacis, c. 57. For its situation and military importance, consult Polybius, V. 58, 59.

der heard of this, he came to war against him: whereupon Ptolemy brought forth *his host*, and met him with a mighty power, and put him to 16 flight. So Alexander fled into Arabia, there to be 17 sheltered; but king Ptolemy was exalted: for Zabdiel[d] the Arabian took off Alexander's head, 18 and sent it unto Ptolemy. King Ptolemy also died[e] the third day after, and they which were in 19 the strong holds were slain one of another. *By this means* Demetrius reigned [f], in the hundred threescore and seventh year.

20 In those days Jonathan gathered together them which were in Judæa, to take the tower which was in Jerusalem: and he made 21 many engines of war against it. Then certain ungodly persons, who hated their own people, went unto the king, and told him that Jonathan be- 22 sieged the tower. Whereof when he heard, he was angry; and immediately removing, he came to Ptolemais, and wrote unto Jonathan, that he should not lay siege to the tower, but come and 23 speak with him at Ptolemais in great haste. Nevertheless, Jonathan, when he heard this, commanded to besiege it *still:* and he chose certain of the elders of Israel, and the priests, and put 24 himself in peril; and taking silver and gold, and raiment, and divers presents besides, he went to

B.C. 145.

---

[d] Josephus calls him Zabdelus: [and in Polybius we read of an Arabian chief named Zabdibelus, who headed the Arabian allies of Antiochus Magnus against Ptolemy Philopator. Polyb. V. 71.] Stephanus Byzantinus calls him Rhabilus; and Diodorus Siculus, Diocles!

[e] Of wounds received in the battle mentioned at verse 15. (Josephus.)

[f] And thenceforward took the surname of Nicator, "the Conqueror."

Ptolemais, unto the king, where he found favour in his sight. And though certain ungodly men of the people had made complaints against him, yet the king entreated him as his predecessors had done before, and promoted him in the sight of all his friends; and confirmed to him the high-priesthood, and all the honours which he had before, and gave him preeminence among his chief friends. Then Jonathan desired the king, that he would make Judæa free from tribute, as also the three governments, with the country of Samaria[g]; and he promised him three hundred talents. So the king consented, and wrote letters unto Jonathan of all these things, after this manner: "King Demetrius unto his brother Jonathan, and unto the nation of the Jews, sendeth greeting: The copy of a letter, which we wrote to our cousin Lasthenes concerning you, we have written also to you, that you may know it. King Demetrius unto his father Lasthenes[h], sendeth greeting: We are determined to do good to the people of the Jews, who are our friends, and keep covenants with us, because of their good-will towards us. Wherefore we have ratified unto them the borders of Judæa, with the three governments of Apherema, and Lydda, and Ramathem, which are added unto Judæa from the country of Samaria[i], and all things appertaining

---

[g] Gr. καὶ τὴν Σαμαρεῖτιν. But probably καὶ is an error for κατὰ, these three governments being *in* and near Samaria, (Grotius). Compare v. 34.

[h] The general of the Cretan forces, who had assisted Demetrius to regain his kingdom. See above, ch. x. 67.

[i] That is, Samaria, Galilee, and Peræa. See also Josephus, Ant. XIII. 8.

B.C. 145.   CHAP. XI.   115

" unto them, for all such as do sacrifice in Jerusa-
" lem, instead of the royal dues which the king
" received of them yearly aforetime out of the
35 " fruits of the earth, and of trees. And as for
" other things which belong unto us, of the tithes
" and customs pertaining unto us, as also the salt-
" pits, and the crown-taxes[k], which are due unto
" us, we discharge them of them all for their re-
36 " lief[l]. And nothing hereof shall be revoked from
37 " this time forth for ever. Now therefore, see
" that you make a copy of these things; and let
" it be delivered unto Jonathan, and set upon the
" holy mount in a conspicuous place."
38 *After this,* when king Demetrius saw that the
land was quiet before him, and that no resistance
was made against him, he sent away all his forces,
every one to his own place, except the bands of
strangers, whom he had gathered from the isles of
the heathen: wherefore all the forces of his fa-
39 thers hated him. Moreover, there was one Tryphon[m], who had been of Alexander's part afore,
who, seeing that all the host murmured against
Demetrius, went to Simalcue[n] the Arabian, who
brought up Antiochus[o] the young son of Alexan-
40 der. And earnestly entreated him to deliver him
this young Antiochus, that he might reign in his
father's stead: he told him therefore all which

[k] See above, at ch. x. 29.
[l] Gr. ἐπαρκῶς: which also may signify " liberally," or " sufficiently."
[m] His name was Diodotus, an Apamæan: he subsequently assumed that of Tryphon.
[n] The readings of this name vary greatly. Josephus calls him Malchus. Possibly the same person is meant who at ver. 17. is called Zabdiel.
[o] Namely, the son of Alexander Balas, by Cleopatra, daughter of Ptolemy: on coming to the throne, he took the surname of Theos.

I 2

Demetrius had done, and how his forces were at enmity with him; and there he remained a long season. In the mean time Jonathan sent unto 41 king Demetrius, that he would cast those of the tower out of Jerusalem, and those also in the fortresses: for they continually fought against Israel. And Demetrius sent unto Jonathan, saying, 42 I will not only do this for thee and thy people, but I will greatly honour thee and thy nation, if opportunity serve. Now therefore thou shalt do 43 well, if thou send me men to help me; for all my forces are gone from me. Upon this, Jonathan 44 sent him three thousand strong men unto Antioch: and when they came to the king, the king was very glad of their coming. Howbeit, they 45 which were of the city gathered themselves together into the midst of the city, to the number of an hundred and twenty thousand men, and would have slain the king. Wherefore the king fled into 46 the court, but they of the city kept the passages of the city, and began to fight. Then the king 47 called to the Jews for help; who came unto him all at once, and dispersing themselves through the city, slew that day in the city to the number of an hundred thousand. Also they set fire on the 48 city, and took many spoils that day, and delivered the king. So when they of the city saw that the 49 Jews had got the city as they would, their courage was abated; wherefore they made supplication to the king, and cried, saying, Grant us peace, 50 and let the Jews cease from assaulting us and the city. With that they cast away their weapons, 51 and made peace: and the Jews were honoured in the sight of the king, and in the sight of all who

were in his realm, and they returned to Jerusa-
52 lem, having great spoils. So king Demetrius sat on the throne of his kingdom, and the land was
53 quiet before him. Nevertheless, he dissembled in all which ever he spake, and estranged himself from Jonathan, neither rewarded he him according to the benefits which he had received of him, but troubled him very sore.

54 After this returned Tryphon, and with him the young child Antiochus, who reigned and
55 was crowned. Then there gathered unto him all the forces which Demetrius had put away, and they fought against Demetrius, who turned
56 his back and fled. Moreover, Tryphon took the
57 elephants, and won Antioch. At that time young Antiochus wrote unto Jonathan, saying, I confirm to thee the high-priesthood, and appoint thee ruler over the four governments[p], and to be one of the
58 king's friends. Upon this he sent him golden vessels to be served[q] in; and gave him leave to drink in gold, and to be clothed in purple, and to
59 wear a golden buckle. His brother Simon also he made captain from *the place, called* the ladder[r] of
60 Tyrus, unto the borders of Egypt. Then Jonathan went forth, and passed over the river, and through the cities *there;* and all the forces of Syria gathered themselves unto him to help him: and when he came to Ascalon, they of the city

B.C. 144.

---

[p] Namely, the three named above, at verse 34, and Ptolemais, mentioned at chap. x. 39.

[q] Gr. χρυσώματα καὶ διακονίαν; literally, "a service of "gold."

[r] Gr. Κλίμαξ, a high mountain so called, lying between Tyre and Ptolemais. See a short description of it in Joseph. Bell. II. 17. The name was applied to other places also. See Polybius V. 72.

met him honourably. From whence he went to Gaza, but they of Gaza shut him out; wherefore he laid siege unto it, and burned the suburbs thereof with fire, and spoiled them. Afterward, when they of Gaza made supplication unto Jonathan, he made peace with them, and took the sons of their chief men for hostages, and sent them to Jerusalem, and passed through the country unto Damascus. Now when Jonathan heard that Demetrius' princes were come to Cades which is in Galilee, with a great power, purposing to remove him out of the country[s];—He went to meet them, and left Simon his brother in the country. Then Simon encamped against Bethsura, and fought against it a long season, and shut it up. But they desired to have peace with him, which he granted them, and then put them out from thence, and took the city, and set a garrison in it. As for Jonathan and his host, they pitched at the water of Gennesar[t], from whence betimes in the morning they gat them to the plain of Nasor. And behold, the host of strangers met them in the plain; who having laid men in ambush for him in the mountains, came themselves over against him. So when they which lay in ambush rose out of their places, and joined battle, all who were of Jonathan's side fled; insomuch that there was not one of them left, except Mattathias *the son* of Absalom, and Judas *the son* of Calphi, the captains of the host. Then Jonathan rent his clothes, and cast earth upon his head, and prayed. Afterwards

---

[s] Or, " from his office:" the Vatican MS. reads, ἀπὸ τῆς χρείας: but the Alexandrian, ἀπὸ τῆς χώρας.
[t] The lake of Gennesareth.

turning again to battle, he put them to flight, and
3 so they ran away. Now when his own men who
had fled saw this, they turned again unto him,
and with him pursued them to Cades, even unto
4 their own tents, and there they camped. So there
were slain of the heathen that day, about three
thousand men: and Jonathan returned to Jerusalem.

CHAPTER XII.

Jonathan renews the league with the Romans and Lacedæmonians. He is made prisoner by Tryphon.

1 Now when Jonathan saw that the time served him, he chose certain men, and sent them to Rome, to confirm and renew the friendship which they
2 had with them. He sent letters also to the Lacedæmonians[a], and to other places for the same pur-
3 pose. So they went unto Rome, and entered into the senate-house, and said, "Jonathan the "high priest, and the people of the Jews, sent us "unto you, to the end ye should renew the friend- "ship which ye had with them, and league, as in
4 "former time." Upon this *the Romans* gave them letters unto the governors of every place, that they should bring them into the land of Judah in peace.
5 And this is the copy of the letters which Jonathan
6 wrote unto the Lacedæmonians: "Jonathan the "high priest, and the elders of the nation, and the "priests, and the other people of the Jews, unto "the Lacedæmonians their brethren, send greet-
7 "ing: There were letters sent in times past unto

[a] The Greek text here and in other passages has Σπαρτιάταις, but there is no ground for supposing that only the inhabitants of Sparta itself are intended.

"Onias[b] the high priest from Darius, who reigned then among you, to signify that ye are our brethren, as the copy here underwritten doth specify. At which time Onias entreated honourably the ambassador who was sent, and received the letters, wherein declaration was made of the league and friendship. Therefore we also, albeit we need none of these things, for that we have the holy books of Scripture in our hands to comfort us, have nevertheless attempted to send unto you, for the renewing of brotherhood and friendship, lest we should become strangers unto you altogether: for there is a long time passed since ye sent unto us. We therefore, at all times, without ceasing, both in our feasts and other convenient days, do remember you in the sacrifices which we offer, and in our prayers; as is right, and as it becometh us to think upon our brethren: and we are right glad of your glory. But *as for us*, many troubles and many wars have environed us; forsomuch as the kings who are round about us, have fought

---

[b] Probably he was the second of that name, the son of Simon the Just.

[c] Josephus (Antiq. XIII. 8.) contends and justly, that the word ought to be *Arius*, not Darius, a name unknown among the Lacedæmonians. In the Greek, as in the English, there is merely the difference of a single letter; and the mistake may have arisen from the similarity of form between Δ and A. Grotius decides *Arius* to be the true reading. A Spartan king of that name is mentioned by Pausanias and Livy: and the chronologers make Arius contemporary with the high priest Onias; namely, the *second* of that name; for, although some writers have attributed the transaction to Onias III, the son of Simon, we must remember that Jonathan's letter speaks of it as of a thing long past; and also, that before Onias III. succeeded to the high-priesthood, the regal government had ceased to exist at Sparta.

"against us. Howbeit, we would not be trouble-
"some unto you, nor to others of our confederates
"and friends in these wars: for we have help from
"heaven which succoureth us, so that we are de-
"livered from our enemies, and our enemies are
"humbled. For this cause we have chosen Nu-
"menius *the son* of Antiochus, and Antipater *the
"son* of Jason, and sent them unto the Romans,
"to renew the amity which we had with them,
"and the former league. We commanded them
"also to go unto you, and to salute you, and to
"deliver you our letters concerning the renewing
"of our brotherhood. Wherefore now ye shall
"do well to give us an answer thereto." And
this is the copy of the letters which Arius sent[d]
to Onias. "Arius king of the Lacedæmonians,
"to Onias the high priest, greeting: It is found
"in writing, that the Lacedæmonians and Jews
"are brethren[e], and that they are of the stock of
"Abraham: now therefore, since this is come to
"our knowledge, ye shall do well to write unto us
"of your welfare. We do write back again to
"you, that your cattle and goods are ours, and
"ours are yours. We do command therefore *our*

[d] The old translation, "which Oniares sent," was unintelligible, and had arisen from a faulty reading, ἣν ἀπέστειλεν Ὀνιάρης, instead of Ὀνίᾳ Ἄρειος. Josephus recites this epistle, with some slight difference, (more in words than matter,) in his Antiquities, XII. 5.

[e] See Shuckford's Connection of Sacred and Profane History, book X. The Lacedæmonians were Dorians, derived from the Pelasgi, who sprung from the descendants of Abraham and Keturah, mentioned in Genesis xxv. The Cretans have been supposed to form the connecting link. See Tacit. Hist. V. 2: and consult a long dissertation on the subject by Calmet, in his "Literal Comment on the "Bible."

"*ambassadors* to make report unto you on this "wise."

Now when Jonathan heard that Demetrius' 24 princes were come to fight against him with a greater host than afore, he removed from Jerusa- 25 lem, and met them in the land of Amathis[f]: for he gave them no respite to invade his country. He sent spies also unto their tents, who came again, 26 and told him, that they had appointed to come upon them in the night-season. Wherefore so 27 soon as the sun was down, Jonathan commanded his men to watch, and to be in arms, that all the night long they might be ready to fight: also he sent forth sentinels round about the host. But 28 when the adversaries heard that Jonathan and his men were ready for battle, they feared and trembled in their hearts, and they kindled fires in their camp[g]. Howbeit, Jonathan and his company 29 knew it not till the morning: for they saw the lights burning. Then Jonathan pursued after 30 them, but overtook them not: for they were gone over the river Eleutherus. Wherefore Jonathan 31 turned aside to the Arabians, who were called Zabadæans[h], and smote them, and took their spoils. And removing thence, he came to Damascus, and 32 so passed through all the country. Simon also 33 went forth, and passed through the country unto Ascalon, and the strong holds there adjoining;

[f] Or, Hamath, on the northern border of the Holy Land, called in Scripture "the en-"tering into Hamath."

[g] Add, "and fled." See in Xenophon's Anabasis, and other instances of this stratagem recorded in Grecian and Roman history. Compare Joseph. Antiq. XIII. 9.

[h] Probably the word ought to be *Nabathæans*, as Josephus writes it. See ch. v. 25.

from whence he turned aside to Joppe, and won
34 it. For he had heard that they would deliver the fortress unto them which took Demetrius' part; wherefore he set a garrison there to keep it.
35 After this came Jonathan home again, and calling the elders of the people together, he consulted with them about building strong holds in Judæa;
36 and making the walls of Jerusalem higher, and raising a great mount between the tower and the city, to separate it from the city, that so it might be alone, that men might neither sell nor buy[i] in
37 it. Upon this they came together, to build up the city; and *part of* the wall toward the brook on the east side was fallen down[k]; and they repaired that
38 which was called Caphenatha. Simon also set up Adida, in Sephela[l], and made it strong with gates and bars.
39 Now Tryphon sought to get the kingdom of Asia, to put the crown on himself, and to stretch forth his hand against Antiochus[m] the king.
40 Howbeit he was afraid that Jonathan would not suffer him, and that he would fight against him; wherefore he sought a way how to take Jonathan,

---

[i] And thus might be compelled to surrender the obnoxious tower through want of provisions. See the result of this manœuvre at ch. xiii. 49, 50, 51.

[k] There is a variety of reading on this passage; Καὶ ἤγγισε τοῦ τείχους τοῦ χειμάρρου, and καὶ ἔπεσεν τοῦ τείχους τ. χ. If the former be adopted, we must translate it, "and their "work approached to the "wall toward the brook."

[l] This word appears to mean *generally*, "a plain." Here it seems to be taken for the southern part of the great plain of Esdraelon mentioned at Judith i. 8, and particularly to denote the open country round Eleutheropolis, a city of eminence in later times, situate to the west of Jerusalem.

[m] See the successful issue of this treachery at ch. xiii. 31.

that he might kill him. So he removed, and came to Bethsan. Then Jonathan went out to meet him with forty thousand men chosen for the battle, and came to Bethsan. Now when Tryphon saw that Jonathan came with so great a force, he durst not stretch his hand against him: but received him honourably, and commended him unto all his friends, and gave him gifts, and commanded his armies to be as obedient unto him as to himself. Unto Jonathan also he said, Why hast thou put all this people to so great trouble, seeing there is no war betwixt us? therefore send them now home again, and choose a few men to wait on thee, and come thou with me to Ptolemais, and I will give it thee, and the rest of the strong holds and forces, and all who have any charge: as for me, I will return and depart: for this is the cause of my coming. So Jonathan believing him, did as he bade him, and sent away his host, who went into the land of Judah. And with himself he retained but three thousand men, of whom he left two thousand in Galilee, and one thousand went with him.

Now as soon as Jonathan entered into Ptolemais, they of Ptolemais shut the gates, and took him, and all them which came with him they slew with the sword. Then sent Tryphon an host of footmen and horsemen into Galilee, and into the great plain, to destroy all Jonathan's company. But when they knew that Jonathan and they which were with him were taken and slain, they encouraged one another, and went close together prepared to fight. They therefore which followed upon them, perceiving that they were ready to

52 fight for their lives, turned back again. Whereupon they all came into the land of Judah peaceably, and there they bewailed Jonathan, and them which were with him, and they were sore afraid;
53 wherefore all Israel made great lamentation. Then all the heathen who were round about them sought to destroy them: for, said they, They have no captain, nor any to help them: now therefore let us make war upon them, and take away their memorial from amongst men.

CHAPTER XIII.

Simon made captain. His acts. Jonathan's death, burial, and monument. Tryphon seizes the kingdom.

1 Now when Simon[a] heard that Tryphon had gathered together a great host, to invade the land
2 of Judah and destroy it; and saw that the people was in great trembling and fear, he went up to
3 Jerusalem, and gathered the people together; and gave them exhortation, saying, Ye yourselves know what great things I and my brethren, and my father's house, have done for the laws and the sanctuary, the battles also and troubles which we
4 have seen. By reason whereof all my brethren are slain for Israel's sake, and I am left alone.
5 Now therefore be it far from me that I should spare mine own life in any time of trouble: for I
6 am no better than my brethren. Doubtless I will avenge my nation and the sanctuary, and our wives and our children: for all the heathen
7 are gathered to destroy us of very malice. And he rekindled the spirit of the people, as soon as

[a] The second son of Mattathias, and elder brother of Judas.

they heard these words. And they answered with a loud voice, saying, Thou art our leader instead of Judas and Jonathan thy brother. Fight thou our battles, and whatsoever thou commandest us, that will we do. So then he gathered together all the men of war, and made haste to finish the walls of Jerusalem, and he fortified it round about. Also he sent Jonathan the *son* of Absalom, and with him a great power, to Joppe: who casting out them which were therein, remained there in it.

So Tryphon removed from Ptolemais with a great power to invade the land of Judah, and Jonathan was with him in ward. But Simon pitched his tents at Adida, over against the plain[b]. Now when Tryphon knew that Simon was risen up instead of his brother Jonathan, and meant to join battle with him, he sent messengers unto him, saying, Whereas we have Jonathan thy brother in hold, it is for money which Jonathan thy brother owed to the king's treasure from the office which he held, that we detain him. Wherefore now send an hundred talents of silver, and two of his sons for hostages, that when he is at liberty he may not revolt from us, and we will let him go. Hereupon Simon, albeit he perceived that they spake deceitfully unto him, yet sent he the money and the children, lest peradventure he should procure to himself great hatred of the people: who might have said, Because I sent him not the money and the children, therefore is *Jonathan* dead. So he sent the children and the hundred talents: howbeit *Tryphon* dissembled,

[b] Namely, of Sephela, mentioned above at ch. xii. 38.

20 neither would he let Jonathan go. And after this came Tryphon to invade the land, and destroy it, going round about by the way which leadeth unto Adora[c]: but Simon and his host marched against
21 him in every place wheresoever he went. Now they which were in the tower, sent messengers unto Tryphon, to the end that he should hasten his coming unto them by the wilderness, and send
22 them victuals. Wherefore Tryphon made ready all his horsemen to come that night: but there fell a very great snow, by reason whereof he came not. So he departed, and came into the country
23 of Galaad. And when he came near to Bascama[d],
24 he slew Jonathan, who was buried there. Afterward Tryphon returned, and went into his own land.
25 Then sent Simon, and took the bones of Jonathan his brother, and buried them in Mo-
26 din the city of his fathers. And all Israel made great lamentation for him, and bewailed him many days.
27 Simon also built a monument upon the sepulchre of his father and his brethren, and raised it aloft to the sight, with polished stone behind and
28 before. Moreover, he set up seven pyramids one against another, for his father and his mother,
29 and his four brethren. And on these he made cunning devices, about the which he set great pillars, and upon the pillars he made all their armour for a perpetual memory, and by the armour

[c] Or Dorah, a town lying in the southern part of Judæa, near the borders of Idumæa.

[d] Calmet judges this to be Bezek, a town not far from Bethsan.

ships carved, that they might be seen by all who sail on the sea. This is the sepulchre which he made at Modin, *and it standeth yet*[e] unto this day.

Now Tryphon dealt deceitfully with the young king Antiochus, and slew him[f]. And he reigned in his stead, and crowned himself king of Asia, and brought a great calamity upon the land.

Then Simon built up the strong holds in Judæa; and fenced them about with high towers, and great walls, and gates, and bars; and laid up victuals in the strong holds. Moreover, Simon chose men, and sent to king Demetrius, to the end he should give the land an immunity, because all which Tryphon did was to spoil[g]. And king Demetrius sent to him according to these words: and answered him, and wrote him a letter, to this effect: "King Demetrius unto Simon the high

30
31
32
33
34
35
36

---

[e] So said Josephus: and so reported Eusebius, in the fourth century after Christ. See Eusebius περὶ τῶν τοπικῶν ὀνομάτων τῶν ἐν τῇ θείᾳ γραφῇ, published (together with a Latin version of it, by St. Jerome) by Vallarsius, from a Greek MS. of the tenth century in the Vatican Library, in vol. III. of the works of St. Jerome, p. 248. Μηδεείμ (lege Μωδεείμ) κώμη πλησίον Διοσπόλεως, ὅθεν ἦσαν οἱ Μακκαβαῖοι, ὧν καὶ τὰ μνήματα εἰς ἔτι νῦν δείκνυται. On which Jerome observes; "Satis itaque "miror quomodo Antiochiæ "eorum reliquias ostendant, "aut quo hoc certo autore sit "creditum." But his editor rightly corrects this slip of the author's memory, by remarking that the brothers, whose sepulchres were at Modin, were the true Maccabees, the sons of Mattathias: but that the martyrs, whose relics were exhibited at Antioch, were the seven brethren tortured to death by Antiochus, to whom the name of *Maccabees* was commonly, though improperly, attributed.

[f] In what manner the death of this young prince was effected, may be seen in Josephus, and in the Epitome of book LV. of Livy.

[g] Literally, "all Tryphon's "doings were robberies."

B.C. 143.   CHAP. XIII.   129

"priest, and friend of kings, as also unto the
"elders and nation of the Jews, sendeth greet-
37 "ing: The golden crown and the *golden* palm-
"branch [h], which ye sent unto us, we have re-
"ceived; and we are ready to make a steadfast
"peace with you; yea, and to write unto our
38 "officers, to grant you immunities. And what-
"soever covenants we have made with you, still
"stand; and the strong holds which ye have
39 "builded, let them be your own. As for any
"oversights or faults committed unto this day, we
"forgive them, and the crown-tax also which ye
"owe us; and if there were any other tribute
40 "paid in Jerusalem, let it be paid no more. And
"if there be any among you meet to be enrolled
"in our court, let them be enrolled, and let there
41 "be peace betwixt us." Thus the yoke of the
heathen was taken away from Israel, in the hun-
42 dred and seventieth year. Then the people of Israel began to write in their instruments and contracts, "In the first year of Simon the great high
"priest, the governor and leader of the Jews."

43 In those days Simon camped against Gaza [i],
and besieged it round about; he made also engines of war [j], and set them by the city, and bat-

[h] Gr. βαϊνήν. But some interpreters think this word signifies "a robe embroidered with palms." Compare 3 Macc. xiv. 4.

[i] Probably we ought to read "Gazara." Compare verses 48 and 53; also ch. xiv. 7.

[j] Gr. ἑλεπόλεις. The helepolis appears to have been a machine of vast size and most formidable power: it was a great favourite with Demetrius, the son of Antigonus; who from its frequent and successful use in sieges took the name of *Poliorcetes*. It is mentioned by several Greek and Latin writers: but the most minute account of its construction is furnished to us by Ammianus Marcellinus, XXIII. 5, in the following terms: "Pro his ari-

K

tered a certain tower, and took it. And they 44 which were in the engines leapt into the city; whereupon there was a great uproar in the city: insomuch that the people of the city rent their 45 clothes, and climbed upon the walls with their

" etum meditamentis jam cre-
" britate despectis, conditur
" machina scriptoribus histo-
" ricis nota, quam helepolim
" Græci cognominamus: cu-
" jus opera diuturna Deme-
" trius Antigoni filius regis,
" Rhodo aliisque urbibus op-
" pugnatis, Poliorcetes est ap-
" pellatus. Ædificatur autem
" hoc modo. Testudo com-
" paginatur immanis, axibus
" roborata longissimis, ferre-
" isque clavis aptata: et con-
" tegitur coriis bubulis virga-
" rumque recenti textura,
" atque limo asperguntur e-
" jus suprema, ut flammeos
" detrectet et missiles casus.
" Conseruntur autem ejus
" frontalibus trisulcæ cuspi-
" des præacutæ, ponderibus
" ferreis graves, qualia nobis
" pictores ostendunt fulmina
" vel fictores, ut quidquid pe-
" tierit aculeis exertis abrum-
" pat. Hanc ita validam mo-
" lem rotis et funibus re-
" gens numerosus intrinsecus
" miles, languidiori murorum
" parti viribus admovet con-
" citis: et nisi depropugnan-
" tium valuerint vires, collisis
" parietibus aditus patefacit
" ingentes." Vitruvius, at book X. chap. 22, describes, somewhat differently, the one used by Demetrius at Rhodes, which he says was 125 feet high, and 60 in width. It was so strongly secured by hair-cloths and raw hides, as to withstand the blow of a stone of 360 pounds weight hurled from a balista. This formidable engine having been rendered useless by the besieged, through a stratagem, was subsequently captured by them and drawn into their city in triumph. Diodorus Siculus, lib. XX. (p. 785, edit. 1607,) mentions another constructed by Demetrius, which was in height 90 cubits, and 45 cubits in width, [nearly the same admeasurements as those given by Vitruvius.] It consisted of nine stories; stood upon four wheels of eight cubits in height: in the several stories were balistæ, catapeltæ, and all sorts of instruments of annoyance, with more than two hundred men to make use of these. This machine was *burnt* by the besieged, at Salamis. Plutarch, in the Life of Demetrius, (tom. V. p. 26, ed. Bryan,) states its height at 66 cubits, and its breadth at 48. The immense weight of the helepolis is also mentioned by Athenæus, X. 3. (p. 415, ed. Casaub.) where he speaks of one being gotten out of a slough, through the powerful music of a piper!

wives and children, and cried with a loud voice,
46 beseeching Simon to grant them peace. And they said, Deal not with us according to our wicked-
47 nesses, but according to thy mercy. So Simon was appeased towards them, and fought no more against them; but put them out of the city, and cleansed the houses wherein the idols were: and so entered into it with songs and thanksgivings.
48 Yea, he put all uncleanness out of it, and placed such men there, as would keep the law; and made it stronger than it was before, and built therein a dwelling-place for himself.
49 They also of the tower in Jerusalem were kept so strait, that they could neither come forth, nor go into the country, nor buy, nor sell: wherefore they were in great distress for want of victuals, and a great number of them perished
50 through famine. Then cried they to Simon, beseeching him that they might have peace: which thing he granted them; and when he had put them out from thence, he cleansed the tower from
51 pollutions: and entered into it the three and twentieth day of the second month, in the hundred seventy and first year, with thanksgiving and branches of palm-trees, and with harps, and cymbals, and with viols, and hymns, and songs: because there was destroyed a great enemy[k] out
52 of Israel. He ordained also, that they should keep that day every year with gladness. Moreover, the hill of the temple, which was by the tower, he

[k] From the time when this tower was erected and garrisoned by Antiochus Epiphanes, (see ch. i. 33—36,) it had been ever " a sore " snare" and " an evil adver- " sary to Israel."

made stronger¹ than it was, and there he dwelt himself with his company. And when Simon saw 53 that John his son was a valiant man, he made him captain of all the hosts; and he dwelt in Gazara.

CHAPTER XIV.

The good deeds of Simon. His fame. Renewal of the league by the Romans and Lacedæmonians.

Now in the hundred threescore and twelfth 1 year, king Demetrius gathered his forces together, and went into Media[a], to get him help to fight against Tryphon. But when Ar- 2 saces, the king of Persia and Media, heard that Demetrius was entered within his borders, he sent one of his princes, to take him alive: who went 3 and smote the host of Demetrius, and took him, and brought him to Arsaces, and he put him in ward.

As for the land *of Judah*, that was quiet all 4 the days of Simon; for he sought the good of his nation in such wise, as that evermore his authority and honour pleased them well. And in addition 5 to all his glory, he took Joppe for an haven, and made it an entrance to the isles of the sea, and 6 enlarged the bounds of his nation, and recovered the country. And gathered together a great number 7 of captives, and had the dominion of Gazara, and Bethsura, and the tower, out of the which he

---

[1] Namely, by lowering the adjoining hill, on which the obnoxious tower had stood. This great undertaking he accomplished by the unceasing labour of his people by day and night during three years. (Josephus.)

[a] By which is meant the countries subject to the Parthians, under Arsaces, (or more properly Mithridates.)

took all impurities; neither was there any who resisted him. Then did they till their ground in peace, and the earth gave her increase, and the trees of the field their fruit. The ancient men sat also in the streets, communing together of good things, and the young men put on glorious and warlike apparel. He provided victuals for the cities, and set in them all manner of munition [b], so that his honourable name was renowned unto the end of the world. He made peace in the lands, and Israel rejoiced with great joy: for every man sat under his vine and his fig-tree, and there was none to fray them: neither was there any left in the land to fight against them: yea, the kings themselves were overthrown in those days. Moreover, he strengthened all those of his people who were brought low: the law he searched out, and every contemner of the law and wicked person he took away. He beautified the sanctuary, and multiplied the vessels of the sanctuary.

Now it was heard at Rome, and as far as Sparta, that Jonathan was dead; and they were very sorry. But as soon as they heard that his brother Simon was made high priest in his stead, and ruled the country, and the cities therein: they wrote unto him in tables of brass, to renew the friendship and league which they had made with Judas and Jonathan his brethren: which writings were read before the congregation at Jerusalem. And this is the copy of the letters which the Lacedæmonians sent: "The rulers of the Lacedæmonians, " and the city, unto Simon the high priest, and " the elders and priests, and residue of the people

[b] Gr. σκεύεσιν ὀχυρώσεως.

" of the Jews, our brethren, *send* greeting: The 21
" ambassadors who were sent unto our people,
" certified us of your glory and honour: wherefore
" we were glad of their coming: and did register 22
" the things which they spake in the council of
" the people, in this manner: Numenius[c] *son* of
" Antiochus, and Antipater *son* of Jason, the Jews'
" ambassadors, came unto us to renew the friend-
" ship which they had with us. And it pleased 23
" the people to entertain the men honourably,
" and to put the copy of their ambassage in the
" appointed records of the people: to the end the
" people of the Lacedæmonians might have a me-
" morial thereof: furthermore, we have written
" a copy thereof unto Simon the high priest."

After this, Simon sent Numenius to Rome, with 24
a great shield of gold of a thousand minæ[d], to confirm the league with them. Whereof when the 25
people heard, they said, What thanks shall we
give to Simon and his sons? For he and his 26
brethren, and the house of his father, have established Israel, and chased away in fight their enemies from them, and confirmed their liberty. So 27
then they wrote *it* in the tables of brass, which
they set upon pillars in mount Sion: and this is
the copy of the writing: "The eighteenth day of
" *the month* Elul[e], in the hundred threescore and
" twelfth year, being the third year of Simon the
" high priest: at Saramel[f] in the great congre- 28

[c] See ch. xii. 16.
[d] Or pounds. If the Attic mina be the weight here meant, it is considered equal to twenty-five Jewish shekels. A shekel *of gold* is one quar-ter of an ounce; of silver, half an ounce.
[e] Nearly answering to our August.
[f] Or, Asaramel. It is not clear what place is intended

" gation of the priests and people, and rulers of
" the nation, and elders of the country, were these
29 " things notified unto us. Forasmuch as often-
" times there have been wars in the country; and
" Simon the son of Mattathias, the son of the sons
" of Jarib, and his brethren, have put themselves
" in jeopardy; and have resisted the enemies of
" their nation, that their sanctuary and law might
" be maintained; and have honoured their nation
30 " with great honour:—(For after that Jonathan,
" having gathered his nation together, and been
31 " their high priest, was added to his people; their
" enemies purposed to invade their country, that
" they might destroy it, and lay hands on the
32 " sanctuary: at which time Simon rose up, and
" fought for his nation, and spent much of his
" own substance, and armed the mighty men of
33 " his nation, and gave them wages, and forti-
" fied the cities of Judæa, together with Bethsura
" which lieth upon the borders of Judæa, where
" the armour of the enemies had been before; and
34 " set a garrison of Jews there. Moreover, he for-
" tified Joppe which lieth upon the sea, and Ga-
" zara which bordereth upon Azotus, where the
" enemies had dwelt before: and placed Jews
" there, and furnished them with all things conve-
35 " nient for the reparation thereof.) The people
" therefore, seeing the acts of Simon, and unto
" what glory he thought to bring his nation,

by this expression. Grotius thinks, "the hall of Millo," mentioned at 1 Kings ix. 24, in which D. Kimchi, a rabbinical commentator, asserts that the public assemblies were formerly holden. It has been conjectured also, that possibly the word is a corrupt reading of "Jerusalem," by a careless transposition of letters. More light is yet wanted on the subject.

the Jews, and to all the people. The contents 2 whereof were these: " King Antiochus to Simon " the high priest, and prince of his nation, and to " the people of the Jews, greeting: Forasmuch as 3 " certain pestilent men[c] have usurped the king- " dom of our fathers, and my purpose is to chal- " lenge it again, that I may restore it to the old " estate, and to that end have gathered a multi- " tude of foreign soldiers together, and prepared " ships of war; my intention also being to go 4 " through the country, that I may punish them " which have destroyed our country, and made " many cities in the kingdom desolate: now there- 5 " fore I confirm unto thee all the immunities " which the kings before me granted thee, and " whatsoever gifts besides they granted. I give 6 " thee leave also to coin money[d] for thy coun-

---

[c] Meaning Tryphon and his supporters.

[d] That the Jews immediately availed themselves of this privilege, we have evidence, in coins both of brass and silver, struck by direction of Simon, which are still remaining in many public and private cabinets. They are of various size, metal, type, and inscription; but, I believe, all agree in bearing the date of their execution, anno 1, 2, 3, or 4: that is, of Simon's government. Two of them, one a silver shekel, the other a small brass piece, are engraved in Wise's " Nummi " Bodleiani," fol. 1750: tab. xv. pp. 93, 215: and these, together with several others, are still preserved in the Bodleian collection. Many are delineated in the " Nummi " Pembrochiani," 4to, 1746. part 2, tab. 85. See also " Relandus de Nummis Sa- " maritanis," 8vo, 1709. Dr. Kennicot has figured and described a brasen piece of the fourth year, at p. 47, 48, 49, of his tract, entitled, " Ob- " servations on the First " Book of Samuel, ch. vi. " 19." 8vo, Oxford, 1768. But this, together with many others, of every year of Simon, and also several attributed to Jonathan, Simon's brother, to John Hyrcanus, to Aristobulus, &c. may be found beautifully engraved, and most elaborately described and discussed, in " Bayerius de Num- " mis Hebræo-Samaritanis,"

7 " try, with thine own stamp. And as concerning
" Jerusalem, and the sanctuary, let them be free[e];
" and all the armour which thou hast made, and
" fortresses which thou hast built, and keepest in
8 " thine hands, let them remain unto thee. And
" if any thing be, or shall be owing to the king,
" let it be forgiven thee from this time forth for
9 " evermore. Furthermore, when we have ob-
" tained our kingdom, we will honour thee, and
" thy nation, and thy temple, with great honour,
" so that your honour shall be known throughout
" the world."
10 In the hundred threescore and fourteenth year went Antiochus into the land of his fathers: and all the forces came together unto him, so that few
11 were left with Tryphon. And king Antiochus pursued him, and he fled unto Do- B.C. 139.
12 ra[f], which lieth by the sea-side. For he saw that troubles came upon him all at once, and that his
13 forces had forsaken him. Then camped Antiochus against Dora, and with him an hundred and

4to, Valentiæ, 1781. Bayer, however, was warmly attacked by Tychsen, another celebrated numismatist, who denied the genuineness of the specimens: but he defended himself with vigour, in " Numo-
" rum Hebræo-Samaritano-
" rum Vindiciæ," 4to, Valentiæ, 1790. Tychsen rejoined; and again was replied to: and the question continued to be agitated for some years afterwards, as may be seen in the Transactions of the Gottingen Academy for 1792, &c.
These two authors, Bayer and Tychsen, furnish ample references to the earlier writers on Oriental coins, as Reland, Swinton, the Pembroke collection, that of Dr. Hunter, to Frœlich, Woide, Gagnier, Barthelemy, &c.; and indeed appear to have exhausted the subject. Those persons who have not access to their works will do well to consult the " Fragments to Calmet," N[os]. 202 and 203.

[e] See above, ch. x. 31.
[f] A town of Phœnicia, situate near mount Carmel; not to be confounded with Adora, mentioned at ch. xiii. 20.

140   BOOK II.   B.C. 139.

twenty thousand men of war, and eight thousand horsemen. And he compassed the city round about, and ships by sea closed up the passage, and he vexed the city by land and by sea, neither suffered he any to go out or in.

In the mean season came Numenius and his company from Rome, having letters to the kings and countries; wherein were written these things: "Lucius[g], consul of the Romans, unto king "Ptolemy, greeting: The Jews' ambassadors, our "friends and confederates, came unto us, to renew "the old friendship[h] and league, being sent from "Simon the high priest, and from the people of "the Jews. And they brought a shield of gold "of a thousand minæ[i]. We thought it good "therefore to write unto the kings and countries, "that they should do them no harm, nor fight "against them, their cities, or countries, nor yet "aid their enemies against them. It seemed also "good to us to receive the shield from them. "If therefore there be any pestilent fellows who "have fled from their country unto you, deliver "them unto Simon the high priest, that he may "punish them according to their own law." The same things wrote he likewise unto Demetrius[k] the king, and Attalus, to Ariarathes, and Arsaces; and to all the countries[l], and to Sampsames[m],

[g] Namely Lucius Calpurnius Piso.

[h] Namely, that which was made with them by Judas Maccabæus, in the year B.C. 161. See above, at ch. viii.

[i] See above, at ch. xiv. 24.

[k] King of Syria. Namely Demetrius Nicator, at this time a prisoner with the Parthians. Attalus, king of Pergamus. Ariarathes, of Cappadocia. Arsaces, (i. e. Mithridates,) of Parthia.

[l] Namely, all those which were on friendly terms with the Romans.

[m] There is an obscurity here.

and the Lacedæmonians, and to Delus, and Myndus, and Sicyon, and Caria, and Samos, and Pamphylia, and Lycia, and Halicarnassus, and Rhodus, and Phaselis, and Cos, and Side, and Aradus, and Gortyna, and Cnidus, and Cyprus, and Cy-
24 rene. And the copy hereof they wrote to Simon
25 the high priest. So Antiochus the king camped against Dora the second *day*, bringing his forces against it continually, and making engines; and he shut up Tryphon, that he could neither go in nor out.

26 And Simon sent him two thousand chosen men to aid him: silver also and gold, and much armour.
27 Nevertheless, he would not receive them, but brake all the covenants which he had made with him
28 afore, and became strange unto him. Furthermore, he sent unto him Athenobius, one of his friends, to commune with him, and say, You withhold Joppe and Gazara, with the tower which is in Jerusa-
29 lem, which are cities of my realm. The borders thereof ye have wasted, and done great hurt in the land, and gotten the dominion of many places
30 within my kingdom. Now therefore deliver up the cities which ye have taken, and the tributes of the places whereof ye have gotten dominion with-
31 out the borders of Judæa: or else, give me for them five hundred talents of silver; and for the harm which you have done, and the tributes of the cities, other five hundred talents: if not, we
32 will come and subdue you in fight. So Athenobius the king's friend came to Jerusalem: and

Grotius, following the Latin version, judges that the Greek text is faulty, and that we ought to read *Lampsacus*, the name of a well-known city of Asia Minor.

when he saw the glory of Simon, and the cupboard of gold, and silver plate, and his great attendance, he was astonished, and told him the king's message. Then answered Simon, and said unto him, 33 We have neither taken other men's land, nor holden that which appertaineth to others, but the inheritance of our fathers, which our enemies had wrongfully in possession a certain time. Where- 34 fore we, having the opportunity, hold the inheritance of our fathers. But as for Joppe and Gazara 35 which thou demandest, *although* they did great harm unto the people in our country, yet will we give an hundred talents for them. Hereunto Athenobius answered him not a word. But re- 36 turned in a rage to the king, and made a report unto him of these speeches, and of the glory of Simon, and of all which he had seen: whereupon the king was exceeding wroth. In the mean time 37 fled Tryphon by ship unto Orthosias[n].

Then the king made Cendebæus captain of the 38 sea-coast, and gave him an host of footmen and horsemen, and commanded him to remove his 39 host toward Judæa: also he commanded him to build up Cedron[o], and to fortify the gates, and to war against the people: but as for the king *himself*, he pursued Tryphon. So Cendebæus came 40 to Jamnia, and began to annoy the people, and to

[n] A maritime town of Phœnicia: seated on or near the river Eleutherus. It was of sufficient importance to coin money in the days of the emperor Adrian. Josephus adds, that Tryphon fled thence to his native place Apamea, where he was taken and slain, having usurped the crown for three years.

[o] Grotius (from the Latin) corrects this to Gedor, or Gedora; which is a town in the south of the Holy Land, bordering on the territory of the Philistines and Idumæa.

invade Judæa, and to take the people prisoners,
41 and slay them. And when he had built up Cedron, he set horsemen there, and an host *of footmen*, to the end that issuing out they might make outroads upon the ways of Judæa, as the king had commanded him.

CHAPTER XVI.

John defeats Cendebæus. Simon and his sons are slain treacherously by Ptolemy son of Abubus.

1 THEN came up John from Gazara, and told Simon his father, what Cendebæus had
2 done. Wherefore Simon called his two eldest sons, Judas and John, and said unto them; I and my brethren, and my father's house, have ever from our youth unto this day fought against the enemies of Israel; and things have prospered so well in our hands, that we have delivered Israel
3 oftentimes. But now I am old, and ye, by *God's* mercy, are of a sufficient age: be ye instead of me and my brother, and go out and fight for our na-
4 tion, and the help from Heaven be with you. So he chose out of the country twenty thousand men of war with horsemen, who went out against Cen-
5 debæus, and rested that night at Modin. And when as they rose in the morning, and went into the plain, behold, a mighty great host both of footmen and horsemen came against them: howbeit
6 there was a water-brook betwixt them. So he and his people pitched over against them: and when he saw that the people were afraid to go over the water-brook, he went over first himself, and then the men seeing him, passed through after
7 him. *That done,* he divided his men, and set the

horsemen in the midst of the footmen: for the enemy's horsemen were very many. Then sounded 8 they with the holy trumpets: whereupon Cendebæus and his host were put to flight, so that many of them were slain, and the remnant fled to the strong hold. At that time was Judas, John's 9 brother, wounded: but John still followed after them, until he came to Cedron[a], which *Cendebæus* had built up. (And they fled even unto the 10 towers in the fields of Azotus;) wherefore he burnt it with fire: so that there were slain of them about two thousand men. Afterward he returned into the land of Judah in peace.

Moreover, Ptolemæus the son of Abubus was 11 made captain over the plain of Jericho, and he had abundance of silver and gold. For he was the high priest's son-in-law. Where- 12 fore his heart being lifted up, he thought to get 13 the country to himself, and thereupon consulted deceitfully against Simon and his sons to destroy them. Now Simon was visiting the cities which 14 were in the country, and taking care for the good ordering of them: at which time he came down himself to Jericho, with his sons Mattathias and Judas, in the hundred threescore and seventh year, in the eleventh month, which is the month Sabat: where the *son* of Abubus receiving them deceit- 15 fully into a little hold, called Docus[b], which he had built, made them a great banquet: howbeit he had hidden men there. So when Simon and 16

---

[a] See the note at ch. xv. 39.

[b] This is said to have been "a strong tower situate *near* "Jericho, the ruins whereof "may be seen to this day." It was also called Dagon; and is mentioned again at 5 Macc. ch. xx.

B.C. 135.   CHAP. XVI.   145

his sons had drunk largely, Ptolemy and his men rose up, and took their weapons, and came upon Simon into the banqueting-place, and slew him, 7 and his two sons, and certain of his servants. In which doing he committed a great treachery, and recompensed evil for good.

8 Then Ptolemy wrote these things, and sent to the king[c], that he should send him an host to aid him, and he would deliver him the country and 9 cities. He sent others also to Gazara to take John: and unto the captains of thousands he sent letters to come unto him, that he might give them 10 silver and gold, and rewards. And others he sent to take Jerusalem, and the mountain of the temple. 11 Now one had run afore to Gazara, and told John that his father and brethren were slain; and (*said* 12 *he*) *Ptolemy* hath sent to slay thee also. Hereof when he heard, he was sore astonished: so he laid hands on them which were come to destroy him, and slew them; for he knew that they sought to make him away.

13 As concerning the rest of the accounts of John, and his wars and worthy deeds which he did, and the building of the walls which he made, and his 14 doings; behold, these are written in the chronicles of his priesthood[d], from the time he was made high priest after his father.

[c] Archbishop Ussher remarks, that from allusions in one or two historians there is reason to think that this treacherous act of Ptolemy was not without the privity of Antiochus.

[d] From which, in all probability, Josephus drew the whole of that information which he has given us concerning these things. See also Macc. book V. ch. xx.—xxvi.

END OF BOOK II.

THE THIRD BOOK OF MACCABEES:

CONTAINING

THE OCCURRENCES OF ABOUT FIFTEEN YEARS, NAMELY, FROM THE ACCESSION OF ANTIOCHUS EPIPHANES TO THE DEATH OF NICANOR.

At the beginning are inserted two letters written at a later period; and likewise the history of Heliodorus' attempt to plunder the Temple.

CHAPTER I.

A letter from the Jews at Jerusalem to their brethren.

1 "THE brethren the Jews which are at Jerusalem, and those in the country of Judæa, wish unto the brethren the Jews which are
2 "throughout Egypt, health and peace: God be gracious unto you, and remember his covenant which he made with Abraham, Isaac, and Jacob,
3 "his faithful servants: and give you all an heart to serve him, and to do his will with a good cou-
4 "rage, and a willing mind; and open your heart in his law and commandments, and send you
5 "peace, and hear your prayers; and be at one with you, and forsake you not in time of trou-
6 "ble. And now we are here praying for you.
7 "In the reign of Demetrius[a] in the hundred three-

B.C. 144.

---

[a] Namely, Demetrius Nicator, the son of Demetrius Soter.

"score and ninth year[b], we the Jews have written "unto you in the extremity of trouble[c]: which "came upon us in these years, from the time that "Jason and his company revolted from the holy "land and kingdom, and burnt the porch, and "shed innocent blood: then we prayed unto the 8 "Lord, and were heard; we offered also sacrifice "and fine flour, and lighted the lamps, and set "forth the loaves. And now, *see* that ye keep 9 "the feast of tabernacles[d] in the month Casleu.

"In the hundred fourscore and eighth year, 10
B.C. "the people who were at Jerusalem, and
125. "in Judæa, and the council, and Judas[e],
"sent greeting and health unto Aristobulus, king
"Ptolemæus'[f] master[g], who was of the stock of the
"anointed priests, and to the Jews who were in
"Egypt. Having been delivered by God from 11
"great perils, we thank him highly, as though we
"had been in battle against the king[h]. For he 12
"cast out[i] them which fought within the holy city.
"For when the leader was come into Persia, and 13
"the army with him which seemed invincible,

---

[b] Namely, of the "Æra of "Contracts," commencing at a period six months later than that which is followed by the author of the preceding book.

[c] Gr. ἐν τῇ θλίψει καὶ ἐν τῇ ἀκμῇ, literally, "in our trouble "and crisis;" but fairly enough translated as above.

[d] See below, ch. x. 6—8.

[e] It does not appear to be ascertained who this Judas was: various opinions concerning him may be seen at one view in Basnage's History of the Jews, book V. ch. 1.

[f] Surnamed Physcon, the seventh sovereign of that name.

[g] Or teacher in philosophy. Aristobulus was a peripatetic philosopher, and is mentioned by Clemens Alexandrinus and Eusebius. (Ussher.)

[h] Namely, Antiochus Epiphanes.

[i] Gr. ἐξέβρασε, literally, "caused to boil over;" that is, "expelled through the "heat and agitation of water," as Suidas explains the word.

"they were slain in the temple of Nanæa[k] by the
14 "treachery of Nanæa's priests. For Antiochus,
"as though he would marry her, came into the
"place, and his friends who were with him, to re-
15 "ceive money in name of a dowry. Which, when
"the priests of Nanæa had set forth, and he was
"entered with a small company into the compass
"of the temple, they shut the temple as soon as
16 "Antiochus was come in: and opening a privy
"door of the roof, they threw stones like thunder-
"bolts, and struck down the captain and his com-
"pany, hewed them in pieces, smote off their
"heads, and cast them to those who were with-
17 "out. Blessed be our God in all things, who
"hath delivered up the ungodly.
18 "Therefore, whereas we are now purposed to
"keep the purification of the temple upon the five
"and twentieth day of *the month* Casleu, we
"thought it necessary to certify you thereof; that
"ye also might keep it, as the *feast* of the taber-
"nacles, and of the fire, *which was given us* when
"Neemias[l] offered sacrifice, after that he had
19 "builded the temple and the altar. For when
"our fathers were led into Persia, the devout
"priests of that time took the fire of the altar
"privily, and hid it in a hollow place of a pit[m]
"without water, where they kept *it* sure, so that
20 "the place was unknown to all men. Now after

---

[k] This appears to be a Persian name for Diana, or perhaps Dea Mater. But see the account given at 2 Macc. vi. 1, &c., and Grotius' note on the place.

[l] See Nehemiah ch. viii: where, however, there is not one syllable concerning the fire here mentioned.

[m] The Greek text here is somewhat obscure: ἐν κοιλώματι φρέατος τάξιν ἔχοντος ἀνύδρου.

"many years, when it pleased God, Neemias being
"sent from the king of Persia, sent some of the
"posterity of those priests who had hid it, for the
"fire: but when they told us they found no fire,
"but thick water; then commanded he them to 21
"draw it up, and to bring it: and when the sa-
"crifices were laid on, Neemias commanded the
"priests to sprinkle the wood and the things laid
"thereupon with the water. When this was 22
"done, and the time came that the sun shone,
"which afore was hid in the cloud, there was a
"great fire kindled, so that every man marvelled.
"And the priests made a prayer whilst the sacri- 23
"fice was consuming, (*I say*,) both the priests and
"all *the rest*, Jonathan beginning, and the rest
"answering thereunto, as Neemias did.

"And the prayer was after this manner; 'O 24
"Lord, Lord God, Creator of all things, who art
"terrible and strong, and righteous, and merciful,
"and the only and gracious King. The only 25
"giver of all things, the only just, almighty, and
"everlasting, thou that deliverest Israel from all
"evil, and didst choose the fathers, and sanctify
"them: receive the sacrifice for thy whole people 26
"Israel, and preserve thine own portion, and
"sanctify it. Gather together those who are 27
"scattered from us; deliver them which serve
"among the heathen; look upon them which are
"despised and abhorred; and let the heathen know
"that thou art our God. Punish them which op- 28
"press us, and with pride do us wrong. Plant thy 29
"people again in thy holy place, as Moses hath
"spoken[n]." And the priests sung psalms of 30

[n] Perhaps the allusion is to Deuteron. xxx. 3—8.

31 " thanksgiving. Now when the sacrifice was
" consumed, Neemias commanded the water which
" was left to be poured° on the great stones.
32 " When this was done, there was kindled a flame:
" but it was consumed by the light which shined
33 " from the altar. So when this matter was known,
" it was told the king of Persia, that in the place
" where the priests who were led away had hid
" the fire, there appeared water, and that Neemias
" and his company had purified the sacrifices
34 " therewith. Then the king enclosing the place,
" made it holy, after he had tried the matter.
35 " And the king took many gifts, and bestowed
36 " thereof on those whom he would gratify. And
" Neemias and his party called this thing Neph-
" thar, which is as much as to say, a cleansing:
" but by the generality it is called Nepthai."

CHAPTER II.

The letter continued.   The author's design in this book.

1   " IT is also found in the records, that Jeremy
" the prophet commanded them which went into
" captivity[a], to take of the fire, as it hath been
2 " signified: and how that the prophet, having
" given them the law, charged them which went
" into captivity not to forget the commandments
" of the Lord; and that they should not err in
" their minds, on beholding images of gold and
3 " silver, with their ornaments. And with other
" such speeches exhorted he them, that the law
4 " should not depart from their hearts. It was

° Gr. ἐκέλευσε λίθους μείζό-
νας κατασχεῖν. The Greek is
obscure. Perhaps for κατασχεῖν
we ought to read καταχέειν.
[a] Gr. τοὺς μεταγινομένους.

" also contained in the *same* writing, that the
" prophet, being warned of God, commanded the
" tabernacle and the ark to go with him, as he
" went forth into the mountain, where Moses
" climbed up, and saw the heritage of God. And 5
" when Jeremy came thither, he found a hollow
" cave; wherein he laid the tabernacle, and the
" ark, and the altar of incense, and so stopped
" the door. And some of those who followed him 6
" came to mark the way, but they could not find
" it. Which, when Jeremy perceived, he blamed 7
" them, saying, As for that place, it shall be un-
" known until the time that God gather his people
" again together, and be merciful unto them.
" Then shall the Lord shew them these things, 8
" and the glory of the Lord shall appear, and the
" cloud also, as it was shewed under Moses, and
" as when Solomon desired that the place might
" be honourably sanctified. It was also declared, 9
" that he, being wise, offered the sacrifice of dedi-
" cation, and of the finishing of the temple. And as 10
" Moses prayed unto the Lord, and the fire came
" down from heaven, and consumed the sacrifices:
" even so prayed Solomon also, and the fire came
" down, and consumed the burnt-offerings. And 11
" Moses said, Because the sin-offering was not
" eaten[b], it was consumed. So also Solomon kept 12
" those eight days.

" The same things also were reported in the 13
" writings and commentaries of Neemias; and
" how he, founding a library, gathered together
" the acts of the kings and the prophets, and of

[b] See Leviticus, ch. x. 16—18.

"David, and the epistles of the kings concerning
14 "the holy gifts. In like manner also Judas
"gathered together all those things which were
"dispersed by reason of the war which we had,
15 "and they remain with us. Wherefore, if ye
"have need thereof, send some to fetch them
16 "unto you. Whereas we then are about to cele-
"brate the purification, we have written unto
"you; and ye shall do well, if ye keep the same
17 "days. But *it is* God who delivered all his
"people, and gave them all an heritage, and the
"kingdom, and the priesthood, and the sanc-
18 "tuary[c], as he promised in the law. For we
"hope in God that he will shortly have mercy
"upon us, and gather us together out of every
"land under heaven, unto the holy place: for he
"hath delivered us out of great troubles, and
19 "hath purified the place."

NOW as concerning Judas Maccabæus, and his
20 brethren, and the purification of the great temple,
and the dedication of the altar; and the wars
21 against Antiochus Epiphanes, and Eupator his
son; and the manifest signs which came from
heaven unto those who behaved themselves manfully to their honour for Judaism: so that being
22 but a few, they overcame the whole country, and
chased barbarous multitudes; and recovered again
the temple renowned all the world over, and freed
the city, and upheld the laws, which were about
23 to be dissolved, the Lord being gracious unto
them with all favour: things which have been
24 declared by Jason of Cyrene in five books—we will
assay to abridge in one volume. For considering

[c] Gr. τὸν ἁγιασμὸν, literally, "sanctification."

the infinite number[d], and the difficulty which they find who desire to enter deeply[e] into the narrations of the story, for the variety of the matter; we have been careful, that they which will read might have delight, and that they which are desirous to commit to memory, might have ease; and that all, into whose hands it comes, may have profit. Indeed to us, who have taken upon us this painful labour of abridging, it was not easy, but a matter of sweat and watching; even as it is no ease unto him who prepareth a banquet, and seeketh the benefit of others: yet for the pleasuring of many we will undertake gladly this painful task; leaving to the author the exact handling of every particular, and labouring to follow the rules[f] of an abridgment. For as the master-builder of a new house must care for the whole building; but he who undertaketh to deck it with painting and sculpture[g], must seek out fit things for the adorning thereof: even so I think it is with us. To stand upon every point, and discourse of all things at large, and to be curious in particulars, belongeth to the first author of the story: but to study brevity, and avoid much labouring of the work, is to be granted to him who will make an abridgment[h]. Here then let us begin the narrative; only adding thus much to

---

[d] Gr. τὸ χύμα τῶν ἀριθμῶν, the multitude, either of events or of narratives to be considered.

[e] Gr. εἰσκυκλεῖσθαι, literally, "to involve themselves."

[f] Gr. ὑπογραμμοῖς, "lines traced for a pattern."

[g] Gr. ἐγκαίειν, "to burn in," meaning, "to paint in encaustic," a species of decoration in which the nations of antiquity delighted to indulge their taste.

[h] Gr. μετάφρασιν, literally, a "transmutation," either into another form or another language.

that which hath been said before; for it is a foolish thing to make a long prologue to a story, and to be short in the story itself.

CHAPTER III.

Heliodorus' attempt to plunder the temple of Jerusalem.

1 Now when the holy city was inhabited with all peace, and the laws were kept very well, because of the godliness of Onias[a] the high
2 priest, and his hatred of wickedness; it came to pass, that even the kings themselves did honour the place, and magnify the temple with their best
3 presents[b]; insomuch that Seleucus[c] king of Asia, of his own revenues, bare all the costs belonging to the services of the sacrifices.
4 But one Simon of the tribe of Benjamin, who was made governor of the temple, fell out with the high priest about evil doings[d] in the
5 city. And when he could not overcome Onias, he went to Apollonius *the son* of Thraseas, who then
6 was governor of Cœlosyria and Phœnice; and told him, that the treasury in Jerusalem was full of infinite sums of money, so that the multitude of their riches was innumerable; and that these did not belong to the account of the sacrifices, but

B.C. 187.

B.C. 186.

B.C. 176.

---

[a] The third of that name, son of Simon II: he succeeded to the high-priesthood in the year 191 B.C.

[b] Gr. ἀποστολαῖς. See Josephus, Antiq. XII. 2, &c. The word occurs in this sense also at 3 Esdras ix. 51. 54. Compare the note [e] at 2 Macc. ii. 19.

[c] Called Philopator, or Soter: he was the son of Antiochus the Great, and elder brother of Antiochus Epiphanes.

[d] Gr. παρανομίας: but several manuscripts read ἀγορανομίας, the office of agoranomus, or ædile: a matter in which it was likely that Simon would raise a quarrel.

that it was possible that all of them might fall into the king's power.

Now when Apollonius came to the king and had shewed him of the money whereof he was told, the king chose out Heliodorus his treasurer [e], and sent him [f] with a commandment to bring away the foresaid money. So forthwith Heliodorus took his journey, under a colour of visiting the cities of Cœlosyria and Phœnice, but indeed to fulfil the king's purpose. And when he was come to Jerusalem, and had been courteously received by the high priest of the city; he told him what intelligence was given of the money, and declared wherefore he came, and asked if these things were so indeed. Then the high priest told him, that there was money laid up for the relief of widows and fatherless children: and some also belonging to Hircanus, *grandson* of Tobias [g], a man of great dignity, and not as that wicked Simon had misinformed: the sum whereof in all was four hundred talents of silver, and two hundred of gold: and that it was altogether impossible that wrong should be done unto them, which had committed it to the holiness of the place, and to the majesty and inviolable sanctity of the temple, honoured over all the world. But Heliodorus, because of the king's commandment given him,

[e] Gr. τὸν ἐπὶ τῶν πραγμάτων. There is a various reading, χρημάτων, which our translators have followed. If we take the other reading, we ought to render it, as the Douay version does, "him who was over his affairs:" but it seems most likely that the *treasurer* would be the officer sent, in a case where the seizing of treasure was the business to be performed.

[f] See Daniel's prophecy concerning the deeds of Seleucus, at ch. xi. 20, &c.

[g] Concerning this man consult Josephus, Antiq. XII. 4.

said, That in any wise, this must be brought into the king's treasury.

14 So at the day which he appointed, he entered in to order the overseeing of this matter: wherefore there was no small agony throughout the
15 whole city. But the priests, prostrating themselves before the altar in their priests' vestments, called unto heaven upon him who made a law concerning things given to be kept, to preserve these sums safely for such as had committed them
16 to be kept. Then whoso had looked the high priest in the face, it would have wounded his heart: for his countenance, and the changing of his colour, declared the inward agony of his mind.
17 For the man was compassed round with a fear, and bodily stupor, by which it was manifest to them which looked upon him, what sorrow he had
18 in his heart. Others ran flocking out of their houses to a general supplication, because the place
19 was like to come into contempt. And the women, girt with sackcloth under their breasts, collected in great numbers in the streets; and the virgins who were kept in, ran some to the gates, and some upon the walls, and others looked out of the win-
20 dows. And all, stretching forth their hands toward
21 heaven, made supplication. Then it was pitiful to see the promiscuous falling down of the multitude, and the fearful expectation of the high priest
22 in great agony. They then called upon the Almighty Lord, to keep the things committed of trust safe and sure for those who had committed
23 them. But Heliodorus was executing that which was decreed.
24 Now as he was there present himself with his

guard about the treasury, the Lord of spirits[h], and the Prince of all power, caused a great apparition; so that all who presumed to come in with him were astonished at the power of God, and fainted, and were sore afraid: for there appeared unto 25 them a horse with a terrible rider upon him, and adorned with a very fair covering; and he ran fiercely, and smote at Heliodorus with his forefeet; and it seemed that he who sat upon the horse had complete armour of gold. Moreover, two other 26 young men appeared before him, notable in strength, excellent in beauty, and splendid in apparel; who stood by him on either side, and scourged him continually, and gave him many sore stripes. And Heliodorus fell suddenly unto 27 the ground, and was compassed with great darkness: but they which were with him took him up, and put him into a litter. Thus him who lately 28 came with a great train, and with all his guard into the said treasury, they carried out, being unable to help himself with his weapons: and manifestly they recognised the power of God. He 29 then, by the hand of God, was cast down, and lay speechless without any hope of life. But they 30 praised the Lord who had miraculously honoured his own place: and the temple, which a little afore was full of fear and trouble, when the Almighty Lord appeared, was filled with joy and gladness. Then straightway certain of Heliodo- 31 rus' friends prayed Onias, that he would call upon the Most High, to grant him his life, who lay utterly at the last gasp. So the high priest, sus- 32

[h] The Greek text varies here, between πνευμάτων and πατέρων.

pecting lest the king should misconceive that some treachery had been done to Heliodorus by the Jews, offered a sacrifice for the health of the man.
33 Now as the high priest was making an atonement, the same young men, in the same clothing, appeared and stood beside Heliodorus; saying, Give Onias the high priest great thanks, insomuch as
34 for his sake the Lord hath granted thee life: and seeing that thou hast been scourged from heaven, declare unto all men the mighty power of God. And when they had spoken these words, they
35 disappeared. So Heliodorus, after he had offered sacrifice unto the Lord, and made great vows unto him who had saved his life, and saluted Onias,
36 returned with his host to the king. Then testified he to all men the works of the great God,
37 which he had seen with his eyes. And when the king asked Heliodorus who might be a fit man to
38 be sent yet once again to Jerusalem, he said; If thou hast any enemy or traitor, send him thither, and thou shalt receive him well scourged, if he escape with his life: for in that place, no doubt,
39 there is an especial power of God. He himself who dwelleth in heaven, hath his eye on that place, and defendeth it; and he beateth and de-
40 stroyeth them which come to hurt it. And the things concerning Heliodorus, and the keeping of the treasury, fell out on this sort.

CHAPTER IV.

Jason is made high priest. He introduces Gentile fashions. He is supplanted by Menelaus. The murder of Onias.

1 BUT the aforesaid Simon, who had been the

betrayer of the money and of his country, spake slanderously of Onias, that it was he who had terrified Heliodorus, and had been the worker of these evils. And him, who was a benefactor of the city, a careful tender of his countrymen, and zealous for the laws, he dared to call a traitor. But when their hatred went so far, that even murders were committed by one of Simon's faction; Onias, seeing the danger of this contention, and that Apollonius, as being the governor of Cœlosyria and Phœnice, did rage, and increase Simon's malice;—went to the king, not to be an accuser of his countrymen, but seeking the good of all, both public and private: for he saw that it was impossible that the state should continue quiet, and Simon leave his folly, unless the king did look thereunto.

But after the death of Seleucus, when Antiochus, called Epiphanes, succeeded to the kingdom; Jason the brother of Onias laboured underhand to be high priest, promising unto the king, by intercession [a], three hundred and threescore talents of silver, and of another revenue eighty talents: besides this, he promised to assign an hundred and fifty more, if he might have licence to set him up a place for exercise [b], and for the training up of youth in the fashions of the heathen, and to inscribe those of Jerusalem citizens of Antioch. Which when the king had granted, and he had gotten into his hand the rule, he forthwith brought his own nation to the Greek

B.C. 175.

[a] Or, " in a conversation:" Gr. δι' ἐντεύξεως.
[b] Gr. γυμνάσιον. Compare 2 Macc. i. 11—15.

11 fashion. And the royal privileges granted of special favour to the Jews, by the means of John the father of Eupolemus, who went ambassador to Rome for amity and aid, he threw aside: and putting down the forms of government which were according to the law, he brought up new
12 customs against the law. For he built gladly a place of exercise under the citadel itself; and bringing into training[c] the chief of the young men, he made them wear a hat.
13 Now such was the height of Greek fashions, and increase of heathenish manners, through the exceeding profaneness of Jason, that ungodly
14 wretch, and not high priest; that the priests had no inclination to serve any more at the altar; but despising the temple, and neglecting the sacrifices, hastened to be partakers of the unlawful allowance in the place of exercise, after the challenge[d]
15 at the Discus; not esteeming the honours of their fathers, but liking the glory of the Grecians best
16 of all. By reason whereof sore calamity came upon them: for they had them to be their enemies and avengers, whose modes they followed so earnestly, and unto whom they desired to be alike
17 in all things. For it is not a light thing to do wickedly against the laws of God: but the time following will declare these things.

B. C. 174.

[c] Gr. τοὺς κρατίστους τῶν ἐφήβων ὑποτάσσων ὑπὸ πέτασον ἦγεν. Here Schleusner suspects the word ὑποτάσσων to be superfluous, having slipped in by error of the copyists from ὑπὸ πέτασον, which followed: and indeed, in one manuscript, the word is wanting: yet, from a quotation from "Hippolytus de Anti-"christo," given by Wesseling in a note on Diodorus Siculus, Eclog. lib. XXXIV. 1. it would appear that ὑποτάσσων must be retained.

[d] Gr. μετὰ τὴν τοῦ δίσκου πρόκλησιν.

Now when the game[e] which was used every fifth year was kept at Tyrus, the king being present, this vile Jason sent sacred messengers[f] from Jerusalem, who were Antiochians, to carry three hundred[g] drachms of silver to the sacrifice of Hercules: which even the bearers thereof thought fit not to bestow upon the sacrifice, because it was not proper, but to reserve for another charge. This money then, in regard of the sender, was appointed to Hercules' sacrifice; but because of the bearers thereof, it was employed to the making of galleys.

Now when Apollonius the *son* of Menestheus was sent into Egypt for the coronation of king Ptolemæus Philometor, Antiochus, understanding him not to be well-affected to his affairs, provided for his own safety: whereupon he came to Joppe, and from thence to Jerusalem: where he was honourably received by Jason, and by the city, and was brought in with torch-light, and with great shoutings: and so afterward went with his host unto Phœnice.

Three years afterward Jason sent Menelaus the foresaid Simon's brother[h], to bear the money unto the king, and to put him in

B.C. 173.

B.C. 172.

---

[e] Which was instituted, not only in Tyre, but in many other places also, in imitation of the Olympic games.

[f] Gr. θεωρούς, so called by Plato, Thucydides, Sophocles, and other classic authors.

[g] Grotius, thinking the sum too small, suggests an emendation, "three thousand." And indeed, three Greek manuscripts read, " three thousand three hundred:" which account is adopted by Vaillant, in his " Historia Regum " Syriæ."

[h] Josephus on the contrary asserts, that he was brother to Onias and Jason; which is much more probable, as he scarcely would have obtained the high-priesthood if he had not been of the family of Aaron.

24 mind of certain necessary matters. But he being brought to the presence of the king, when he had magnified him for the glorious appearance of his power, got the priesthood to himself, offering more than Jason by three hundred talents of sil-
25 ver. So he came with the king's mandate, bringing nothing worthy the high-priesthood, but having the fury of a cruel tyrant, and the rage of a
26 savage beast. Then Jason, who had undermined his own brother, being undermined[i] by another, was compelled to flee into the country of the Am-
27 monites. So Menelaus obtained the authority: but as for the money which he had promised unto the king, he took no good order for it, albeit Sos-
28 tratus the ruler of the castle required it: for unto him appertained the gathering of the customs. Wherefore they were both called before the king.
29 Now Menelaus left his brother Lysimachus in his stead in the priesthood; and Sostratus *left* Crates,
30 who was governor of the Cyprians. While those things were in doing, they of Tarsus and Mallos[k] made insurrection, because they were given to the
31 king's concubine called Antiochis. Then came the king in all haste to appease matters, leaving Andronicus, a man in authority, for his deputy.
32 Now Menelaus, supposing that he had gotten a convenient time, stole certain vessels of gold out of the temple; and gave some to Andronicus, and some he sold at Tyrus, and the
33 cities round about. Which when Onias knew of a

[i] Gr. ὑπονοθεύσας, and ὑπονοθευθείς. The expressions strictly apply to a case where an illegitimate person is substituted for a legitimate or proper one.

[k] Two cities of Cilicia.

surety, he reproved him, and withdrew himself into a sanctuary¹ at Daphne, which lieth by Antiochia. Wherefore Menelaus taking Andronicus apart, prayed him to get Onias into his hands; who being persuaded thereunto, and coming to Onias in deceit, gave him his right hand with oaths; and though he were suspected *by him*, yet persuaded he him to come forth from the sanctuary: whom forthwith he shut up *and slew* without regard of justice. For the which cause not only the Jews, but many also of other nations took great indignation, and were much grieved for the unjust murder of the man.

And when the king was come again from the places about Cilicia, the Jews who were in the city, and certain of the Greeks who abhorred the fact also, complained because Onias was slain without cause. Therefore Antiochus was heartily sorry, and moved to pity, and wept, because of the sober and orderly behaviour of him who was dead. And being inflamed with anger, forthwith he took away Andronicus his purple, and rent off his clothes; and leading him through the whole city unto that very place where he had committed impiety against Onias, there slew heᵐ the bloodstained murderer. Thus the Lord awarded him his punishment, as he had deserved.

---

¹ Namely, of Apollo, who was worshipped with much solemnity at this Daphne, near Antioch in Syria. This asylum is noticed by Strabo, and is expressly named on some coins of Antioch.

ᵐ Gr. τὸν μαιφόνον ἀπεκόσμησε: the verb may signify either "to strip off the raiment," or "to kill:" but the stripping has been mentioned already in an earlier portion of this verse.

39 Now when many sacrileges had been committed in the city by Lysimachus, with the consent of Menelaus, and the report thereof was spread abroad, the multitude gathered themselves together against Lysimachus, many vessels of gold 40 being already carried away. Whereupon the common people rising, and being filled with rage, Lysimachus armed about three thousand men, and began first to offer violence; one Auranus being the leader, a man far gone in years, and no less in 41 folly. They then seeing the attempt of Lysimachus, some of them caught stones, some clubs; others taking handfuls of dust which was next at hand, cast them all together upon Lysimachus, 42 and those who were with him. Thus many of them they wounded, and some they struck to the ground, and all *of them* they forced to flee: but as for the church-robber himself, him they killed 43 beside the treasury. Of these matters therefore there was an accusation laid against Menelaus.

44 Now when the king came to Tyrus, three men who were sent from the council pleaded the cause 45 before him: but Menelaus being now convicted, promised Ptolemy[n] the *son* of Dorymenes to give him much money, if he would pacify the king to- 46 wards him. Whereupon Ptolemy taking the king aside into a certain gallery[o], as it were to take 47 the air, brought him to be of another mind. Insomuch that he discharged Menelaus from the accusations; who, notwithstanding, was cause of all

[n] For whom see 2 Macc. iii. 38, where he is reckoned one of the three "mighty men of the king's friends."

[o] Gr. περίστυλον, a place surrounded by pillars, a colonnade.

the mischief: and those poor men, who, if they had told their cause, yea, before the Scythians, should have been judged innocent, them he condemned to death. Thus they who spake up in defence of the city, and of the people, and of the holy vessels, quickly suffered an unjust punishment. Wherefore even they of Tyrus, moved with hatred with that wicked deed, caused them to be honourably buried. And so through the covetousness of them who were in power, Menelaus remained still in authority, increasing in malice, and being a great traitor[p] to the citizens.

CHAPTER V.

Jason's cruelties, and death. Antiochus defeats the Jews, and plunders the temple.

ABOUT the same time Antiochus prepared his second[a] expedition into Egypt: and then it happened, that through all the city, for the space almost of forty days, there were seen horsemen[b] running in the air, robed in cloth of gold, and armed with lances, like a band of soldiers; and troops of horsemen in array, encountering and running one against another, with shaking of

[p] Gr. ἐπίβουλος, lying in wait for any opportunity of injuring or annoying them.

[a] Compare Daniel xi. 29. Respecting his *first* expedition, which was in the preceding year, see 2 Macc. i. 17.

[b] The ingenious and fanciful Dr. Darwin, in the additional notes to his "Botanic "Garden," adduces this passage in proof of the antiquity of the appearance of the *Northern Lights;* of which phænomenon he considers this to be " such a description as " might probably be given by " an ignorant and alarmed " people." (Note 1, on Meteors.) Josephus describes similar appearances in the heavens a short time previously to the destruction of Jerusalem by Titus. Compare 5 Macc. iii. 7.

shields, and multitude of pikes, and drawing of swords, and casting of darts, and glittering of golden ornaments, and armour of all sorts. Wherefore every man prayed, that that apparition might turn to good.

Now when there was gone forth a false rumour, as though Antiochus had been dead, Jason took not less than a thousand men, and suddenly made an assault upon the city: and they which were upon the walls, being drawn back, and the city at length taken, Menelaus fled into the castle. But Jason slew his own citizens without mercy, (not considering that success against his own kindred would be the worst kind of success[c]; but thinking that he was erecting trophies over his enemies, and not over his own countrymen.) Howbeit, for all this he obtained not the authority, but at the last received shame for the reward of his treason, and fled again[d] into the country of the Ammonites. In the end therefore he had an unhappy return, being accused[e] before Aretas the king of the Arabians, fleeing from city to city, pursued of all men, hated as a forsaker of the laws; and being had in abomination, as a public executioner of his country and countrymen, he was cast out into Egypt. Thus he, who had driven many out of their country, perished in a strange land, retiring to the Lacedæmonians, and thinking *there* to find shelter, by reason of his

[c] The every-way unfortunate results of civil war are alluded to and deplored by more than one of the Greek and Latin poets.

[d] See above, ch. iv. 26.

[e] The Greek text reads ἐγκλεισθεὶς, " shut up and " watched:" but Grotius judges that the true reading is ἐγκληθείς: in this he is followed by Schleusner.

kindred. And he who had cast out many unburied, 10 had none to mourn for him, nor any solemn funerals at all, nor sepulchre with his fathers.

Now when this which was done came to the 11 king's ear, he thought that Judæa had revolted: whereupon removing out of Egypt [f] in a furious mind, he took the city by force of arms; and com- 12 manded his men of war to cut down unsparingly such as they met, and to slay such as went up upon the houses. Thus there was killing of young 13 and old, making away of men, women, and children, slaying of virgins and infants. And there 14 were destroyed within the space of three whole days, fourscore thousand; whereof forty thousand were slain in the conflict; and no fewer were sold than slain. Yet was he not content with this, but 15 presumed to go into the most holy temple of all the world; having for his guide Menelaus, that traitor to the laws and to his country. And tak- 16 ing the holy vessels with polluted hands, and with profane hands pulling down the things which had been dedicated by other kings to the augmentation, and glory, and honour of the place, he gave them away [g]. And so haughty was Antiochus in 17 mind, not considering that the Lord was angry for a while for the sins of them who dwelt in the city, and therefore his eye was not upon the place. For had they not been formerly wrapped in many 18 sins, this man, as soon as he had come, had forthwith been scourged, and turned back from his presumption, as Heliodorus was, who was sent by Seleucus the king to inspect the treasury. Never- 19

[f] Compare 2 Macc. i. 20.
[g] Gr. ἐπεδίδου: the sense is not perfectly clear.

theless, God did not choose the people for the place's sake, but the place for the people's sake.

20 And therefore the place itself, which was partaker with them of the adversity which happened to the nation, did afterward communicate in the benefits sent from the Lord: and as it was forsaken in the wrath of the Almighty, so again, the great Lord being reconciled, it was reestablished with all glory.

21 So when Antiochus had carried out[h] of the temple a thousand and eight hundred talents, he departed in all haste unto Antiochia; weening in his pride to make the land navigable, and the sea passable on foot[i]: such was the haughtiness of his mind.

22 And he left governors to vex the nation: at Jerusalem, Philip, for his country a Phrygian, and for manners more barbarous than he who placed him

23 there; and at Garizim, Andronicus; and besides, Menelaus, who, worse than all the rest, bare an heavy hand over the citizens, having a malicious

24 mind against his countrymen the Jews. He sent also that detestable ringleader Apollonius[k], with an army of two and twenty thousand, B.C. 168. commanding him to slay all those who were in their best age, and to sell the women, and the

25 younger persons. Who coming to Jerusalem, and pretending peace, did forbear till the holy day of the sabbath; when taking the Jews keeping holy day, he commanded his men to arm themselves.

26 And so he slew all them which were gone to the

[h] Compare 2 Macc. i. 23, 24.
[i] Like another Xerxes; whose attempts of this kind, at mount Athos and at the Hellespont, are recorded by Herodotus, book VII. ch. 22—24; and 33—36.
[k] Compare 2 Macc. i. 29—32.

public worship; and running through the city with weapons, slaughtered great multitudes. But 27 Judas Maccabæus, with nine others, or thereabout, withdrew himself into the wilderness[1]; and lived in the mountains after the manner of beasts, with his company, who fed on herbs continually, that they might not be partakers of the pollution.

CHAPTER VI.

Antiochus persecutes the Jews. The courage and death of Eleazar.

Not long after this, the king sent an old man 1 of Athens[a], to compel the Jews to depart from the laws of their fathers, and not to live after the laws of God: and to pollute also 2 the temple in Jerusalem, and to call it the temple of Jupiter Olympius; and that in Garizim, of Jupiter the defender of strangers[b], as indeed they

B.C. 167.

---

[1] Compare 2 Macc. ii. 27—30.

[a] Grotius (following the Latin version) judges that the true reading is not Ἀθηναῖον but Ἀντιόχειον; which indeed would be much more apposite, seeing that many of the Jews at this time had been enrolled citizens of Antioch. I perceive that the authors of the "Universal History" consider Ἀθηναῖον as a proper name, and have rendered it "Athenens, "an old minister, well versed "in all the heathenish rites "as well as in cruelty."

[b] But Josephus says, "Ju-"piter Hellenius," Ant. XII. 5. It is notorious that Antiochus Epiphanes was a most zealous worshipper of *all new* gods: see Michaelis' supplementa ad Lexica Heb. tom. II. p. 1857, who refers to Athenæus; in which author we find the following account. (Lib. V. p. 194, 195, ed. Casaubon.) Ἐν δὲ ταῖς πρὸς τὰς πόλεις θυσίαις, καὶ ταῖς πρὸς τοὺς θεοὺς τιμαῖς, πάντας ὑπερέβαλλε τοὺς βεβασιλευκότας.—Τὸ δὲ τῶν ἀγαλμάτων πλῆθος οὐ δυνατὸν ἐξηγήσασθαι· πάντων γὰρ τῶν παρ' ἀνθρώποις λεγομένων ἢ νομιζομένων θεῶν ἢ δαιμόνων, προσέτι δὲ ἡρώων, εἴδωλα διήγετο, τὰ μὲν κεχρυσωμένα, τὰ δὲ ἠμφιεσμένα στολαῖς διαχρύσοις. All this took place at his grand festival at Daphne: and Athenæus adds, that the expence was supplied partly from the sums of which he

3 were[c] who dwelt in the place. And sore and grievous, even to the common people, was the
4 presence[d] of this mischief. For the temple was filled with riot and revelling, by the Gentiles; who dallied with harlots, and had to do with women within the sacred precincts; and besides that,
5 brought in things which were not lawful. The altar also was filled with profane things, which
6 the law forbiddeth. Neither was it lawful for a man to keep sabbath-days, or the feasts of his forefathers, or to profess himself at all to be a
7 Jew. And in the day of the king's birth every month they were brought by bitter constraint to eat of the sacrifices; and when the feast of Bacchus was kept, the Jews were compelled to go in
8 procession to Bacchus, carrying ivy[e]. Moreover, there went out a decree to the neighbour cities of the Grecians, by the suggestion of Ptolemy[f], against the Jews, that they should observe the same mode of living, and be partakers of their
9 sacrifices: and whoso would not conform themselves to the manners of the Greeks, should be put to death. Then might a man have seen the pre-
10 sent misery. For there were two women[g] brought who had circumcised their children; whom when they had openly led round about the city, the babes hanging at their breasts, they cast them
11 down headlong from the wall. And others who

had defrauded Ptolemy Philometor while a boy, partly from the contributions of his friends, and partly from the many temples which he had robbed. Ἱεροσυλήκει δὲ καὶ τὰ πλεῖστα τῶν Ἱερῶν.

[c] Gr. καθὼς ἐτύγχανον.

[d] Gr. ἡ ἐπίστασις: signifying both the coming on, and continuance, of the evil.

[e] Compare 1 Macc. ii. 19, and the note there.

[f] See above, ch. iv. 45.

[g] Compare 2 Macc. i. 60—63.

had run together into caves near by, to keep the sabbath-day secretly, being discovered to Philip[h], were all burnt together; because they scrupled to defend themselves, for the honour of the most sacred day.

Now I beseech those who meet with this book, that they be not discouraged for these calamities; but that they judge those punishments not to be for the destruction, but for a chastening, of our nation. For it is a token of his great goodness, when wicked doers are not suffered any long time, but forthwith fall into punishments. For not as with other nations, whom the Lord patiently forbeareth to punish, till they be come to the fulness of their sins, so dealeth he with us. Lest that, being come to the height of sin, afterwards he should take vengeance on us. And therefore he never withdraweth his mercy from us. And though he chasten with adversity, yet doth he never forsake his people. But let this be said by way of remembrance. But we must come to the declaring of the matter in few words.

Eleazar, one of the principal scribes, an aged man, and of a very well-favoured countenance, was constrained to open his mouth, and to eat swine's flesh. But he choosing rather to die gloriously, than to live stained with such an abomination, spit it forth, and came of his own accord to the torment. As it behoved them to come, who are resolute to stand out against such things as are not lawful for love of life to be tasted. But they which had the charge of that wicked feast, for the old acquaintance they had with the

[h] For an account of Philip, see ch. v. 22.

man, taking him aside, besought him to bring
flesh of his own provision, such as was lawful for
him to use, and make as if he did eat of the flesh
taken from the sacrifice commanded by the king;
22 that in so doing he might be delivered from death,
and for the old friendship with them, find favour.
23 But he, taking on him a discreet consideration,
and as became his age, and the excellency of his
ancient years, and the honour of his grey head
whereunto he was come[i], and his most honest education from a child, or rather the holy law made
and given by God; answered accordingly, and
desired them straightways to send him to the
24 grave. For it becometh not our age (*said he*) to
dissemble, whereby many young persons might
think that Eleazar, being fourscore years old and
25 ten, were now gone to a strange religion: and so
they through mine hypocrisy, and desire to live
a little time, and a moment longer, should be led
astray by me, and I should get to myself a stain
26 and pollution upon my old age. For even though
for the present time I should be delivered from
the punishment of men: yet should I not escape
the hand of the Almighty, neither alive nor dead.
27 Wherefore now manfully exchanging this life, I
will shew myself such an one, as mine age re-
28 quireth; and leave a noble example to such as be
young, to die willingly and courageously a noble
death, for the venerable and holy laws. And
when he had said these words, immediately he
29 went to the torment: they which led him, changing the good-will they bare him a little before,
into hatred, because the foresaid speeches, as they

[i] Gr. τῆς ἐπικτήτου καὶ ἐπιφανοῦς πολιᾶς.

thought, were madness. And when he was ready 30 to die with stripes, he groaned, and said; It is manifest unto the Lord, who hath the holy knowledge, that whereas I might have been delivered from death, I *now* endure sore pains in body, by being beaten; but in soul am well content to suffer these things, because I fear him. And thus 31 this man died, leaving his death for an example of a noble courage, and a memorial of virtue, not only unto young men, but unto the generality of his nation.

CHAPTER VII.

The constancy and death of seven brethren and their mother.

It came to pass also, that seven brethren with 1 their mother were taken, and compelled by the king, to taste swine's flesh forbidden by the law, and were tormented with scourges and whips. But one of them who spake first, said thus; What 2 wouldest thou ask or learn of us? we are ready to die, *rather* than to transgress the laws of our fathers. Then the king, being in a rage, command- 3 ed to heat the pans and caldrons hot. Which 4 forthwith being heated, he commanded to cut out the tongue of him who spake first; and having scalped him[a], to cut off the utmost parts of his body, the rest of his brethren and his mother looking on. Now when he was thus maimed in 5 all his members, he commanded him, being yet alive, to be brought to the fire, and to be fried in the pan. And as the vapour of the pan was dis-

---

[a] Or, "flayed:" Gr. περισκυθίσαντας: but the former is perhaps nearer to the meaning of the original word.

persed for a good space, they exhorted one another with the mother, to die manfully, saying
6 thus; The Lord God looketh upon us, and in truth hath comfort in us, as Moses in his song, which witnessed to their faces, declared, saying [b],
7 "And he shall be comforted in his servants." So when the first was dead after this manner, they brought the second to the cruel torture [c]: and when they had pulled off the skin of his head with the hair, they asked him, Wilt thou eat before thou be punished throughout every member
8 of thy body? But he answered in his own language, and said, No. Wherefore he also received the remainder of the torment as the former did.
9 And when he was at the last gasp, he said, Thou like a fury takest us out of this present life, but the King of the world shall raise us up, who have died for his laws, unto an eternal resurrection of
10 life. After him was the third scornfully ill-treated: and when he was required, he put out his tongue, and that right soon; and held forth his
11 hands manfully, and said courageously, These I had from Heaven; and for His laws I despise [d] them, and from Him I hope to receive them again.
12 Insomuch that the king himself, and they which were with him, marvelled at the young man's courage, for that he nothing regarded the pains.
13 Now when this man was dead also, they tormented
14 and mangled the fourth in like manner. And be-

[b] Compare Deut. xxxii. 36.
[c] Gr. ἐμπαιγμόν; which word (together with its verb ἐμπαίζω) denotes severity of usage mixed with scorn and contumely. It was usually rendered "a mocking-stock" by the former translators.
[d] Gr. ὑπερορῶ, "I leave "them out of consideration;" or, "I make no account of "them."

ing at the point of death, he said thus; It is good, being put to death by men, to look for hope from God, to be raised up again by Him: as for thee, thou shalt have no resurrection to life. After- 15 ward they brought up the fifth also, and mangled him. Then looked he unto *the king*, and said, 16 Thou having power over men, thyself being corruptible, doest what thou wilt; yet think not that our nation is forsaken by God: but abide a while, 17 and behold his great power, how he will torment thee and thy seed. After him also they brought 18 the sixth, who being ready to die, said; Be not deceived without cause: for we suffer these things for ourselves, having sinned[e] against our God: therefore marvellous things are done *unto us*. But 19 think not thou, who hast taken in hand to strive against God, that thou shalt escape unpunished.

But the mother was admirable above all, and 20 worthy of honourable memory: for when she saw her seven sons slain within the space of one day, she bare it with a good courage, because of the hope which she had in the Lord. Yea, she ex- 21 horted every one of them in her own language, filled with courageous spirits: and stirring up her womanish thoughts with a manly spirit, she said unto them; I cannot tell how ye came into my 22 womb; for I neither gave you breath nor life, neither was it I who formed the members of every one of you. But doubtless, the Creator of the 23 world, who formed the generation of man, and found out the beginning of all things, will also of his own mercy give you breath and life again, as

---

[e] Compare 2 Macc. ii. 13; also see below, verse 32, 33.

ye now regard not your own selves for his law's sake.

24 Now Antiochus thinking himself despised, and suspecting it to be a reproachful speech, whilst the youngest was yet alive, did not only exhort him by words, but also assured him with oaths, that he would make him both a rich and an enviable man, if he would turn from the laws of his fathers; and that also he would take him for his
25 friend, and trust him with affairs. But when the young man would in no case hearken unto him, the king called his mother, and exhorted her that she would counsel the young man to save his life.
26 And when he had exhorted her with many words, she promised him that she would persuade her
27 son. But she bowing herself towards him, laughing the cruel tyrant to scorn, spake in her country language on this manner: " O my son, have pity " upon me who bare thee nine months in my " womb, and gave thee suck three years[f], and " nourished thee, and brought thee up unto this
28 " age, and endured the troubles of education. I " beseech thee, my son, look upon the heaven and " the earth, and all which is therein, and consider " that God made them of things which were not; " and so was the race of men made likewise.
29 " Fear not this executioner; but being worthy of " thy brethren, take thy death, that I may receive
30 " thee again in mercy with thy brethren." Whilst she was yet speaking, the young man said, " Whom wait ye for? I will not obey the king's " commandment: but I will obey the command-

---

[f] Observe the long period of giving suck here stated.

"ment of the law which was given unto our fa-
"thers by Moses. And thou, who hast been the 31
"author of all mischief against the Hebrews, shalt
"not escape the hands of God. For we suffer be- 32
"cause of our sins. And though the living Lord 33
"be angry with us a little while, for our chasten-
"ing and correction, yet shall he be reconciled
"again to his servants. But thou, O godless man, 34
"and of all other most abominable, be not lifted
"up without a cause, puffing up thyself with un-
"certain hopes, lifting up thy hand against the
"servants *of God*: for thou hast not yet escaped 35
"the judgment of Almighty God, who seeth all
"things. For our brethren, who now have suf- 36
"fered a short pain, are dead under God's cove-
"nant of everlasting life: but thou, through the
"judgment of God, shalt receive just punishment
"for thy pride. But I, as my brethren, offer up 37
"my body and life for the laws of our fathers, be-
"seeching God that he would speedily be merci-
"ful unto our nation, and that thou by torments
"and plagues mayest confess that he alone is
"God; and that in me and my brethren, the 38
"wrath of the Almighty, which is justly brought
"upon all our nation, may cease."

Then the king, being in a rage, handled him 39
worse than all the rest, taking it grievously that
he had mocked. So this man died undefiled, put- 40
ting his whole trust in the Lord. Last of all, 41
after the sons, the mother died. Let this be 42
enough now to have spoken[g] concerning the idolatrous feasts, and the extreme tortures.

[g] See the circumstances related in this chapter, detailed more at large in the fourth book of Maccabees.

CHAPTER VIII.

The exploits of Judas. His victory over Nicanor.

1 THEN Judas Maccabæus, and they which were with him, went privily into the towns, and called their kinsfolks together; and taking unto them all such as continued in the Jews' re-
2 ligion, assembled about six thousand men: and they called upon the Lord, that he would look upon the people which was trodden down by all, and also pity the temple profaned by ungodly
3 men: and that he would have compassion upon the city, sore defaced, and ready to be laid even with the ground, and hear the blood which cried
4 unto him: and remember the wicked slaughter of harmless infants[a], and the blasphemies committed against his name; and that he would shew his
5 hatred against the wicked. Now when Maccabæus had his company about him, he could not be withstood by the heathen: for the wrath of
6 the Lord was turned into mercy. Therefore he came at unawares, and burnt up towns and cities; and got into his hands the most commodious places, and overcame and put to flight no small
7 number of his enemies. But specially took he advantage of the night for such privy attempts, insomuch that a fame of his manliness was spread every where.
8 So when Philip[b] saw that this man increased by little and little, and that things prospered with

Likewise a perusal of the eloquent and spirit-stirring oration of Gregory Nazianzen on this subject (Orat. XXII.) would amply repay the reader for his pains.

[a] Compare book II. ch. i. 61.
[b] See ch. v. 22.

him still more and more; he wrote unto Ptolemæus the governor[c] of Cœlosyria and Phœnice, to yield more aid to the king's affairs. And forthwith 9 chusing Nicanor the *son* of Patroclus, one of his special friends, he sent him with no fewer than twenty thousand of all nations under him, to root out the whole generation of the Jews; and with him he joined also Gorgias a captain, who in matters of war had great experience. So Nicanor un- 10 dertook to make so much money of the captive Jews, as should defray the tribute of two thousand talents, which the king was to pay[d] to the Romans. Wherefore immediately he sent to the 11 cities upon the sea-coast, inviting them to a sale of the captive Jews; and promising that they should have fourscore and ten bodies for one talent; not expecting the vengeance which was about to follow upon him from the Almighty God.

Now when word was brought unto Judas of 12 Nicanor's coming, and he had imparted unto those who were with him that the army was at hand; they which were fearful, and distrusted the justice 13 of God, fled, and conveyed themselves away. Others sold all which they had left, and withal 14 besought the Lord to deliver them, being sold by the wicked Nicanor, before they met together: and if not for their own sakes, yet for the cove- 15 nants he had made with their fathers, and for his

---

[c] That is, governor under Apollonius.

[d] Namely, according to the stipulations of a treaty which had been made between the Romans and Antiochus the Great, after the defeat of the latter. The particulars of this transaction are related by Polybius and Livy.

holy and glorious name's sake, by which they were called.

16 So Maccabæus, calling together those who remained with him, unto the number of six thousand, exhorted them not to be stricken with terror of the enemy; nor to fear the great multitude of the heathen, who came wrongfully against them,
17 but to fight manfully: and to set before their eyes the injury which they had unjustly done to the holy place, and the cruel handling of the city, whereof they made a mockery, and also the taking
18 away of the government of their forefathers. For they (*said he*) trust in their weapons[e] and boldness; but our confidence is in the Almighty God, who with a nod can cast down both them which
19 come against us, and also all the world. Moreover, he recounted unto them what helps their forefathers had found; and how they were delivered, when under Sennacherib an hundred four-
20 score and five thousand perished[f]. And he told them of the battle which they had in Babylon with the Galatians[g]; how they came but eight thousand in all to the business, with four thousand Macedonians; and that the Macedonians being perplexed, the eight thousand destroyed an hundred and twenty thousand, through the help which they had from heaven, and so received a
21 great booty. Thus when he had made them bold

---

[e] Judas here almost repeats the very words of David, at Psalm xx. 7: "Some trust "in chariots, and some in "horses: but we will re- "member the name of the "Lord our God."

[f] See the history of this transaction at 2 Kings xix. 35.

[g] That is, the Asiatic Gauls; for an account of whom see the note at book II. ch. viii. 2.

with these words, and ready to die for the laws and the country, he divided his army into four parts: and joined with himself his own brethren, 22 leaders of each band, *to wit,* Simon, and Joseph[h], and Jonathan, giving each one fifteen hundred men. Also *he appointed* Eleazar[i] to read the 23 holy book: and when he had given them this watchword, " The help of God;" himself leading the first band, he joined battle with Nicanor. And by the help of the Almighty they slew above 24 nine thousand of their enemies, and wounded and maimed the most part of Nicanor's host, and so put all to flight: and took the money of those 25 who had come to buy them, and pursued them far: but being pressed for time, they returned. 26 For it was the day before the sabbath, and therefore they did not long continue to pursue them.

So when they had gathered their armour to- 27 gether, and spoiled their enemies, they occupied themselves about the sabbath; yielding exceeding great praise and thanks to the Lord, who had preserved them unto that day, and distilled[k] upon them this the beginning of his mercy. And 28 after the sabbath, when they had given part of the spoils to the maimed, and the widows, and orphans; the residue they divided among themselves and their servants. When this was done, 29

[h] He is called Joannan at 2 Macc. ii. 2.

[i] The Greek text of this clause is rather obscure: Ἔτι δὲ καὶ Ἐλεάζαρον, παραγνοὺς τὴν ἱερὰν βίβλον, καὶ δοὺς, κ. τ. λ. which Grotius would correct to Ἐλεαζάρου παραναγνοὺς, " quum prælegisset de Eleazaro," " after reading to them concerning Eleazar;" namely, to kindle their courage by his example.

[k] See the same expression used at Deuteron. xxxii. 2, " My speech shall distil as " the dew."

and they had made a common supplication, they besought the merciful Lord to be reconciled with his servants for ever.

30 Moreover, of those who were with Timotheus and Bacchides, who fought against them, they slew above twenty thousand; and very easily won high and strong holds, and divided amongst themselves many spoils more; and made the maimed, orphans, widows, yea, and the aged also, equal 31 in spoils with themselves. And when they had gathered their armour together, they laid it all up carefully in convenient places; and the remnant of 32 the spoils they brought to Jerusalem. They slew also Philarches that wicked person, who was with Timotheus, and had annoyed the Jews many 33 ways. Furthermore, at such time as they kept the feast for the victory in their country, they burnt Callisthenes[1], who had set fire upon the holy gates, who was fled into a little house, who thus received a reward meet for his wickedness.

34 As for that wicked wretch Nicanor, who had brought a thousand merchants to buy the Jews; 35 he was, through the help of the Lord, brought down by them of whom he made least account; and putting off his glorious apparel, and discharging his company, he came like a fugitive servant through the midland unto Antioch, having very great misadventure, for that his host was 36 destroyed. Thus he, who took upon him to make good to the Romans their tribute, by means of the captives in Jerusalem, told abroad, that the Jews had God to fight for them; and therefore

---

[1] The Vatican manuscript adds here, "and certain others."

they could not be hurt, because they followed the laws which he had appointed them.

CHAPTER IX.

Antiochus' sickness and death.

ABOUT that time came Antiochus in disorder out of the country of Persia. For he had entered the *city* called Persepolis[a], and went about to rob the temple, and to hold the city; whereupon the multitude advancing betook themselves to a resistance by arms: and so it happened that Antiochus, being put to flight by the inhabitants, made a dishonourable retreat.

Now while he was at Ecbatana[b], news was brought him of what had happened unto Nicanor and Timotheus. Then swelling with anger, he thought to avenge upon the Jews the disgrace done unto him by those who made him flee. Therefore commanded he his charioteer to drive without ceasing, and to dispatch the journey, the judgment of God now following him. For he had spoken proudly in this sort: " I will make " Jerusalem a common buryingplace[c] of the Jews,

---

[a] The chief city of the Persian empire; for descriptions of which see Q. Curtius and Diodorus Siculus. But compare 2 Macc. vi. 1; where this occurrence is said to have taken place in Elymais.

[b] A renowned city, the ancient capital of Media. Its origin and structure are detailed by Herodotus, I. 98.

[c] Gr. Πολυάνδριον Ἰουδαίων Ἱεροσόλυμα ποιήσω. That this threat contained within it a degree of insult as well as injury, we perceive on observing from Greek classic authors that the word πολυάνδριον conveyed the idea of any thing rather than an *honourable* place of sepulture. Ælian relates of the Lacedæmonian women, that they examined the bodies of their sons who had fallen in battle; and if the majority of their wounds were in front, proving that they had fought well and died nobly, they were delighted, and with pride τοὺς

5 "when I come thither." But the all-seeing Lord, the God of Israel, smote him with an incurable and invisible plague; for as soon as he had spoken these words, a pain of the bowels, which was remediless, came upon him, and sore torments of
6 the inner parts; and that most justly: for he had tormented other men's bowels with many and
7 strange torments. Howbeit he nothing at all ceased from his bragging, but still was filled with pride, breathing out fire in his rage against the Jews, and commanding to hasten the journey: but it came to pass that he fell down from his chariot, which was borne along violently; so that having a sore fall, all the members of his body were dislocated.
8 And thus he, who a little afore thought he might command the waves of the sea, (so proud was he beyond the condition of man,) and weigh the high mountains in a balance, was now cast on the ground, and carried in a horse-litter, shewing
9 forth unto all the manifest power of God. So that the worms rose up out of the body of this wicked man; and whiles he lived in pains and torments, his flesh fell away, and the filthiness of his
10 smell was noisome to all his army. And the man, who thought a little afore he could reach to the stars of heaven, no man could endure to carry, for his intolerable stink.

παῖδας εἰς τὰς πατρῴας ἔφερον τάφους. But if the wounds were in the back, from which a suspicion of their courage might arise, ἐνταῦθα αἰδούμεναι, καὶ θρηνοῦσαι, καὶ ὡς ἔνι μάλιστα λαθεῖν σπεύδουσαι, ἀπηλλάττοντο, καταλιποῦσαι τοὺς νεκροὺς ἐν τῷ πολυανδρίῳ θάψαι. Read the note of Perizonius on the passage; who appositely quotes Jeremiah xxvi. 23, where king Jehoiakim is related to have slain Uriah, and to have cast his dead body *into the graves of the common people.*

Here therefore, being plagued, he began to 11
leave off his great pride; and to come to the knowledge *of himself* by the scourge of God, his pain
increasing every moment. And when he himself 12
could not abide his own smell, he said these
words; "It is meet to be subject unto God, and
" that a man who is mortal should not proudly
" think of himself as if he were God." This wicked 13
person vowed also unto the Lord, (who now no
more would have mercy upon him,) saying thus;
That the holy city (to the which he was going in 14
haste, to lay it even with the ground, and to make
it a common buryingplace) he would set at
liberty. And as touching the Jews, whom he 15
had judged not worthy to be so much as buried,
but to be cast out with their children, to be devoured by the fowls and wild beasts; he would
make them all equals to the citizens of Athens [d].
And the holy temple, which before he had spoiled, 16
he would garnish with goodly gifts; and restore
all the holy vessels, with many more; and out of
his own revenue defray the charges belonging to
the sacrifices: yea, and that also he would become 17
a Jew himself, and go through every place which
was inhabited, declaring the power of God. But 18
for all this his pains would not cease: for the just
judgment of God was come upon him: therefore
despairing of his health, he wrote unto the Jews
the letters underwritten, bearing the form of a
supplication, and containing as follows:

[d] Probably here (as before, at ch. vi. 1.) is a misreading, of *Athens* for *Antioch*: the words being abbreviated might have been mistaken by the copyist: the freedom of *Antioch* we have seen conferred upon the Jews; viz. at ch. iv. 9, and vi. 1: where see the note.

19 "Antiochus, king and governor, to the good
"Jews his citizens, wisheth much joy, health, and
20 "prosperity. If ye and your children fare well,
"and your affairs be to your contentment, I give
"very great thanks to God, having my hope in
21 "heaven. As for me, I was sick, or else I would
"have remembered kindly your honour and good-
"will. Returning out of Persia, and being taken
"with a grievous disease, I thought it necessary to
22 "care for the common safety of all: not despairing
"of myself, but having great hope to escape this
23 "sickness. But considering that even my father,
"at what time he led an army into the high
24 "countries, appointed a successor; to the end that
"if any thing fell out contrary to expectation, or if
"any tidings were brought which were grievous,
"they of the land, knowing to whom the public
25 "affairs were left, might not be troubled. And
"moreover, considering how that the princes who
"are borderers and neighbours unto my kingdom,
"wait for opportunities, and expect what shall be
"the event; I have appointed my son Antiochus
"king, whom I often committed and commended
"unto many of you, when I went up into the
"high provinces; to whom I have written as
26 "followeth: therefore I pray and request you
"to remember the benefits which I have done
"unto you generally, and in special; and that
"every man will be still faithful to me and my
27 "son. For I am persuaded that he, following
"my intentions, will behave towards you equitably
"and graciously."

28 Thus the murderer and blasphemer, having suffered most grievously, as he entreated other

men, so died he a miserable death in a strange country in the mountains. And Philip, who was brought up with him, carried away his body; who also fearing the son of Antiochus, betook himself into Egypt to Ptolemæus Philometor. 29

CHAPTER X.

Judas purifies the temple. His valiant acts.

Now Maccabæus and his company, the Lord guiding them, recovered the temple and the city; but the altars which the heathen had built in the open street, and also the chapels, they pulled down. And having cleansed the temple, they made another altar; and striking stones they took fire out of them, and offered a sacrifice after two years[a], and set forth incense, and lights, and shew-bread. When that was done, they fell flat down, and besought the Lord that they might come no more into such troubles; but if they sinned any more against him, that he himself would chasten[b] them with mercy; and that they might not be delivered unto the blasphemous and barbarous nations. Now upon the same day that the temple had been profaned by strangers, it happened that on the same day the purification of it took place; even the five and twentieth day of the same month, which is Casleu. And they kept eight days with gladness, as in the feast of 1 2 3 4 5 6

B.C. 165.

---

[a] Surely we ought to read *three* instead of *two;* for so the history requires. Compare 2 Macc. iv. 52, 53; and Josephus. Grotius sanctions this correction; and he is supported by one Greek MS.

[b] Compare David's petition to the same effect, after he had been betrayed into the folly of numbering Israel and Judah, as recorded at 2 Samuel xxiv. 14. See also 1 Macc. ii. 17: vi. 10.

the tabernacles; remembering that not long afore they had holden[c] the feast of the tabernacles, when as they wandered in the mountains and dens like 7 wild beasts. Therefore they bare branches, and fair boughs, and palms also; and sang psalms unto Him who had given them good success in cleansing 8 his place. They ordained also, by a common statute and decree, That every year those days should be kept by the whole nation of the Jews. 9 And this was the end of Antiochus called Epiphanes.

10 But now will we declare the acts of Antiochus Eupator, who was the son of this wicked man; collecting briefly the calamities of the 11 wars. For when he was come to the crown, he set one Lysias over the affairs of his realm; and *appointed him* chief governor of Cœlosyria and 12 Phœnice. For Ptolemæus, who was called Macron[d], chusing rather to do justice unto the Jews, for the wrong which had been done unto them, 13 endeavoured to continue peace with them. Whereupon being accused by *the king's* friends before Eupator, and called traitor every where, because he had left Cyprus, which Philometor had committed unto him, and departed to Antiochus Epiphanes; and seeing that he was in no honourable place[e], he was so discouraged, that he poisoned himself, and died.

B.C. 164.

[c] The sense is rather, that they had passed the day of that feast in wandering like beasts over the mountains; instead of being able to keep it with due solemnity, and in peace.

[d] The same who is mentioned above, at ch. iv. 45; and viii. 8; as being the son of Dorymenes.

[e] Gr. μητ' εὐγενῆ τὴν ἐξουσίαν ἔχων.

But when Gorgias was made governor of the strong holds, he hired soldiers, and nourished war continually with the Jews: and therewithal the Idumæans, having gotten into their hands the most commodious fortresses, kept the Jews occupied; and receiving those who were banished from Jerusalem, they went about to nourish war. Then they which were with Maccabæus made supplication, and besought God that he would be their helper; and so they ran with violence upon the strong holds[f] of the Idumæans: and assaulting them valiantly, they won the holds; and kept off all who fought upon the wall, and slew all who fell into their hands, and killed no fewer than twenty thousand. And because certain (no fewer than nine thousand) were fled together into two very strong castles, having all manner of things convenient to *sustain* the siege; Maccabæus left Simon and Joseph, and Zacchæus also, and them which were with him, who were enough to besiege them; and departed himself unto those places which more needed his help. Now Simon and his company being led with covetousness, were persuaded for money, (through certain of those who were in the castle,) and took seventy thousand drachms, and let some of them escape. But when it was told Maccabæus what was done, he called the governors of the people together; and accused those men, that they had sold their brethren for money, and set their enemies free to fight against them. So he slew those who were found traitors, and immediately took the two castles. And

---

[f] Namely Acrabattine; as related at 2 Macc. v. 3.

having good success with his weapons in all things he took in hand, he slew in the two strong holds more than twenty thousand.

24 Now Timotheus, whom the Jews had overcome[g] before; when he had gathered a great multitude of foreign forces, and horses out of Asia not a few, came as though he would take Judæa by force of
25 arms. But when he drew near, Maccabæus and his company turned themselves to pray unto God, and sprinkled earth upon their heads, and girded
26 their loins with sackcloth; and fell down at the foot of the altar, and besought him to be merciful to them, and to be an enemy to their enemies, and an adversary to their adversaries, as the law de-
27 clareth[h]. So after the prayer, they took their weapons, and went on further from the city: and when they drew near to their enemies, they kept
28 by themselves. Now the sun being newly risen, they joined both together; the one part having together with their virtue their refuge also unto the Lord, for a pledge of success and victory: the other side making their courage leader of their
29 battle. But when the battle waxed strong, there appeared unto the enemies from heaven five comely men upon horses, with bridles of gold;
30 and two of them led the Jews, and took Maccabæus betwixt them, and covered him on every side with their complete armour, and kept him safe; but shot arrows and lightnings against the enemies: so that being confounded with blindness,

[g] Compare 2 Macc. v. 6, 7.
[h] Viz. at Deut. xxviii. 7; "The Lord shall cause thine "enemies that rise up against "thee to be smitten before "thy face: they shall come "out against thee one way, "and flee before thee seven "ways."

and filled with confusion, they were cut to pieces. And there were slain *of footmen* twenty thousand 31 and five hundred, and six hundred horsemen.

As for Timotheus himself, he fled into the hold 32 called Gazara[i], a very strong garrison, of which Chæreas was governor. But Maccabæus and his 33 company laid siege against the fortress courageously four days. And they which were within, 34 trusting to the strength of the place, blasphemed exceedingly, and uttered wicked words. Nevertheless, upon the fifth day early twenty young 35 men of Maccabæus' company, inflamed with anger because of the blasphemies, assaulted the wall manfully, and with a fierce courage killed all whom they met withal. Others likewise ascending 36 after them, whiles they were busied with them which were within, burnt the towers, and kindling fires, burnt the blasphemers alive; and others broke open the gates, and having received in the rest of the army, took the city: and killed Timo- 37 theus, who was hid in a certain pit, and Chæreas his brother, with Apollophanes. When this was 38 done, they praised the Lord with psalms and thanksgiving, who had done so great things for Israel, and given them the victory.

CHAPTER XI.

The acts of Lysias. Letters of Antiochus and of the Romans.

NOT long after this, Lysias the king's[a] protec- 1 tor and cousin, who also managed the affairs, took sore displeasure for the things which were done.

[i] See 2 Macc. v. 8; vii. 45.
[a] Namely, young Antiochus Eupator.

2 And when he had gathered about fourscore thousand *men*, with all the horsemen, he came against the Jews, thinking to make the city an habitation
3 for the Gentiles; and to make a gain of the temple, as of the other chapels of the heathen, and to
4 set the high-priesthood to sale every year: not at all considering the power of God, but puffed up with his ten thousands of footmen, and his thousands of horsemen, and his fourscore elephants.
5 So he came to Judæa, and drew near to Bethsura, which was a strong town, but distant from Jerusalem about five furlongs; and he laid sore siege
6 unto it. Now when Maccabæus and his company heard that he besieged the holds, they and all the people with lamentation and tears besought the Lord, that he would send a good angel to deliver
7 Israel. Then Maccabæus himself first of all took up weapons, exhorting the others that they would jeopard themselves together with him to help their brethren: so they went forth together with
8 a willing mind. And as they were at Jerusalem, there appeared going before them on horseback, one in white clothing, shaking a panoply of gold.
9 Then they praised the merciful God, all together, and took heart; insomuch that they were ready, not only to fight with men, but with most cruel
10 beasts, and to pierce through walls of iron. Thus they marched forward in their array, having a helper from heaven: for the Lord was merciful
11 unto them. And giving a charge upon their enemies like lions, they slew eleven thousand *footmen*, and sixteen hundred horsemen, and put all
12 the others to flight. The greater part of them

also being wounded escaped naked[b]; and Lysias himself fled away shamefully, and so escaped. Who, as he was a man of understanding, casting with himself what loss he had had; and considering that the Hebrews could not be overcome, because the Almighty God helped them; he sent unto them, and persuaded them to agree to all reasonable *conditions*, and *promised* that he would persuade the king that he must needs be a friend unto them. Then Maccabæus consented to all which Lysias desired, being careful of the common good; and whatsoever Maccabæus wrote unto Lysias concerning the Jews, the king granted it.

For there were letters written unto the Jews from Lysias to this effect: " Lysias unto the peo-
" ple of the Jews, *sendeth* greeting: John and
" Absalom, who were sent from you, delivered
" me the petition subscribed, and made the re-
" quest for the performance of the contents there-
" of. Therefore what things soever were meet to
" be reported to the king, I have declared them,
" and he hath granted as much as might be. If
" then ye will keep yourselves loyal to the state,
" hereafter also will I endeavour to be a means of
" your good. But of the particulars I have given
" order, both to these, and the others who came
" from me, to commune with you. Fare ye well.
" The hundred and eight and fortieth year, the
" four and twentieth day of *the month* Dioscorin-
" thius[c]."

---

[b] Gr. γυμνοὶ, that is, "without their armour:" having thrown away their weapons, for the greater facility of escape.

[c] No such name of a month

B.C. 164.   CHAP. XI.   195

22 Now the king's letters contained these words: " King Antiochus unto his brother Lysias, *sendeth*
23 " greeting: Since our father is translated unto the " gods, our will is, that they which are in our " realm live quietly, that every one may attend
24 " upon his own affairs. We understand also, that " the Jews did not agree to our father's bringing " them to the Grecian customs, but had rather " keep their own manner of living: for the which " cause they require that their own laws may be
25 " allowed to them. Desiring therefore that this " nation also shall be in rest, we have determined " to restore them their temple, that they may live " according to the customs of their forefathers.
26 " Thou shalt do well therefore to send unto them, " and grant them peace[d]; that when they are cer- " tified of our mind, they may be of good com- " fort, and ever go cheerfully about their own " affairs."
27 And the letter of the king unto the nation of the Jews was after this manner: " King Anti- " ochus *sendeth* greeting unto the council, and the
28 " rest of the Jews: If ye fare well, we have our
29 " desire; we are also in good health. Menelaus " declared unto us, that your desire was to return
30 " home, and to follow your own business: where-

---

is known. The Latin version reads *Dioscorus*. Grotius believes that the reading is faulty, and ought to be Δίου, (one of the Macedonian months,) which the copyist may have mistaken for an abbreviated word, and supplied at his own discretion. Archbishop Ussher believes it to be an intercalary month, the same as Adar-Nisan, or Dyster-Xanthicus, which occurs in Esther iii. 7, in a Greek MS. now in the British Museum, (MS. Holmes, N°. 93.)

[d] The Greek phrase here, and in many following passages, is, δοὺς δεξιάς.

o 2

"fore they which will depart shall have safe con-
"duct, with security, till the thirtieth day of Xan-
"thicus. And the Jews shall use their own kind 31
"of meats, and laws, as before; and none of them
"any manner of ways shall be molested for things
"ignorantly done. I have sent also Menelaus, 32
"that he may comfort you. Fare ye well. In 33
"the hundred forty and eighth year, and in the
"fifteenth day of *the month* Xanthicus."

The Romans also sent unto them a letter con- 34
taining these words: "Quintus Memmius, and
"Titus Manlius, ambassadors of the Romans, *send*
"greeting unto the people of the Jews: Whatso- 35
"ever Lysias the king's cousin hath granted,
"therewith we also are well pleased. But touch- 36
"ing such things as he judged to be referred to
"the king, after ye have advised thereof, send
"one forthwith, that we may declare as it is con-
"venient for you: for we are now going to An-
"tioch. Therefore send some with speed, that 37
"we may know what is your mind. Farewell. 38
"This hundred and eight and fortieth year, the
"fifteenth day of *the month* Xanthicus [f]."

CHAPTER XII.

Judas defeats Timotheus and Gorgias. He takes many cities.

WHEN these covenants were made, Lysias went 1
unto the king, and the Jews were about their hus-
bandry. But of the governors of several places, 2

---

[e] Answering to our April.

[f] The abridgment of Jason's history has been thought by some to end with this chapter; and the remainder of the book to have been composed from other sources.

Timotheus[a], and Apollonius the *son* of Gennæus, also Hieronymus, and Demophon, and besides them Nicanor the governor of Cyprus, would not suffer them to be quiet, and live in peace.

3 The men of Joppe also did such an ungodly deed as this: they prayed the Jews who dwelt among them to go with their wives and children into the boats which they had prepared, as though 4 they had meant them no hurt. Who accepted of it according to the common decree of the city, as being desirous to live in peace, and suspecting nothing: but when they were gone forth into the deep, they drowned[b] no less than two hundred of them.

5 When Judas heard of this cruelty done unto his countrymen, he commanded those who were with 6 him *to make them ready*. And calling upon God the righteous Judge, he came against those murderers of his brethren; and burnt the haven by night, and set the boats on fire, and those who 7 fled thither he slew. But when the town was shut up, he retreated, with a determination to come again and root out the whole state and peo- 8 ple of Joppe. But when he heard that the Jamnites[c] were minded to do in like manner unto the 9 Jews who dwelt among them; he came upon the Jamnites also by night, and set fire on the haven, and the navy; so that the light of the fire was

---

[a] Compare 2 Macc. v. 6, 37; 3 Macc. viii. 30, 32; x. 37.

[b] Josephus relates a similar act of cruelty practised by the Galilæans against those who were favourers of Herod. (Antiq. XIV. 27.)

[c] Jamnia was another seaport town, near Joppe. See book II. ch. iv. 15, and the note there.

seen at Jerusalem, two hundred and forty furlongs off.

Now when they were gone from thence nine furlongs, in their journey towards Timotheus, no fewer than five thousand *men on foot*, and five hundred horsemen of the Arabians set upon him. Whereupon there was a very sore battle; but Judas' side, by the help of God, got the victory; so that the Nomades[d] of Arabia being overcome, besought Judas for peace, promising both to give him cattle, and to assist him in other matters. Then Judas, thinking indeed that they would be profitable in many things, granted them peace: and having received assurance of this, they departed to their tents.

He went also about to take a certain city, which was strongly secured by bridges, and fenced about with walls, and inhabited by people of divers countries; and the name of it was Caspis[e]. But they which were within it, put such trust in the strength of the walls and provision of victuals, that they behaved themselves rudely towards Judas and his company; railing also and blaspheming, and uttering such words as were not to be spoken. Wherefore Judas with his company, calling upon the great Lord of the world, (who without any rams or engines of war, did cast

---

[d] "Wanderers," so called from their roving unsettled mode of life; their custom being not to reside in towns or in any fixed spot, but to move from place to place at pleasure, according to the convenience of pasturage for their cattle. From this word *Nomades*, the Latin authors afterwards called them *Numidæ*.

[e] Or Casphon, as it is called at 2 Macc. v. 36: probably the place designated is Heshbon.

down Jericho[f] in the time of Joshua,) gave a
16 fierce assault against the walls; and took the city by the will of God, and made unspeakable slaughters; insomuch that a lake two furlongs broad, near adjoining thereunto, being filled full, appeared to be running with blood.
17 Then departed they from thence seven hundred and fifty furlongs, and came to Characa unto
18 the Jews who are called Tubieni[g]. But as for Timotheus, they found him not in the places: for before he had dispatched any thing, he departed from thence, having left a very strong garrison in
19 a certain hold. Howbeit, Dositheus and Sosipater, who were of Maccabæus's captains, went forth, and slew those whom Timotheus had left in the fortress, above ten thousand men.
20 And Maccabæus ranged his army by bands, and set them over the bands; and went against Timotheus, who had about him an hundred and twenty thousand men of foot, and two thousand and five
21 hundred horsemen. Now when Timotheus had knowledge of Judas' coming, he sent the women and children, and the other baggage, unto a fortress called Carnion[h]; (for the post was hard to besiege, and uneasy to come unto, by reason of the
22 straitness of all the places;) but when Judas his first band came in sight, the enemies (being smitten with fear and terror, through the appearing of Him who seeth all things) fled amain; one running this way, another that way, so as that they were often hurt by their own men, and wounded with
23 the points of their own swords. Judas also was

[f] Compare Joshua vi. 20.
[g] See at 2 Macc. v. 13.
[h] Or Carnaim. Compare 2 Macc. v. 43.

very earnest in pursuing them, killing those wicked wretches, of whom he slew about thirty thousand men. Moreover, Timotheus himself fell into the hands of Dositheus and Sosipater, whom he besought with much craft to let him go with his life; because he had many of the Jews' parents, and the brethren of some of them, who, if they put him to death, should not be regarded. So when he had confirmed the agreement[i] with many words, that he would restore these without hurt, they let him go, for the saving of their brethren.

Then Maccabæus marched forth to Carnion, and to the temple of Atargatis[k]; and there he slew five and twenty thousand persons. And after he had put to flight and destroyed them, Judas removed the host towards Ephron[l], a strong city, wherein Lysias abode and a great multitude of divers nations, and the strong young men kept the walls, and defended them mightily: wherein also was great provision of engines and darts.

---

[i] Gr. ὁρισμόν: the same word occurs at Daniel vi. 10, and 12; where it is translated, *a writing* or *decree*.

[k] This deity, called also Dercetis, or Derceto, by the Greeks, was worshipped extensively throughout Phœnicia and Babylonia. Lucian describes her image as being half woman half fish, like Dagon of the Philistines; and indeed she has been considered to be the same deity (for in these the sexes were holden changeable at pleasure). Diodorus Siculus mentions that a statue of it at Ascalon had the *face* only of a woman, all the rest of the body, &c. being like a fish. The name is said to signify, "a mag-"nificent fish." See Selden, de Diis Syris. Dercetis and her worship is mentioned by Ovid, Metamorphos. IV. 45. And it is noticed in the Fragments to Calmet, (from the Asiatic Researches, vol. IV.) that the name Antargati occurs as the Sanskrit appellation of one of the Chaldæan deities.

[l] Compare 2 Macc. v. 46.

28 But when Judas and his company had called upon almighty God, (who with his power breaketh the strength of his enemies,) they won the city, and slew twenty and five thousand of them which were within.

29 From thence they departed to Scythopolis[m], which lieth six hundred furlongs from Jerusalem.

30 But when the Jews who dwelt there had testified that the Scythopolitans dwelt lovingly with them, and entreated them kindly in the time of their ad-

31 versity; they gave them thanks, desiring them to be friendly still unto them: and so they came to Jerusalem, the feast of the weeks approaching.

32 And after the *feast* called Pentecost, they went[n] forth against Gorgias the governor of Idumæa[o];

33 who came out with three thousand men of foot,

34 and four hundred horsemen. And it happened that in their fighting together, a few of the Jews

35 were slain. At which time Dositheus, one of Bacenor's company, who was on horseback, and a strong man, pressed close upon Gorgias, and taking hold of his coat, drew him by force; and when he would have taken that cursed man alive, a horseman of Thracia coming upon him, smote off his shoulder[p], so that Gorgias escaped

36 unto Marisa[q]. Now when Gorgias[r] and his men

[m] The same which at 2 Macc. v. 52, is called Bethsan. See the note there.

[n] Namely, Joseph the son of Zacharias, and Azarias, whom Judas had left in charge of the people, while he himself was gone on a military expedition. Compare 2 Macc. v. 18.

[o] Beyond doubt the reading is faulty, and ought to be *Jamnia*, as at 2 Macc. v. 58. Josephus warrants this correction.

[p] More properly, "his arm at the shoulder."

[q] A town or fortress of Judah, near to Eleutheropolis.

[r] There is here a remarkable variety among the MSS.

had fought long, and were weary; Judas called upon the Lord, that he would shew himself to be their helper, and leader of the battle. And with 37 that he began in his own language, and sung psalms with a loud voice; and rushing unawares upon Gorgias and his men, he put them to flight. So Judas gathered his host, and came into the 38 city Odollam^s. And when the seventh day came, they purified themselves, (as the custom was,) and kept the sabbath in the same place.

And upon the day following, as the use had 39 been^t, Judas and his company came to take up the bodies of them which were slain, and to bury them with their kinsmen in their fathers' graves. Now under the coats of every one who was slain, 40 they found things^u consecrated to the idols of the Jamnites, which are forbidden^x the Jews by the law. Then every man saw that this was the cause wherefore they were slain. All men there- 41 fore praising the Lord the righteous Judge, who had opened the things that were hid, betook them- 42 selves unto prayer; and besought him, that the sin committed might wholly be put out of remembrance. Besides, that noble Judas exhorted the people to keep themselves from sin; forsomuch as they saw before their eyes the things which came

---

some reading Ἐσδριν, Ἐσραν, Ἐξρει, or Ἐσδρην: which Grotius judges ought to be Ἐφρὼν, the city mentioned at ver. 27. Archbishop Ussher takes Esdris for one of Judas' captains.

^s Query whether this be the same as Adullam, mentioned at Genesis xxxviii. 12.?

^t The Greek text varies, between καθ ὃν τρόπον, and καθ ὃν χρόνον, τὸ τῆς χρείας ἐγεγόνει. The latter would signify " when all which was " necessary had been done."

^u See the same offence and its punishment recorded at Joshua vii. 4—26.

^x See Deuteron. vii. 5.

to pass, for the sins of those who were slain.
43 And when he had made a gathering throughout the company ⁷ to the sum of two thousand ᶻ drachms of silver, he sent it to Jerusalem to offer a sin-offering, doing therein very well, and properly, in that he was mindful of the resurrection;
44 (for if he had not hoped that they which were slain should have risen again, it had been superfluous
45 and vain to pray for the dead;) and also *in that* he perceived that there was great favour laid up for those who died godly. (It was an holy and good thought.) Whereupon he made an expiation for the dead, that they might be delivered from sin.

CHAPTER XIII.

The battles of Judas with Antiochus Eupator. Peace made.

1 IN the hundred forty and ninth year it was told Judas that Antiochus Eupator was coming with a great power into Judæa:
2 and with him Lysias his protector and ruler of his affairs, having each of them a Grecian power, of footmen an hundred and ten thousand, and horsemen five thousand and three hundred, and elephants two and twenty, and three hundred chariots armed with scythes.
3 Menelaus also joined himself with them, and with great dissimulation encouraged Antiochus; not for the safeguard of his country, but because

---

ʸ Gr. κατ' ἀνδρολογίαν, "man by man."

Verses 43—45.] It deserves to be noticed, that no mention of any such offering or idea, as that which is inserted here, is found either in the Second Book of Maccabees, or in the Fifth, although the same portion of the history is there treated of.

ᶻ Three Greek manuscripts read "three thousand."

he thought to have been made governor. But 4 the King of kings moved Antiochus' mind against this wicked wretch; and when Lysias informed the king that this man was the cause of all mischief, the king commanded to bring him unto Berœa, and to put him to death, as the manner is in that place. Now there is in that place a tower 5 of fifty cubits high, full of ashes; and it had a round instrument[a], which on every side hanged down into the ashes. And whosoever was con- 6 demned of sacrilege, or had committed any other grievous crime, there did all men thrust him unto death. Such a death it happened that wicked 7 Menelaus to die, not having so much as burial in the earth; and that most justly: for insomuch as 8 he had committed many sins about the altar, whose fire and ashes were holy, he received his death in ashes.

Now the king came with a barbarous and 9 haughty mind, to do far worse to the Jews than had been done in his father's time. Which things 10 when Judas perceived, he commanded the multitude to call upon the Lord night and day; that if ever at any other time, he would now also help

[a] Gr. ὄργανον περιφερές. The passage is rather obscure: but it seems that the tower contained a *wheel* in contact with the ashes, on which the culprit was tied, and then whirled round till he was suffocated. See the word ὄργανον again used to signify a wheel, in 4 Macc. ix. 19, 20. A similar mode of destruction is mentioned by Valerius Maximus, (IX. 2. sect. 6.) who states that Darius Ochus of Persia, wishing to get rid of some obnoxious chiefs, devised a novel mode of punishment, to save himself from violating the letter of a previous oath: "Septum altis pa-
" rietibus locum cinere com-
" plevit, suppositoque tigno
" prominente, benigne cibo et
" potione exceptos in eo col-
" locabat; e quo somno sopiti
" in illam insidiosam conge-
" riem decidebant."

them, being at the point to be deprived of their law, of their country, and of the holy temple: 11 and that he would not suffer the people, which lately had been refreshed a little, to become again 12 subject to the blasphemous nations. So when they had all done this together, and besought the merciful Lord with weeping and fasting and lying flat upon the ground three days long; Judas, having exhorted them, commanded they should be in 13 readiness. And being apart with the elders, he determined, before the king's host should enter into Judæa, and get possession of the city, to go forth, and try the matter *in fight*, by the help of the 14 Lord. So when he had committed *all* to the Creator of the world, and exhorted his soldiers to fight manfully, even unto death, for the laws, the temple, the city, the country, and the commonwealth, he 15 camped by Modin. And having given the watchword to them that were about him, " Victory is " of God;" with the most valiant and choice young men, he attacked the king's tent by night, and slew in the camp about four thousand men, and the chiefest of the elephants, with all who 16 were upon him [b]. And at last they filled the camp with fear and tumult, and departed with good 17 success. This was done in the break of the day, because the protection of the Lord did help him.

18 Now when the king had taken a taste of the

[b] There is some obscurity in the Greek text, καὶ τὸν πρωτεύοντα τῶν ἐλεφάντων σὺν τῷ κατ' οἰκίαν ὄχλῳ συνέθηκε. [There is a various reading, ὄντι for ὄχλῳ.] Grotius translates it, " and he added, (to the slain,) " him who was director of " the Elephants, with all his " retinue." Bochart understands the elephant himself, not his governor, to be spoken of ; and corrects the reading to τὸν πρωτεύοντα τῶν ἐλεφάντων ὃς σὺν τῷ κατ' οἰκίαν ὄχλῳ συνέθηκε.

manliness of the Jews, he went about to take the holds by policy; and marched towards Bethsura, 19 which was a strong garrison of the Jews: but he was put to flight, failed, and lost some of his men: and Judas conveyed unto them which were 20 in it such things as were necessary. But Rho- 21 docus, who was in the Jews' host, disclosed the secrets to the enemies; therefore he was sought out, and taken, and put in prison. The king 22 treated with them in Bethsura the second time, gave his hand, took theirs, departed, fought with Judas and his men, was overcome; heard that 23 Philip, who was left over the affairs in Antioch, had shaken off his allegiance; was confounded *at it*, entreated the Jews, submitted himself, and sware to all just conditions, agreed with them, and offered sacrifice, honoured the temple, and dealt kindly with the place; and accepted well of 24 Maccabæus, made him principal governor from Ptolemais unto the Gerrhenians[c]; came to Ptole- 25 mais: the people there were grieved by reason of the covenants; for they stormed, because they wished to make their covenants void. Lysias 26 went up to the judgment-seat, said as much as could be in defence of the cause, persuaded, pacified, made them well-affected, returned to Antioch. Thus it went touching the king's coming and departing.

CHAPTER XIV[a].

The attempts of Nicanor against the Jews.

AFTER three years[b] was Judas with his com- 1

[c] Who dwelt on the borders of Egypt.
[a] Compare this chapter with 2 Macc. vii.
[b] Namely, from the commencement of Antiochus' reign.

pany informed that Demetrius the *son* of Seleucus, having entered by the haven of Tripolis 2 with a great power and navy, had gained possession of the country, and killed Antiochus, and Lysias his protector.

3 Now one Alcimus, who had been high priest, and had defiled himself wilfully in the times of their mingling[c] *with the Gentiles*, perceiving that by no means he could save himself, nor have any 4 more access to the holy altar; came to king Demetrius in the hundred and one and fiftieth year, presenting unto him a crown of gold, and a palm, and also of the golden boughs which were used solemnly in the temple: and so that day he held 5 his peace. Howbeit, having gotten opportunity to further his foolish enterprise, *and* being called into council by Demetrius, and asked how the Jews stood affected, and what they intended, he 6 answered thereunto; "Those of the Jews who are " called Assidæans[d], (whose captain is Judas Mac-" cabæus,) nourish war, and are seditious, and will 7 " not let the realm be in quietness. Wherefore I, " being deprived of mine ancestors' honour, (I " mean the high-priesthood,) am now come hi-8 " ther: first verily for the unfeigned care I have " of things pertaining to the king; and secondly, " even for that I intend the good of mine own " countrymen: for all our nation is in no small " misery, through the unadvised dealing of them 9 " aforesaid. Wherefore, O king, seeing thou

[c] Gr. ἐπιμιξίας: but many MSS. read ἀμιξίας, as at verse 38 of this chapter. The two readings and passages deserve to be compared, as doubtless one and the same thing is intended in both.

[d] Concerning these men, see 2 Macc. ii. 42. and vii. 13.

"knowest all these things, be careful for the country and our nation, which is pressed[e] on every side, according to the affable clemency which thou readily shewest unto all. For as long as Judas liveth, it is not possible that the state should be quiet."

This was no sooner spoken by him, but the rest of his friends, being maliciously set against Judas, did more incense Demetrius. And forthwith calling Nicanor, who had been master of the elephants, and making him governor over Judæa, he sent him forth; commanding him to slay Judas, and to scatter them which were with him, and to make Alcimus high priest of the most high temple. Then the heathen who had fled out of Judæa from Judas, came to Nicanor by flocks, thinking the harm and calamities of the Jews would be their welfare. Now when *the Jews* heard of Nicanor's coming, and the intended invasion of the heathen, they cast earth upon their heads, and made supplication to him who had established his people for ever, and who always helpeth his own portion with manifestation of his presence. So at the commandment of the captain they removed straightways from thence, and came near unto them, at the town of Dessau[f].

Now Simon, Judas' brother, had joined battle with Nicanor, but was somewhat discomfited through the sudden silence[g] of his enemies.

---

[e] Gr. τοῦ περιϊσταμένου γένους ἡμῶν, "surrounded and pressed on all sides." The verb is used in this passive sense by Polybius.

[f] Its precise situation is not known.

[g] Gr. ἀφασίαν. This expression is used by Polybius: still the sense is obscure.

18 Nevertheless, Nicanor hearing of the manliness of Judas and his men, and the courageousness which they had to fight for their country, declined to try
19 the matter by the sword. Wherefore he sent Posidonius, and Theodotus, and Mattathias, to make
20 peace. So when they had taken long advisement thereupon, and the captain had made the multitude acquainted therewith, and it appeared that they were all of one mind, they consented to the
21 covenant; and appointed a day to meet in together by themselves: and *when* the day came, and
22 particular seats were set for each of them; Judas placed armed men, ready in convenient places, lest some treachery should be suddenly practised by the enemies: so they held a peaceable conference.
23 Now Nicanor abode in Jerusalem, and did no hurt, but sent away the people which had been
24 gathered together in flocks. And he had Judas ever in his presence; *for* he was affectionately in-
25 clined towards him. He prayed him also to take a wife, and to beget children: so he married, was
26 quiet, and took part [h] of this social life. But Alcimus perceiving the love which was betwixt them, and considering the covenants which were made, took himself away; and came to Demetrius, and told him that Nicanor was not well affected

Grotius would meet the difficulty by reading ἐφόδειαν, and Biel by ἄφιξιν: but the MSS. give no countenance to either emendation.

[h] Gr. ἐκοινώνησεν βίου, "he "entered upon domestic life." In the first book of Maccabees, iv. 6, the phrase βίου κοινωνία occurs, denoting " a " married life." Most of the old translators interpret the passage as meaning that Judas and Nicanor thenceforward *lived together*.

towards the state; for that he had ordained Judas, a traitor to his realm, to be his successor. Then the king being in a rage, and provoked 27 with the accusations of the most wicked man, wrote to Nicanor, signifying that he was much displeased with the covenants, and commanding him that he should send Maccabæus prisoner in all haste unto Antioch.

When this came to Nicanor's hearing, he was 28 much confounded in himself, and took it grievously that he should make void the articles which were agreed upon, the man being in no fault. But because there was no way 29 of resisting the king, he watched his time to accomplish this thing by policy. But when Maccabæus 30 saw that Nicanor began to be churlish unto him, and that he entreated him more roughly than he was wont, perceiving that such sour behaviour came not of good, he gathered together not a few of his men, and withdrew himself secretly from Nicanor. But the other, finding that 31 he was notably prevented by Judas' policy, came into the great and holy temple; and while the priests were offering the ordinary sacrifices, com- 32 manded them to deliver *him* the man. And when they sware that they could not tell where the 33 man was whom he sought, he stretched out his right hand toward the temple, and made an oath in this manner; If ye will not deliver me Judas as a prisoner, I will lay this temple of God even with the ground, and I will break down the altar, and erect here a notable temple unto Bacchus.

After these words he departed. Then the 34

priests lifted up their hands towards heaven, and besought Him who was ever a defender of their
35 nation, saying in this manner; Thou, O Lord of all things, who hast need of nothing[i], wast pleased that the temple of thine habitation should be
36 among us; therefore now, O holy Lord of all holiness, keep this house ever undefiled, which lately was cleansed[k].

37 Now was there accused unto Nicanor one Rhazis, one of the elders of Jerusalem, a lover of his countrymen, and a man of very good report, who for his kindness was called a father of the Jews.
38 For in the former times, when they mingled not[1] themselves with the Gentiles, he had been accused of Judaism, and did boldly jeopard his body and life with all vehemency for the religion of the
39 Jews. So Nicanor, willing to declare the hate which he bare unto the Jews, sent above five hun-
40 dred men of war to take him. For he thought
41 by taking him, to do *the Jews* much hurt. Now when the multitude would have taken the tower, and violently broken into the outer door, and commanded to bring fire and burn the doors, he being surrounded on every side, fell upon his sword;
42 chusing rather to die manfully, than to come into the hands of the wicked, to be abused otherwise
43 than beseemed his noble birth: but missing his stroke through the hurry of the conflict, the multitude also rushing within the doors, he ran boldly

---

[i] See the same expression used at 1 Macc. ii. 9.

[k] The common version adds here, " and stop every un-" righteous mouth." But these words are wholly wanting in almost every Greek manuscript.

[l] Gr. ἀμιξίας. Compare this expression with verse 3 above.

up to the wall, and cast himself down manfully amongst the thickest of them. But they quickly 44 giving back, and a space being made, he fell down upon the middle of his belly[m]. Nevertheless, 45 while there was yet breath within him, being inflamed with anger, he rose up; and though his blood gushed out like spouts of water, and his wounds were grievous, yet he ran through the midst of the throng; and standing upon a certain steep rock, when as his blood was now quite gone, 46 he held forth his bowels, and taking them in both his hands, he cast them upon the throng; and calling upon the Lord of life and spirit to restore him those again, he thus died.

CHAPTER XV.

The defeat of Nicanor. His death.

But Nicanor, hearing that Judas and his com- 1 pany were in the strong places about Samaria, devised without any danger to set upon them on the sabbath-day. Nevertheless, the Jews who were 2 compelled to go with him, said; O destroy not so cruelly and barbarously, but give honour to that day, which He who seeth all things hath honoured with holiness above *other days*. Then the most 3 abandoned wretch demanded, If there existed a Mighty One in heaven, who had commanded the sabbath-day to be kept. And when they said, 4 There is, the living Lord: he is the mighty One

---

[m] Gr. ἦλθε κατὰ μέσον τὸν κενεῶνα· or, as before translated, "into the midst of the "void place;" for the word κενεών is thought to bear both significations: but the wounded condition of the man, as described in the following verse, seems to determine in favour of that rendering which I have adopted.

in heaven, who commanded the seventh day to be
5 kept: then said the other, And I also am mighty upon earth, and I command to take arms, and to do the king's business: yet he obtained not to
6 have his wicked will done. So Nicanor, lifting up his neck in all haughtiness, determined to set up a public trophy of his victory over Judas and them which were with him.
7 But Maccabæus had ever sure confidence that
8 he should obtain help from the Lord: wherefore he exhorted his people not to fear the coming of the heathen against them, but to remember the help which in former times they had received from heaven; and now to expect the victory and aid which should come unto them from the Al-
9 mighty. And so comforting them out of the law and the prophets, and withal putting them in mind of the battles which they had won afore,
10 he made them more cheerful. And when he had stirred up their minds, he gave them their charge; shewing them therewithal the perfidy of the hea-
11 then, and the breach of oaths. Thus he armed every one of them, not so much with defence of shields and spears, as with the comfort of good words: and besides that, telling them a dream worthy to be believed for a true vision [a], he re-
12 joiced them all [not a little]. And this was his vision: That Onias, who had been high priest, a virtuous and a good man, reverend in deportment, gentle in manners, well spoken also, and exercised from a child in all points of virtue, holding up

[a] Gr. ὕπαρ τι. There is a various reading, ὑπέρ τι, which is respectably supported by MSS.

his hands, prayed over the whole body of the Jews. This done, that in like manner there appeared a man with grey hairs, and exceeding glorious, and that about him there was a certain wonderful and most excellent majesty. Then Onias answered, saying, This is a lover of thy brethren, who prayeth much for the people, and for the holy city, *to wit*, Jeremias the prophet of God. Whereupon Jeremias holding forth his right hand, gave to Judas a sword of gold, and in giving it, spake thus; Take this holy sword, a gift from God, with which thou shalt defeat[b] the adversaries.

Thus being well comforted by the words of Judas, which were very good, and able to stir them up to valour, and to encourage the hearts of the young men, they determined not to pitch camp; but courageously to set upon them, and manfully to try the matter by conflict; because both the city, and the sanctuary, and the temple, were in danger. For their anxiety for their wives and their children, their brethren and kinsfolks, was in less account with them: but the greatest and principal fear was for the holy temple. Also there was no slight anxiety among those who were collected together in the city, being troubled for the conflict abroad. And now, when as all looked forward to the approaching trial, and the enemies were already come near, and the army was set in array, and the beasts placed in a convenient position, and the horsemen drawn up on the wings; Maccabæus, seeing the coming of the

[b] Gr. θραύσεις, a word used in this sense by Polybius.

multitude, and the divers preparations of armour, and the fierceness of the beasts, stretched out his hands towards heaven, and called upon the Lord who worketh wonders[c]; knowing that victory cometh not by arms, but even as it seemeth good to him, he giveth the victory to such as are
22 worthy. Therefore in his prayer he said after this manner; "O Lord, thou didst send thine angel
" in the time of Ezekias king of Judæa, and didst
" slay in the host of Sennacherib an hundred
23 " fourscore and five thousand. Wherefore now
" also, O Lord of heaven, send a good angel be-
24 " fore us, for a fear and a dread *unto them;* and
" through the might of thine arm, let those be
" stricken with terror who come against thy holy
" people to blaspheme." And he ended thus.
25 Then Nicanor, and they which were with him,
26 came forward with trumpets and songs. But Judas and his company encountered the enemies
27 with invocation and prayer. So that fighting with their hands, and praying unto God with their hearts, they slew no less than thirty and five thousand men: for through the appearance of God they were greatly cheered.
28 Now when the battle was done, returning again with joy, they discovered that Nicanor lay dead
29 in all his armour. Then making a great shout, and a noise, they praised the Mighty One in their
30 own language. And *Judas,* who was ever the chief defender of the citizens, both in body and mind, and who continued his love[d] towards his

[c] The Vatican manuscript adds here τὸν κατόπτην, "the " beholder *of all things.*"

[d] Gr. ὁ τὴν τῆς ἡλικίας εὔνοιαν εἰς τοὺς ὁμοεθνεῖς διαφυλάξας.

countrymen all his life, commanded to strike off Nicanor's head, and his hand, with his shoulder, and bring them to Jerusalem. So when he had arrived there, and had called them of his nation together, and set the priests before the altar, he sent for them which were of the tower; and shewed them vile Nicanor's head, and the hand of that blasphemer, which with proud brags he had stretched out against the holy temple of the Almighty. And when he had cut out the tongue of that ungodly Nicanor, he commanded that they should give it by pieces unto the fowls, and hang up the reward[e] of his madness before the temple. So every man praised toward the heaven the glorious Lord, saying, Blessed be He who hath kept his own place undefiled. He hanged also Nicanor's head upon the tower, an evident and manifest sign unto all of the help of the Lord.

And they all ordained with a common decree, in no case to let that day pass without solemnity, but to celebrate the thirteenth day of the twelfth month, which in the Syrian tongue is called Adar, the day before Mardocheus' day[f]. It having gone thus with Nicanor, and from that time forth the city continuing in the power of the Hebrews, I also here will end my discourse.

And if *I have done* well, and appropriately[g] to my arrangement of the story, it is that which I desired: but if slenderly and meanly, it is that

---

[e] Gr. ἐπίχειρον, a word used by Polybius in this sense. Schleusner contends that it ought to be translated *arm;* but I think his arguments will not bear examination.

[f] Namely, the feast of Purim, mentioned at Esther ix. 28, 59.

[g] Gr. εὐθίκτως, an expression used by Polybius.

39 which I could attain unto. For, as to drink wine alone, or in like manner again water, is hurtful; and as wine mingled with water is pleasant, and affords an agreeable delight: even so the fit framing of a discourse delighteth the ears of them which read the story. And here shall be the end.

It deserves remark, that in Coverdale's translation of the Bible, first printed in 1535, likewise in Matthew's, 1537, in Cranmer's, 1539, also in the various reprints of these editions, the last two verses of this book are wanting: nor have I found them in any English Bible earlier than the Genevan of 1560, and the Bishops' of 1568.

END OF BOOK III.

THE FOURTH BOOK

OF

MACCABEES:

CONTAINING

REFLECTIONS ON RELIGIOUS PRINCIPLE: LIKEWISE AN ACCOUNT OF HELIODORUS' ATTEMPT TO PLUNDER THE TEMPLE: AND THE HISTORY OF ELEAZAR AND THE SEVEN BRETHREN PERSECUTED EVEN TO DEATH FOR THEIR ADHERENCE TO RELIGION.

CHAPTER I.

On the power of Religious Principle.

1 As I am about to discuss a most philosophical subject, *namely*, whether religious principle[a] be perfect master of the Passions; I should be advising you well *by desiring* that with all readiness
2 of mind you give attention to philosophy. For in truth, Reason is necessary to every person, as a preliminary step to Science: and moreover it contains within itself the recommendation of *excelling*

---

[a] This book is commonly spoken of as a treatise "on "the government of *Reason:*" on consideration, I have judged it best to distinguish as under, the four following words, which are of constant occurrence throughout the work. Λόγος I translate, *Reason*: λογισμὸς, *Principle*: εὐσεβὴς λογισμὸς, *Religious Principle*: εὐλογιστία, *Rectitude of Principle*.

in the highest virtue, I mean, in Prudence. Now 3 if Principle appears to have dominion over those passions which are impediments to Temperance, such as gluttony and sensual desire: it also ap- 4 pears to lord it over those which stand in the way of Justice, such as habitual depravity [b]; and likewise over those which interfere with Fortitude, namely, Anger, and Pain, and Fear.

How happens it then, perhaps some may say, 5 that if Principle is superior to the passions, it does not obtain the sovereignty over Forgetfulness and Ignorance? This their attempt at argument is ridiculous. For Principle does not prevail against 6 those passions which belong to itself [c], *and are defects of its own nature;* but against such as are opposed to Justice, and Fortitude, and Temperance, and Prudence [d]: and *even* against these it prevails not in such degree as to destroy them, but *only* so as not to yield to, *or be guided by* them.

This fact indeed I might prove to you by argu- 7 ments from many other sources, that Principle is absolute sovereign of the Passions: but I may de- 8 monstrate it with much greater effect, from the magnanimity of those persons who suffered death in defence of virtue, namely, Eleazar, and the seven brethren and their mother. For all these, 9 by their contempt of sufferings even unto death [e], have given demonstration that Principle does possess controul over the Passions. For their virtues, 10

---

[b] Gr. κακοήθεια.
[c] Gr. τῶν ἑαυτοῦ παθῶν.
[d] These words are omitted by Josephus. (edit. Haverkamp.)
[e] After these words Josephus adds, " in defence of the laws of God, and by despising even their own lives for the sake of religion."

therefore, it is my business to praise these men, who, together with their mother, died at this juncture for the sake of that which is right: and for the honours which they have acquired, I must congratulate and think them happy.

11 For they, having obtained admiration for their fortitude and patience, not only from men in general, but even from those who had shamefully ill-treated them[f], became the means of putting a stop to that tyranny which was exercised against their nation; having conquered the tyrant by their patient endurance, so that their country was purged and cleansed by the expiatory sacrifice which they offered.

12 But I may now proceed at once to discuss the point in question, commencing by speaking generally to the argument, as is our custom; and then will go on to discourse concerning these persons in particular, giving glory to the all-wise God.

13 The question, then, which we have to determine, is, "whether Principle be complete master
14 " of the Passions." Let us define, therefore, and explain, what is Principle, and what is Passion. Also, how many sorts of Passions there are; and whether Principle extends its dominion to all of these.

15 Principle then is, "Intellect accompanied *and* "*guided* by sound reason, chusing and ordering
16 " aright[g] a life directed by wisdom." And Wisdom is, "The knowledge of affairs both divine and
17 " human, and of their causes." But this is *attained by* the discipline and instruction of the law:

[f] Compare ch. xvii. 16.
[g] Gr. προτίμων τὸν σοφίας βίον. [var. lect. λόγον.]

by which instruction we learn to receive divine matters with becoming reverence, and human affairs agreeably to their apparent utility. Now of wisdom there are *four* species, Prudence, Justice, Fortitude, and Temperance; and the most influential[h] of them all is Prudence; by means of which indeed Principle obtains that mastery which it exercises over the Passions.

Of the Passions [*or affections*] the two most comprehensive are Pleasure and Pain: and each of these affects [both the body and[i]] the mind. There are also numerous affections which accompany and follow these leading passions, of Pleasure and Pain. Before Pleasure goes Desire: and after Pleasure comes Joy. Before Pain is Fear: and after Pain comes Sorrow. Anger[k] is an affection which partakes both of pleasure and pain, *as will be perceived* if any one carefully observes it whenever it comes upon him. There exists also in Pleasure a malignant evil habit, which is the most various and versatile of all the affections. In the mind it exhibits itself under the form of arrogance, and avarice, love of vainglory, love of quarrelling, want of good faith, and envy. And in the body it is greediness, and gluttony, and selfish enjoyment[l].

[h] So Cicero pronounces of it, that, of the four virtues, this "maxime naturam attin-" git humanam." De Officiis, I. c. 6.

[i] The words within brackets are wanting in the Oxford Septuagint, 8vo. 1817, but they are necessary to complete the sense, as may appear from ver. 27, 28. infra. Grabe's edition, taken from the Alexandrian MS., contains them.

[k] The same account of Anger is given by Aristotle, in the second book of his Rhetoric. Ἔστω ὀργὴ ὄρεξις μετὰ λύπης τιμωρίας,—καὶ πάσῃ ὀργῇ ἕπεσθαί τινα ἡδονήν.

[l] Gr. μονοφαγία. Though this substantive is not found (perhaps) in classic authors,

28 As therefore there are two direct main shoots of the body and mind, namely, Pleasure and Pain; so are there many side-shoots springing up from
29 these affections. Each of which shoots Principle, that universal husbandman, pruning on every side[m], and scraping off, and tying up, and watering, and changing about in every way, cultivates and improves the materials both of the morals and af-
30 fections. For Principle truly is the leader of the Virtues; but of the Passions it is the monarch.
31 Observe now, first of all, from those acts which are obstructive to Temperance, how completely
32 Principle is ruler over the Passions. For instance, Temperance is "The conquering of our desires."
33 Of the desires, some have reference to the mind, and some to the body; and over both of these,
34 Principle appears to bear sway. For from what cause *is it, that*, when we are urged on to forbidden kinds[n] of food, we turn away from the pleasures which these are calculated to afford? Is it not, that Principle is able to restrain and rule
35 these appetites? such at least is my opinion. And therefore, when we long for fishes, and fowls, and fourfooted animals, and every kind of food which is forbidden to us by the law, it is through the mastery of Principle that we abstain from them.

yet both the verb μονοφαγέω and the adjective μονοφάγος occur in Athenæus: and in Aristophanes (Vesp. 923), we have a person styled κυνῶν ἁπάντων ἄνδρα μονοφαγίστατον.

[m] Gr. περικαθαίρων τε καὶ ἀποκνίζων, καὶ περιπλέκων, καὶ ἐπάρδων, καὶ πάντα τρόπον μετοχετεύων, κ. τ. λ. The text of the Oxford edition, 1817, 8vo. is extremely faulty here, and indeed in very many other passages.

[n] The author of this book is here speaking as a Jew, to Jews. See the particulars of the prohibitions to which he alludes, at Leviticus, ch. iii. vii. xi. and Deuter. ch. xiv.

For the affections of our appetites are restrained 36 and turned into another direction by sobriety of mind; and all the movements of the body are kept in check[o] by Principle.

CHAPTER II.

Particular illustrations of the strength of Principle.

AND where is the wonder of all this? if *even* 1 the desires of the soul are disappointed, when brought into competition with the pursuit of that which is honourable and right? Yet on this 2 ground the self-controuling Joseph[a] is extolled; that through the Principle which ruled in his mind, he overcame the temptation to sensual indulgence. For he, being youthful and fully ripe 3 for sexual intercourse, quelled through Principle the impetuous ardour of his passions.

And not only does Principle seem to vanquish 4 the stimulus of sensual indulgence, but also that of desire of every kind. For instance, the Law 5 says [b], " Thou shalt not covet thy neighbour's " wife, nor any thing which is thy neighbour's." And now, since the Law has enjoined us not to 6 covet, I may the more easily persuade you that Principle is able to overcome the desires, even as it masters those passions which are preventive of Justice. For how is a man reclaimed, who through 7 parsimony habitually lives by himself[c], and is a

[o] Gr. φιμοῦνται, are led as by a halter.
[a] See Genesis xxxix.
[b] Namely, at Exodus xx. 17.
[c] The sordid baseness of this habit is alluded to and reproved by Job, who thus imprecates on himself: " *If* " *I have eaten my morsel my-* " *self alone*, and the father- " less hath not eaten thereof, " —then let mine arm fall " from my shoulder-blade,

glutton and a drunkard[d]; unless it be evident
8 that Principle is lord over the passions? But as
soon as any man regulates his life by the Law,—
although he be a miser, he does violence to his
own disposition; lending money without interest
to those who are in need, and forfeiting[e] the money lent when the weeks *of the sabbatical year*
9 come on. And though a man be naturally parsimonious, he becomes obedient to the Law through
Principle; neither gathering up[f] the last ears of
his harvest, nor gleaning the remnant of his vineyards: and in other points of his conduct it is
easy to see that it is Principle which conquers his
10 passions. For the Law prevails even over affection towards parents; not surrendering the cause
11 of Virtue *even* on their account. It also prevails
over conjugal affection; condemning it whenever
12 it seems contrary to law. It controuls likewise
the affection *of parents* towards their children,
punishing them for any vice. And it is master
over the intercourse between friends, reproving
them for any evil doings.
13 And do not think this to be incredible, when
Principle is able to overcome even enmity, by
14 means of the Law: not *permitting us* to cut down
the fruit-trees[g] belonging to the enemies, but pre-

" and mine arm be broken
" from the bone." Job xxxi.
17, 23. See above, ch. i. 27.

[d] Gr. μονοφάγος τις ἂν τὸ ἦθος, καὶ γαστρίμαργος, καὶ μέθυσος.

[e] Gr. καὶ τὸ δάνειον τῶν ἑβδομάδων ἐνστασῶν χρεοκοπούμενος. The allusion seems to be to the sabbatical year, or year of jubilee, the provisions of which are detailed in Leviticus, ch. xxv.

[f] See Leviticus xix. 9, 10; xxiii. 22; Deut. xxiv. 19, 21.

[g] See this injunction laid upon the Israelites at Deut. xx. 19, where they are called " trees for meat." Josephus, in his second book against

serving their property from those who were destroying it, and helping to build up again the things which had fallen.

And even over the more violent passions Principle appears to bear rule; namely, the love of empire, and vain-glory, and boasting, and ostentation, and envy. For all these malignant passions a sober mind subdues and repels, as likewise it behaves towards anger; for even this it masters. For example; Moses, when enraged with Dathan and Abiram, did nothing against them in anger[h], but disciplined his mind under Principle. For the sober mind, as I observed, is able to prevail against the passions: and some of them it can change, and others utterly annul[i]. For on what other ground does our most wise father Jacob[k] reprove Simeon and Levi, for having slain the whole tribe of the Sichemites contrary to good Principle; saying, "Cursed be their anger?" For, if Principle had not possessed the power of subduing Anger, he would not have spoken thus. For when God formed man, He planted around him a variety both of passions and of moral feelings. And then over all He set the intellectual Mind *as* on a throne[l], for a holy director by means of the

---

Apion, has a parallel passage: 'Ἐπιεικῆ δὲ καὶ τὰ πρὸς τοὺς πολεμίους εἶναι κριθέντα· οὐδὲ γὰρ ἐᾷ [ὁ νόμος] τὴν γῆν αὐτῶν πυρπολεῖν, οὐδὲ κόπτειν ἥμερα δένδρα συγκεχώρηκεν.

[h] See this verified (in Numbers xvi.) of the man who "was very meek, above "all the men which were up-"on the face of the earth."

[i] These two verses (17, 18.) do not occur in Josephus' text.

[k] See Genesis xxxiv. and xlix.

[l] Gr. καὶ τηνικαῦτα δὲ περὶ πάντων τὸν ἱερὸν ἡγεμόνα νοῦν διὰ τῶν ἔνδον αἰσθητηρίων ἐνεθρόνισεν.

CHAPTER III.

The argument illustrated by example.

1 How then happens it, any one may say, that if Principle subdues the passions, it does not obtain the mastery over forgetfulness and ignorance?
2 But this reasoning is perfectly ridiculous: for Principle does not appear to have dominion over those passions which are connected with itself, but
3 over those which belong to the body. For instance, any one of you may not be able wholly to eradicate Desire; but nevertheless *your* Principle is able to effect so much as this, that you be not
4 enslaved by *that* desire. Any one of us may not be able to root quite out of his mind Anger: but still, he may be able, *by means of Reason*, to lend
5 aid[a] towards subduing his anger. Any one of you may not be able to eradicate a vicious propensity: but Principle is able to assist him, so that he
6 shall not be bowed down by this propensity. For Principle is not an eradicator of the Passions, but their antagonist and opponent.
7 And this we may illustrate more forcibly by
8 the thirst of king David[b]. For when David had been engaged with the Philistines during a whole day, and had slain many of them, in company

---

[a] Gr. βοηθῆσαι τῷ θυμῷ. This use of the verb βοηθέω we have in Polybius; βοηθεῖν ταῖς νόσοις καὶ ταῖς αἰτίαις τοῦ βλάπτειν τὸ σῶμα. Lib. XI. 25.

[b] See the history of this transaction at 2 Sam. xxiii. 15, &c.

with the soldiers of his nation: when evening was come, perspiring and greatly fatigued, he came to the royal tent, around which the whole body of his chief mighty men[c] had encamped. All the rest, then, employed themselves about their supper: but the king, being exceedingly thirsty, although he had at hand abundance of water from the fountain, could not assuage his thirst with this: but a certain unaccountable longing for water which was in the enemy's camp, increasing tortured[d] him, and relaxing consumed him. Wherefore when his guards were concerned at this longing of the king, two[e] brave young soldiers, feeling respect for this his desire, armed themselves; and taking an urn, passed over the enemies' ramparts. And having escaped the notice of those who watched the gates, they passed through the whole camp of the enemy in search of it. And having discovered the fountain by their valour, they brought from it a draught for the king. But he, though parched up with thirst, considered how great danger it would be to his soul to drink water, which must be reckoned equal to so much blood[f]. Wherefore, placing his

---

[c] Gr. τῶν προγόνων. The Latin translator of Josephus renders it simply "militum." "Προγόνων, quasi primæ no-"bilitatis viri, maximeque "conspicui invicta fortitudi-"ne, quam eis Sacer Textus "ibi adscribit,"—is Combefisius' note upon the passage in Haverkamp's edition of Josephus.

[d] Gr. ἐπιτείνουσα συνέφρυγε, καὶ λύουσα κατέφλεγεν. The sense appears to be, that the feeling alternately increased and relaxed, and at each stage was accompanied by much torment to the king's mind.

[e] The Scripture informs us that there were "*three:*" see 2 Sam. xxiii. 16.

[f] "And David longed, and "said, O that one would give "me drink of the water of "the well of Bethlehem,

Principle in opposition to his desire, he poured
18 out the cup *as an offering* to God. For the sober
mind is able to overcome the pressure of the pas-
19 sions; and to extinguish the flames of lusts; and
to vanquish bodily pains, however excessive; and,
by honourable uprightness of Principle, to reject
with scorn all *assumed* dominion of the Passions.
20 But the occasion now invites us to the demon-
strative proof from history of this theory
of sober Principle.
21 For, when our fathers were enjoying complete
peace[g] through their strict observance of the Law,
and were prospering; so that even the king of
Asia, Seleucus Nicanor, both assigned them money for the service of the temple, and approved
and permitted their constitution and form of go-
22 vernment: then certain persons, attempting inno-
vations against the general unanimity of sentiment, fell into calamities[h] in various ways.

"which is by the gate! And the three mighty men brake through the host of the Philistines, and drew water out of the well of Bethlehem that was by the gate, and took it, and brought it to David: nevertheless he would not drink thereof, but poured it out unto the Lord. And he said, Be it far from me, O Lord, that I should do this: is not this the blood of the men that went in jeopardy of their lives? therefore he would not drink it." 2 Samuel xxiii. 15—17.

[g] This narrative commences about the year 187 before Christ, when Seleucus Philopator was king of Syria; Ptolemy Epiphanes king of Egypt; and Onias, the son of Simon, high priest of the Jews. Compare 3 Macc. iii.

[h] Gr. πολυτρόποις ἐχρήσαντο συμφοραῖς. But this text is probably faulty: the sense seems to be, that, through the ill-advised attempts of some few persons, *the whole nation* was brought into calamity.

CHAPTER IV.

The attempt of Apollonius. The beginning of Antiochus' ill-will to the Jews.

For a certain man named Simon, who was opposed in politics to Onias, then holding the high-priesthood for his life, an upright and honourable man,—after that by every kind of accusation thrown out to the hurt of his nation, he could do him no harm; fled away, with the design of betraying his country, *to the enemy.* Wherefore, when he was come to Apollonius[a], the military governor of Syria and Phœnice and Cilicia, he said: " Being well affected towards " the interests of the king, I am come to inform " you that many immense sums[b] of private money " are hoarded up in the treasuries in Jerusalem, " which monies have no connexion with the tem- " ple, but belong of right to king Seleucus."

Apollonius, coming to the knowledge of these particulars, praises Simon for his affectionate regard for the king; and, going up to Seleucus, apprised him of this accumulated treasure. And when he had received a commission respecting it, taking his attendant troops, and quickly returning into our country with the accursed Simon and a most powerful army; he proclaimed that he was come at the king's command, to take away from

---

[a] Compare the history of this transaction with the accounts given in the other books; namely, at 3 Macc. iii. 5, &c. 5 Macc. i. 2. Both these books state that the person sent was Heliodorus, not Apollonius: but this latter name is mentioned (as archbishop Ussher observes) in the *Fasti Siculi*.

[b] Gr. πολλὰς μυριάδας.

the treasury the money which belonged to individuals. And when our nation was indignant at this speech, and spake up against it; thinking it were extremely hard that they who had confided their deposits to the sacred treasury should be deprived of them; they prepared what resistance they could. But Apollonius with threats departed for the temple. But the priests, with the women and children in the temple, having besought God to protect the holy place which was thus contemned; and while Apollonius with his armed forces was going up to the seizure of the treasure;—there appeared from heaven angels[c], riding on horses, glittering all over in their armour, and filling his troops with great fear and trembling. And Apollonius, falling down half dead upon the floor of that court of the temple which is open to all[d] nations, stretched forth his hands to heaven, and with tears besought the Hebrews, that by offering up prayers for him they would appease the heavenly host. [For he owned that he had sinned, so as even to be worthy of death; and that, if he were preserved, he would proclaim abroad to all men the blessedness of the holy place[e].]

Onias the high priest, induced by these words, and on other grounds being anxious that king Seleucus should not think that Apollonius had been thus laid hold on by human stratagem and

[c] Compare the account given in 3 Macc. iii. which differs in a few particulars: for example, Heliodorus, not Apollonius, is there made the principal actor.

[d] Namely, that which was called "the court of the Gentiles."

[e] This verse does not occur in Josephus.

not by Divine vengeance, prayed for him. And he, being thus unexpectedly preserved from death, departed, intending to shew unto the king[f] the things which had happened to him.

But when king Seleucus was dead, his son Antiochus Epiphanes succeeded[g] to his kingdom, a haughty and wicked man[h]. Who, having deposed Onias from the high-priesthood, appointed his brother Jason high priest: who had covenanted, if Antiochus would give him the authority, to pay him[i] every year three thousand six hundred and sixty talents. And *the king* gave him authority to be high priest, and to be civil ruler of the nation. Who both changed the way of living of the Jewish people, and led them aside by strange policies to all kinds of transgression of their law. So that he not only erected a gymnasium on the very citadel of our country, but also put a stop[k] to the service of the temple. At which things Divine Justice being provoked, caused Antiochus himself to be their enemy.

For when he was in Egypt warring with Ptolemy[l], and had heard that, on a report of his death being circulated, the men of Jeru-

---

[f] Compare 3 Macc. iii. 36—39.

[g] Namely, in the year before Christ 175.

[h] See his character drawn at 2 Macc. i. 10, and the notes there.

[i] If the figures here given be correct, the money promised yearly to Antiochus amounts to the enormous sum of one hundred and thirty one thousand three hundred and ninety pounds, of our money!

[k] See this predicted at Daniel xi. 31, and its fulfilment detailed more fully at 2 Macc. i. 39. 41, &c.

[l] Ptolemy Philometor. Antiochus wishing " to have the " dominion of two realms," (see 2 Macc. i. 16.) entered into Egypt, and made war against Ptolemy, and defeated him, anno Seleucid. 143. B.C. 170.

B. C. 167.   CHAP. V.   233

salem had most exceedingly rejoiced [m], he marched against them with all speed. And when he had defeated them, he made a decree, that if any of them were seen living according to the laws and customs of their country, they should be put to death. And when he could in no way accomplish by his decrees the dissolution of that affection which the people bore to their own law; but saw that all his threats and punishments were rendered vain: so that even women [n], because they had circumcised their children, were thrown down a precipice, together with their infants, being previously aware that they would suffer this punishment *if they ventured to circumcise:* when therefore his decrees were treated with contempt by the people, he in person compelled by tortures every individual of the nation, by tasting forbidden and unclean meats [o], to abjure the Jewish religion.

CHAPTER V.

Eleazar brought forward. His eloquent address to the king.

1 THE tyrant Antiochus [a], then, sitting in state with his attendants on a certain elevated spot, and his armed troops standing round them on every side;—commanded his guards to

About B.C. 167.

[m] Gr. ὡς ἔνι μάλιστα χαίροιεν. Respecting their supposed joy, see 3 Macc. v. 5. and 11.

[n] Compare 3 Macc. vi. 10.

[o] How strong a contrast does this present to the conduct of his predecessor Antiochus the Great: who, in his eager desire to benefit and please the Jews, forbade that any of the meats which their law pronounced to be unclean should even be brought within the precincts of the city. See Josephus, Antiq. XII. 3.

[a] This persecution of Eleazar and the rest is thought to have taken place in the year before Christ 167. Compare 3 Macc. vi. 18, &c.

seize every individual of the Hebrews, and to compel him to taste swine's flesh[b], and things offered to idols[c]. And that if any persons re- 3 fused to eat this unclean food, they should be tortured to death upon the wheel.

And when many had been seized, a Hebrew 4 named Eleazar, a chief man among the people, by family a priest, by profession a lawyer[d], and advanced in years, and from his age known to many of those about the king, was brought out near to him. And Antiochus seeing him, said; "Old 5 "man, I would advise you, before your torments "begin, to eat of the swine's flesh and save your "life: for I respect your age and grey hairs; 6 "which, although you have had for so long a "time, you do not seem to me to understand phi- "losophy, since you adhere to the superstition of "the Jews. For why, since nature has freely 7 "given you the excellent food of this animal's "flesh, do you abhor it? For truly it is absurd 8 "not to enjoy things which are agreeable, without "conveying any disgrace; and unjust to turn our- "selves away from the favours of nature. But 9 "you seem to me likely to do a thing still more "senseless, if, from a vain affectation of follow- "ing Truth, you will further proceed to hold me "in contempt, to your own punishment. Will 10

---

[b] It is of course remembered that this food was expressly and by name forbidden to the Jews by God. See Leviticus xi. 7.

[c] Gr. εἰδωλόθυτα, which, we remember, were at a subsequent period forbidden to the early Christian converts, by an express ordinance of the Apostles. See Acts xv. 29.

[d] Gr. νομικός: the same word occurs in the New Testament, and designates a Jewish divine, or expounder of the Scriptures.

"you not wake up from this foolish philosophy of
11 "yours? And will you not chase away the de-
"ception of your reasonings; and, having re-
"gained a mind worthy of your years, follow a
"philosophy which unites expediency with truth?
12 "and, receiving thankfully my benevolent ex-
13 "hortation, have pity on your old age? For
"consider this also; that, if there be any Power
"which watches over this your religious system,
"it would pardon you for every transgression of
"the law which was committed through com-
"pulsion."

14 While the tyrant in this manner exhorted him
to the unallowed eating of flesh, Eleazar requested
15 leave[e] to speak. And having received permission,
he commenced publicly addressing the people
thus:

16 "We, O Antiochus, who are persuaded that we
"conduct ourselves agreeably to a divine law,
"think no duty more imperative than that of a
17 "full obedience[f] to our law. On which account
"we deem it wrong to offend against it in any
18 "manner. And yet, even if our law were not in
"truth divine, as you imagine, (but we on the
"contrary hold it to be divine,) not even in that
"case would it be lawful for us to annul that
19 "character which we have for piety. Do not

[e] Gr. λόγον ᾔτησεν.
[f] Gr. εὐπειθείας. Schleusner conjectures that we ought to read ἀπειθείας, *disobedience*: but, besides that all the MSS. are opposed to such a change, the received text obtains a strong confirmation from the following passage of Josephus, (contra Apionem, I.) Speaking of the moral habits of the Jews, Josephus says; Μαλίστα δὲ πάντων περὶ παιδοτροφίαν φιλοκαλοῦντες, καὶ τὸ φυλάττειν τοὺς νόμους καὶ τὴν κατὰ τούτους παραδεδομένην εὐσέβειαν ἔργον ἀναγκαιότατον παντὸς τοῦ βίου πεποιημένοι.

"think therefore, that this is a small offence, if
"we should eat of things which are unclean. For 20
"to transgress in small matters or in great is
"equal *in guilt;* for by each of these the law
"is equally holden at nought.

"And you deride our philosophy, as though we 21
"live in it without good reason for so doing.
"Yet it throughly teaches us temperance, so that 22
"we master all the pleasures and desires: and it
"exercises us in fortitude, so that we willingly
"undergo every toil[g]: and it instructs us in jus- 23
"tice, so that in all our behaviour we give what
"is due: and it teaches us to be pious, so that
"we worship the only living God in a manner
"becoming his greatness.

"Wherefore we eat not unclean meats: for, 24
"believing that the law was constituted by God,
"we know that the Creator of the world sympa-
"thises with our nature in the framing of his
"laws. And those things which will suit our na- 25
"tures he has permitted us to eat; but the meats
"which would prove the contrary, he has for-
"bidden us to use.

"But you, tyrannically, not only force us to 26
"transgress the law, but also to eat, that you
"may still further have to laugh at this eating of
"unclean things which is most odious to us. But 27

---

[g] The Greek text of verses 22 and 23 is greatly obscured by careless pointing and printing in the Oxford edition: it ought to stand thus: Σωφροσύνην τε γὰρ ἡμᾶς ἐκδιδάσκει, ὥστε πασῶν τῶν ἡδονῶν καὶ ἐπιθυμιῶν κρατεῖν: Καὶ ἀνδρείαν ἐξασκεῖ, ὥστε πάντα πόνον ἑκουσίως ὑπομένειν. Καὶ δικαιοσύνην παιδεύει, ὥστε διὰ πάντων τῶν ἠθῶν ἰσονομεῖν. Καὶ εὐσεβείαν διδάσκει, ὥστε μόνον τὸν ὄντα Θεὸν σέβειν μεγαλοπρεπῶς. Thus the four parts are complete, and answer to each other.

" this laughter you never shall enjoy against me:
" nor will I violate the sacred oaths of my fore-
28 " fathers concerning the keeping of the law. Not
" even if you pluck out my eyes, and consume
29 " my entrails in the fire. I am not so old and
" devoid of spirit, but that my principle is still vi-
30 " gorous in religion's cause. Against this, pre-
" pare your racks, and kindle the fire still more
" fiercely[g]. I will not so far compassionate my
" old age, as for my own individual sake to pull
31 " down the law of my country. I will not fail
" thee, O law, my instructor! I will not forsake
32 " thee, O beloved self-controul! nor will I shame
" thee, O philosophic reason! nor will I renounce
" thee, O honoured priesthood and science of the
33 " law! Nor shall you pollute my reverend mouth
" in old age, nor the advanced years of a life
34 " passed in obedience[h] to the law. My fathers
" shall receive me pure, not having been afraid of
35 " your violence even unto death. For indeed
" over the ungodly you will tyrannize: but over
" my religious principles you shall not obtain do-
" minion, neither by your arguments nor your
" deeds."

CHAPTER VI.

Eleazar's sufferings; and death. Reflections on it.

1 WHEN Eleazar had in this manner eloquently answered[a] the tyrant's exhortations, the guards surrounded him, and drew him with violence to
2 the instruments of torture. And first of all they

[g] See Daniel iii. 19.
[h] Gr. οὐδὲ νομίμου βίου ἡλικίαν, a phrase which scarcely admits a close translation into English; as indeed is frequently the case throughout this book.
[a] Gr. ἀντιρητορεύσαντα.

stripped[b] the old man, arrayed as he was in the becoming garb of piety. Then, having bound his arms to each side of his body, they disfigured him with scourges: a herald on each side crying out aloud, "Obey the commands of the king." But Eleazar, truly noble and high-minded, regarded it not in the least, as though he were tortured only in a dream. But lifting up his eyes on high to heaven, the old man was stript of his flesh by the whips, and streamed down with blood, and his flanks were laid open by wounds. And though he fell to the ground, because his body could not support the pains, he still retained his strength of principle upright and unbending.

Then one of the savage guards leaping upon his belly kicked[c] it, to make him rise up after he had fallen. But he supported the pain, and regarded not the violence, and patiently endured the ill usage. And, like a fine spirited champion[d] at the Grecian games, the old man enduring stripes conquered his tormentors. And though his face was wet with perspiration, and he sorely gasped for breath; yet he was admired, even by those who tortured him, for his hardihood.

Wherefore, partly in pity for his age; partly feeling sympathy for their former acquaintance with him, and partly in admiration of his constancy; some of the king's attendants came up to him and said: Why, Eleazar, will you destroy[e] yourself by all these evils? we will bring you

---

[b] Gr. περιέδυσαν τὸν γηραιὸν ἐκκεκοσμημένον περὶ τὴν εὐσέβειαν εὐσχημοσύνην.

[c] Gr. λὰξ εἰς τοὺς κενεῶνας ἐναλλόμενος ἔτυπτεν.

[d] Gr. Ἀθλητής.

[e] There is a variety of reading in the Greek: ἀπολλεῖς, ὑποβάλλεις, παραβάλλεις.

some dressed meat[f], and do you save yourself by pretending to have tasted some of the swine's flesh.

13 But Eleazar, as if tortured[g] still more cruelly
14 by this advice, cried out: "Let not us, who are "children of Abraham, be so foolish as through "weakness of mind to play a part which is dis-
15 "creditable to us. Absurd indeed it would be, if "having lived to old age in conformity with the "truth, and preserving a good character agreeably "to the law[h], we now should change *our course:*
16 "and ourselves should become a pattern of im- "piety to the young, by being an example of eat-
17 "ing unclean meats. It would be disgraceful, if "we should still live on for some short time; and "this, being derided by all men for our coward-
18 "ice. While by the tyrant we shall be despised "as spiritless, and shall not have defended our di-
19 "vine law unto the death. Wherefore, do you, "O ye children of Abraham, die nobly in defence "of *your* religion. But you, ye guards of the ty- "rant, why do you make delay[i]?"
20 When they beheld him thus high-spirited in

---

[f] Gr. τῶν ἠψημένων, so that by the outward appearance it could not be distinguished.

[g] We have here exhibited by Eleazar a portion of that spirit which animated St. Paul, when his friends, alarmed for his safety, besought him not to go up to Jerusalem: "What mean ye to "weep and to break mine "heart? for I am ready not "to be bound only, but also "to die at Jerusalem for the "name of the Lord Jesus." Acts xxi. 13.

[h] Gr. δόξαν νομίμως φυλάσσοντες.

[i] Thus, in 3 Macc. vii. 30, the youngest of the seven sons, when led out to punishment and warmed by the pious address of his mother, exclaimed, "Whom wait ye "for? I will not obey the "king's commandment: but "I will obey the command- "ment of the law that was "given unto our fathers by "Moses."

the midst of his troubles; and that he did not change at all through their compassion of him, they carried him to the fire. Then with their horrid instruments they threw him on the pile of fire to burn him, and poured stinking liquids into his nostrils. But he, being now completely burnt to the bones, and about to expire, lifted up his eyes to God, and said: "Thou knowest, O God, "that whereas I might have saved myself, I am "dying by fiery torments for the law's sake. "Therefore be merciful to thy people, being satis- "fied with the punishment suffered by me for "them. Make my blood[k] a purification for them, "and accept my life an offering instead of theirs." And having uttered these words, the holy man died nobly in his torments; and, even to the tortures of death, stood fast in his principle for the sake of the law.

Confessedly therefore religious Principle is lord over the passions. For if the passions had overpowered principle, I would have given to them the testimony of such mastery. But now, since principle has overcome the passions, to it we give, as is becoming, the rank and power of sovereignty. And it is just that we should own that the mastery belongs to principle, since it prevails over pains inflicted from without[1]. Nay, to say other-

[k] Gr. Καθάρσιον αὐτῶν ποιή-σον τὸ ἐμὸν αἷμα. So, at 3 Macc. vii. 37, "I, as my "brethren, offer up my body "and life for the laws of our "fathers, beseeching God that "he would speedily be mer- "ciful unto our nation: and "that in me and my brethren "the wrath of the Almighty, "which is justly brought "upon all our nation, may "cease."—For the use and meaning of the word καθάρ-σιον, see Ælian. Var. Hist. XIV. 7: and compare the Oration of Æschines against Timarchus, sect. 23.

[1] Gr. τῶν ἔξωθεν ἀλγηδόνων.

wise would be ridiculous: and I demonstrate, that Principle not only conquers pains, but likewise that it is master over pleasures, and does not give way to these.

CHAPTER VII.

Reflections on the sufferings and constancy of Eleazar.

1 FOR the principle of our father Eleazar, as an excellent pilot, steering the ship of piety through
2 the stormy sea of passions;—though ill-used by the tyrant's threats, and overwhelmed by the tem-
3 pestuous waves of tortures;—by no means turned aside the rudder of piety, until it sailed in safely
4 to the harbour of immortal victory. No city ever so held out, when besieged by numerous and varied engines of war, as did that holy man, while his sacred life was assailed with scourgings and racks; *and* he conquered his besiegers, through
5 the principle of piety which shielded him. For father Eleazar, stretching out his firm determination as a rocky promontory[a], broke to pieces around it the raging billows of the passions.
6 O Priest worthy of the priesthood! thou didst not pollute thy holy teeth, nor defile with polluted meat thy stomach[b] which admitted only that which was holy and clean. O thou harmonizer[c] with the law, and disciple[d] of a divine philo-
7 sophy! Such ought those to be, who put in practice[e] the law at the cost of their own life, and

---

[a] See a somewhat similar figure of speech below, at ch. xiii. 6.

[b] Gr. τὴν θεοσέβειαν καὶ καθαρισμὸν χωρήσασαν γαστέρα.

[c] Gr. σύμφωνε νόμου; which does not well admit a close translation into English.

[d] Gr. φιλόσοφε θείου λόγου.

[e] The Greek text varies, between δημουργοῦντας and λειτουργοῦντας.

with generous exertions defend it by sufferings even unto death. You, O father, by your endur- 8 ance have gloriously established[f] our adherence to the law; and by your correct behaviour have magnified our sanctity; and by your deeds have added credit to our profession of divine philosophy.

O aged man, of more strength than the tor- 9 tures! O old man of more energy than the fire! Eleazar, thou greatest monarch of the passions!

For, as our father Aaron, armed with a censer, 10 running through the midst of the congregation[g], vanquished the angel who was consuming them with fire: so Eleazar, a descendant of Aaron, 11 though he was being devoured by fire, yet swerved not aside from his principle. And, what is most 12 to be admired, being an old man, the energies of his body being now weakened, and his flesh now hanging loosely about him, and his nerves also spent with exertion, he became young again in spirit through principle; and by the principle[h] which animated Isaac, he defeated the many-headed torture. O happy old age! venerable gray 13 hairs, and life obedient to the law! which the sure seal of death has consummated! Wherefore, 14 if an old man through religion has despised torments even unto death, beyond all dispute religious Principle is governor of the passions.

[f] Gr. τὴν εὐνομίαν ἡμῶν διὰ τῶν ὑπομονῶν εἰς δόξαν ἐκύρωσας, καὶ τὴν ἁγιστίαν σεμνολογήσας οὐ κατέλυσας, καὶ διὰ τῶν ἔργων ἐπιστοποίησας τοὺς τῆς θείας φιλοσοφίας λόγους.

[g] Gr. ἐθνοπλήθους. But there is a various reading, which as to sense seems preferable, διὰ τοῦ ἐθνοπλήκτου πυρὸς, "through the fire, which was "consuming the congrega-"tion." See Numbers xvi. 44.

[h] This last clause is wanting in some MSS.

15 But perhaps some persons may say, that all men do not subdue their passions[i]; because all
16 indeed do not possess this prudent principle. But as many as pay regard to piety with all their heart, these alone are able to overcome the affec-
17 tions of the flesh. Who believe that to God they do not die: for, *even* as our forefathers Abra-
18 ham[k], Isaac, and Jacob, they live to God. It does not therefore contradict *our assertion*, if that some men through weakness of principle appear to be governed by their passions. For who, that piously follows the whole rule of philosophy, and trusts in God, and knows that it is a blessed thing to endure every pain for virtue's sake, would not overcome his passions, in the cause of reli-
19 gion? For the wise and temperate man alone is the brave controller of the passions.

CHAPTER VIII.

Seven brethren, with their mother, are brought forth to the torture.

1 THROUGH this it was, that even boys, governing their conduct by religious principle, overcame still severer torments.

2 For when the tyrant was signally defeated in his first attempt, not having been able to force the old

3 man to eat unclean meats; then in violent anger he commanded to bring others of the grown-up[a] Hebrew captives: and, if they would eat the unclean

---

[i] It seems that the supposed objection terminates here, and that the remainder of the sentence comprises the author's answer to such an argument.

[k] See Exodus iii. 6. and St. Matthew xxii. 32; Mark xii. 26.

[a] Gr. ἐκ τῆς ἡλικίας τῶν Ἑβραίων.

food, to let them go when they had eaten; but, if they refused, to torment them with greater severity.

The tyrant having given these orders, there were brought forward seven brethren [b], together with their aged mother, handsome and modest youths, and ingenuous, and altogether graceful in appearance. Whom when the tyrant beheld encircling their mother as in a dance, he was pleased with them; and being struck with their fair and ingenuous appearance, he smiled upon them, and having called them near to him, said; "O young "men, I have an affectionate admiration of the "beauty of each of you: and greatly respecting "so numerous a band of brothers, I not only ad- "vise you not to fall into the same madness with "that old man who was recently tortured: but "moreover I counsel you to yield, and to enjoy "my friendship: for, as I have the power [c] to "punish those who disobey my commands, so "have I also *power* to confer favours upon those "who are obedient to me. Trust to me [d] there- "fore, and you shall receive stations of authority [e] "in my affairs, after you have renounced the or- "dinance of the policy of your fathers [f]: and

---

[b] Rufinus, in his Latin paraphrase of this book, relates that the mother's name was Solomona, and those of the sons, Maccabæus, Aber, Machir, Judas, Achaz, Areth, Jacob: from their eldest brother these youths obtained commonly the appellation of "the Maccabæan brethren." [Ussher.]

[c] The same argument, we remember, was addressed by Pilate to our blessed Saviour. See St. John xix. 10.

[d] Gr. Πιστεύσατε: but a preferable various reading is πεισθέντες, "obeying."

[e] Gr. ἀρχὰς ἡγεμονικάς.

[f] Gr. τὸν πάτριον ὑμῶν τῆς πολιτείας θεσμόν.

"adopting the Grecian mode [g] of life, and living "according to it, enjoy your youth *with all its* "*delights*. For, if you dispose me to anger by "your disobedience, you will compel me, with "dreadful punishments, to destroy every one of "you by tortures. Have mercy therefore on your- "selves, whom even I an enemy pity on account "of your youthful age and your fair forms. Will "you not take this into consideration, that if you "disobey, there is nothing in store for you but to "die in the midst of torments?"

And thus saying, he commanded the instruments of torture to be brought forward; that even by terror he might persuade them to eat the unclean meats. And when his guards brought out the wheels, and dislocating racks, and pullies [h], and catapeltæ, and caldrons, and frying-pans, and rings, and iron fetters, and wedges, and materials for kindling fire: the tyrant went on to say; "Young men, be afraid: and that just "Deity, whom you worship, will pardon you for "having transgressed upon compulsion." But they, *though* hearing seductive words, and beholding terrible things [i], not only were not afraid, but even replied to the tyrant's arguments; and, by the excellence of their reasoning, demolished his power.

[g] For former accounts of this policy of Antiochus towards the Jews, see 2 Macc. i. 12—14; and 3 Macc. iii. 9—19; v. 1—11.

[h] Gr. τροχαντῆρας. It is not easy to say exactly what the τροχαντὴρ was: the lexicons give no information whatsoever. For all these implements of torture, the reader may consult "Gallo- "nius de Martyrum cruci- "atibus," 8vo. 1668.

[i] *Ὤν οὐ μόνον ἡ βλαβὴ ἠδύνατο συνεκτρίψαι αὐτοὺς, ἀλλὰ καὶ ἡ ὄψις ἐκφοβήσασα διολέσαι.* Sapient. Salomon. cap. xi. 19.

Now let us consider the matter *closely*. If there had been among them any who were weak-minded and void of courage, what sort of words would they have used? would they not have been these? " O wretched and most foolish that we are! when " the king exhorts and invites us to accept his " kindness, shall we not obey him? Why do we " amuse ourselves with vain desires, and venture " on a disobedience which will *only* bring our " death? Brethren, shall we not fear these im- " plements of torture, and reflect on the threats " of torment, and fly from this vain-glory and " fatal ostentation? Let us have mercy on our " own prime of life, and compassion on our mo- " ther's age: and let us consider, that by disobe- " dience we shall instantly die. But Divine Justice " itself will pardon us, that we were afraid of the " king through *stern* necessity.

" Why do we withdraw ourselves from a most " delightful life, and deprive ourselves of the world " with its enjoyments? Let us not struggle against " necessity; nor seek vain-glory in our own tor- " ments. Not even the law itself adjudges us to " death, for having against our wills[k] dreaded " the instruments of torture. From whence has " so great a love of strife settled itself in us, and " a fatal obstinacy delights us, when we might " live unmolested[l] by obeying the king?"

But nothing of this kind did the young men say, nor even thought of it, when they were on the point of being tortured: for they were regard-

---

[k] Gr. ὁ νόμος—ἀκουσίους. Another reading is, ὁ ναὸς ἑκουσίως: but the former appears far preferable.
[l] Gr. μετὰ ἀταραξίας (var. lect. ἀδείας).

less ᵐ of suffering, and superior to a sense of pain.
29 So that, as soon as the tyrant had ceased from advising them to eat the unclean meats, they all with one voice, as if from one mind, spake *thus* unto him.

CHAPTER IX.

The noble address of the young men. The first and second are put to death.

1 " Why waitest thou [a], O tyrant? for we are
 " prepared to die, *rather* than transgress the com-
2 " mands of our fathers. For we feel, and justly,
 " that we disgrace our ancestors, if we follow not
 " obedience to the law and Moses [b] as our guide.
3 " Do not, O tyrant, who advisest us to violate the
 " law;—do not, while you hate us, pity us more
4 " than we pity ourselves. For we consider your
 " compassionate wish, that we should save our
 " lives by transgressing the law, to be worse than
5 " death [c] itself. And you think to frighten us,
 " threatening us with a death by torture, as
 " though we had not lately learned [d] this from
6 " Eleazar. But if aged men of the Hebrews have
 " died, and even after enduring torturings, for re-
 " ligion's sake; with more justice we young men
 " ought to die, despising the torments of your
 " persecutions, which even the old man, who is
 " our instructor, overcame.

[m] The Greek word is περίφρονες, but it is manifest that this must be understood as if it were ὑπέρφρονες.

[a] Compare ch. vi. 19, above. This prompt and resolute reply breathes the same spirit as was exhibited at an earlier period to king Nebuchadnezzar by Shadrach, Meshach, and Abednego, when they were exposed to a similar alternative, of idolatry or death.

[b] The Greek text varies, between Μωϋσῆ and γνώσει.

[c] Compare ch. vi. 13, and the note there.

[d] The Greek is μαθὸν, which probably ought to be μαθόντας.

" Make the experiment, therefore, O tyrant! 7 " and even if you take away our lives for reli" gion's sake, think not that you hurt us by these " torments. For we indeed, through this suffer- 8 " ing and endurance, shall *hereafter* receive the " rewards of virtue; and shall be [e] with God, in " whose cause we are suffering. But you, on 9 " account of the wilful foul murder of us, shall " suffer from Divine vengeance eternal torment " by fire."

When they had thus spoken, the tyrant was 10 not only vexed with them as disobedient, but also was wroth with them as *being* ungrateful[f] persons. So that the guards being commanded 11 brought out the eldest of them; and having rent off his coat, they bound his hands and arms to each side of his body with leather thongs. And when 12 they had tired themselves by beating him with scourges, producing no effect, they threw him upon the wheel. Upon the circumference of which the 13 noble youth being extended had his joints dislocated. And *while* he was being fractured in every 14 limb, he inveighed *against Antiochus*, saying: " O most foul tyrant, enemy of heavenly justice, 15 " and cruel-minded; you do not maltreat me in " this manner *for* having committed murder or " sacrilege, but for standing up in defence of the

---

[e] The last clause of this verse is omitted in the Oxford 8vo. Septuagint of 1817: but it occurs in Grabe's edition, taken from the Alexandrian MS.

[f] It is probable that he felt personally nettled, at having taken in vain the trouble of expressing his anxiety for their welfare, and offering them life and security on terms which he fancied must be accepted joyfully; but which they, from a principle of religion, spurned with the bitterest contempt.

16 " Divine Law." And when the guards said, " Consent to eat, that you may be released from
17 " torments;" he said to them, " Your wheel, O ye " accursed ministers, is not so powerful as to " break[g] my Principle. Cut up my limbs, and " burn my flesh, and wrench my joints asunder.
18 " For throughout all your tortures I will cause " you to believe that the children of the Hebrews " alone are invincible in virtue's cause."
19 As he was saying this, they placed fire under him[h]; and turned the wheel about with great
20 violence, extending him at length upon it. And the wheel was besprinkled with blood on every side; and the heap of hot coals was extinguished by the droppings of gore; and pieces of his flesh
21 flew about the axles of the machine. And although he already had the frame of his bones wrenched and mangled, the high-minded youth, true son[i] of Abraham, never uttered a groan.
22 But, as if he were being transformed by fire into
23 immortality, he nobly endured the rackings: saying, " Follow my example, brethren: desert not[k] " the post of honour which my life exhibits; nor " forswear your fraternal fellowship with me in
24 " magnanimity. War a holy and noble warfare[l]

[g] Gr. ἆξαι. But Josephus has ἆγξαι, "to choke," or "stifle." Either of the two expressions is sufficiently apposite.

[h] The text of this verse in the edition of 1817 is thus: Ταῦτα λέγοντες εἰς πῦρ ἐπέτρωσαν, καὶ διερεθίζοντες, τὸν τροχὸν προσεπικατέτεινον· which is probably corrupt, and ought to be (as in Grabe), Ταῦτα λέγοντι πῦρ ὑπέστρωσαν, καὶ διηρέθισαν τὸν τροχὸν προσεπικατατείνοντες.

[i] Gr. Ἀβραμιαῖος νεανίας.

[k] Gr. μή μου τὸν αἰῶνα λειποτακτήσητε, a phrase which does not admit a close rendering into English.

[l] Gr. ἱερὰν καὶ εὐγενῆ στρατείαν στρατεύσασθε. Precisely the same advice, and almost in the selfsame words, is

" for Religion ; by which means the providence of
" our Just Father, becoming appeased towards
" our nation, may take vengeance on the execrable
" tyrant." And having spoken thus, the holy ad- 25
mirable youth breathed out his soul.

And when all had wondered at his persevering 26
spirit, the officers brought out the one who was
next to him in age; and having fitted on themselves iron gauntlets [m] with sharp nails, they bound
him to the machines *called* catapeltæ. And 27
when, on asking whether he would consent to eat
before he were tortured, they heard his noble sentiment; tearing him with the iron claws from the 28
muscles *of his neck*, the savage beasts like panthers[n] drew off all the flesh to the chin, and the
skin of his head. But he with gravity bearing 29
this pain, said: How pleasant is every form of
death in behalf of our country's Religion! And to 30
the tyrant he said, "Do you not think, most in-
" human of all tyrants, that you are now suffer-
" ing torments greater than mine, on seeing the
" haughty calculations of your tyranny defeated
" by our endurance in Religion's cause? For I 31
" truly lighten my own pains with the delights
" which virtue yields. But you are tormented
" with the apprehensions of impiety: and you
" shall not escape, O most infamous tyrant, the
" Divine wrath!"

given by St. Paul to Timothy, ἵνα στρατεύῃ τὴν καλὴν στρατείαν. 1 Tim. i. 18.

[m] Gr. σιδηρᾶς χεῖρας. The officers or executioners put on these gloves, or gauntlets, or claws, that they might tear his flesh from the bones, as shewn at verse 28.

[n] Gr. οἱ παρδάλειοι θῆρες. Athenæus uses the word παρδαλώδης to express the same idea. The metaphor is fami-liar to most of the Greek classic authors.

CHAPTER X.

The third and fourth brothers are put to death.

1 AND when this one had undergone a memorable[a] death, the third was brought forward, being much intreated by many that he would taste *the* 2 *meats*, and save his life. But he, crying aloud, said: "Do ye not know that the same father begat "and the same mother bare me, as those who just "now have died; and that I was educated in the 3 "same opinions? I will not abjure[b] the honourable "tie of brotherhood. Wherefore, if ye have ready "any species of punishment, apply it to my body: "for my mind, even if you wish it, you cannot 4 "reach." But they, grievously disliking his freedom of speech, wrenched his hands and feet with dislocating engines; and straining him by the 5 joints, pulled his limbs asunder. And they fractured his fingers, and his arms, and his legs, and 6 his elbows[c]. And not being able to choke him by any means, dragging off[d] his skin together with the tips of his fingers, they flayed him entirely, and immediately brought him to the wheel. 7 Round about which[e], while he was dislocated, *even* to the back bone, he beheld the pieces of his

---

[a] Gr. τὸν ἀοίδιμον, "worthy "of song." The same expression is repeated at verse 13.

[b] According to the intreaty of his elder brother, given above, at ver. 23 of the preceding chapter.

[c] Gr. ἀγκῶνας. The word βραχίονας had gone before: and by these two probably are meant both the upper and lower joints of the arms.

[d] Gr. περισύραντες τὸ δέρμα σὺν ἄκραις ταῖς τῶν δακτύλων κορυφαῖς ἀπεσκύθιζον. In book III. ch. vii. 4, we have the word περισκυθίσαντας, which appears to bear precisely the same meaning as ἀποσκυθίζω in this passage.

[e] Gr. περὶ ὃν ἐκ σφονδύλων ἐκμελιζόμενος ἑώρα κ. τ. λ.

flesh flying about, and streams of blood flowing from his entrails. And, being at the point of death, he said, " We indeed, O abominable tyrant, suffer these things through our *religious* education and virtue towards God : but you, for your impiety and foul murders, shall endure interminable torments."

And after that he had died in a manner worthy of his brethren, they dragged forward the fourth; saying, " Do not you be mad with the same madness as your brethren: but obey the king, and save yourself." But he said to them, " You have no fire of so intense[f] a power against me, that I should quake with fear. *No!* by the blessed death of my brethren, and the eternal destruction *which awaits* the tyrant, and the praiseworthy life of the righteous, I will not renounce[g] our honourable brotherhood. Devise new tortures, O tyrant! that even after these *also* you may learn that I am the brother of those *men* who have been tormented before *me*." On hearing these words, the bloodthirsty, murderous, and most abominable Antiochus commanded to cut out his tongue. But he said, " Even though you take away my organ of speech, yet God heareth even the silent. Behold, my tongue is ready loosed before you; cut it off: for you shall not further *be able to* cut away our fixed Principle[h] as *you do to* our tongue. With pleasure, for

---

[f] Gr. οὐκ οὕτως καυστικώτερον ἔχετε κατ' ἐμοῦ τὸ πῦρ: or the sense may be, your fire cannot be *more* consuming against me, than it has been found against my brethren who have already endured it.

[g] See above, ver. 3, and the note there.

[h] Gr. τὸν λογισμὸν ἡμῶν γλωσσοτομήσεις.

"God's sake, we suffer amputation of our limbs.
19 " But you God shall speedily visit with ven-
" geance; since you cut out that tongue which
" was wont to hymn the strains of Divine
" praises."

CHAPTER XI.

The death of the fifth and sixth brothers.

1 AND after this *youth* also had died, being miserably mangled in torments, the fifth leaped for-
2 ward, saying; "I am not about, O tyrant, to beg
" escape from the torturing which is inflicted on
3 " us for virtue's sake. But of my own accord I
" have come forward, that having put me also to
" death, you may owe to heavenly justice a debt
4 " of vengeance for still more enormities. O thou
" hater of virtue, and of the human race! what
" have we done, that thou destroyest us after this
5 " merciless manner? Does it seem to you wrong
" that we venerate the universal Creator, and live
6 " according to his most virtuous law? This con-
" duct, surely, deserves honours rather than tor-
" tures. [If (at least[a]) you had ever felt any of
" the desires of men, and had entertained a hope
" of salvation from God. But lo! now, being
" estranged from God, you persecute those who
" are reverent towards Him."]
7 While he was uttering these words, the guards
having bound him, dragged him to the catapelta:
8 to which tying him by the knees, and making

[a] This part, to the end of the verse, is omitted by Josephus. The sense at present is imperfect, and requires to be completed by the insertion of the words, " you would have been sensible of this," if, &c.

these fast with iron fetters, they twisted[b] his loins upon the wedge of the wheel; on which being wholly disjointed, he curled round the wheel like a scorpion [or snake], and was pulled limb from limb. In this manner, being both hard pressed for breath, and crushed in his body, he said: " Involuntarily, O tyrant, you bestow on us fair " favours, giving us opportunity, by more nobly " borne sufferings, to exhibit our endurance in " defence of the law."

And when he also was dead, the sixth was brought out, a mere youth: who, when the tyrant asked if he would eat and save himself, replied: " I indeed in age am younger than my brethren, " but in purpose of mind I am their equal. For " we, having been brought forth and educated in " the same manner, ought alike to die in defence " of the same *cause*. So that if you chuse to tor- " ment us because we eat not unclean food, tor- " ment."

When he had thus spoken, they brought him to the rack: stretched on which, with his limbs strained and his spine disjointed, he was roasted from beneath. And having heated sharp spits, they applied them to his back; and piercing through his sides, they burned away his entrails. But he, while thus tormented, said; " O holy " noble trial, to which so many brothers of us " being called, to be exercised in sufferings for

---

[b] The Greek text of this verse is somewhat difficult of interpretation: τὴν ὀσφὺν αὐτοῦ περὶ τὸν τροχαῖον σφῆνα κατέκαμψαν· περὶ ὃν ὅλος ἐπὶ τὸν τροχὸν σκορπίου τρόπον ἀνακλώμενος ἐξεμελίζετο. It may mean, that he was broken into as many pieces as there are joints in the tail of a scorpion.

18 " religion's sake, have not been overcome! For
" righteous knowledge[c], armed with honour and
19 " virtue, O tyrant, is invincible. I shall soon die,
" *and be* with my brethren: and so will you[d], O
" tyrant, *shortly*, having brought upon yourself a
20 " severe avenging fiend. O thou inventor of new
" torments[e], and enemy of those who are truly
" religious, we six youths have demolished thy
21 " tyrannic sway. For is it not a demolishing of
" you, that you have not been able to persuade
" away our Principle, nor to force us to the eat-
22 " ing of unclean food? Your fire to us is cold:
" your catapeltæ give no pain : and your violence
23 " is powerless. For the guards, not of a tyrant,
" but of the Divine Law, are our protectors ;
" through this, we retain our Principle unsub-
" dued."

CHAPTER XII.

The speech, and death, of the seventh brother.

1 AND when he also, having been thrown into
a caldron, had died blessedly, the seventh came
2 forward, the youngest of all: whom the tyrant
commiserating, although he had been sorely put
to shame by his brethren; seeing him already
bound in chains, he sent for him to come nearer,
3 and endeavoured to advise him, saying: " You

[c] Gr. ἡ εὐσεβὴς ἐπιστήμη καλοκᾳγαθίᾳ καθωπλισμένη. The punctuation in this and the next two verses is very faulty in the edition of 1817, and obstructs the sense.

[d] The Greek text is obscure here. It may mean, that " I myself shall bring " upon you a severe avenger."

[e] See the same character given of Antiochus at 3 Macc. ix. 6. " He had tormented " other men's bowels with " many *and strange* tor- " ments."

"see now the result of your brethren's folly; for "through disobedience they have been racked "and are dead: and you yourself, unless you "obey, shall, after horrible tortures, die forthwith "before your time[a]. But, if you will be per- "suaded, you shall be our friend, and shall take "a lead in the affairs of the kingdom."

And having thus exhorted him, he sent for the boy's mother; that having condoled with her on the loss of so many sons, he might rouse her to save *one*[b] *at least*, by making this surviving one obedient. But he, after that his mother had exhorted him in the Hebrew tongue, (as we shall relate in a short time) said; "Let me go, that I "may speak to the king and to all his friends "with him." And they, the king and his friends, rejoicing exceedingly at the youth's announcement, quickly set him free. And he, running close up to the frying-pans, said: "Unholy tyrant, "most impious of all wicked wretches! are you "not ashamed, having received from God worldly "good things and a kingdom, to slay his servants, "and to rack those who practise piety? For "which things, the Divine vengeance is keeping "you in store for a more intense and eternal fire "and torments, which shall not cease from you "for ever. Were you not ashamed, O most sa- "vage wretch, being a man yourself, to cut out "the tongues of men formed with like passions[c],

---

[a] Gr. πρὸ ὥρας; or it may mean, "within this very "hour."

[b] Gr. παρορμήσειεν ἐπὶ τὴν σωτηρίαν.

[c] Gr. τοὺς ὁμοιοπαθεῖς; the expression used to the men of Lystra by St. Paul: see Acts xiv. 15.

" and composed of the same elements [d]; and
" shamefully to misuse and torment them in this
12 " manner? They, however, having died nobly,
13 " have fulfilled their piety towards God. But
" you, wretch, shall miserably suffer [e], for having
" slain without cause the champions of virtue.
14 " Wherefore I, (continued he,) being myself about
" to die, do not desert the testimony [f] of my bre-
15 " thren. [And I invoke the God of my fathers,
" that He will be merciful to my family. But
" you He will punish, both in this life and after
" death [g]."]
16 And having prayed thus against *the tyrant*, he threw himself into the frying-pans, and so expired.

CHAPTER XIII.

Reflections on the above-mentioned occurrence.

1 Now if these seven brethren despised sufferings even unto death, it is confessed on all sides that religious Principle is absolute master of the
2 passions. For as, if being enslaved by their passions, they had eaten the unclean meat, we should have said that they were vanquished by these
3 *passions;* so now it is not so: but through that principle which we have commended [a], by God's
4 help they overcame their passions. And it is impossible to overlook this victorious generalship [b] of

[d] So at Acts xvii. 26, St. Paul declares, that God "hath " made of one blood all na-" tions of the earth."

[e] Gr. κακὸς κακῶς οἰμώξεις, a phrase sufficiently familiar to the readers of the Greek dramatic poets.

[f] The Greek text varies, between μαρτυρίας and ἀριστείας, " noble conduct."

[g] This verse is omitted by Josephus.

[a] Gr. τῷ ἐπαινουμένῳ λογισμῷ παρὰ Θεῷ περιεγένοντο τ. π.

[b] Or sovereignty. Gr. τὴν ἡγεμονίαν τῆς διανοίας.

settled purpose: for it prevailed over both passion and sufferings. How then can we avoid conceding to these men the conquest of their passions through rectitude of principle, who shrank not from the pains of fire? For like as towers[c] placed at the mouths of harbours, breaking the threats of the waves, afford a calm sea to those who are sailing into port; so that sevenfold[d] barrier, the right principle of these youths, having fortified the harbour of piety, conquered the headstrong violence of *their* passions. For having formed a holy band of piety, they animated each other, saying; "Brothers! let us die like brothers, in de-"fence of the law. Let us imitate the three "young men[e] in Assyria, who despised the fur-"nace equally torturing[f] to them all. Let us "not shrink from shewing forth our piety." And one said, "Take courage, brother:" and another, "Endure nobly." And another, putting them in remembrance, said, "Remember whence ye are, "and by what father's hand Isaac through his "piety submitted to be offered for a victim." And one and all looking on *each other*, cheerful and full of confidence, said; "Let us with all our "heart sacrifice ourselves to God who gave us "our lives, and let us make our bodies serviceable "for the preservation of the law. Let us not fear

[c] Gr. Καθάπερ γὰρ προβλῆτες λιμένων πύργοι. Thus in the Ajax of Sophocles the projecting rock of Sunium is called πόντου πρόβλημα ἁλίκλυστον. See a metaphor of the same kind above at ch. vii. 5.

[d] Gr. ἡ ἑπτάπυργος τῶν νεανίσκων εὐλογιστία.

[e] Namely, those mentioned in the book of Daniel.

[f] Gr. ἰσοπάλιδος καμίνου. Or perhaps the expression may mean, "equal to those tor-"tures which are prepared "for us;" so that they have set us an honourable example.

"him who appears to kill the body[g]. For a great
"trial and danger to the soul is laid up for those
13 "who transgress the commandment of God. Let
"us therefore arm ourselves with that mastery[h]
"over the passions which divine principle sup-
14 "plies. For when we shall have suffered thus,
"Abraham and Isaac and Jacob will receive us
"into their bosoms[i], and all the fathers will
15 "praise us." And to each one of their brethren
who was dragged along, the rest said; "Do not
"disgrace us, brother; nor disappoint *the just*
"*hopes of* those who have died before us."

16 Now you are not ignorant of the charm *and
spell* of brotherhood, which divine and allwise
Providence has imparted through fathers to their
children, and which it has implanted even from
17 the mother's womb. In which these brothers having remained an equal time, and being formed in
the same period, and increasing in growth from
the same blood, and being completed with the
18 same life, and brought forth after equal periods,
and drinking milk from the same fountains,—on
those accounts the affectionate souls are nourished[k] up together in the embraces of *the same*
19 bosom; and increase *in affection* more and more
by this bringing up together, and by daily intercourse, and by the rest of their education, and by

---

[g] Thus our blessed Saviour instructs his disciples: "Fear "not them which kill the "body, but are not able to "kill the soul," &c. Matt. x. 28.

[h] Gr. τῇ τοῦ θείου λογισμοῦ παθοκρατείᾳ.

[i] Compare Luke xvi. 22, 23.

[k] Gr. ἀφ' ὧν συντρέφονται ἐν ἐναγκαλισμάτων, [sed lege ἀγκαλαῖς μαστῶν] φιλάδελφοι ψυχαί. The text is rather obscure: and beyond all doubt the reading of the edition of 1817 is corrupt.

that study and practice (which we use) of the law of God.

Brotherly affection therefore, being thus full of sympathy, *even in ordinary cases*, these seven brethren had between themselves a still more strongly sympathetic unanimity. For having been educated in the same law, and having practised the same virtues, and being brought up together in a life of righteousness, they loved[1] each other with still greater ardour. For a similar zeal for all which was right and honourable, added intensity to their mutual accordance. For by the addition of piety, it made brotherly affection more than ever desirable to them. But yet, although nature, and familiarity, and virtuous morals, had combined to increase in them the *already* strong ties of brotherhood; those who were left of *them* endured to behold their brethren, who were cruelly used for their religion, tortured even unto death.

CHAPTER XIV.

Reflections on the noble conduct of the youths, and on their mother's sufferings.

AND more than this, they were even encouraging them on to the cruel treatment: so that they not only disregarded those pains, but likewise overcame the affections of brotherly love. O principles, more kingly than a king! more liberal than the liberal minded [a]! O sacred and harmonious agreement of the seven brethren in religion! Not one of the seven youths shewed cowardice, nor

---

[1] The edition of 1817 is again faulty here. βασιλικώτεροι, καὶ ἐλευθέρων ἐλευθερώτεροι.

[a] Gr. Ὦ βασιλέως λογισμοὶ

shrank back from death. But all, as if they were running the road to immortality, hastened to the
4 death by torture. For, as the hands and feet move in accordance with the directions of the mind: so these holy youths, being moved by religion[b], as by one immortal soul, joined in undergoing death for its sake.
5 O most holy sevenfold band[c] of accordant bro-
6 thers! For, as the seven days of creation revolving formed the circle of the week: so these youths formed a circling band of piety, overcom-
7 ing the fear of *the tyrant's* torments. Now we, *even* at hearing the affliction of those young men, are struck with horror; but they, not only seeing, and not only hearing the threatening words on the spot, but also suffering *the effect of those threats*, endured it; and this, through the pains
8 of fire. Than which, what can be more painful? for the power of fire, being sharp and rapid, quickly consumes the bodies.
9 And think it not marvellous, that the principle of those men prevailed amidst their torments; when even a woman's mind despised pains still
10 more varied. For the mother[d] of those seven

[b] The Greek text here is not quite clear.

[c] There is a degree of obscurity about the Greek text of this passage: Ὦ παναγία ἡ συμφώνων ἀδελφῶν ἑβδομάς· καθάπερ γὰρ ἑπτὰ τῆς κοσμοποιίας ἡμέραι περὶ τὴν εὐσέβειαν· οὕτως περὶ τὴν ἑβδομάδα χορεύοντες οἱ μείρακες ἐκύκλουν τὸν τῶν βασάνων φόβον καταλύοντες. L'Estrange paraphrases it thus: "For as the seven days in which the world was created give us the idea of God, and shew the perfection of his majesty and goodness; so do these seven renowned martyrs, by running the whole circle of pains and tortures, compose one finished piece of constancy and courage; and teach us that perfection of fortitude which banishes the slavish fear of death."

[d] Augustin thus expresses himself on the subject of this

young men endured *equal* rackings over every one of her children. And consider now, how extensive and variously entwined[e] is the ardour of parental affection, drawing every creature to a sympathy with its own offspring. Since even irrational animals entertain towards their young the same sympathy and affection as human beings. For instance, among birds, those which are domesticated and wander about *our* houses, defend their young. And those which make nests and hatch young on the tops of mountains, and in the crags of valleys, and the hollows and tops of trees, hinder any one from approaching them. And even if they are unable to prevent this;—flying around[f] them, in agony of affection, calling out in their peculiar note, they succour their offspring in whatever manner they are able. And why need we shew by *example of* irrational animals the sympathy which exists towards our children? when even bees, at the season of making honey, drive away those who approach them; and pierce with their sting, as with a sword, those who go near to their hive, and defend themselves even unto death.

CHAPTER XV.

An eulogy of the mother, for her most noble behaviour.

NEVERTHELESS[a], sympathy for her children

---

verse : " Isti in se singuli " sentiendo, illa videndo in " omnibus passa est. Facta " mater septem martyrum, " septies martyr." (Augustini Sermo de Maccabæis, Op. tom. V. p. 851. ed. Benedictin.)

[e] Gr. πολύπλοκος: there is a various reading, πολύτεκνος: but the former is to be preferred.

[f] Thus, in that fine simile in the second book of the Iliad, it is said, Μήτηρ δ' ἀμφεποτᾶτο ὀδυρομένη φίλα τέκνα.

[a] The Greek text in these two verses is confused, and probably faulty.

did not move aside *from her fixed purpose* the mother of the young men, who had a spirit[b] equal to that of her *forefather* Abraham. O Principle, sovereign of the passions! and Piety, dearer to a mother than *even* her children! The mother, when two things were set before her; religion, or the saving of her sons for a time, according to the tyrant's promise; rather chose religion, which saveth to eternal life[c] with God.

O! in what way can I morally pourtray[d] the affections of parents to their children? which wondrously stamp[e] a similarity, both of mind and form, on that small distinctive character *which each possesses*, namely, of *being* a child! as mothers especially sympathise more strongly than fathers in the sufferings of their children. For inasmuch as mothers are more tender-minded and more fond[f] of that which is born of them, so much more affection do they bear towards their children. But this mother of the seven *youths* was more fond of her children than all mothers: who, growing in affection towards them through seven child-births, and forced by her many pains with each one to have a sympathy of feeling with

---

[b] Gr. τὴν Ἀβραὰμ ὁμόψυχον.

[c] How closely does this sentiment correspond with the comforting address of our Saviour to his disciples, as given at Matth. x. 39; xvi. 25; Luke xvii. 33; and John xii. 25. "He that loveth his life "shall lose it: and he that "hateth his life in this world "shall keep it unto life eter- "nal."

[d] Gr. ἠθολογήσαιμ' ἄν.

[e] The meaning of this passage is not very clear. The text is, ψυχῆς τε καὶ μορφῆς ὁμοιότητα εἰς μικρὸν παιδὸς χαρακτῆρα θαυμάσιον ἐναποσφραγίζοντα, μάλιστα διὰ τὸ πάθος, τοῖς γεννηθεῖσιν τὰς μητέρας τῶν πατέρων καθεστάναι συμπαθεστέρας. There is some variety of reading in the latter part of the verse.

[f] The Greek varies, between φιλογονώτεραι and πολυγονώτεραι: but the latter can scarcely be maintained.

them; yet through the fear of God regarded not the temporary saving of her sons[g].

Not but that, on account of her sons' noble con- 8 duct, and their obedience to the law, she felt a still greater yearning of affection towards them. For they were both just, and temperate, and 9 brave, and high-minded, and fond of their brothers; and fond of their mother to such a degree that they obeyed her even unto death, by keeping the injunctions of the law. But yet, although there 10 were so many circumstances of affection which drew on a mother to sympathy: in the case of no one of them were the various tortures able to turn astray her principle. But each child separately, 11 and all of them together, the mother *actually* encouraged to the death for religion's sake.

O holy disposition, and charms of parental love, 12 and affectionate feeling[h], and the influence[i] of having bred up children, and the indomitable affections of mothers! The mother beholding[k] them 13 one by one racked and burned, changed not herself, through religion. She beheld the flesh of 14 her children consuming in the fire, and their toes and fingers quivering on the ground, and the flesh of their heads *stripped off*[l], even down to the beards, *and* hanging down like masks.

[g] The Greek text of this verse is very faulty, in the edition of 1817.

[h] Gr. σύνεσις: but the edit. 1817, reads γονεῦσιν.

[i] The Greek text gives the single word τροφεία, with a conciseness of expression which our language will not reach.

[k] Gregory Nazianzen, in his fine animated oration on this subject, thus powerfully describes the moral courage of this parent: ʽΗν οὐδὲν ἔκαμψεν οὐδ' ἐμαλάκισεν—οὐκ ἀρθρέμβολα προτεινόμενα, οὐ τροχοὶ——οὐ σάρκες ξαινόμεναι, οὐχ αἵματος ὀχετοὶ ῥέοντες. (Orat. XXII. de Maccabæis, p. 400. edit. Paris. fol. 1609.)

[l] See above, ch. ix. 28.

15 O mother, who at this instant wast tried by severer pangs than in thy bearing of them! O thou woman, who alone hast brought forth entire
16 holiness! Thy first-born expiring did not move thee: nor the second, piteously regarding thee in his torments: nor the third, yielding up his
17 breath. Nor, when thou didst behold the eyes of each of them fiercely glaring on[m] the tortures destined for them, and their nostrils snuffing up the gale[n] of their own death,—didst thou weep!
18 When thou beheldest flesh upon flesh of thy children chopped in pieces, hands after hands amputated, and heads upon heads cut off, and corpse falling upon corpse; and sawest the lately happy band of thy children made a common sepulchre[o] by these tortures,—thou didst not shed one tear.
19 Not so powerfully do the melodies of the sirens nor the notes of swans attract the hearers to listening, as did the voices of these children in
20 torments calling on their mother. With what and how great tortures was the mother *herself* tormented, while her sons were being tortured by

---

[m] Gr. ταυρηδὸν ὁρῶντας. Thus we read in the Medea of Euripides, ἀποτεταύρωται δμῶσιν: and again,—εἶδον ὄμμα νιν ταυρουμένην: and in Aristophanes, (Ran. 804.) ἔβλεψε γοῦν ταυρηδὸν ἐγκύψας κάτω. Also, in the Phædo of Plato, Socrates on receiving the cup of hemlock, is described as ὥσπερ εἰώθει ταυρηδὸν ὑποβλέψας πρὸς τὸν ἄνθρωπον, κ. τ. λ. In this latter passage, however, the sense seems to be *somewhat* different, and the expression may refer to a *fixed steady look*, rather than to a fierce or determined one. The Greek classics furnish many cognate expressions: in Ælian we have σεμνὸν καὶ βλοσυρὸν ὁρᾶν; and again τιτανῶδες βλέπειν. (Var. Hist. XII. 21. et Fragm.)—and ἀρρενωπὸν καὶ γοργὸν βλέπειν. (Var. Hist. II. 44. XIII. 1.) &c. &c.

[n] Gr. προσημειουμένους, literally, "presignifying."

[o] Gr. πολυάνδριον. Compare 3 Macc. ix. 4, and the note on that passage.

racks and burning irons! But religious Principle, 21 having in the midst of sufferings manfully nerved her mind, gave her energy to look beyond the temporary calls of parental love. Though she 22 beheld the destruction of seven sons [p]: the noble mother stripped off all these *feelings*, through her faith towards God. For perceiving in her own 23 mind, as in a council-chamber, powerful advisers, namely, nature, and parentage, and maternal affection, and the rackings of her children; the 24 mother, holding two votes [q], one fatal to her children, the other preservative *of them*, decided not for a preservation which would save her seven sons for a short time; but, being a true daughter of Abraham, she was mindful of religious constancy [r].

[p] Josephus adds here, "and "the complicated variety of "their tortures," καὶ τὴν τῶν στρεβλῶν πολύπλοκον ποικιλίαν. And the text, if not absolutely corrupt, is certainly imperfect without the insertion, as may be perceived; Καίπερ ἑπτὰ τέκνων ὁρῶσα ἀπώλειαν,—ἃς πάσας ἡ γενναία μήτηρ ἐξέδυσεν διὰ τὴν πρὸς Θεὸν πίστιν.

[q] In all cases which were to be determined by suffrage, it was customary among the Greeks for each person to have two ψῆφοι, or tickets; one of which was called ψῆφος σώζουσα, being favourable to the party under judgment, the other ψῆφος καθαιροῦσα, which rejected or condemned him, as the case might be. See Lysias, Orat. XIII. There were also two methods of giving these votes; one, the ψῆφος φανερὰ, where the vote was openly and publicly given; the other, ψῆφος ἀφανὴς, where the ticket was privately put into an urn, to be afterwards drawn out with many others, but without its being known who had voted either one way or the other. (See the above passage of Lysias; also an instance of the ψῆφος φανερὰ, in Thucydides IV. 74.) The former of these modes resembles our parliamentary and public votings; the latter is equivalent to the vote by ballot.

[r] An example of nearly similar heroism is recorded in the fifth book of Maccabees, chapter xx; where the mother of John Hyrcanus, having

25 O mother of a nation, avenger of the law, champion of religion, and conqueress in a struggle
26 of affections! O thou who wast more noble in endurance than males, more manly than men in patience! For, as the ark of Noah in the universal deluge, bearing in it the entire world, sus-
27 tained the violent waves: so thou, observer of the law, *though* overwhelmed on all sides by a deluge of troubles, and hard pressed by violent winds, *namely*, the tortures of thy sons,—didst nobly sustain the storms for religion's sake.

CHAPTER XVI.

The praises of the mother of the seven brethren.

1 IF then a woman, and she an old one, and the mother of seven children, endured to behold the tortures of her children even unto death: confessedly religious Principle is perfect master of the passions.
2 Now I have shewn, that not only men have mastered the passions, but even that a woman
3 nobly disregarded the greatest torments. And not so furious were Daniel's lions; nor so fiercely flamed the furnace of Misael with most devouring[a] fire; as the natural love of her children burned *in*

---

been taken prisoner with two of her sons, by Ptolemy, who had basely murdered their father Simon at a banquet, is brought on the wall of a town where Hyrcanus was besieging Ptolemy, and threatened with her own death and that of her sons, unless Hyrcanus would raise the siege. She however exhorts him manfully to continue his assault, and accordingly is put to death soon after by the tyrant.

[a] Gr. λαβροτάτῳ πυρί: which Pindar calls Σέλας λάβρον Ἀφαίστου. (Pyth. III. 69.) The same phrase is used by Oppian.

"for God's sake. Do you therefore, having the 20
"same faith towards God, make no complaint.
"For it is unreasonable that they who are in-
"structed in religion should not bear up against
"troubles."

With these arguments the mother of the seven 21
encouraging each one of her sons, persuaded them
to die rather than transgress the command of
God: especially as they knew this, that those who 22
die in God's cause *really* live to God[h], as Abraham, and Isaac, and Jacob, and all the patriarchs.

CHAPTER XVII.

The praises of the mother continued.

MOREOVER, some of the guards related, that 1
when she herself was about to be seized and put
to death, in order that nobody might touch[a] her
person, she threw herself[b] upon the pile. O mo- 2
ther, who with thy seven sons hast overthrown
the tyrant's violence, and defeated his wicked devices; and hast demonstrated the nobleness of

"the souls of thine enemies
"the Lord thy God shall
"*sling out*, as out of the mid-
"dle of a sling." 1 Samuel
xxv. 29.

[h] According to the words of our Saviour, "Now that
"the dead are raised, even
"Moses shewed at the bush,
"when he calleth the Lord
"the God of Abraham, and
"the God of Isaac, and the
"God of Jacob. For He is
"not a God of the dead, but
"of the living; for all live
"to Him." Luke xx. 37.

[a] So in the Hecuba of Euripides, when Polyxena, the daughter of Priam, is about to be offered as a sacrifice, she desires the surrounding guards to retire, and not venture to touch her: 'Εκοῦσα θνήσκω· μήτις ἅψηται χροὸς τοῦ 'μοῦ.

[b] The author of the preceding book gives no particulars of the death of the mother; but merely says, "Last
"of all, after the sons, the
"mother died." Later writers have asserted that she underwent the same or even greater torments.

3 Faith! For thou, as a house[c] firmly supported on the pillar of thy children, didst bear without bend-
4 ing the shock of *the tyrant's* tortures. Be of good cheer, therefore, O holy-minded mother, having a firm hope[d] in God of *a reward* for thy endurance.
5 Not so majestic stands the moon in heaven, surrounded by the stars; as thou, having robed in the light[e] of religion thy seven sons, equal to stars, art become honourable in God's sight, and
6 with them art fixed in heaven. For the generation of thy family was truly from the son[f] of *Abraham*.
7 Now if it were in my power to pourtray[g], as in a picture, thy religious story, would not men shudder at beholding the mother of seven children undergoing in the cause of religion various tor-
8 tures even unto death? And indeed it would be right moreover to inscribe upon the tomb itself these words, which are set down for a memorial
9 to those of *our* nation: " Here are entombed an " aged priest, and an aged woman, and seven sons, " through the violence of a tyrant, who wished to
10 " destroy the civil polity of the Hebrews. Who " also have avenged[h] their nation, looking unto " God, and enduring the torments unto death."

[c] Josephus differs here slightly from the text; and his reading gives a less perplexed construction, though the meaning is evidently alike in both.

[d] Gr. τὴν ἐλπίδα τῆς ὑπομονῆς γενναίως [var. lect. βεβαίαν] ἔχουσα πρὸς Θεόν.

[e] Gr. ὡς σὺ τοὺς ἰσαστέρους ἑπτὰ παῖδας φωταγωγήσασα πρὸς τὴν εὐσέβειαν ἔντιμος καθέστηκας Θεῷ.

[f] The Greek text varies between παιδὸς and πατρός.

[g] Gr. ὥσπερ ἐπὶ πίνακός τινος ζωγραφῆσαι τὴν τῆς ἱστορίας σου εὐσέβειαν [qu. τῆς εὐσεβείας σου ἱστορίαν?] The edition of 1817 is defective here.

[h] Or, have vindicated the character of their nation. Gr. ἐξεδίκησαν. Compare ver. 19, below.

For in truth the struggle which was made by 11 them was divine. For at that time Virtue directed the games[i], adjudging the victory by endurance, in immortality, in eternal life. And the 13 first combatant[k] was Eleazar: and the mother of the seven children was in the struggle: and the brothers were combatants. Their antagonist was, 14 the tyrant; and the spectators were, the world and the human race. And religion was declared 15 conqueror, and she crowned her own champions.

Who did not admire the champions of divine 16 legislation? Who were not astonished *at them*? The tyrant himself[l], at all events, and all his council, most exceedingly wondered at their patient endurance. Through which also they now 17 are standing beside the throne of God, and are leading a life of blessedness. For Moses truly 18 has said[m], "and all his saints are in thy hand."

They, therefore, having been sanctified through 19 God, have been honoured not only with this honour, but also *with the additional praise* that through their exertions the enemy did not overcome our nation: and that the tyrant was pu- 20 nished, and the country was cleansed *from sin;* they having become as it were a devoted offering[n] for the sin of the nation. And through the blood 21 of those pious men, and their propitiatory death,

---

[i] Gr. Ἠθλοθέτει γὰρ τότε ἀρετὴ δι' ὑπομονῆς δοκιμάζουσα τὸ νῖκος ἐν ἀφθαρσίᾳ ἐν ζωῇ πολυχρονίῳ. The entire imagery is taken from the public games of Greece.

[k] So Gregory Nazianzen expresses himself on the subject: προηγωνίσατο πατὴρ, ἐπαγωνιοῦνται παῖδες. Orat. XXII.

[l] See above, ch. i. 11.

[m] At Deuter. xxxiii. 3.

[n] Gr. ἀντίψυχον. Compare ch. i. 11, and vi. 24; with the note there.

Divine Providence effectually saved Israel, which before was overwhelmed with evils.

22 For the tyrant Antiochus, beholding the bravery of their virtue, and their patience under torments, proclaimed their constancy by a herald, for
23 an example to his own soldiers. And he kept them *in his service* as noble and brave men, both for pitched battle and for siege of cities: and *by their aid* he routed and vanquished all his enemies.

CHAPTER XVIII.

The victorious result of their constancy. The mother's speech to her children.

1 O YE Israelites, descendants of the seed of Abraham, obey this law, and in every way ob-
2 serve religion. Knowing that religious Principle is lord over the passions: and not only over troubles from within, but likewise over those which are from without.

3 By which means those youths, exposing their lives to sufferings for religion, not only were admired by men, but also were deemed worthy of a
4 divine inheritance. And through them the nation obtained peace; and having reestablished in the country the wholesome observance of the laws, it
5 effectually dislodged its enemies. And the tyrant Antiochus was both punished on earth, and *now*
6 after his death is still enduring punishment. For, when he could by no means prevail *so far as* to compel the inhabitants of Jerusalem to adopt Gentile customs[a], and to live in a manner strange[b] to
7 the usages of their country: he forthwith de-

[a] Gr. ἀλλοφυλῆσαι.   [b] Compare book II. ch. i. 44.

parted from Jerusalem[c], and led his army against the Persians. [B. C. 166.]

[d] That righteous woman, the mother of the seven young men, said thus also to her children: "I formerly was a pure virgin, and did not go "out from my father's house; but kept within [e] "the walled building. No ravisher, the despoiler "of unprotected innocence, ruined me in the field[f]: "nor did the seducer, the deceitful serpent [g], cor-

[c] Compare 2 Macc. iii. 27—31. 3 Macc. ix. 1, 2.

[d] All which follows after the seventh verse is believed to have been written by a different author.

[e] Gr. ἐφύλασσον τὴν ᾠκοδομημένην πλευρὰν, the meaning of which expression is ambiguous.

[f] See Deut. xxii. 25.

[g] Is this *merely* a metaphorical expression? or does it cover a less obvious meaning? Can it allude to any of those strange opinions concerning the serpent in Paradise, which are known to have prevailed in various ages of the world?

The heresy of the Ophitæ, who worshipped the serpent as a god, is mentioned by Origen in his sixth book against Celsus, and is described by Epiphanius, (Hæres. 37.) — Tertullian (adversus Valentinianos, cap. 2.) calls it, "Ille a primordio *Divinæ* "*imaginis prædo.*" Tennison, in his Discourse on Idolatry, (4to. 1678, p. 354,) speaks of "good angels ap- "pearing *like the most emi- "nent sort of winged ser- "pents, with beautiful faces,* "*it may be, of men,*" &c. And again; "If the seraphim "had not appeared in some "such form, it would be very "difficult to give any tolera- "ble account of the tempta- "tion of Adam and Eve by "a dæmon in the shape of a "serpent. That serpent is "ridiculously painted in the "form of a creeping one be- "fore the fall: and it is im- "possible to conceive our "first parents so stupid as to "have entered into discourse "with such a creature with- "out any astonishment." Ibid.

It is well known to those who are conversant in such matters, that in ancient illuminated biblical manuscripts, the serpent, while tempting Eve, is often drawn *with the face of a very handsome young man.* And there are pictures, by Michael Angelo and others, representing it with a human face, sometimes male, sometimes also female. The same thing is seen on ancient carvings, which decorate both the outsides and insides of our churches.

Mercerus, in his Commentary on Genesis, ch. iii. re-

"rupt my virginity: but I remained with a hus-
11 "band during the flower of my age. And when
"these my children had grown up, their father
"died: happy indeed *was he:* for having passed
"a life of abundance of fine children, he escaped
"the painful period of being deprived [h] of them.
12 "Who, while he was yet with you, used to teach
13 "you the law and the prophets. And he read to
"us of Abel, who was murdered by Cain: and of
"Isaac, who was offered for a burnt-offering: and
14 "of Joseph, who was in prison. He told us also
"of the zealous Phineas: and he taught you the
"*story of* Ananias, Azarias, and Misael. And he
"used to glorify Daniel, who was in the den of
15 "lions; whom also he pronounced blessed. And
"he reminded you of the scripture of Esaias [i],
"which says, 'When thou walkest through the
16 "fire, the flame shall not burn thee.' He chanted
"to you David [k], the writer of the hymns, who
"says, 'Many are the afflictions of the righteous,
17 "and the Lord shall deliver him out of all.' He
"recited to us the Proverbs of Solomon, who saith [l],

lates the opinion of some Jewish doctors, (but to which he himself does not assent,) in the following words: "He-"bræorum quidam, quod ego "alienum puto, serpentem "inquiunt vidisse eos soboli "procreandæ operam dantes, "et inde eam appetiisse: sed "spiritus est Satanas, nec in "serpentem ut mulierem ap-"peteret competere poterat." Whether there be any connexion between this opinion of the rabbins, and the expression in the text, I do not feel myself able to decide.—Quære. Will the literature of *Holland* furnish us with any lights upon this subject?

[h] The Greek text has here two elegant and concise expressions, put in opposition to each other; εὐτεκνίας βίον, and ἀτεκνίας καιρὸν, which we are *compelled* to paraphrase, our language not furnishing a literal translation of them.

[i] Namely, at ch. xliii. 2.
[k] In Psalm xxxiv. 19.
[l] Viz. at Prov. iii. 18.

"'He is a tree of life to all those who do his will.'
"He bare witness to Ezechiel[m], who saith, 'Shall 18
"these dry bones live?' For he did not forget 19
"the song which Moses taught[n], which teacheth
"and saith; 'I will kill, and I will make alive.
"This is your life, and the prolonging[o] of your
"days.'"

O! bitter was that day, yet not *really* bitter[p], 20 when the bitter tyrant of the Gentiles kindled the fire under his savage caldrons, and with boiling fury brought to the catapelta and to all his torments the seven sons of the daughter of Abraham. Their eyeballs he blinded; and their tongues he 21 cut out; and he slew them with various torments. For which deeds Divine Justice pursued, and will 22 pursue, the accursed *sinner*. But the sons of Abra- 23 ham, with their victorious mother, are gathered together to the land of their fathers, having received again pure and immortal souls from God. To whom be glory for ever and ever. Amen. 24

[m] Gr. ἐπιστοποιεῖτο. See Ezech. xxxvii. 3.
[n] Namely, at Deut. xxxii. 39, 47.
[o] The Greek varies, between μακρότης and μακαριότης: but the *former* agrees with the passage as it stands in the book of Deuteronomy.
[p] Gr. Ὦ πικρᾶς τῆς τότε ἡμέρας, καὶ οὐ πικρᾶς, a mode of expression familiarly used by the Greek dramatic writers.

END OF BOOK IV.

THE FIFTH BOOK

OF

MACCABEES:

CONTAINING

A RECORD OF EVENTS FROM THE TRANSLATION OF THE HEBREW SCRIPTURES INTO GREEK UNDER PTOLEMY PHILADELPHUS, (B.C. 277,) TO THE DEATH OF HEROD'S TWO SONS, IN THE FIFTH OR SIXTH YEAR BEFORE CHRIST.

PREFACE (from the Paris Polyglott Bible.)

THIS book, from the first to the sixteenth chapter inclusive, is entitled, " The Second Book of " Maccabees according to the translation of the " Hebrews," as may be seen at the end of ch. xvi. The remainder of it is entitled simply, " The Se-" cond Book of Maccabees," the series of chapters being continued from the preceding portion. But, since the work agrees neither with the Syriac text, which is considered of the highest authority among the Orientals, nor with the Greek, nor with the Vulgate version, (although it exists in almost all the Oriental manuscripts), we have placed it at the end of this Bible, and moreover without its points: both, that it may not be supposed by any one that we include it among the canonical books;

and also, because the Second Book of Maccabees, which is reckoned canonical, still remains to us entire, though under the name of " The First " Book."

You have however in this book some particulars extracted from the first and from the second: also some others which perhaps have never yet been made public; which we trust may not be without some degree of pleasure to you: inasmuch as the entire book is a sort of continuation of the history, carried down from the very Maccabees to the reign of Herod and the government of Pilate[a], and consequently to the time of Christ our Lord.

Lastly, we wish you to understand that we have copied the text with that scrupulous exactness, that we have not changed even those things which easily might have been altered for the better.

CHAPTER I.[b]

The attempt of Heliodorus on the treasury.

It was ordained by the kings[c] of the Grecian Gentiles that large sums of money should be sent into the holy city[d] every year, and

---

[a] This appears to be a mistake, as will be seen on reference to the note at ch. lix. 25.

[b] Compare this chapter with 3 Macc. iii.

[c] Namely, by Seleucus Nicanor, Antiochus the Second, Antiochus the Great, and also Seleucus IV, surnamed Soter, or Philopator, the son of Antiochus the Great.

[d] Among the peculiarities of expression observable in this Fifth Book, are to be reckoned " the house of " God," or " the holy house," instead of " the temple ;" " the holy city," or " the " city of the holy house,"

should be delivered to the priests, that they might add it to the treasury of the house of God, as money for the receivers of alms [orphans] and for widows.

2 Now Seleucus[e] was king in Macedonia[f]: and he had a friend[g], one of his captains, who was called Heliodorus. This man was sent to spoil the treasury, and to take whatever
3 money was therein. When this was noised abroad, it created great grief among the citizens; and they were afraid lest Heliodorus should pro-
4 ceed to greater lengths; as they had not sufficient power to prevent him from executing his orders.
5 Wherefore they all fly to God *for aid*, and ordained a general fast, and supplicated with humi-
6 lity, bowing of the knees, and great wailing; putting on sackcloth, and rolling themselves in ashes, with Onias[h] the high priest and the other princes and elders, even to the common people, and wo-
7 men and children. And on the next day Heliodorus came into the house of God, with a train of followers; and entered into the house with his foot

B.C. 176.

for Jerusalem; and "the "land (or region) of the "holy house," to designate "Judæa." The other more usual appellations do sometimes occur, but very seldom. About this title, "the holy "city," a phrase which is used frequently in the Old Testament, and likewise in St. Matthew and the book of Revelation, much has been written by commentators; and the reader, desirous of fuller information on the point, is referred to Calmet and Prideaux.

[e] Namely, Seleucus IV.

[f] And of Syria also; by which means he possessed the sovereignty of Judæa.

[g] In 3 Macc. iii. Heliodorus is called *treasurer* to the king.

[h] Namely, Onias III.— N.B. I have generally judged it superfluous to make mention, in the notes on *this* book, of persons previously named and described in any of the former books.

soldiers, he himself being on horseback, and was in search of the money. But the great and good 8 God[i] sent a loud, terrible voice upon him; and he saw a person armed with weapons of war, riding on a large horse, *and* advancing against him: wherefore he was seized with fear and trembling: 9 and that person came up to him, and pulled him off from his saddle[k], and struck him with violence to the earth. So that being exceedingly terror- 10 struck, and frightened out of his senses, he became dumb. But when his attendants saw what had 11 befallen him, and could perceive no one who had done these things unto him, they carried him with all haste down to his own house: and he remained 12 during several days, neither speaking nor taking any food. Wherefore the chief men of his friends 13 went to Onias the priest, beseeching him to be appeased towards him, and to implore the great and good God that He would not punish him. Which thing Onias did; and Heliodorus was 14 healed of his disease. And he saw *in a vision* the 15 person, whom he had seen in the sanctuary, commanding him to go to Onias the priest, and to salute him, and pay him becoming honour; telling him, that the great and good God had heard his prayers, and had healed him at Onias' request. Heliodorus therefore hastened to Onias the priest, 16

---

[i] This phrase, "Deus Op- "timus Maximus," occurs continually, and is peculiar to this one book of Maccabees: the same phrase, as we learn from Hottinger, is usual in the Samaritan Chronicle. (Hottingeri Exercitationes Antimorin. p. 66. 4to. 1644.)

[k] Or horsecloth, or housing, Lat. *sagma;* which is the word used by the Latin Vulgate at Leviticus xv. 9. where our translators read " sad- " dle."

whom falling down he saluted; and gave him money of various kinds[1], requesting him to add it to that which was in the treasury.

17 Then he went from Jerusalem into the country of Macedonia, and related to king Seleucus what had happened to him; entreating that he would not compel him[m] to become his representative at
18 Jerusalem. Wherefore the king wondered at the things which Heliodorus mentioned to him; and commanded him to publish them to the world.
19 And he took care that his men should be removed and sent away from Jerusalem, increasing the gifts which he used to send thither annually, on
20 account of what had befallen Heliodorus. And the kings added more to the money which they ordered to be given to the priests, that it might be spent on the orphans and widows; also to that which was to be spent on the sacrifices.

CHAPTER II[a].

The history of the translation of the twenty-four books out of the Hebrew tongue into the Greek tongue, for Ptolemy king of Egypt.

1 THERE was a man of Macedon named Ptolemy, endued with knowledge and understanding; whom, as he dwelt in Egypt, the

---

[1] Lat. denarios et drachmas.

[m] Compare ver. 38 of book III. ch. iii.

[a] See a more full and minute account of these transactions in Josephus, Ant. XII. 2. See also the history of the same by Aristeas, or Justin Martyr, or Epiphanius; or consult Ussher, Hodius, or the observations in Calmet.

It is obvious to every reader, that the events of this chapter precede in order of time those related in ch. i. But I give the book exactly as I find it.

Egyptians made king over the country of Egypt. Wherefore he, being possessed with a desire of 2 seeking out *various* knowledge, collected all the books of wise men from every quarter. And be- 3 ing anxious to obtain " the Twenty-four[b] Books," he wrote to the high priest in Jerusalem, to send him seventy elders from among those who were most skilled in those books; and he sent to the priest a letter, with a present. So 4 when the king's letter came to the priest, he chose out seventy learned men, and sent them, together with a man named Eleazar[c], one excelling in religion, science, and learning: who departed into Egypt. And when their approach was made 5 known to the king, he commanded seventy lodgings to be prepared, and the men to be there entertained. He also ordered a secretary to be ap- 6 pointed for each one, who should take down the interpretation of these books in the Greek character and language. He likewise forbade that any 7 one of these should hold communication with any

[b] It is well known that the Hebrews usually called their scriptures by the name of " the *twenty-two* books," answering to the number of their letters, but not *twenty-four*, as stated by the author of this fifth book.

[c] Josephus takes no notice of any such person being sent: but the name of the high priest at this period was Eleazar; so that possibly some confusion of names may have arisen from this circumstance. But see below, ch. iv. ver. 1. where Eleazar, who is tortured for his religion, is said to have formerly gone with the doctors unto Ptolemy. The chronology however will not permit us to assent to this. Eleazar is indeed there stated to be a man of ninety years of age; but still, the translation of the Scriptures at Alexandria occurred ninety years before that persecution under Antiochus, in which Eleazar was put to death.

of his fellows; lest they should agree together
8 to make any change in those books. So the secretaries took down from every one of them the
9 translation of " the Twenty-four Books." And when the translations were finished, Eleazar brought them to the king; and compared them together in his presence: on which comparison,
10 they were found to agree. Upon which the king was exceeding glad, and ordered a large sum of money to be divided amongst the party. But Eleazar *himself* he rewarded with a munificent recompense.

11 He also on that day set free every captive which was found in Egypt, of the tribe of Judah and of Benjamin, that they might return to their
12 own country Syria. The number of them was
13 about one hundred and thirty thousand. Moreover, he ordered money to be distributed among them, so that several denarii came to the share of each person; who, receiving these, departed into
14 their own land. Then he commanded a great table to be made of the purest gold, which should be large enough to contain a representation of the whole land of Egypt, and a picture of the Nile, from the commencement of its stream to the end of it in Egypt, with its various divisions through
15 the country, and how it laves the whole land. He also ordered the table to be set with many precious
16 stones. And this table was made; and its carving was finished, and it was set with precious stones: and it was carried into the city of Jerusalem, a
17 present to the magnificent house. And, arriving in safety, it was placed in the house, according to
18 the king's command. And truly men never be-

held its like, for the beauty of the pictures, and the excellence of the workmanship.

CHAPTER III.[a]

The history of the Jews. A relation of what befell the Jews under king Antiochus; and what battles took place between them and his captains; and to what lengths he at last proceeded.

THERE was a certain man of the kings of Macedon, who was called Antiochus[b]; among whose deeds was this: that when Ptolemy the abovementioned king of Egypt was dead, he went with his armies to attack the second[c] Ptolemy. And, having conquered and slain Ptolemy, he won his country[d] Egypt, and took possession of it. From hence, as his affairs gained an accession of strength, he subdued a great part of the earth; the king of Persia and others paying him obedience. Wherefore his heart was lifted up: and being puffed up with pride, he commanded images to be made after his own likeness; that men should worship them, to his glorifying and honour. And when these were made, he sent messengers into all the regions of his empire, commanding them to be worshipped and adored. To these commands the nations assented, fearing and dreading his tyranny.

Now there were at that time in Judæa three

B.C. 170.

1
2
3
4
5
6

---

[a] Compare with this chapter 2 Macc. i. 3 Macc. v. Joseph. Antiq. XII. 6, 7. Bell. I. 1.

[b] Namely, Antiochus Epiphanes.

[c] Or rather, "the succeeding:" for as the king intended here is Ptolemy Philometor, the epithet "second" is incorrectly applied, he being in fact the *sixth* of the Ptolemies.

[d] As had been predicted by the prophet Daniel, ch. xi. 25.

men, the very worst of all mortals; and each of them had, as it were, a connexion in the same sort of vice. The name of one of these three was Menelaus[e]; of the second, Simeon[f]; of the third, 7 Alcimus[g]. And about that time there appeared[h] certain images, which the citizens of Jerusalem beheld in the air for the space of forty days: they were the appearances of men riding on fiery horses 8 fighting with each other. So those impious men went to Antiochus, to obtain from him some authority, that they might perpetrate with ease whatever they wished, of whoredom, *and* plundering of men's goods; and in short, might rule over the rest, and might keep them in subjection. 9 And they said to him, "O king, there have ap-
" peared lately in the air over Jerusalem fiery
" horsemen, contending with each other: and on
" that account the Hebrews have rejoiced, saying,
" that this portended the death of king Antio-
10 " chus." Which words the king believing, being filled with rage, he marched to Jerusalem in the shortest possible time; and came upon the nation 11 not at all forewarned of his approach. And his men attacked the inhabitants, and slew them with the sword, making a very great slaughter[i]; many also they wounded, and a great multitude they led 12 into captivity. But some escaping fled into the

[e] The brother of Jesus, or Jason; for an account of whom see 3 Macc. iv.
[f] Or Simon, mentioned at 3 Macc. iii. and iv.
[g] Who was afterwards made high priest. See 2 Macc. vii.
[h] Compare 3 Macc. v. 2.
[i] The author of the third book of Maccabees reports, that " there were destroyed " within the space of three " whole days fourscore thou- " sand; whereof forty thou- " sand were slain in the con- " flict, and no fewer sold than " slain," ch. v. 14.

mountains and woods, where they continued a long time, feeding upon herbs.

After this, Antiochus determined to depart from the country. But the evil which he had done to the nation did not suffice him: but he left as his substitute a man named Fælix[k], enjoining him to compel the Jews to worship his image, and to eat swine's flesh. Which Fælix did, sending for the people to obey the king in the things which he had commanded him. But they refused to do the things whereunto they were called; wherefore he slew a great multitude of them; preserving those wicked wretches and their family, and raising their dignity.

CHAPTER IV.[a]

The history of the death of Eleazar the priest.

AFTERWARDS was seized Eleazar, who had gone with the doctors unto Ptolemy[b], and was then a very old man, ninety years of age; and he was placed before Fælix; who said to him, "Eleazar, truly you are a wise and pru-
"dent man; and indeed I have loved you for
"many years, and therefore I should not wish
"your death: therefore obey the king, and wor-
"ship his image, and eat of his sacrifices, and de-
"part in safety." To whom Eleazar replied;
"I am not about to forsake my obedience to God,

---

[k] This appears to be either *Philip*, whom Antiochus is said (at 3 Macc. v. 22.) to have left governor at Jerusalem; or else, "the old man "of Athens" mentioned at 3 Macc. vi. 1, as being sent by him "to compel the Jews to "depart from the laws of "their fathers."

[a] Compare this chapter with 3 Macc. vi. 18—31. and with 4 Macc. v. and vi.

[b] See above, ii. 4.

5 " in order to obey the king." And Fælix, coming
" up, whispered to him, "Take care to send for
" some one to bring you flesh from your own of-
6 " ferings, which place upon my table: and eat
" some part of that in the presence of the people,
" that they may know that you have obeyed the
" king: and you will save your life, without any
7 " harm done to your religion." Eleazar answered
him, " I do not obey God under any kind of fraud,
" but rather I will endure this *your* violence. For
" inasmuch as I am an old man of ninety years,
" my bones are now weakened, and my body has
8 " wasted away. If I therefore shall with a brave
" spirit endure those *torments*, from which even
" the bravest young men shrink back in fear; my
" people and the youths of my nation will bravely
9 " imitate me, and will say; 'How is it that we
" may not endure the pains, which one, who is in-
" ferior to us in strength, and less substantial in
10 " flesh and bones, has undergone?' which indeed
" will be better for me, than to deceive them by a
11 " feigned obedience to the king: for they will
" *then* say, 'If that decrepid old man, wise and
" prudent as he is, is clinging to life and overcome
" by the pain of temporary matters[c], abdicating
" his religion; truly that will be lawful for us
" which was lawful for him, since he is an old
" man and a wise one, and one whom we ought
12 " to follow.' Wherefore I would rather die, leav-
" ing to them a constancy in religion and patience
" against tyranny; than live, after having weak-
" ened their constancy in obeying their Lord and

[c] Or, " is afflicted by the painful thought of bidding adieu
" to temporal affairs."

" following his commands; so that through me
" they may be rendered happy, not unhappy."

Now when Fælix had heard the determination 13
of Eleazar, he was violently enraged with him,
and commanded him to be tortured in a variety
of ways: so that he came into the most desperate
mortal struggle, and said; " Thou, O God, 14
" knowest that I might have delivered myself
" from the *troubles* into which I have fallen, by
" obeying another *rather* than Thee. This how- 15
" ever I have not done; but I have preferred
" obeying Thee, and have esteemed all the vio-
" lence offered me as light, for the sake of con-
" stancy in obedience to Thee. And now I think 16
" little of the things which have happened to me
" according to thy good pleasure, and support
" them as well as I can. I therefore pray Thee, 17
" that Thou wilt accept this from me, and cause
" me to die before I become weaker in endurance."
And God heard his prayers; and immediately he 18
died. But he left his people devoted to the wor- 19
ship of their God, and endued with a sound fortitude, and perseverance in religion, and patience
to bear up against the trials which awaited them.

CHAPTER V[a].
The history of the death of the seven brethren.

AFTER this, seven brothers were seized, and their 1
mother; and they were sent to the king; for he
had not yet gone far away from Jerusalem. And 2
when they had been carried to the king, one of
them was brought into his presence; whom he

[a] Compare with this chapter, 3 Macc. vii. and 4 Macc. viii—xii.

3 ordered to renounce his religion: but he refusing said to him, "If you think to teach us the truth
4 "*for the first time*, the matter is not so: for truth
" is that which we have learned from our fathers,
" and by which we have bound ourselves to em-
" brace the worship of God only, and constantly
" to observe the law; and from this we in no
5 " wise will depart." And king Antiochus was angry at these words, and commanded an iron frying pan to be brought, and to be placed on the
6 fire. Then he ordered the young man's tongue to be cut out, and his hands and feet to be cut off, and the skin of his head to be flayed off, and to be placed in the pan: and they did so to him.
7 Then he commanded a large brazen caldron to be brought and set over the fire, into which the
8 rest of his body was thrown. And when the man was near dying, he ordered the fire to be removed from him, that he might be tortured the longer: intending by these acts to terrify his
9 mother and his brethren. But in fact by this he gave them additional courage and strength, to maintain their religion with constancy, and to bear all those torments which tyranny could inflict upon them.
10 So when the first was dead, the second was brought before him: to whom some of the attendants said, " Obey those orders which the king
" will give you, lest you perish even as your bro-
11 " ther perished." But he answered, " I am not
" weaker in spirit than my brother, nor behind
" him in my faith. Bring forward your fire and
" sword; and do not diminish ought of that which
" you did to my brother." And they did to him

as had been done to his brother. And he called 12
out to the king, and said to him; " Hear, O thou
" monster of cruelty towards men, and know that
" thou gainest nothing of ours except our bodies;
" but our souls thou dost by no means obtain;
" and these shortly will go to their Creator, whom 13
" He will restore to their bodies, when He shall
" raise to life[b] the dead men of his nation and the
" slain ones of his people."

And the third was brought out; who beckon- 14
ing with his hand said to the king; " Why dost
" thou frighten us, O enemy? know that this is 15
" sent upon us from heaven, which also we under-
" go *as such,* giving thanks to God, and from Him
" we hope for our reward." And the king, and 16
those who stood near him, admired the courage of
the youth, and the firmness of his mind, and his
fair discourse. Then he gave orders, and he was
slain.

And the fourth was brought out, who said: 17
" For God's religion we set our lives to sale, and
" hire them out, that we may require payment
" from Him, on that day when you shall have no
" excuse in the judgment, and shall not be able
" to endure your tortures." The king commanded, 18
and he was put to death.

And the fifth was brought out, who said to him; 19
" Think not within thyself that God has forsaken
" us, because of the things which He has sent

---

[b] There appears here a manifest allusion to the words of the prophet Isaiah, ch. xxvi. 19, " Thy dead men shall live, " together with my dead body " shall they arise. Awake and " sing, ye that dwell in dust: " for thy dew is as the dew " of herbs, and the earth shall " cast out the dead." Also, to a striking passage in Ezechiel, ch. xxxvii. 1—14.

20 " upon us. But truly his will is, to shew us
" honour and love by these things; and He will
21 " avenge us of thee and of thy posterity." And
the king commanded, and he was slain.
22 And the sixth was brought out, who said; " I
" confess indeed my offences to God, but I believe
" that they shall be forgiven me through *this* my
23 " death. But you have now opposed God, by
" slaying those who embrace His religion: and
" surely He will repay you according to your
" works, and will root you out from his earth."
And he gave orders for him, and he was slain.
24 And the seventh was brought out, who was a
25 boy. Then his mother arose, fearless and unmoved, and looked upon[c] the corpses of her chil-
26 dren: and she said, "My sons, I know not how I
" conceived each one of you, when I did conceive
" him. Nor had I the power of giving him
" breath; or of bringing him forth to the light
" of this world; or of bestowing on him courage
27 " and understanding: but indeed the great and
" good God himself formed him according to his
" own will: and gave to him a form according to
28 " his good pleasure: and brought him into the
" world by his power; appointing to him a term
" of life, and good rules, and a dispensation *of re-*
29 " *ligion,* as it pleaseth Him. But you now have
" sold to God your bodies which he himself form-
" ed, and your souls which he created: and you
" have acquiesced in his judgments which he
30 " hath decreed. Wherefore, happy are ye, in the
" things which happily you have obtained; and

[c] Compare what is related of her firmness and fortitude, in book IV. ch. xv. 13—23.

" blessed are ye, for the things in which you
" have been victorious."

Now Antiochus had supposed, when he beheld 31
her rise up, that she had done this through being
overcome by fear for her child; and he wholly
thought that she was about to enjoin him obedience to the king, that he might not perish as his
brethren had perished. But when he had heard 32
her words, he was ashamed, and blushed, and
commanded the boy to be brought to him; that
he might exhort him, and persuade him to love
life, and deter him from death: lest all those 33
should be seen to oppose his authority, and very
many others should follow their example. There- 34
fore, when he was brought to him, he exhorted
him by discourse, and promised him riches, and
sware to him that he would make him viceroy to
himself. But when the boy was not at all moved 35
by his words, and took no heed of them; the
king turned to his mother, and said to her;
" Happy woman, pity this thy son, whom alone 36
" thou hast surviving; and exhort him to comply
" with my orders, and to escape those *sufferings*
" which have happened to his brethren." And 37
she said, " Bring him hither, that I may exhort
" him in the words of God."

And when they had brought him to her, she 38
went aside from the crowd: then she kissed him,
and laughed to scorn the things which had been
said to her by Antiochus: and then said to him; 39
" My son, come now, be obedient to me, because
" I have brought you forth, and suckled you, and
" educated you, and taught you divine religion.
" Look up now to the heaven, and the earth, and 40

"the water, and the fire; and understand that
"the one true God himself created these; and
"formed man of flesh and blood, who lives a
41 "short time, and then will die. Wherefore fear
"the true God, who dieth not: and obey the true
42 "*Being*, who changeth not his promises: and fear
"not this mere giant [d]: and die for God's religion,
43 "as your brothers have died. For if you could
"see, my son, their honourable dwelling-place,
"and the light of their habitation [e], and to what
"glory they have attained, you would not endure
44 "not to follow them: and in truth I also hope
"that the great and good God will prepare me,
"and that I shall closely follow you."
45 Then said the boy; "Know ye that I *will* obey
"God, and will not obey the commands of Anti-
"ochus: wherefore, delay not to let me follow
"my brothers; hinder me not from departing to
46 "the place whither they have gone." Then to
the king he said; "Woe to thee from God! whither
"wilt thou fly from Him? where wilt thou seek
"for refuge? or whose help wilt thou implore,
"that He may not take vengeance on thee?

[d] Lat. "Gigantem vulga-
"rem."

[e] This circumstance, as be-
tokening a state of comfort
and happiness, is frequently
brought forward in the holy
Scriptures. Thus, while ac-
tual darkness overspread the
land of Egypt, we read that
"all the children of Israel
"had *light* in their dwell-
"ings." Exod. x. 23. And
the same expression, in a figure, is of constant occurrence: "that David my ser-
"vant may have a *light* al-
"ways:"—"the *light* shall
"shine on thy ways:"—
"Lord, lift thou up the *light*
"of thy countenance upon
"us:"—"The Lord is my
"*light*," &c. &c. &c. So St.
Paul speaks of "the inherit-
"ance of the saints in *light*."
But I do not purpose to quote
the *New Testament* here. See
below, verse 48.

"Truly thou hast done us a kindness, when thou 47 "hadst designed to do us evil: thou hast done "evil to thine own soul, and hast destroyed it, "while thou thoughtest to do it good. Now we 48 "are on our way to a life which death shall never "follow; and shall dwell in light which dark- "ness shall never put away. But your dwelling 49 "shall be in the infernal regions, with exquisite "punishments from God. And I trust, that the 50 "wrath of God will depart from his people, on "account of what we have suffered for them: but 51 "that you He will torment in this world, and "bring you to a wretched death; and that after- "wards you will depart into eternal torments."

And Antiochus was angry, seeing that the boy 52 opposed his authority; wherefore he commanded him to be tortured even more than his brothers. And this was done, and he died. But their mo- 53 ther intreated God, and besought Him that she might follow her sons; and immediately she died.

Then Antiochus departed into his country Ma- 54 cedonia: and he wrote to Fælix, and to the other governors [f] in Syria, that they should slay all the Jews, except those who should embrace his reli- gion. And his servants obeyed his command, 55 putting a multitude of men to death.

CHAPTER VI [a].

The history of Mattathias the high priest, the son of Jochanan, who is the son of Hesmai [b] the priest.

A CERTAIN man named Mattathias, the son of 1

[f] See 3 Macc. v. 22—24.
[a] Compare this chapter with 2 Macc. ii.; Joseph. Antiq. XII. 8.; Bell. I. 1.
[b] Called by Josephus, "As- "samonæus:" compare the note on book II. ch. ii. 1.

Jochanan, fled to one of the mountains which were fortified. And the men who were scattered abroad fled thither to him: and some concealed
2 themselves in secluded places. But after that Antiochus had departed to a greater distance from the country, Mattathias sent his son Judas se-
3 cretly into the cities of Judah; to certify them of his own and his people's health, and to desire that as many as were inspired with courage, magnanimity, and zeal for religion, for their wives, and their children, should come unto him.
4 And certain of the higher orders of the people, who had stayed behind, went out to him: who,
5 when they were come to him, said to them; "Nothing is left to us, but prayer to God, and confidence in Him, and a fight with our enemies, if perhaps God will give us assistance and the vic-
6 "tory over them." And the people assented to the opinion of Mattathias, and they acted according to it.
7 And it was told to Fælix; and he marched
8 against them with a great army. And word was brought to him, while on his march, that about a thousand of the people of the Jews, men and women mixed, were assembled together, and dwelling in a certain cave, that they might be enabled
9 to preserve their own way of worship. And he turned aside to them with some part of his troops, sending the commanders of his men with the rest
10 of the army against Mattathias. Now Fælix demanded from those who were in the cave, that they should come out to him, and consent to enter
11 into his religion; but they refused. Whereupon

he threatened that he would put smoke[c] under them; and they endured that, and did not come out to him; and he put smoke under them, and they all died.

And when the generals of his army were march- 12 ing against Mattathias, and came even to him, he being ready for battle; one of the generals, of 13 noble blood, went to him, proposing to him to obey the king, and that he should not oppose his authority; so that he himself might live, and those who were with him, and might not perish. To whom he said; " I indeed obey God the true 14 " king: but do you obey your king, and do what- " soever seems good to you." And he ceased from speaking. And they began to lay snares for him. 15 And there came a certain man, of the worst of 16 the Jews who were with them, and excited them to march against him and to prepare war. And 17 Mattathias rushed on him with his drawn sword, and cut off the Jew's head: then he struck the general[d], to whom the Jew was speaking, and slew him also.

But Mattathias' companions, seeing what he 18 had done, hastened to him; and they burst into the camp of the enemy, slaying great numbers of them, and put them to flight: afterwards they pursued the fugitives, until they slew the whole of them.

After this, Mattathias blew the trumpet, and 19

---

[c] Namely, that he would kindle fires in the cave's mouth, and thus smother them with the smoke.

[d] Josephus states the name of this general (or "commis- "sioner," as he is called at 2 Macc. ii. 25) to be Apelles.

proclaimed an expedition against Fælix. And he and his companions entered into the land of Judah, and took possession of very many of their cities. And the most high God gave them rest by his hands from the generals of Antiochus: and they returned to the observance of their own religion: and the bands of their enemies retreated from before them.

CHAPTER VII[a].

The account of the death of Mattathias, and the acts of Judas his son after him.

Now Mattathias became infirm. And when he was near to death, he called his sons, who were five, and said unto them: "I " know of a certainty that very many and great " wars will be kindled in the land of Judah, for " the sake [or, by reason] of those matters for " which the great and good God has stirred " us up to wage war against our enemies. But " I charge you that you fear God, and trust " in him, and be zealous of the law, and the " sanctuary, and the people also; and prepare " yourselves to wage war against its enemies: " and fear not death, because, without doubt, this " is decreed unto all men. So that, if God shall " make you victorious, you have at once obtained " that which you were longing for: but if you " fall, that is no loss to you in his sight."

And Mattathias died and was buried; and his sons did according to that which he had com-

---

[a] Compare this chapter with 2 Macc. ii. 49, &c. iii. iv. 3 Macc. viii. Joseph. Antiq. XII. 8—11. Bell. I. 1.

manded them. And they agreed to make their brother Judas their leader. Now Judas their 7 brother was the best in counsel, and bravest in strength of them all. And an army was sent 8 against them by Fælix[b], under a man who was called Seron[c], whom Judas with his company put to flight, and he slew great numbers. And the 9 fame of Judas was spread abroad, and increased greatly in the ears *of men:* and all the nations which were round about him feared him exceedingly.

And it was told to king Antiochus what Matta- 10 thias and his son Judas had done. News of this 11 came also to the king of the Persians; so that he played false with Antiochus, departing from his friendship, following the example of Judas. Which 12 giving Antiochus a great deal of uneasiness, he called to him one of his household officers named Lysias[d], a stout and brave man, and said to him;
" I have now determined to go into the land of 13
" Persia to make war; and I wish to leave behind
" me my son in my stead; and to take with me
" the half of my army, and to leave the remainder
" with my son: and behold I have given to you 14
" the governance of my son, and the governance
" of the men whom I leave with him. And 15
" verily you know what Mattathias and Judas
" have done to my friends and my subjects.
" Wherefore, send one to lead a powerful army 16

---

[b] The second book of Maccabees, ch. iii. 10. calls him Apollonius.
[c] He is called " a prince " of the army of Syria," at
2 Macc. iii. 13.
[d] "A nobleman, and one " of the blood royal," book II. ch. iii. 32.

"into the land of Judah; and command him to "attack the land of Judah with the sword, and to "root them out, and to demolish their dwellings, "and to destroy all traces of them."

17 Then Antiochus departed into the country of
18 Persia. But Lysias made ready three hardy and brave generals, skilled in war; of whom one was named Ptolemy[e], a second Nicanor, and the third
19 Gorgias. And with them he sent forty thousand chosen troops and seven thousand horsemen. He also charged them to bring with them an army of Syrians, and Philistines; and ordered them to
20 root out the Jews entirely. And they marched forth, carrying with them a multitude of merchants, that they might sell to them the captives which they were about to obtain from among the Jews.
21 But tidings of this came to Judas the son of Mattathias; and he went to the house of the
22 great and good God; and assembled his men, and enjoined them a fast, and supplications, and prayers to the great and good God; and charged that they should beseech Him for victory against their enemies; which thing they did.
23 After this, Judas collecting his men, appointed over each thousand a chief[f], and likewise over each hundred, and over each fifty, and over each
24 ten. Then he commanded proclamation to be made by trumpet throughout his army, that whosoever was fearful, and whomsoever God commanded to be dismissed from the army, he should

---

[e] At book II. ch. iii. 38, these three generals are styled, "mighty men of the king's "friends."
[f] Compare 2 Macc. iii. 55, 56.

return home. And great numbers returned; and there remained with them seven thousand stout and brave men, skilled in wars and accustomed thereto; nor had any one of them ever fled: and they marched against their enemies. But when they had drawn nigh to them, Judas prayed to his Lord, intreating Him that He would turn away from him the malice of his enemy; and that He would assist him, and render him victorious. Then he commanded the priests to sound the trumpets, which they did: and all his men called upon God, and rushed upon the army of Nicanor. And God gave them victory over them, and they turned him and his men to flight, killing of them nine thousand men, and the rest were dispersed. And Judas and his company returned to Nicanor's camp, and made spoil of it; and plundered very much property of the merchants, and sent it to be divided among the sick.

This battle took place on the sixth day of the week; wherefore Judas and his men remained on the same spot until the sabbath-day had passed. Then they marched against Ptolemy and Gorgias, whom they found and defeated, and gained a victory over them, slaying twenty thousand of their troops. And Ptolemy and Gorgias fled; whom Judas and his company pursued; yet he could not overtake them, because they betook themselves into a city of two idols[g], and fortified themselves therein with the remnant of their army. And Judas attacked Fælix; and he was put to flight before him. And Judas pursued him.

---

[g] The corresponding part of book III. states, that the place to which Nicanor fled was *Antioch*.

Who, coming to a certain house which was nigh at hand, entered into it and closed the doors, for 34 it was a fortified house. And Judas commanded, and he set fire to it; and the house was burned, and Fælix was burned[h] in it. So Judas took vengeance on him for Eleazar and the others 35 whom Fælix had put to death. Afterwards the people returned to the slain, and took their spoils and their armour; but the best of the prey they 36 sent into the Holy Land. But Nicanor departed in disguise unknown, and returned to Lysias, and told him all which had happened to him and his company.

CHAPTER VIII.[a]

The relation of Antiochus' return, and of his going into the land of Judah, and of the disease which fell on him, of which he died in his journey.

1 But Antiochus returned out of the country of Persia, flying, with his army disbanded. 2 And when he had learned what had happened to his army which Lysias had sent forth, and to all his men, he went out with a large 3 army, marching to the land of Judah. Now when in his progress he had reached the middle of his journey, God smote his troops with most mighty 4 weapons: but this could not stop him from his journey; but he persisted in it, uttering all sorts of insolence against God, and saying that no one could turn him aside, nor hinder him from his de-

---

[h] At 3 Macc. viii. 33, the person burned is called Callisthenes!

[a] Compare with this chapter 2 Macc. vi; 3 Macc. ix; Joseph. Antiq. XII. 13.

termined purposes. Wherefore the great and good 5 God smote him also with ulcers which attacked the whole of his body: but even yet he did not desist, nor refrain from his journey; but was 6 more filled with wrath, and inflamed with an eager desire to obtain what he had determined on, and to carry his resolution into effect.

Now there were in his army very many ele- 7 phants. It so happened that one of these ran away, and made a bellowing: upon which the horses which were drawing the couch on which Antiochus lay, ran off, and threw him out. And, 8 as he was fat and corpulent, his limbs were bruised, and some of his joints were dislocated. And the bad 9 smell of his ulcers, which already sent forth a fœtid odour, was so much increased, that neither he himself could longer endure it, nor could those who came near him. So when he fell, his ser- 10 vants took him up, and carried him upon their shoulders: but as the foul smell grew worse, they threw him down and departed to a distance.

Therefore, perceiving the evils which sur- 11 rounded him, he believed for certain that all that punishment had come upon him from the great and good God; by reason of the injury and the tyranny which he had used towards the Hebrews, and the unjust shedding of their blood. In fear 12 therefore he turned himself to God, and, confessing his sins, said; " O God, in truth I deserve " the things [b] which Thou hast sent upon me:

---

[b] See Josephus' remark upon Polybius' account of the cause of Antiochus' death; in ch. 13 of his XIIth book of Antiquities. In fact, both Polybius and Josephus recognize the same principle, while they attribute this death to

" and indeed just art Thou[c] in thy judgments;
13 " Thou humblest him who is exalted, and bring-
" est down him who is puffed up: but thine is
" greatness, and magnificence, and majesty, and
14 " prowess. Truly, I own, I have oppressed the
" people, and have both acted and decreed tyran-
15 " nically against them. Forgive, I pray Thee, O
" God, this my error; and wipe out my sin, and
" bestow on me my health: and my care shall be
" to fill the treasury of thy house with gold and
16 " silver: and to strew[d] the floor of the house of
" thy sanctuary with purple vestments; and to
" be circumcised; and to proclaim throughout all
" my kingdom, that Thou only art the true God,
" without any partner, and that there is no God
" besides thee."

17 But God did not hear his prayers, nor accept his supplication: but his troubles so increased on him that he voided his bowels: and his ulcers increased to that degree, that his flesh dropt off
18 from his body. Then he died, and was buried in his place. And his son reigned in his stead, whose name was Eupator.

different causes: Polybius, a Greek heathen, considered it a just recompense for his attempt to plunder the temple of Diana; while Josephus, a Jew, regarded it as an example of Divine vengeance, punishing his spoliation of the temple of God at Jerusalem.

[c] The author here borrows the words of the 119th Psalm: " Righteous art Thou, O " Lord, and upright are Thy " judgments."

[d] Similar to this act of thanksgiving was the *Lectisternium* of the Romans, when after a victory couches were solemnly placed and spread for the images of their gods, as if about to partake of a feast.

CHAPTER IX.[a]

The history of the eight days of dedication.

WHEN Judas had put to flight Ptolemy, and Nicanor, and Gorgias, and had slain their men; he himself and his troops returned into the country[b] of the holy house. And he commanded all the altars to be destroyed which Antiochus had ordered to be built: and he removed all the idols which were in the sanctuary: and they built up a new altar, and he commanded sacrifices to be offered upon that. They prayed also to the great and good God, that He would bring forth the holy fire[c] which might remain upon the altar: and fire came out from some stones of the altar, and burned up the wood and the sacrifices; and from it fire continued on the altar until the third carrying into captivity[d]. And then they kept the festival of the new altar[e] for eight days, beginning on the twenty-fifth day of the month Casleu. And then they placed bread[f] on the table of the house of God, and lighted the lamps of the

---

[a] Compare 2 Macc. iv. 36, &c. 3 Macc. x. Joseph. Antiq. XII. 11. There is an irregularity here in the order of the narrative; this cleansing and dedication having preceded the death of king Antiochus, and indeed having contributed to his trouble of mind, as is shewn at 2 Macc. vii. 7.

[b] Concerning this phrase, see the note upon chap. i. 1. above.

[c] Compare 3 Macc. i. 19—22: and ii. 10.

[d] There can be little doubt that the author alludes to the last general captivity under Titus; although the expression, "the third," is often applied to an earlier visitation of that kind. (See Calmet.) This phrase may serve in some degree to mark the probable age of the book. Compare ch. xxi. 30. and liii. 8.

[e] The same festival which Josephus calls "the feast of lights." Ant. XII. 7.

[f] Namely, the shew-bread.

8 candlestick. And on each of these eight days they assembled together for prayer and praise: and moreover they appointed it an ordinance for every year to come.

CHAPTER X.[a]

The history of Judas' battles with Gorgias and Ptolemy.

1 Now after the days of dedication, Judas marched into the country of the Idumæans, to the mountain Sarah[b]: for Gorgias was staying
2 there. And Gorgias went out against him with a great army, and there were sore battles betwixt them; and there fell of Gorgias' men twenty thou-
3 sand. And Gorgias fled to Ptolemy[c] into the land of the west[d], (for Antiochus had made him governor of that country, and there he was stay-
4 ing,) and told him what had befallen him. Whereupon Ptolemy went forth with an army, in which were a hundred and twenty thousand men of Ma-
5 cedonia and the east. And he went on until he came to the country of Giares, (*that is to say, Gilead,*) and the parts adjacent; and he slew great
6 numbers of the Jews. So they wrote to Judas, telling him what had happened to them, begging him to come and defeat Ptolemy and drive him
7 away from them. And their letter reached him at the same time that a letter came to him from

B. C. 164.

[a] Compare this with 2 Macc. v; 3 Macc. x; Joseph. Antiq. XII. 12.

[b] Perhaps a continuation of that chain which in Scripture is called "mount Seir:" compare ch. xxi. 29. xxxv. 4: and read the note at ch. xlix. 20. By the parallel passages, in book II. ch. v. 65, and book III. ch. x. 14, 15, we know that Gorgias at this time was in the neighbourhood of Idumæa.

[c] The Third Book of Maccabees calls him *Timotheus*, throughout the chapter, and so does Josephus.

[d] Namely, Philistia, and the western coast of Judæa.

the inhabitants of the mountain[e] of Galilee likewise, informing him how the Macedonians who were at Tyre and Sidon had now united against them, and had attacked them, killing several.

Now when Judas had read both the letters, he called together his men, and shewed them the contents of the letters, and appointed a fast and supplication. After this, he ordered his brother Simeon to take with him three thousand men of the Jews, and to march with all speed to the mountain of Galilee, and to quell the Macedonians who were there. And Simeon went. But Judas hastened to encounter Ptolemy. And Simeon attacked the Macedonians unexpectedly, and slew of them eight thousand men, and gave rest to the Galilæans.

But Judas marched on until he came up with Gorgias and Ptolemy; pressing them and besieging them: and *the two armies* encountered, and very fierce battles took place betwixt them. For Ptolemy headed a numerous, stout, and brave body of men. But Judas was accompanied by a very small band: yet, as the people who were with him consisted of the bravest and strongest *troops*, he steadily resisted, and the battle between them lasted long, and grew very sore. Wherefore Judas called out to the great and good God, and invoked his *aid*. And he related [f] that he had seen five youthful horsemen, three of whom fought

---

[e] Or rather, "the mountainous district."

[f] Lat. "Meminit." The third book states, not that Judas alone saw this vision, and related it to his troops; but that the thing itself was seen by the whole of the enemy's army.

against Ptolemy's army, and two stood near him-
17 self. Whom when he viewed attentively, they
18 seemed to him to be angels of God. Wherefore his heart was comforted, and the hearts of his companions; and making frequent assaults upon the enemy, they put them to flight, and slew
19 great multitudes of them. And the number of those who were slain of Ptolemy's army, from the beginning of this battle until the end, was twenty thousand and five hundred.

20 After these things, Ptolemy and his men fled to the sea-coast; while Judas pursued them, and
21 slew as many of them as he caught. But Ptolemy fled to Gaza, and remained there; and the men
22 of Chalisam [g] came to him. And Judas marched against them; and when he found them, he defeated them: and Ptolemy's men were dispersed, but he himself fled to Gaza [h], and there fortified
23 himself. And Judas' men pursued the flying body, and slew great numbers of them. And Judas and the men who were with him marched straight to Gaza, and he pitched his camp and besieged it.
24 And Judas' men returned to him; and they who were left of Ptolemy's forces went up upon the fortification, and abused Judas with much revil-
25 ing. And the fighting between them and Judas'. troops lasted for five days. But when the fifth

[g] Who these are, I am not able to specify with any certainty: perhaps the inhabitants of Kulzum, a small town on the sea-coast of Egypt.

[h] Probably Gazara, as stated at 3 Macc. x. 32. Yet both Gaza and Gazara were near to the sea-coast: and at 2 Macc. v. 65, we read that Judas proceeded from Hebron into the land of the Philistines, and passed through Samaria: in which case he might have visited both of these towns.

day was come, the people continued to cast reproaches upon Judas, and to revile his religion: whereupon twenty of Judas' men grew angry; who taking shields on their left hands, and swords in their right, and having with them a man bearing a ladder which they had made, marched until they came to the wall: and eighteen of them stood and threw darts at those who were on the wall; and two, hastening to the wall, raised up the ladder, and by it mounted. But certain of those who were there, perceiving that they had ascended, and that their companions had followed, and also had gone down from the wall into the city, descended from the wall after them: whom *Judas' men* defeated, slaying great numbers of their enemies. But the army of Judas pressed forward to the gate of the city; and the twenty began to run toward the gate that they might open it: but they were driven thence most fiercely; wherefore they called out with loud cries. Judas therefore and his men knew that they had come near to the gate: and the battle grew sore both without the gate and within. And Judas and his men attacked the gate with fire, and it fell down; and the people perished, and the men who had reviled Judas, were taken, and he commanded them to be brought out and burned[i]. Moreover he commanded the city to be utterly smitten with the sword; and the slaughter continued in it for two days, and then it was wasted with fire.

But Ptolemy fled; nor were tidings of him

[i] These particulars of the siege and capture of this place are expressly assigned, not to Gaza but Gazara, in book III. x. 32—36.

heard at that time; because that he had changed his clothes, and concealed himself in one of the
34 pits [k], and no account of him was had. But his two brothers were taken, and brought to Judas;
35 and he ordered them to be beheaded. After this he went into the land of the sanctuary, with abundance of spoil; and both he and his company offered prayers therein, giving thanks to God for the benefits which they had received.

CHAPTER XI.[a]

The relation of the battle between Judas and Lysias the general of Eupator, after the death of king Antiochus.

1 THE name of Antiochus, of whom mention has been made above, was Epiphanius: but the name of his son who reigned after him was Eupator, who also was named Antiochus.
2 And when the battles of Judas with these generals had taken place, they [b] wrote on the subject to Eupator; who sent with Lysias, his cousin's son, a large army, in which were eighty thousand
3 horsemen and eighty elephants. Who coming to a city which is called Bethner [c], pitched their camp around it, and besieged it, because it was
4 a large city, and much people was therein. And Lysias raised engines of war around it, and began
5 to besiege the inhabitants: which being told to

---

[k] Compare book III. x. 37.

[a] Compare with this the account given at 3 Macc. xi. and xii.

[b] Namely, some of the king's troops who still held the tower in Jerusalem, together with "some ungodly men " of Israel, who joined them- " selves unto them," as related at 2 Macc. vi. 18—27.

[c] The same place as Bethsura, so often mentioned in books II. and III. and Bethzur, named in the books of Joshua and Chronicles.

Judas, he himself and his company went out to some fortified mountains[d]; and there they abode; lest if they remained in any city, Lysias should come and besiege it, and should overpower them. Judas therefore collected his company, and resolved to march with them to Lysias' camp, after they should have gone to the house of God and offered sacrifices in it; beseeching the great and good God to turn away from them the malice of their enemies, and to grant them victory over them: which thing they did. After this, they marched from the region of the holy house to Bethner. For they had designed to come upon the army suddenly, and to defeat it without a struggle.

Now men say, that there appeared to *Judas* a certain personage between heaven and earth, riding on a fiery horse, and holding in his hand a large spear, with which he smote the army of the Gentiles[e]. So that what they had seen gave them additional courage and spirits. And they made haste and charged the army, and slew great numbers of its men. Wherefore the *enemy's* army was troubled and thrown into the greatest confusion, and the whole of it betook itself to a confused flight. And the sword of Judas and his company pressed sore upon them; and he slew of them eleven thousand footmen, and sixteen hundred horsemen. Lysias also was chased, with his company, to a distant place, in which he remained in safety.

And he sent to Judas, *desiring him* to be sub-

[d] Probably in the neighbourhood of Bathzacharias, mentioned at 2 Macc. vi. 32.
[e] Literally, "of the Greeks."

ject to the king, retaining his own and his people's religion: to whom Judas consented in this matter, until word could be written to the king, and an answer of his agreeing thereto could be received. *And Judas wrote concerning this business:* Lysias also wrote to the king, informing him of what had happened, and what proof he had had of the strength and bravery of the *Jewish* nation; and that a continuation of wars with them would exterminate *his* men, as these beforementioned had been exterminated: he told him also their agreement, and his own waiting until he should receive a letter to say what he must do. To whom the king replied, that it seemed right to him to make peace with the nation *of the Jews,* taking away that stumblingblock concerning the exercise of their religion: for that this very thing had incited them to the revolts, and to the attacks made on his predecessors. He also commanded him to make with them a treaty of peace and obedience; so that no obstacles should be thrown in their way in the matter of religion. He wrote also to Judas, and to all the Jews who were in the land of Judah, according to this effect: and this *peace* continued between them for some space of time.

CHAPTER XII.

An account of the beginning of the power of the Romans, and of the enlargement of their empire.

1 AT this same time, of which we have been speaking, the affairs of the Romans began to be exalted: that the great and good God might fulfil that which Daniel the prophet (to whom be

peace[a]) had foretold[b] concerning the fourth empire. There was also at this time a certain most munificent king in Africa, whose name was Annibal[c]. And the royal seat of his empire was Carthage. He determined to take possession of the kingdom of the Romans: wherefore they united to oppose him, and wars were multiplied between them, so that they fought eighteen[d] battles in the space of ten years; and they were not able to drive him out of their country, by reason of his innumerable army and people. They determined therefore to raise a large force selected from their bravest troops and armies, and to attack Annibal in war, and to persevere until they should turn away his forces from them. Which thing truly they did: and they placed at the head of their armies two most renowned men; the name of one was Æmilius, and of the other Varro. Who meeting Annibal engaged with him; and there were slain of their army ninety thousand men; and of Annibal's army forty thousand men were slain. Æmilius also was killed in that battle[e].

[a] This same expression occurs in the Samaritan Chronicle: and it is remarked by Hottinger, that this formula of blessing is constantly added by the Arabian writers, after mentioning the name of any prophet. (*Hottingeri Exercitationes Antimorinianæ*, 4to. 1644. p. 65, 66.)

[b] Namely, in ch. xi. of his prophecy.

[c] For confirmation or correction of this whole account, respecting the beginning and enlargement of the power of Rome, the reader who is desirous of particular information, will, of course, refer to the approved Roman historians.

[d] In fact, the engagements between the contending powers were far more numerous than is here stated; the author of the book perhaps considered alone those battles which were attended by important results.

[e] The battle mentioned is that of Cannæ, well known to have been attended by the

B.C. 163. CHAP. XII. 313

7 But Varro fled into a certain very large and strong city called Venusia: him Annibal did not pursue; but he marched to Rome, to take it, and
8 there to remain. So he lay before it for eight days, and began to build houses opposite to it;
9 which when the citizens saw, they deliberated on entering into a peace and treaty with him, and on surrendering the country.
10 But there was among them a certain young man named Scipio, (for the Romans at that time were without a king, and the entire administration of their affairs was committed to three hundred and twenty[f] men, over whom presided a
11 person who was called senior[g] or elder.) Scipio therefore comes to these, and persuaded them not to trust to Annibal nor to submission to him. To whom they answered, that they did not trust him,
12 but that they were unable to resist him. To whom he said; the country of Africa is wholly destitute of soldiers, because that they are all *here* with Annibal: give me therefore a troop of chosen
13 men, that I may go into Africa: and I will perform such feats in it, that when tidings of them shall reach him, perhaps he will quit you, and you will be freed from him, and will be in peace: and having retrieved and strengthened your resources, if he should prepare to return, you will be able to oppose him.
14 And the advice of Scipio appeared to them to

most disastrous results to the Romans; the consuls Æmilius Paulus and Terentius Varro being defeated with immense loss, and the former falling on the field of battle.

[f] See 3 Macc. viii. 15. and the note there.

[g] His title was *princeps senatus*, a post of great dignity and honour, but unaccompanied by any extraordinary power.

be right; and they committed to him thirty thousand of their bravest men. And he proceeded into Africa. And Asdrubal the brother of Annibal met him, and fought with him; whom Scipio defeated[h], and cut off his head, and took it, with the rest of the prey, and returned to Rome.

And mounting upon the rampart, he called to Annibal, and said: How will you be able to prevail against this our country, when you are not able to expel me from your own land, to which I have gone: I have destroyed it, and have killed your brother, and have brought away his head. Then he threw the head to him. Which being brought to Annibal and recognised by him, he was increased in fury and anger against the people, and sware that he would not depart till he had taken Rome.

But the citizens, to withdraw him from them, and keep him in check, took counsel to send back Scipio to besiege and attack Carthage. And Scipio returned with his army into Africa: and they pitched their camp around Carthage, and besieged it with a most active siege. Wherefore the inhabitants wrote to Annibal, saying, You are coveting a foreign country, which you know not whether you will be able to win or not: but there has come to your own country one who is endeavouring to gain possession of it. Wherefore, if you delay coming, we will surrender to him the country, and will give up your family and all your

---

[h] It will be immediately perceived that there is considerable incorrectness in this narrative: Hasdrubal was defeated and slain, not in Africa, but in Italy; and not by Scipio, but by the two consuls Marcus Livius and Claudius Nero.

substance and your treasures; that we and our property may go unhurt.

22 Now when this letter was brought to him, he departed from Rome; and hastened till he came 23 into Africa: and Scipio went forward and met him, and fought a most fierce battle with him three times, and there were slain fifty thousand of 24 his men. But Annibal, being put to flight, retired into the land of Egypt[i]; whom Scipio pursued, and took him prisoner[k], and returned to 25 Africa. And when he was there, Annibal disdained to be seen by the Africans; wherefore he took poison and died.

26 And Scipio won the country of Africa, and possessed himself of all the goods, and servants, and 27 treasures of Annibal. By which means the fame of the Romans was magnified, and their power from that time began to receive increase.

CHAPTER XIII.[a]

An account of the letter of the Romans to Judas, and of the treaty which took place between them.

1 "FROM the elder and three hundred and twenty "governors, unto Judas, general of the army, 2 "and to the Jews. Health be to you. We

[i] Here again is an error of the author: Hannibal did not fly into Egypt, but sailed for Tyrus to Antiochus, king of Syria; whom not finding there he followed, till he joined him at Antioch.

[k] This part of the narrative again is incorrect. Hannibal was not taken prisoner by Scipio; nor did he die in Africa; but on being likely to be delivered up to the Romans by Prusias, king of Bithynia, at whose court he had taken shelter after the defeat of his friend Antiochus, he took poison, rather than fall into the hands of his old inveterate enemies.

[a] Compare with this 2 Macc. viii. 24, &c. Joseph. Antiq. XII. 17.

"have already heard of your victories, and cou-
"rage, and endurance in war; whereof we rejoice.
"We have also understood that you have entered
"into an agreement with Antiochus. We write 3
"to you to this effect, that you should be friends
"to us, and not to the Greeks who have done
"you harm: moreover we intend to go to An-
"tioch, and to make war upon its inhabitants:
"wherefore make haste to acquaint us with whom 4
"you are at enmity, and with whom you have a
"league of friendship; that we may act accord-
"ingly."

THE COPY OF THE TREATY.

"This is the treaty made by the elder and 5
"three hundred and twenty[k] governors with Ju-
"das, general of the army, and the Jews; that
"they should be joined to the Romans, and that
"the Romans and Jews may be of one mind in
"wars and victories for ever. Now if war should 6
"come upon the Romans, Judas and his people
"shall help them, giving no aid to the enemies of
"the Romans, by provisions or by any kind of
"weapons. And when war shall come upon the 7
"Jews, the Romans shall help them to the utmost
"of their power, giving no aid to their enemies
"by assistance of any kind. And as the Jews are 8
"bound to the Romans, so likewise are the Ro-
"mans to the Jews, without any increase or de-
"crease."

And Judas and his people accepted this; and 9
the treaty stood, and continued between them and
the Romans for a long time.

[k] See the note on 3 Macc. viii. 15.

CHAPTER XIV.[a]

An account of the battle which took place between Judas, Ptolemy, and Gorgias.

1 AFTER this, Ptolemy collected an hundred and twenty thousand men, and a thousand horsemen, and they went after Judas. And Judas met him with ten thousand men, and routed him, 2 and *many* of Ptolemy's men were slain. And he besought Judas, and humbly entreated him to let him escape with his life; and swore that he would never more make war against him, and that he would shew kindness to the Jews who were in all 3 his countries. And Judas had compassion on him, and let him go; and Ptolemy adhered to his oath.

4 But Gorgias having collected three thousand men from mount Sarah[b], (*that is, of Idumæa,*) and four hundred horsemen, met Judas, and slew the captain of his army and certain of his men. 5 Then Judas and his men advanced towards them; and Gorgias was put to flight, and the greater part of his army was killed or fled: and he was sought for, and no tidings were heard of him; but it is reported that he fell in the battle.

---

[a] Quære, whether the latter part of this chapter relates to the occurrences detailed at 3 Macc. xii. 32—37? The battle recorded in the former part, I do not trace in the other books: but something like it occurred, not indeed with Ptolemy, but with Antiochus Eupator, at book III. ch. xiii. 6—24. That transaction, however, seems rather to be referred to in the following chapter of this book.

[b] See above, ch. x. 1.

CHAPTER XV.[a]

An account of the dissolution of the treaty which Antiochus had made with Judas, and of his march (together with Lysias his cousin's son) with a great army, and of his wars.

But when word was brought to Antiochus Eupator that Judas' affairs had gained strength, and what victories he had gained, he was very angry; and broke the treaty which he had made with Judas, and collected a large army, in which were twenty-two elephants: and he marched with Lysias his cousin's son into the country of Judah, directing his course to the city Beth-ner[b], before which he pitched his camp, and besieged it. Now when this was reported to Judas, he and all the elders of the children of Israel met together, and prayed to the great and good God, offering many sacrifices; which being finished, Judas proceeded with the leaders of his forces, and came into the camp by night, and made a sudden attack upon it, and slew of the enemy four thousand men and one of the elephants: and he returned to his own camp until the dawn of day should begin to break. Then each army was drawn out, and the battle grew fierce between them. And Judas perceived one of the elephants with golden trappings, and he supposed that the king was sitting upon him: so he called his men, and said to them, Which of

---

[a] Compare 2 Macc. vi; 3 Macc. xiii; Joseph. Ant. XII. 14, 15; Bell. I. 1.

[b] See above, ch. xi. 3, 9. There can be no doubt that the place meant is Bethsura, as in the corresponding passages of the second and third books.

8 you will go out and kill this elephant? And a young man, one of his servants[c], who was called Eleazar, went out and rushed upon the *enemy's* line, slaying on the right and left, so that the men
9 turned aside out of his view; and he went forward until he came even to the elephant; and creeping under him, he cut open his belly; and the elephant fell down upon him, and he died. So the king perceiving this, commanded to sound
10 a retreat; and it was done. And the amount of men of the higher rank slain that day in the battle was eight hundred men, besides those of the common men who were slain, and those who had been killed during the night.
11 Then it was told the king, that a certain man of his friends named Philip[d] had revolted from him: and that Demetrius[e] the son of Seleucus had gone forth from Rome with a great army of Romans, intending to take the kingdom out of his
12 hand. At which being much affrighted, he sent to Judas concerning making peace between them: to which Judas assented; and Antiochus and Lysias his cousin's son sware to him, that they
13 would never more make war upon him. And the king displayed a large sum of money, and gave it
14 to Judas for a present to the house of God. The king also commanded Menelaus to be seized, one

---

[c] This appears to be erroneous, as from all other accounts we are informed that this exploit was performed by his own *brother*, Eleazar, surnamed Avaran.

[d] Compare the account given of this Philip and his connexion with the king, at 2 Macc. vi. 14 and 55; and 3 Macc. ix. 29.

[e] For particulars concerning him, see 2 Macc. vii. 1, and the note there.

of the three[f] wicked men who had brought evil on the Jews in the days of Antiochus his father; and he ordered him to be carried up to a lofty tower, and to be thrown headlong thence; which was done. For by this the king designed to gratify the Jews, since this man was one of their chief enemies, and had slain great numbers of them.

CHAPTER XVI.[a]

The history of the arrival at Antioch of Demetrius the son of Seleucus, and of his defeating Eupator.

AFTER these things, king Eupator marched into the country of Macedonia, and then returned to Antioch. Whom Demetrius attacked with an army of Romans, and defeated, and slew, together with Lysias his cousin's son; and he reigned at Antioch. But to him went Alcimus, the leader of those three[b] wicked men; who, coming into his presence, prostrated himself before him, and wept most vehemently, and said; "O king, Judas and his company have been slaying great numbers of us; because, having deserted their religion, we have embraced the religion of the king. Wherefore, O king, assist us against them, and avenge us on them." Then he made the Jews go to him, and incensed him; suggesting to them such things as might provoke Demetrius, and irritate him to fit out an army to vanquish Judas. To whom the king giving heed,

---

[f] See above, ch. iii. 6. The particulars of his death are related more at large at 3 Macc. xiii. 3—8.

[a] Compare 2 Macc. vii; 3 Macc. xiv. xv; Joseph. Ant. XII. 17.

[b] See above, ch. iii. 6, and xv. 14.

sent a general named Nicanor[c], with a great army
and an abundant supply of weapons of war. And when Nicanor had come into the Holy Land, he sent messengers to Judas to come to him; and did not disclose that he had come to conquer the nation, but stated that he came only on account of the peace which was made between him and the nation, and that they[d] *also* were under obedience to the Romans. And Judas went out to him with a certain number of his men, who were endued with strength and courage: and he commanded them not to go far from him, lest Demetrius[e] might lay a snare for him.

10 When therefore he had met Demetrius, he saluted him; and, a seat being placed for each of them, they sat down, and Demetrius conversed with him as he pleased: afterwards each of them went into a tent which *the troops* had erected for him.

11 And Nicanor and Judas departed into the Holy City, and there dwelt together: and a firm friendship grew up between them: which being made known to Alcimus, he went to Demetrius and incensed him against Judas, and persuaded him to write and command Nicanor to send Judas to him bound in chains. But tidings of this came to Judas, and he went out from the city by night, and departed to Sebaste[f], and sent to

[c] Compare 3 Macc. xiv. 12.
[d] That is to say, that Demetrius, as well as the Jews, was in amity with the Romans; so that no danger was to be apprehended by them from him.
[e] Probably we ought to read here, and in the following verse, *Nicanor*; as it does not appear from the history that Demetrius was present in person. Compare the other accounts, as given in 2 Macc. vii. and 3 Macc. xiv.
[f] That is, *Samaria*; it had

his companions to come to him. And when 14 they were come, he sounded the trumpet, and commanded them to prepare themselves to attack Nicanor. But Nicanor sought Judas with great 15 diligence, and could learn no tidings of him. Wherefore he went to the house of God, requiring 16 of the priests to give him up to him, that he might send him bound in chains to the king: but they sware that he had not come into the house of God. Whereupon he abused both them and the 17 house of God, and spake insolently of the temple, and threatened that he would demolish it from the very foundations; and departed in a rage. He also took care to search all the houses of the Holy City. Likewise he sent his men to the 18 house of a certain excellent man[g], who had been seized in the time of Antiochus, and put to extreme torture; but after the death of Antiochus the Jews increased his authority and greatly honoured him. And when the messengers of 19 Nicanor came to him, he feared lest he should meet with the same treatment which he had received from Antiochus; wherefore he laid hands on himself. When this was told to Judas, he was 20 very sorry and much afflicted: and he sent to Nicanor, saying; "Do not seek me in the city, for " I am not there : therefore come forth to me, that " we may meet each other, either in the plains or " in the mountains, as you chuse." And Nicanor 21 went forth to him, and Judas met him with

not *yet* obtained this appellation, but at a subsequent period was so named by Herod the Great. See below, ch. xxi. 28.

[g] Namely Rhazis, mentioned at 3 Macc. xiv. 37.

these words: "O God, it was Thou who didst ex-
"terminate the army of king Sennacherib; and
"he indeed was greater than this man, in fame,
22 "in empire, and in the multitude of his host: and
"Thou didst deliver Ezechiah king of Judah
"from him, when he had trusted in Thee and
"prayed to Thee: deliver us, I pray thee, O God,
"from his malice, and make us victorious over
"him."
23 Then he made ready himself for battle, and advanced to Nicanor, saying, "Take care of your-
24 "self, it is to you I come." And Nicanor turned his back and fled: and Judas pursuing smote him on the shoulders, which he divided; and his men
25 were put to flight. And there fell of them on that day thirty thousand: and the inhabitants of the cities went out and slew them, so that they
26 left not one of them. And they decreed that that day should be every year a day of thanksgiving to the great and good God, and a day of gladness, and of feasting, and of drinking.

['Thus far is finished the Second[h] Book from the translation of the Hebrews.]

CHAPTER XVII.[a]

An account of the death of Judas.

1 BUT when nearly the same season of the year came round, Bacchides went forth with thirty

[h] Here indeed ends the history, so far as is contained in the third (usually *second*) book: the second (first) book carries the accounts down to the death of Simon, the brother of Judas.

[a] Compare 2 Macc. ix. 1—22. Joseph. Antiq. XII. 18, 19.

thousand of the bravest of the Macedonians; and came upon Judas without any tidings thereof coming to him, when he was in a certain city called Lalis[b], with three thousand men: wherefore most of those who were with him fled; and there remained with him eight hundred men, and his brothers Simeon and Jonathan. But those who remained with Judas were the strongest and bravest, and who had already endured much in the several battles which he had fought. And Judas and his company went out to *meet* Bacchides and his army.

And Bacchides divided his army, placing fifteen thousand on the right hand of Judas and his company, and fifteen thousand on their left. Then each part shouted against Judas and his company. Who attentively regarding each, perceived that the *enemy's* strongest and bravest troops were on the right, and found out that Bacchides himself was there among them. Judas likewise divided his company, and took the bravest of them with him, and gave the rest to his brothers. Then he made a charge upon those on the right, and he with his company slew about two thousand men. Then perceiving Bacchides, he directed his eyes and steps towards him, and slew all the bravest men who were about him. And he in person with his company sustained the multitudes which pressed upon him, felling to the ground the greater part of them, and he came near to Bacchides.

[b] At book II. ch. ix. 5, this is called *Eleasa:* where the Vulgate reads *Laisa*, as if it might be *Laish*, mentioned in the book of Isaiah.—According to Calmet, it is a place near to Beroea, or rather Berzetho, a small city of the tribe of Benjamin.

11 Whom when Bacchides saw coming towards him like a lion, brandishing in his hand a large sword stained with blood, he was excessively afraid of
12 him, and trembled, and fled out of his sight. And Judas with his company pursued him, and they slew his people with the sword, so that they put to death the greater part of those fifteen thousand: and Bacchides fled even to Ashdod[c].
13 And the fifteen thousand which were on Judas' left, followed him, and attacked Judas, to whom by this time were come his brothers and those
14 who were with them, greatly fatigued. And those fifteen thousand rushed upon them, and a very great battle took place between them and Judas; and there fell on both sides a certain number of slain, in which number was Judas.
15 Whom his brothers carried and buried beside the sepulchre of Mattathias his father, [God be merciful to them]; and the children of Israel bewailed
16 him many days. Now the time of his governing was seven years, and Jonathan his brother succeeded him in the government.

CHAPTER XVIII.[a]

The history of Jonathan the son of Mattathias.

1 AND Jonathan succeeded his brother, and he went to Jordan with a small number *of men*; which when Bacchides heard of, he marched

B.C. 160.

[c] Josephus says, "to a certain mountain called Aza," which appears a preferable reading; as the town of Ashdod (Azotus) may perhaps be thought too distant from the field of battle. But compare 2 Macc. ix. 15. and xvi. 10.

[a] Compare 2 Macc. ix. 28—72. See the acts of Jonathan detailed more at large at 2 Macc. ix. 28, to xii. and in Joseph. Antiq. XIII. 1—10.

to him with a large army. And when Jonathan 2 saw him, his men swam over Jordan; and Bacchides and his army followed them, and surrounded them. But Jonathan rushed on Bac- 3 chides; and as the men gave way to Jonathan, he and his company went out from the midst of them, and departed to Beersheba [b]: and his bro- 4 ther Simeon joined him, and they abode there; and they repaired whatever of the fortifications had fallen down, and they fortified themselves there.

But Bacchides marched to them, and besieged 5 them: and Jonathan and his brother, and they which were with them, went out to him by night, and slew great numbers of his army, and burned the battering rams and engines of war; and 6 his army was dispersed, and Bacchides fled into the desert. And Jonathan and Simeon, and the men who were with him, pursued and took him. Who, 7 when he saw Jonathan, knew that his death was near: wherefore he proclaimed peace with Jonathan, and sware that he would never more make war upon him, and moreover, that he would restore the whole of the captives which he had taken of the army of Judas. And Jonathan gave 8 him his hand, and departed from him: nor after this was there any more war between them. And not long after this [c], Jonathan died, and his brother Simeon succeeded him.

B.C. 158.

---

[b] Quære whether we ought to read Bethbasi, as the place mentioned at 2 Macc. ix. 62?

[c] This is not expressed with sufficient accuracy; nor indeed is the chronology satisfactorily settled. Jonathan is said to have lived thirteen or fourteen years after making peace with Bacchides, and to have been slain by Tryphon in the year B. C. 144. And

B.C. 144.   CHAP. XIX.   327

CHAPTER XIX.[a]

The history of Simeon the son of Mattathias.

1 THEN Simeon the son of Mattathias succeeded to the government; and he gathered together all those who remained of the army
2 of Judas: and his affairs prospered, and he subdued all those who had exercised hostility against the Jews after the death of his brother Judas; and he behaved well towards his people, and the matters of his country were rightly ordered.
3 Wherefore Antiochus[b] attacked him, and also Demetrius the son of Seleucus; and sent a great
4 army against him: to meet which, Simeon and his two sons went out; and he divided his army into two parts, one of which he kept with himself,
5 and gave the other to his sons. Then he and they which were with him went to the army; and he sent his two sons and their followers by another way, and appointed with them to attack the army
6 at a given time. After this, he met the army of Antiochus, and attacked it, and began to prevail against it: and his two sons came when the battle had now begun, and the fight grew fierce, and they
7 came round the rear of the army. And Antiochus' army, being placed between two armies, was cut to pieces, nor did a single man of them escape: nor did Antiochus return any more to fight with

yet Josephus, Antiq. XIII. 11, states that he ruled only *four* years! Compare the account of his settlement of the affairs of Jerusalem for some years, at 2 Macc. ix. 73. to xii. 48.

[a] Compare 2 Macc. xiii—xvi. Joseph. Antiq. XIII. 11—14.
[b] Simon was first attacked by Tryphon; and subsequently by Cendebæus under orders from Antiochus.

Simeon. And peace and quietness continued 8 among the Jews all the days of Simeon. And the time of his government was two years[c]. Then 9 Ptolemy his son-in-law rushed on him, and slew him, at a certain feast[d] where he was present. And he seized his wife and his two sons. And Simeon's son, whose name was Hyrcanus, was set in his father's place.

[Here ends the history as given in the two books usually attached to our Bibles.]

CHAPTER XX.[a]

The history of Hyrcanus the son of Simeon.

Now Simeon, while he was yet alive[b], had ap- 1 pointed Jochanan his son to be captain; and having gathered to him very many troops, he sent him to vanquish a certain man who had come out against him, and was called Hyrcanus[c]. Now he was a man of great fame, 2 powerful in strength, and of an ancient sovereignty. Whom Jonathan encountered, and de- 3 feated: wherefore Simeon named his son Jochanan Hyrcanus; on account of his slaying Hyrcanus, and gaining a victory over him.

B.C. 135.

[c] Instead of this, we rather ought to read *nine* years, namely, from 144 to 135 B.C.

[d] Namely, at the castle of Docus near Jericho, as related at 2 Macc. xvi. 15.

[a] Compare Josephus, Antiq. XIII. 15.

[b] See 2 Macc. xiii. 53.

[c] Others say that he gained the name by a victory over the Hyrcanians. See Eusebii Chronicon, and Sulpitius Severus. Calmet thinks that the person designated by the name Hyrcanus was Cendebæus, the general of king Antiochus; whom John defeated near Modin, as is related at 2 Macc. xvi.

4 But when this Hyrcanus had heard that Ptolemy had killed his father, he was afraid of Ptolemy, and fled to Gaza[d]: and Ptolemy pursued him
5 with many followers. But the citizens of Gaza helped Hyrcanus, and shut the gates of their city, and hindered Ptolemy from reaching Hyrcanus.
6 And Ptolemy returned, and departed to Dagon[e], having with him the mother of Hyrcanus and his two brothers. Now Dagon had at that time a strongly fortified castle.
7 But Hyrcanus went to the Holy House[f], and offered sacrifices, and succeeded his father: and he collected a large army and went to *attack* Ptolemy. Wherefore Ptolemy shut the gate of Dagon upon himself and his company, and fortified himself
8 therein. And Hyrcanus besieged him, and made an iron ram to batter the wall, and to open it:
9 and the battle between them lasted long, and Hyrcanus prevailed against Ptolemy, and went up
10 close to the castle, and almost took it. When Ptolemy therefore saw this, he commanded the mother of Hyrcanus and his two brothers to be brought out upon the wall, and to be tortured
11 most severely; which was done to them. But Hyrcanus, seeing this, stood still; and fearing that they would be put to death, desisted from fighting.
12 To whom his mother called out, and said; " My

[d] Here, as in many former places, the names of Gaza and Gazara appear to have been interchanged. Compare 3 Macc. xvi. 19, 21.

[e] Josephus states this to be " one of the fortresses above " Jericho." It was also called Docus, and was the place where Simon was slain by Ptolemy his son-in-law. See 2 Macc. xvi. 15.

[f] Hottinger remarks, that this is the expression used to designate the temple of Jerusalem by all Oriental writers, sacred and profane. (Exercitt. Antimorin. 4to. 1644. p. 66.)

"son, do not be moved by love and filial piety towards me and your brethren, in preference to your father: nor on account of our captivity be weakened in your desire of avenging him; but demand satisfaction for the rights of your father and mine, to the utmost of your power. But that which you fear for us from that tyrant, he will necessarily do to us at all events: wherefore press forward your siege without any intermission."

When therefore Hyrcanus had heard the words of his mother, he urged on the siege: wherefore Ptolemy increased the tortures of his mother and his brothers; and sware that he would throw them headlong from the castle, as often as Hyrcanus came near to the wall. Therefore Hyrcanus feared, lest he should be the cause of their death; and he returned to his camp, still continuing the siege of Ptolemy. Now it happened, that the feast of tabernacles was at hand[g]; wherefore Hyrcanus went into the city of the Holy House, that he might be present at the feast and the solemnity and the sacrifices. And when Ptolemy knew that he had departed to the Holy City, and was detained there, he seized upon the mother of Hyrcanus and his brothers, and slew them; and he fled into a place[h] whither Hyrcanus could not come.

---

[g] Josephus states, that the departure of Hyrcanus, and the consequent protraction of the siege, was owing to the coming on of *the sabbatical year*.

[h] Namely, to Philadelphia; where a friend of his called Zeno (and Cotylas) had seized upon the sovereignty. [Josephus.]

CHAPTER XXI.[a]

The history of the going up of Antiochus to the city of the Holy House, to fight with Hyrcanus.

1 Now when Antiochus had heard that Simeon was dead, he collected an army, and marched
2 until he came to the city of the Holy House: and he encamped around it, and besieged it, designing to take it by force: but he could not, by reason of the height and strength of the walls, and the mul-
3 titude of warriors who were in it. But by God's will he was restrained from *winning* it: for he had betaken himself to the northern side of the city, and had built there an hundred and thirty
4 towers opposite to the wall; and had caused men to mount them, to fight with those who should
5 endeavour to go up upon the walls of the city. He also appointed men to dig up the earth in a certain spot, till they came to the foundation of the wall: which finding to be of wood, they burned it with fire, and a very large portion of the wall fell down.
6 And Hyrcanus' men opposed them, and prevented them from entering, keeping guard over
7 the ruined portion; and Hyrcanus went out with the better part of his fighting men against the army of Antiochus, and defeated them with great
8 slaughter. And Antiochus and his men were routed; whom Hyrcanus with his troops pursued, till they had driven them away from the city.
9 Then, returning to the towers which Antiochus had built, they destroyed them; and abode in the

[a] Compare Josephus, Antiq. XIII. 16, 17.

city, and around it. But Antiochus encamped in 10 a certain place, which was distant from the city of the house of God about two furlongs.

And at the approach of the feast of tabernacles 11 Hyrcanus sent ambassadors to him, to treat for a truce until the solemnity should be passed; which he granted him; and sent victims, and gold and silver[b], to the house of God. And Hyrcanus com- 12 manded the priests to receive what Antiochus had sent; and they did so. Now when Hyrcanus and 13 the priests saw the reverence of Antiochus towards the temple of God, he sent ambassadors to him, to treat for peace. To which Antiochus 14 agreed; and he went to Jerusalem: and Hyrcanus meeting him, they entered the city together. And 15 Hyrcanus made a feast for Antiochus and his princes; and they did eat and drink together; and he made him a present of three hundred talents of gold: and each of them agreed[c] with his 16 companion about peace and rendering assistance, and Antiochus departed into his own country.

But it is related, that Hyrcanus opened the 17 treasury[d], which had been *made* by some kings of the sons of David, [to whom be peace,] and he brought out thence a great sum of money, and left

---

[b] Josephus forcibly contrasts this behaviour of the king with that of Antiochus Epiphanes, when he had become master of the city. See 2 Macc. i. 44—60. From this exhibition of liberality, the Jews gave to Antiochus the surname of Ριυs.

[c] Namely, on certain conditions, which may be seen in Diodorus Siculus, and Josephus.

[d] Josephus states, that he opened the sepulchre of David, and took thence three thousand talents; with which he hired a body of mercenary troops; being the first Jewish prince who did this. Compare also Joseph. Antiq. VII. 12.

as much in it, consigning it to its former state of
18 secrecy. Then he built up and repaired that part of the wall which had fallen down; and he provided carefully for the convenience and advantage of his flock, and behaved himself uprightly towards them.

19 Now when Antiochus had come into his own country, he determined to go and fight with the king of Persia[e], for he had re-
20 volted from the time of the first Antiochus: and he sent ambassadors to Hyrcanus, that he should go to him; and Hyrcanus went with him, and
21 departed into the country of Persia. And an army of the Persians met him, and fought with him; whom Antiochus putting to flight defeated
22 and put to the sword. Then he stayed in the place where he was, and erected a wonderful building[f], that it might be a memorial of him in
23 their country. And after some time he went forward to meet the king of the Persians; and Hyr-

B. C. 131.

---

[e] Rather, Phraates king of *Parthia*, who still detained Demetrius Nicator a prisoner. It is observable that the author of this book, in common with almost all the later Greek and Roman historians, uses the terms *Persians* and *Parthians* as synonymous. Indeed it has been contended that the difference is more nominal than real; since the Parthians originally were comprised within the Persian empire; and after that had been brought under the sway of the Macedonian princes, Arsaces revolted with a large district, and established himself as an independent monarch; and the family of the Arsacidæ, having acquired both wealth and power, held possession of their throne during a period of no less than 482 years. On the indifferent use of the words *Persian* and *Parthian*, see archbishop Ussher, *in Notis ad Ignatii Acta*, p. 36. (4to. Lond. 1647.) And for the origin and a short history of that people, consult Justin's History, books 41 and 42.

[f] He erected a trophy on the banks of the river Lycus, where he had conquered Indates the Parthian general.

canus remained behind, by reason of the sabbath, which Pentecost immediately followed. And the king of Persia and Antiochus met; and very great battles took place between them, in which Antiochus and many of his army were slain[g]. 24

And when news of this was brought to Hyrcanus, he marched[h] into the country of Syria, and on his journey besieged Halepus[i]: and the citizens surrendered to him, paying him tribute; and he departed from them, and returned into the Holy City, and remained there for some days. 25
B. C. 130. 26

Then he departed into the country of Samaria, and fought against Neapolis[k]; but the citizens hindered him from entering into it. And he destroyed whatever buildings they had on mount Jezabel[l], and the temple; which was done two hundred years after that Sanballat[m] the Samaritan had built it. He also slew the priests who were in Sebaste[n]. And he marched into the country of Idumæa, that is, the mountains Sarah[o], 27
B. C. 129. 28
29

[g] Authors are not agreed whether he fell in battle or afterwards: he was succeeded by his brother Demetrius Nicator, whom Phraates had set free at the time of Antiochus' invasion. [Josephus.]

[h] From this period the Jews refused to acknowledge any Macedonian or Syrian king.

[i] The town now called Aleppo.

[k] The town which anciently was called Shechem, or Sichem, being the principal city of Samaria. It still bears the name of Napolose, or Naplouse. See a description of its present state in "Clarke's Travels."

[l] That is, mount Ebal, or more properly Garizim.

[m] See the history of this transaction in Josephus, Antiq. XI. 8.

[n] The city of Samaria obtained this name under the reign of Herod the Great, who enlarged, adorned, and fortified it. See Joseph. Ant. XV. 11; Bell. I. 16.

[o] Probably the same as "Seir," so often mentioned in Scripture. See above, ch. x. 1; xiv. 4; also xlix. 20.

and they surrendered to him: with whom he stipulated that they should be circumcised and adopt the religion of Torah (*or the Mosaic law*). And they agreed with him, and were circumcised, and became Jews, and were confirmed in this *practice* even till the destruction of the second house [p].

And Hyrcanus went on to all the surrounding nations; and they all submitted to him, and at the same time entered into an agreement of peace and obedience.

He also sent ambassadors to the Romans, writing to them concerning the renewal of the league [q] which was between them. When therefore his ambassadors had come to the Romans, they honoured them; and appointed them a seat of dignity; and gave attention to the embassy on account of which they had come; and despatched their business, and replied to his letter.

B. C. 128.

CHAPTER XXII.[a]

The copy of the Romans' letter to Hyrcanus.

"FROM the elder, and his three hundred and
" twenty governors, to Hyrcanus the king
" of Judah, health. Your letter has even
" now reached us, on reading which we rejoiced;
" and we have questioned your ambassadors con-
" cerning the state of your affairs. Also we have
" acknowledged their place of dignity in science,

B. C. 127.

---

[p] This expression clearly informs us that the author of this book, whoever he may have been, lived after A. D. 70.

[q] See above, 2 Macc. viii. and xii.

[a] Compare Josephus, Ant. XIII. 17; but his account varies in some particulars from that which is given here.

"moral discipline, and the virtues; and we have honoured them, and made them sit in the presence of our elder: who has been careful to transact all their business, giving command that all the cities which Antiochus had taken away by force should be restored to you; and that every obstacle to the exercise of your religion should be removed; and that all should be made void which Antiochus had decreed against you. He has also commanded that all the cities which he had taken should continue faithful to you; he has likewise given orders by letter to all his provinces, that your ambassadors should be treated with respect and honour. Moreover he has sent with them an ambassador to you named Cynæus, bearing a letter; to whom also he has entrusted an embassy, that he might treat with you in person."

Therefore when this epistle of the Romans had reached Hyrcanus, he began to be styled king, being formerly called high priest: and thus the royal and sacerdotal dignities were united in him. And he was the first who was called king among the chiefs of the Jews in the time of the second house.

B.C. 126.

CHAPTER XXIII.[a]

The history of the wars of Hyrcanus with the Samaritans.

Now Hyrcanus marched to Sebaste, and besieged the Samaritans[b] who were therein, for a

---

[a] Compare Josephus, Ant. XIII. 18.

[b] They were subjects of Syria; whose two princes, Antiochus Gryphus and Antiochus Cyzicenus, being engaged in continual quarrels with each other, gave Hyrca-

long time; till he reduced them to such straits, that they were compelled to feed upon every
2 kind of dead carcass. Nevertheless they bore this patiently, fearing his sword, and trusting to the Macedonians and Egyptians, whose aid
3 they had implored. In the mean time comes on the great fast, at which Hyrcanus must be present in the Holy House, to offer sacrifices on that day.
4 Wherefore he substituted his two sons, Antigonus and Aristobulus, as commanders of the army; leaving them orders to besiege the Samaritans,
5 and reduce them to extremities. Likewise he commanded the army to obey his sons, and to execute their orders: and he departed to the city of the Holy House.
6 Moreover Antiochus[c] the Macedonian marched to help the inhabitants of Sebaste; and tidings of it were brought to the two sons of Hyrcanus;
7 who, having substituted a general to conduct the siege of Sebaste, went to meet Antiochus; whom they encountered and routed, and returned to Se-
8 baste. There came likewise out of Egypt Lythras[d], the son of queen Cleopatra, to help the
9 Samaritans. When news of this was brought to Hyrcanus, he went to meet him, the solemnity being now past: whom when he met, he encoun-

nus opportunity of revenging himself for some former injuries alleged to have been committed by the Samaritans upon the Jews.

[c] Namely, Antiochus IX. surnamed Cyzicenus.

[d] That is, Ptolemy Lathyrus, the son of Ptolemy Physcon and Cleopatra: he began to reign, conjointly with his mother, in the year B.C. 116. He brought about 6000 soldiers with him, and began by plundering several parts of Judæa; hoping thereby to draw off Hyrcanus from the siege.

tered most fiercely, and slew very many of his men: and Lythras was put to flight; nor did the Egyptians any more after this return to give assistance to the Samaritans. And king Hyrcanus returned to Sebaste, and pressed sore on it, till he took it with the sword, and slew those of its citizens who were remaining, and utterly destroyed it, and pulled down its walls.

B.C. 110.

10
11

CHAPTER XXIV.[a]

The history of Lythras the son of Cleopatra, and of his marching out against his mother in Egypt.

LYTHRAS the son of Cleopatra, having become strong in goods and in men, revolted from Cleopatra his mother; the chief men of the kingdom being his abettors. Therefore Cleopatra, having sent for two Jews, one of whom was called Chelcias, and the other Hananias[b], placed them at the head of those princes of Egypt who remained on her side, and made them both generals of the Egyptian army. Now they managed all matters well with the common people, and conducted the affairs of the empire with wisdom. Them Cleopatra sent to fight with Lythras; who going to him made war, and routed him,

B.C. 105.

1
2
3
4

---

[a] Compare Joseph. Ant. XIII. 18. See also XIII. 20.

[b] Josephus states these to be the sons of that Onias, who, by leave of Ptolemy and Cleopatra, had built in Egypt a temple to God, after the pattern of the temple of Jerusalem; being moved to this by remembering the prophecy of Isaiah at ch. xix. 19: "In that day shall there be an altar to the Lord in the midst of the land of Egypt, and a pillar at the border thereof to the Lord." See the particulars of the history detailed at Joseph. Ant. XIII. 6.

putting his men to flight: and he fled to Cyprus, and there remained, with a few who adhered to him.

CHAPTER XXV.[a]

An account of the Jewish sects at this time.

1 At that time there were three sects among the Jews. One, of the Pharisees, that is, "the
2 "separated," or religious; whose rule it was, to maintain whatever was contained in the law, according to the expositions of their fore-
3 fathers. The second, that of the Sadducees; and these are followers of a certain man of the doctors,
4 by name Sadoc; whose rule it was, to maintain according to the things found in the text of the law, and of which there is demonstration in the Scripture itself; but not that which is not extant
5 in the text, nor is proved from it. The third sect was that of the Hasdanim[b], or those who studied the virtues: but the author of *this* book[c] did not make mention of their rule, *nor do we know it except in* so far as it is discovered by their
6 name: for they applied themselves to such practices as came near to the more eminent virtues; namely, to select from those two other rules what-

---

[a] Compare Josephus, Ant. XIII. 9; XVII. 3; XVIII. 2; and especially Bell. II. 7.

[b] Or Assidæans, mentioned at 2 Macc. ii. 42; vii. 13; 3 Macc. xiv. 6. Some think them to be the same with the *Essenes*, described by Josephus (Bell. II. 7.) and by others; for whose collected observations the reader is referred to Calmet's Dictionary of the Bible. In the eighth volume of the Critici Sacri (edit. 1660) is a specific tract on the subject, by J. Drusius, which deserves to be consulted.

[c] This expression is to be remarked, but I cannot furnish the solution. See it again at ch. xxv. 5; and at the close of the book, ch. lix. 96.

ever was most safe in belief, most sure and guarded.

Hyrcanus at first was one of the Pharisees; afterwards he went over to the Sadducees; because that one of the Pharisees had said to him, it is not lawful for you to be high priest, because your mother was a captive before she bare you, in the days of Antiochus: but it becometh not that the son of a captive should be high priest. And this conversation took place in the presence of the chief men of the Pharisees; which was the cause of his going over to the rule of the Sadducees. Now the Sadducees were at enmity with the Pharisees; wherefore they kept up differences betwixt one another, and they prevailed on him so far, as to slay great numbers of the Pharisees. And the trouble came to such a height, that wars and many evils continued among them for a great length of time.

CHAPTER XXVI.[a]

The account of Hyrcanus' death, and of the time of his reign.

Hyrcanus had three sons, namely, Antigonus, Aristobulus, and Alexander. And Hyrcanus loved Antigonus and Aristobulus; but Alexander was odious to him. And on a time he saw in a dream, that of his sons, Alexander would reign after his death; and this gave him uneasiness. And he did not think fit, while he lived, to set up either of the sons whom he loved, on account of his vision; nor to appoint Alexander

[a] Compare Josephus, Ant. XIII. 18; Bell. I. 3.

B.C. 10⁶⁄₇.   CHAP. XXVII.   341

5 king, because he was disliked by him. Wherefore he deferred the business; that after his death it might take that turn which should please the great and good God.

6 Now the Jews had been, in the time of his father and uncles, united in affection towards them; and prompt to obey them, on account of their subduing of their enemies, and the excellent feats
7 which they performed. They also continued united in affection to Hyrcanus; until the slaughter of the Pharisees was committed by him, and the rooting out of the Jews, and the
8 civil wars on account of religion. From hence sprung perpetual enmities, and ceaseless evils, and many murders. Which was the reason why many
9 detested Hyrcanus. Now the time of his reign was thirty-one[b] years, and he died.

B.C. 106.

CHAPTER XXVII.[a]

The history of Aristobulus the son of Hyrcanus.

1 HYRCANUS being dead, his son Aristobulus succeeded him on the throne; who displayed haughtiness, pride, and power; and placed on his head a large crown, in contempt of
2 the crown of the sacred priesthood. Now he was affectionately inclined towards his brother Antigonus, whom he preferred[b] to all his friends: but his brother Alexander he kept in prison, as also

B.C. 104.

---

[b] Josephus, in one book, says thirty-one years; in another, thirty-three: but archbishop Ussher allows him only twenty-nine years' reign; in which case we must place his death in B.C. 107.

[a] Compare Joseph. Ant. XIII. 19; Bell. I. 3.

[b] And advanced him to a share of the regal power.

z 3

his mother[c], by reason of her love for Alexander. And he sent[d] his brother Antigonus, who fought against him, and conquered him, with all his abettors and troops, which he put to flight, and returned into the city of the Holy House. This happened while Aristobulus lay sick. When therefore Antigonus was on his way to the city, the sickness of his brother was reported to him; who, entering the city, went to the house of God, to give thanks for the mercy shewn in his deliverance from the enemy, and to beseech the great and good God to restore health to his brother. Therefore certain of those who were adversaries and haters of Antigonus go to Aristobulus and say; In sooth the news of your sickness was carried to your brother, and behold he is coming with his partisans, armed; and is now gone into the sanctuary to make to himself friends, that he may come suddenly upon you and slay you. And king Aristobulus was afraid to take any hasty step against his brother respecting that which had been told him, till he should know the correctness of the intelligence. Wherefore he commanded all his attendants to post themselves arm-

---

[c] Josephus adds, that he suffered her to die of hunger while in prison!

[d] There is every appearance of an hiatus between the second and third verses of this chapter: against *whom* did Aristobulus send his brother Antigonus? not against Alexander, for he was in prison. But we read in Josephus, that at this particular time Antigonus made an expedition into Ituræa, part of which he conquered and added to Judæa; so that possibly a sentence (or more) may have been omitted, in which was mentioned the leader of the Ituræans whom Antigonus encountered with such success. The text, as it stands at present, is scarcely intelligible.

ed in a certain place, from which whoever came
9 to his palace could not turn aside. He likewise
ordered it to be publicly proclaimed, that no one
wearing arms of any kind should come to the
10 king into the court, without being bidden. After
this, he sent to Antigonus, ordering him to come
to him: whereupon Antigonus took off his arms
11 in obedience to the king. In the mean time there
comes to him a messenger from the wife of his
brother[c] Aristobulus, (who hated him,) saying to
12 him; The king says to you, "I have now heard
" of the beauty of your dress when you entered
" the city, and am desirous of beholding you thus
" habited; wherefore come to me in that form,
13 " that I may be gratified in seeing you." And
Antigonus doubted not that this message was
from the king, as the messenger had reported;
14 and that he did not wish to put him on the same
footing with others as to the laying aside their
arms: and he went to him in that manner and
15 dress. And when he had come to that place in
which king Aristobulus had commanded his men
to post themselves, with orders to kill any person
16 who should come thither armed; and when the
men saw him wearing his arms;—they rushed on
him, and instantly slew him; and his blood flowed
17 over the marble *pavement* on that spot. And the
cry of men grew loud, and their weeping and lamentation was magnified, grieving over the death
of Antigonus, for his beauty, and the elegance of
his discourse, and his exploits.
18 So the king, hearing the noise of the men,

[c] Salome, called also Alexandra.

enquired concerning it; and found that Antigonus had been slain; which caused him the greatest sorrow, both for the affection which he bare towards him, and because he did not deserve this fate: and he perceived that a snare had been laid for his brother: and he cried aloud, and wept exceedingly; and smote his breast unceasingly; so that some blood-vessels of his breast were burst, and the blood flowed out of his mouth. But his attendants and the chief of his friends came to him, consoling him, and appeasing and soothing him, so as to restrain him from this action; being apprehensive that he would die, as he was weak, and was almost expiring under that which he had *already* done.

And they took a golden basin, to receive the blood which gushed forth at his mouth; and they sent the basin, with the blood which was in it, by one of the attendants to a physician, that he might see it, and advise what was to be done for him. And the page went with the basin: and when he came to the place where Antigonus had been slain, and his blood had flowed about, the page slipped, and fell; and spilled the king's blood which was in the basin over the blood of his murdered brother. And the page returned with the basin, and told the courtiers what had happened; who abused and reviled him; while he justified himself, and sware that he had not designedly or voluntarily done this. But when the king heard them quarrelling, he asked to be told what they were saying: and they held their tongues: but when he threatened them, they told him. Who then said, " Praise be to the Just

"Judge, who hath shed the blood of the oppressor
29 " over the blood of the oppressed." Then he groaned, and forthwith expired. And the time of
30 his reign was one full year. And all his flock lamented him; for he was noble-minded, victorious[e], and liberal: and his brother Alexander reigned in his stead.

CHAPTER XXVIII.[a]

The account of Alexander the son of Hyrcanus.

1 AFTER that Aristobulus was dead, his brother Alexander was released from his fetters; and being brought out of prison, succeeded
2 to the throne. Now the governor of the city Acche[b] (*which is Ptolemais*) had rebelled; and had sent messengers to Lythras the son of Cleopatra, requesting that he would aid him, and take
3 him under his protection; but he for a long time refused, fearing *a recurrence of* the things which
4 he had before suffered[c] from Hyrcanus. But the messenger gave him courage by means of the succours promised by the lord of Tyre, of Sidon, and others. And Lythras marched with thirty
5 thousand men: and the report of it was brought to Alexander, who anticipated him at Ptolemais, and attacked it; and the citizens of Ptolemais shut the gate in his face, and endeavoured to keep

B.C. 105.

---

[e] He became memorable for subduing Ituræa, a part of Arabia Petræa, lying on the eastern side of Jordan, and compelling its inhabitants to adopt the customs of the Jews. See above, v. 3.—Ituræa is mentioned at Luke iii. 1. and its renown in archery is celebrated by the Roman poets. See also Strabo, lib. XVI.

[a] Compare Joseph. Antiq. XIII. 20, 21. Bell. I. 3.

[b] See the note on 2 Macc. v. 22.

[c] See above, ch. xxiii. 10.

him out. Wherefore Alexander straitened them, and continued to besiege them; until he was informed of the marching of Lythras: then he retired from before them, Lythras with his troops being at hand.

Now there was among the citizens of Ptolemais an old man[d] of acknowledged authority, who persuaded the citizens not to permit Lythras to enter their city, nor to take on themselves obedience to him, since he was of a different religion. He also said to them, Far more advantageous to you in every way will be submission to Alexander, who is of the same religion, than submission to Lythras: nor did he cease, until they agreed to his sentiments. And they prevented Lythras from entering Ptolemais, refusing submission to him. And Lythras was perplexed in his affairs, nor did he take counsel what was best for him to do.

And this was told to the king of Sidon[e], and he sent messengers to him, that he should help him in the war against Alexander; that either they might defeat him, or *take* some of his cities, and thus punish him; and thus Lythras might return into his own country, after performing deeds which might render him formidable; which in truth would be more to his advantage than to return without having effected his purpose. And this was told to Alexander; who sent to Lythras an honourable embassy with a very valuable pre-

---

[d] Josephus informs us that the name of this sage counsellor was Demænetus.

[e] This appears from Josephus to be Zoïlus, who had also taken possession of the neighbouring posts, Strato's Tower, (afterwards called Cæsarea,) and Dora.

B.C. 104.   CHAP. XXVIII.   347

sent, and proposed to him not to aid the king of
13 Sidon. And Lythras accepted Alexander's pre-
14 sent, agreeing to his request. But Alexander
marched to Sidon, and fought against its sovereign;
and God made him victorious over him, and he
slew great numbers of his men; and having put
him to flight, gained possession of his country.

15 After this, Alexander sent messengers to Cleopatra, that she should come with an army against Lythras her son; and that he also B.C. 104. would march with his army against him, and would
16 deliver him a prisoner to her. Which when Lythras found out, he departed into the mountain of Galilee[f], and slew great numbers of the inhabitants, and carried away ten thousand captives: a great
17 number of his own men also were slain. From thence he marched even till he came to Jordan, and there encamped; that his men and horses might rest themselves, and afterwards he might march to Jerusalem to fight with Alexander.
18 This was told to Alexander; who went against him with fifty thousand men, of whom six thousand had shields of brass: and it is said that each
19 of those could resist any number of men. And he attacked him at the Jordan, and engaged with him there; but did not obtain the victory, because he trusted in his men, and had placed his confidence in their number.
20 But with Lythras there were men very skilful in battles[g] and in drawing up armies; who ad-

[f] Where falling suddenly upon a town called Asochis, he mastered it, and departed, loaded with abundance of captives and other spoil. (Josephus.)

[g] Josephus particularly names Philostephanus, as the

vised him to divide his forces into two parts, so that one might be with Lythras and his company prepared for battle, and the other part might be with another captain of their company. And he fought even until noon, and great numbers of his men were slain. And his friend advanced, with the remainder of the army which was with him, whose strength was yet entire, against Alexander and his men, who were by this time overcome with fatigue: and he dealt with them as he pleased, and slew great multitudes of them; and Alexander and the men who had remained with him fled into the city of the Holy House.

Lythras also departed towards evening into a certain town near at hand; and by chance some Jewish women with their children met him; and he commanded some of the children to be killed, and their flesh to be dressed, pretending that there were some in his army who fed on human flesh; designing by these acts to strike the inhabitants of the country with a dread of his troops.

After this came Cleopatra; whom Alexander met, and told her what Lythras had done to his army, and appointed to go with her in search of him. Which being told to Lythras, he fled to a place where was a station of his ships; going on board which, he returned to Cyprus; and Cleopatra returned into Egypt.

But at the end of the year Alexander marched against Gaza; because its chief[h] had revolted from him, and had sent to a certain king of the

---

man whose skilful tactics eventually gained Ptolemy the battle.

[h] Josephus records his name, Apollodotus; and the brother, who treacherously slew him, (ver. 31,) was called Lysimachus.

Arabians named Hartas[i] to assist him; who con-
29 sented to do so, and marched towards Gaza: this was told to Alexander; who leaving some of his men before Gaza, marched against Hartas, and
30 engaged him, and put him to flight. Then he returned to Gaza, and lying sore upon it, took it at
31 the end of a year. But the cause of his taking it was the brother of that chief; who
32 coming suddenly on him, slew him. When the citizens sought to kill him, he collected his friends, and went to the gate of the city, and addressed Alexander, begging that on giving security for his life and the lives of his friends, he would enter
33 the city; which Alexander promising, entered Gaza, and slew its inhabitants, and overthrew the temple which was in it, and burned the gilded idol which was in the temple.
34 After which he departed to the city of the Holy House, and there celebrated the feast of taber-
35 nacles. And when the feast was past, he made himself ready against Hartas, whom he encoun-
36 tered, and slew a great number of his men: and Hartas' affairs were much straitened and crippled, and he feared his own utter extinction. Wherefore suing to Alexander for his life, he yielded
37 him obedience, and paid him tributes. And Alex-

---

[i] Such is the spelling given; but the name is properly *Aretas*. This appears to have been an appellative name among the Arabian sovereigns; as we read of an Aretas in 3 Macc. v. 7, at the year B. C. 170: of another, B. C. 66. (see below, ch. xxxv): and a grandson of this last occurs in St. Paul's second Epistle to the Corinthians; who, having married the daughter of Herod Antipas, held the sovereignty of Damascus, and endeavoured to intercept the apostle; whose friends secured him by letting him down in a basket from the city-wall. See 2 Cor. xi. 32; and Acts ix. 24.

ander departed from him, and marched against Hemath[k] and Tyre, and took them; and having received tribute from the inhabitants, he returned into the city of the Holy House.

CHAPTER XXIX.[a]

An account of the battles which took place between the Pharisees and Sadducees.

AFTERWARDS evils arose between the Pharisees and Sadducees, and continued by the space of six years[b]. And Alexander helped the Sadducees against the Pharisees, of whom there were slain within six years fifty thousand. Wherefore between these two sects the state of things was reduced to utter destruction[c], and their enmity was completely confirmed. So Alexander, having sent for the elder men of each sect, spake kindly to them, and advised a reconciliation. But they answered him, "In truth you, in our opinion, "are worthy of death[d], for the abundance of in-"nocent blood *which you have shed:* wherefore "let there be nothing between us but the sword." Then after this, they began to shew their enmity openly, sending messengers to Demetrius[e] *the king*

---

[k] Josephus calls it Amathus, "the strongest of all "the fortresses on the river "Jordan." Some chronologers place this event three years before the capture of Gaza.

[a] Compare Josephus, Antiq. XIII. 21, 22. Bell. I. 3.

[b] Tacitus is supposed to allude to this civil strife, in the fifth book of his Histories, ch. 8.

[c] Or, "these two sects were "bent on nothing less than "the extermination of each "other."

[d] Josephus relates, that when he asked the Jews what he could do to oblige them, they unanimously desired him "to go and kill himself."

[e] Namely, Demetrius III. who, conjointly with Philip, was at that time sovereign of Syria; or, as in the text, of Macedon.

of Macedon, that he should come to them with an
7 army; promising that they would assist him against Alexander and his party, and would reduce the Hebrews to submission to the Macedonians. And Demetrius marched to them with a large army.
8 Which also was told to Alexander; who sent a person to hire six thousand Macedonians, B.C. 89. whom joining to his own forces he ad-
9 vanced against Demetrius. Many also of the
10 Jews, Pharisees, went over to Demetrius. And Demetrius sent secretly persons to those Macedonians who were with Alexander, to seduce them from him; but they hearkened not unto him.
11 Alexander also sent secretly men to the Jews who were with Demetrius, to turn them to his side; but neither did these do as he would have them.
12 And Alexander and Demetrius met, and fought a battle; in which all Alexander's men fell, and he
13 escaped alone into the land of Judah. But when his men heard it whispered that he had escaped in safety, and found out the place where he was;
14 there assembled unto him about six thousand men of the bravest of the sons of Israel; and many of those, who had revolted to Demetrius, joined them-
15 selves to him. Afterwards men flocked to him from every side; and he returned to give battle to Demetrius with a numerous force, and put him to flight: and Demetrius returned into his own country.
16 And Alexander marched against him to Antioch, and besieged it three years: and B.C. 84. when Demetrius came out to fight, Alex-
17 ander conquered him and slew him: and he de-

parted from the city, and returned to Jerusalem to his citizens; who magnified him, honouring and praising him for having defeated his enemies. And the Jews agreed to submit to him, and his heart was at rest: and he sent his armies against all his enemies, whom he put to flight, and gained the victory over them. He also gained possession of the mountains of Sarah, and the country of Ammon, and Moab, and the country of the Philistines, and all the parts which were in the hands of the Arabians who fought with him, even to the bounds of the desert. And the affairs of his kingdom were ruled aright; and he placed his people and his country in a state of safety.

CHAPTER XXX.[a]
The account of the death of Alexander the son of Hyrcanus.

AFTERWARDS king Alexander fell sick with a quartan fever, for three whole years. But when the governor of a city named Ragaba[b] revolted from him, he led thither a powerful army, taking with him his wife and family, and besieged the city. But when it was on the point of being taken, his disease increased and his strength declined; and his wife, who was named Alexandra, lost all hope of his recovery: who going up to him said; "You know now what "differences there are between you and the Pha-"risees: and your two sons are little boys, and I "am a woman, and altogether we shall not be

[a] Compare Joseph. Antiq. XIII. 23.
[b] Josephus calls it a fortress beyond Jordan, in the country of the Gerasenes.

"able to resist them: what advice therefore do
5 "you give to me and them?" He said to her,
"My advice is, that you persevere against the
6 "city till it be taken, which will be shortly. And
"when it shall have been won, establish its go-
"vernment according as the other cities have
7 "been established. But towards all these people,
"pretend that I am sick; and whatever you do,
"pretend that you do it at my suggestion; and
"reveal my death to those servants on whom you
8 "can depend. And when you shall have finished
"these matters, go into the city of the Holy House,
"having previously dried and embalmed my
"body with spices; and fill the place where I lie
"with many perfumes, that no unpleasant smell
9 "may proceed from me. And when the affairs of
"the country are settled, go thence, and roll me
"up in abundance of perfumes, and carry me into
10 "the palace, as if sick: and when I am there,
"send for the principal men of the Pharisees;
"and when they come, honour them, and speak
11 "good words to them: then say, Alexander is al-
"ready dead, and behold I give him up to you,
"do with him whatever seems good to you: and
"I from henceforth will behave to you as you
12 "shall please. For if you do this, I know very
"well that they will do nothing to me and you,
"except that which is good; and the people will
"follow them, and your affairs will be ordered
"aright after my death, and you will reign se-
"curely until your two sons be grown up."
13 After this, Alexander died; and his wife concealed his death; and when the city was taken,
she returned to Jerusalem; and having sent for

the chief men of the Pharisees, she addressed them as Alexander had advised her. To whom they replied, that Alexander had been their king, and they had been his people; and they spoke to her with all affection, and promised to place her at the head of their government. Then they went out and collected men; and taking Alexander's body, they carried it forth magnificently to its burial: and they sent for men to appoint Alexandra queen; with whose concurrence she was *so* appointed. And the years of Alexander's reign were twenty-seven.

CHAPTER XXXI.[a]

The history of queen Alexandra.

Now while Alexandra reigned, she called to her the chief men of the Pharisees, and commanded them to write to all those of their sect who had fled[b] into Egypt and other parts, in the days of Hyrcanus and of Alexander, that they should return into the land of Judah. And she shewed them her favourable inclination towards them, and did not oppose herself to their rites, nor forbid their ceremonies, as Alexander and Hyrcanus had forbidden them. She also released all of them who were detained in prison. And they came together from every quarter; and the Sadducees forbore offering them any violence. And their affairs were well ordered, and their condition became improved by the removal of quarrels.

[a] Compare Josephus, Ant. XIII. 24. Bell. I. 4.
[b] See Josephus, Ant. XIII. 22.

6 But when Hyrcanus and Aristobulus the two sons of Alexander grew up, *the queen* made Hyrcanus high priest, for he was meek, mild, and
7 honest: but Aristobulus she made general of the army, for he was stout, brave, and high-spirited; and she also gave to him the army of the Sadducees: but she did not think it meet to appoint
8 him king, as he was still a boy. Moreover she sent to all those who paid tribute to Alexander, and took their kings' sons, whom she detained near her as hostages; and they continued uninterruptedly in their obedience to her, paying tribute
9 every year. And she walked uprightly with her people, distributing justice, and commanding her people to do the same. Wherefore there was a lasting peace between the parties, and she gained their good-will.

CHAPTER XXXII.[a]

An account of the things which were done to the Sadducees by the Pharisees in the time of Alexandra.

1 THERE was among the Sadducees a chief man, who had been promoted by Alexander, named Diogenes, who formerly had induced him to slay eight hundred[b] men of the Pha-
2 risees. Therefore the leaders of the Pharisees come to Alexandra, and remind her of what Diogenes had done, asking her leave to slay him; which she gave: and they, having it, slew many
3 Sadducees together with him. Which the Sadducees taking very much to heart, went to Aristo-

[a] Compare Josephus, Ant. XIII. 24. Bell. I. 4.
[b] See the account of this massacre in Josephus, Ant. XIII. 22.

bulus; and, taking him with them, went to the
queen, and said to her: " You are aware what 4
" terrible and heavy things we have undergone,
" and the many wars and battles which we have
" fought, in aid of Alexander and his father Hyr-
" canus. Wherefore it was not meet to trample 5
" on our rights, and to lift up the hand of our
" enemies over us, and to lower our dignities; for 6
" a matter of this kind will not be hidden from
" Hartas and others of your enemies; who have
" experienced our bravery, and have not been able
" to resist us, and their hearts have been filled
" with the fear of us. When therefore they shall 7
" perceive what you have done to us, they will
" imagine that our hearts are devising plans
" against you; of which when they shall be cer-
" tified, trust that they will play false towards
" you. Nor will we endure to be killed by the 8
" Pharisees, like sheep. Therefore, either restrain 9
" their malice from us, or allow us to go out from
" the city into some of the towns of Judah." And 10
she said to them, " Do this, that their annoyance
" to you may be prevented." And the Sadducees 11
went forth of the city; and their chiefs departed
with the men of war who adhered to them; and
went with their cattle to those of the towns of
Judah which they had selected [c], and dwelt in
them; and there were joined to them those who 12
were devoted to virtue, (i. e. *the Hasdanim*[d].)

[c] Josephus relates that she confided to them the fortresses throughout the country, with the exception of three, wherein her chief valuables were deposited.

[d] See above, the note on ch. xxv. 5.

CHAPTER XXXIII.[a]

The account of the death of Alexandra.

1 AFTER these things, Alexandra fell into a dis-
2 ease, of which she died. And when her recovery was almost despaired of, her son Aristobulus went out from Jerusalem by night,
3 attended by his servant: and he departed to Gabatha[b], to a certain chief man among the Saddu-
4 cees, one of his friends; and taking him with him, he proceeded to the cities where the Sadducees dwelt; and opened to them his purpose, and exhorted them to go out with him, and to be his allies in war against his brother and the Phari-
5 sees, and to appoint him king. To whom they assenting[c], openly played false with Alexandra, collecting men from every quarter to join Aristobulus.
6 When the fame of these things reached Hyrcanus the son of Alexandra, the high priest, and the elders of the Pharisees, they went to Alexandra, sick as she was, and related the matter to her;
7 pressing on her the great fear which they had for her and her son Hyrcanus, from Aristobulus and
8 those who were with him. To whom she answered; "I truly am near death, so that it is "more proper and profitable for me to attend to "my own affairs; what therefore can I do, being

---

[a] Compare Josephus, Ant. XIII. 24. Bell. I. 4.

[b] Josephus says, *Agaba;* and that the name of his friend was Galœstes.

[c] Josephus states, that his proposal was so well received, that within fifteen days he gained over to his cause two and twenty towns.

" situated thus? But my men, and my goods, and my arms, are with you and in your hands; therefore order the business as it seemeth to you right, imploring the aid of God upon your matters, and asking deliverance from Him." Then she died. The amount of her age was seventy-three years; and the time of her reign nine years.

CHAPTER XXXIV.[a]

The account of Aristobulus' attack on his brother Hyrcanus, after Alexandra's death.

WHEN Aristobulus departed from Jerusalem in the days of Alexandra, he left his wife and children in Jerusalem. But when the news of his departure reached Alexandra, she confined them in a certain house, setting a guard over them. But when Alexandra was dead, Hyrcanus called them to him, and behaved kindly to them, and took care of them; that they might deliver him from his brother, if haply he should conquer him. Then Aristobulus led out a great army as far as to Jordan; and Hyrcanus went out against him with an army of Pharisees. And when the two armies had encountered, great numbers of Hyrcanus' army were slain; and Hyrcanus, and the remainder of his army, took to flight. Whom Aristobulus and his troops pursuing, slew every one whom they caught, excepting those who surrendered themselves. Then Hyrcanus retreated into the Holy City; whither also arrived Aristobulus and his army; and he surrounded it on every side with his tents, and attempted by stra-

[a] Compare Josephus, Ant. XIV. 1. Bell. I. 4.

8 tagem to destroy the fortification. And the elders of Judah, and the elders of the priests, went out to him, and forbade his doing what he had designed; requesting him to dismiss from his mind whatever hostile feeling he had towards his bro-
9 ther: to which proposal he assented. Then it was agreed between them that Aristobulus should be king over Judah, and Hyrcanus should be high priest[b] in the house of God, and next to the king
10 *in dignity*. And Aristobulus assented to these terms, and entered the city, and had an interview with his brother in the house of God; and they took an oath together to ratify those terms which
11 the elders had mutually agreed on. So Aristobulus was made king, and Hyrcanus was ranked
12 next unto him. And men were at peace, and the affairs of these two brothers were rightly ordered, and the state of their people and of their country became one of tranquillity.

CHAPTER XXXV.[a]

The account of Antipater, (that is, Herod the king,) and of the seditions and battles which he kindled between Hyrcanus and Aristobulus.

1 THERE was a man of the Jews, of the sons[b] of certain of those who went up out of Babylon with

[b] It is observable, that Josephus takes no notice of this circumstance; but states, that Hyrcanus consented to live *entirely* as a private person.
[a] Compare Josephus, Ant. XIV. 2, 3. Bell. I. 5.
[b] See Josephus on this point: also Abp. Ussher's observation at the year B. C. 72, in his "Annals." In truth, the Jews could never bring themselves to regard Herod as one of their own blood and brethren, notwithstanding all his acts of munificence and public splendour.

Ezra the priest, *named* Antipater. And he was 2 wise, prudent, acute, brave, and high-minded, of a good disposition, kind, and courteous; also rich, and possessing many houses, goods, and flocks.

This man king Alexander had made governor 3 of the country of the Idumæans, from whence he had taken a wife; by whom he had four sons, namely, Phaselus, Herod, who reigned over Judah, Pheroras, and Josephus. Afterwards, being 4 removed from the mountains of Sarah[c], that is, the country of the Idumæans, in the days of Alexander, he dwelt in the city of the Holy House: and 5 Hyrcanus loved him, and was much inclined towards him: wherefore Aristobulus sought to kill him; which, however, he did not accomplish.

So Antipater was excessively afraid of Aristo- 6 bulus, and for that reason began secretly to plot against Aristobulus' kingdom. He went there- 7 fore to the principal men of the kingdom, and having gotten from them a pledge of secrecy respecting the matters which he was about to communicate, he began to talk to them of the infa- 8 mous life of Aristobulus, his tyranny, his impiety, and the bloodshed which he had caused, and his usurpation of the throne, of which his elder brother was more worthy. Then he bade them be- 9 ware of the great and good God, unless they took away the tyrant's ruling hand, and restored what was due to their rightful sovereign. Nor was 10 there left a single one of the chief men, whom he did not overreach, and incline to submit to Hyrcanus, seducing them from their obedience to Aris-

---

[c] See above, ch. x. 1. and the note there.

tobulus, Hyrcanus knowing nothing of the mat-
11 ter: but Antipater ascribed[d] all this to him, being unwilling to tell him before he had established the thing.
12 Therefore, when he had fully settled this business with the people, he went to Hyrcanus, and
13 said to him; Truly your brother is greatly afraid of you, because he sees that his estate will be nowise secure while you are alive; on which account he is seeking about for an opportunity to
14 slay you, and will not suffer you to live. But Hyrcanus did not give credence to him, because of the goodness and sincerity of his heart. Wherefore Antipater repeated this discourse to him
15 again and again. Also he gave large sums of money to the persons in whom Hyrcanus placed confidence, and agreed with them that they should tell him similar things to what Antipater had
16 mentioned; only *taking care* that he should not imagine that they knew that Antipater had been
17 speaking to him *on the subject*. So Hyrcanus believed their words; and was induced to devise a plan by which he might be delivered from his brother.
18 When therefore Antipater spoke again to him of the matter, he informed him that the truth of his words was now manifest to him, and that he knew that he had advised him well; and he asked his counsel in this affair.
19 And Antipater advised him to go out of the city

---

[d] That is to say, he sounded all these chief men of the kingdom, causing them to believe that it was done with the privity, if not by the express command, of Hyrcanus.

to some one in whom he could confide, and who might be able to aid and assist him? And Antipater went to Hartam[e], and agreed with him that he should receive Hyrcanus as a guest when he came, since he was rather afraid of dwelling with his brother. At which Hartam rejoiced, and came into the plan, and agreed with Antipater that in no case would he deliver up Hyrcanus and Antipater to their enemies, and that he would assist and protect them. And he returned to Jerusalem, and made known to Hyrcanus what he had done, and *how* he had agreed with Hartam concerning their going to him. Wherefore both of them went out of the city by night, and went to Hartam, and remained with him for some time.

Then Antipater began to persuade Hartam to lead forth an army with Hyrcanus, to reduce and capture his brother Aristobulus. But Hartam declined prosecuting this plan, fearing that he had not strength to resist Aristobulus. But Antipater ceased not to shew him that the business with Aristobulus was easy, and to urge him to it by arguments of the treasure *to be gained*, and by the greatness of glory *which he would acquire*, and the memory *which he would leave behind*

---

[e] Or Hartas. In this manner is the name spelled throughout; but the person designated is Aretas, king of Arabia Petræa; whose capital city was Petra, once a place of consequence, now an almost unknown heap of wondrous ruins. Its early history is briefly touched by Diodorus Siculus, II. c. 48, and XIX. c. 95. [See it described, under the name of Wadi-moosa, by the recent travellers, Legh and Burckhardt.] Aretas was afterwards defeated and made prisoner by Pompey. On the name, see note on ch. xxviii. 28.—Plutarch calls him βασιλεὺς τῶν περὶ τὴν Πέτραν Ἀράβων.

27 *him:* until he consented to march; yet upon condition that Hyrcanus would restore to him whatever cities and towns[f] belonging to him his father
28 Alexander had taken away. To which Hyrcanus agreeing and completing the treaty, Hartam marched (and Hyrcanus with him) with fifty thousand horse and foot soldiers, bending his course to the country of Judah: against whom
29 Aristobulus went forth and engaged them. And when the fight had become fierce, many of Aristo-
30 bulus' army went over to Hyrcanus. Which Aristobulus perceiving, sounded a retreat, and returned to his camp, fearing lest his whole army should gradually slip away *to the enemy*, and thus
31 he himself should be taken prisoner. But when night was coming on, Aristobulus departed from
32 the camp alone, and went to the Holy City. And when on break of day his departure became known to the army, the greater part of them joined themselves to Hyrcanus, and the rest dis-
33 persed and went their ways. But Hyrcanus, Hartam, and Antipater, went straight to the city of the Holy House, carrying with them a large
34 army; and they found Aristobulus already prepared for a siege; for he had closed the gates of the city, and had placed men on the ramparts to
35 defend them. And Hyrcanus and Hartam encamped with their forces against the city, and besieged it.

[f] Josephus tells us that these were twelve in number, and he recites their names.

CHAPTER XXXVI.[a]

The history of Gneus, general of the army of the Romans.

Now it happened, that Gneus[b], general of the army of the Romans, went forth to fight with Tyrcanes[c] the Armenian: for the citizens of Damascus, and Hames[d], and Halepum[e], and the rest of them of Syria who are belonging to the Armenians, had lately rebelled against the Romans: and on that account Gneus had sent Scaurus to Damascus and to its territories, to take possession of them; which thing was told to Aristobulus and Hyrcanus. Therefore Aristobulus sent ambassadors to Scaurus, and much money, requesting him to come to him with an army, and assist him against Hyrcanus. Hyrcanus also sent ambassadors to him, requesting his aid against Aristobulus; but he did not send him a present.

But Scaurus refused to go to either of them: but he wrote to Hartam, ordering him to retire with his army from the city of the Holy House, and forbade him to give help to Hyrcanus against his brother; and threatened that he would come into his country with an army of Romans and Syrians, unless he obeyed. Now when this letter had reached Hartam, he immediately retired from the city: Hyrcanus also retreated; whom Aristo-

---

[a] Compare Joseph. Antiq. XIV. 4—8. Bell. I. 5.

[b] That is, Cneius Pompeius.

[c] That is, Tigranes, who had been elected king of Syria, after the joint reign of Demetrius III. and Philip, in preference to any prince of the Syrian line.

[d] Probably Hamath, or Emesa, a city on the river Orontes.

[e] Aleppo, as above mentioned at ch. xxi. 25.

bulus pursued with a certain number of his troops, and overtook them, and engaged them[f]: and a great number of the Arabians were slain in that battle, and very many of the Jews: and Aristobulus returned into the Holy City.

10 In the mean time, Gneus reached Damascus; to whom Aristobulus sent, by the hand of a man named Nicomedes[g], a garden and vineyard[h] of gold, altogether weighing five hundred talents, with a most rich present; and besought him to
11 assist him against Hyrcanus. Hyrcanus also sent
12 Antipater to Pompey, with the like request. And Pompey (who is Gneus) was inclined to help Ari-
13 stobulus. Which when Antipater saw, he watched an opportunity that he might speak with Pompey
14 alone, and said to him: "In truth, that *present* "which you have received from Aristobulus needs "not be restored to him, even though you should
15 "not assist him; yet Hyrcanus offers *you* twice "so much: and Aristobulus will not be able to "bring the Jews into subjection to you, but this
16 "Hyrcanus will do." And Pompey supposed the matter to be so as Antipater had said; and rejoiced *to think* that he could bring the Jews under
17 his dominion. Wherefore he said to Antipater, "I will assist your friend against Aristobulus; al-

---

[f] At a place called Papyro. (Josephus).

[g] Josephus calls him Nicodemus.

[h] Josephus states, that he himself had seen this ornament and read the inscription on it, in the temple of Jupiter Capitolinus at Rome. From this splendid ornament, or rather, perhaps, from the magnificent vine of gold and jewels with which Herod decorated the outer gate of his newly erected temple, may have sprung the idea which is mentioned by Tacitus, in the fifth book of his History, that the Jews were worshippers of Bacchus.

"though I may pretend to help him against you, that he may entrust himself to me. For I am sure, that as soon as he shall find out that I am giving aid to his brother against him, he will play false with all his men, and will take care of himself, and his business will be much longer delayed. But I will send for him, and will go with him into the Holy City, and then will so act that your friend shall obtain his right; but with this condition, that he shall pay us an annual tribute."

THE MESSENGER OF ARISTOBULUS.

After this, having sent for Nicomedes, he said to him; "Go to your master, and tell him, that I have consented to his request; and carry him my letter, and say to him, that he must come to me in haste without delay, for I am waiting for him." And he wrote a letter to Aristobulus, of which this is a copy:

"From Gneus, general of the army of the Romans, to king Aristobulus, heir to the throne and high-priesthood, health be to you. Your garden and vine of gold have arrived; and I have received them, and have sent them to the elder and governors; which they have accepted and have placed in the temple[i] at Rome, returning you thanks. They have written, moreover, that I should assist you, and appoint you king over the Jews. If therefore you think fit to come to me with all speed, that I may go up

---

[i] Namely, of Jupiter Capitolinus; agreeably to that which is related in the note on verse 10, above.

B.C. 63.   CHAP. XXXVI.   367

"with you to the Holy City, and fulfil your
"wishes, I will do so."

26 And Nicomedes departed to Aristobulus with the
letter of Gneus. And Antipater, returning to Hyrcanus, told him of the promise of B.C. 63.
27 Gneus, advising him to go to Damascus. So Hyrcanus went to Damascus: Aristobulus went also: and they met at Damascus in the audience-room of Pompey, (that is, Gneus;) and Antipater and the
28 elders of the Jews said to Gneus; "Know, most
"illustrious general, that this Aristobulus has
"been dealing falsely towards us, and has usurped
"by the sword the kingdom of his brother Hyr-
"canus, who is more worthy of it *than he*, seeing
"that he is the elder brother, and of a better and
29 "more correct way of life. And it was not enough
"for him to oppress his brother, but he has op-
"pressed all the nations which are round about
"us; shedding their blood and pillaging their
"goods unjustly, and keeping up enmities be-
"tween us and them, a thing which we abhor."
30 Then stood up a thousand aged men, attesting the truth of his words.
31 And Aristobulus said, "Truly this my brother
"is a better man than I; but I did not seek for
"the throne, until I saw that all those who had
"been subject to our father Alexander were deal-
"ing falsely with us after his death, knowing the
32 "inability of my brother. Which when I looked
"into, I perceived that it was my duty to under-
"take the sovereignty, in that I was better *than*
"*he* in matters of war, and by that was better
33 "suited for preserving the monarchy: and I
"went to war with all those who dealt falsely

"with us, and reduced them to obedience: and this was the command of our father before his death." And he brought forward witnesses who attested the truth of his words.

After these things Pompey departed from the city Damascus, journeying to the Holy House. But Antipater sent privately to the inhabitants of the cities which Aristobulus had won, exciting them to complain to Gneus, setting forth the tyranny which he had exercised over them; which thing they did. And Gneus ordered him to write them a testimonial of their freedom, and *to say* that he would in no wise trouble them more; which truly he did, and the nations were released from their obedience to the Jews.

But when Aristobulus saw what Gneus had done to him, he and his men departed by night from Gneus' army without acquainting him with it, and went on to the city of the Holy House: and Gneus followed him till he came to the city of the Holy House, around which he encamped. But when he beheld the height of the walls, and the strength of its buildings, and the multitude of men who were in it, and the mountains which encircled it, he perceived that flattery and cunning would be more serviceable against Aristobulus than acts of provocation: wherefore he sent ambassadors to him, that he should come out to him, promising him safe conduct: and Aristobulus went out to him; whom Gneus received kindly, not saying a word about his former doings. After this Aristobulus said to Gneus, "I wish that you would aid me against my brother, giving my enemies no power over me; and for

"this you shall have whatsoever you wish."
43 Gneus replied, "If you wish this, bring to me "whatever money and precious stones are in the "temple, and I will put you in possession of "what you wish." And Aristobulus said to him,
44 "Undoubtedly this I will do." And Gneus sent a captain named Gabinius[j] with a great number of men, to receive whatever of gold and jewels
45 there was in the temple. But the citizens and the priests refused to permit this: wherefore they resisted Gabinius, killing many of his men and of
46 his friends, and drove him out of the city. Upon which, Gneus, being wrath with Aristobulus, threw him into prison.
47 Then he marched with his army, to force his way into the city and enter it. But a great body of the citizens going forth, hindered him from doing this, by slaying great numbers of his men.
48 And in truth, the numbers, the spirit, and the bravery of the nation, which he had seen, frightened him; so that, being alarmed at these, he had resolved to retire from them, had not mischievous quarrels arisen in the city between the friends of Aristobulus and the friends of Hyr-
49 canus. For some of them wished to open the gates to Pompey, but others were averse to this. Wherefore they came to blows on this account;

[j] Aulus Gabinius attained the dignity of consul: being a friend of Pompey, he was employed in Judæa: for the act of replacing Ptolemy on the throne of Egypt, as related below at ch. xl. 15—20, he was accused at Rome, and at Pompey's request was publicly defended by Cicero. That oration is not now extant; but we are made acquainted with the circumstance by what is said in the oration for Rabirius Posthumus, which in fact is a sort of second part of the same cause or trial.

and as this state of things increased *rather than diminished*, the war continued. Which Pompey noticing, beset with his army the gate of the city: and as some of the people opened a wicket to him, he entered[k], and took possession of the king's palace; but could not gain the temple, because the priests had closed the doors, and had secured the approaches by *armed* men. Against these he sent men to attack them from every side, and they put them to flight. And his friends coming to the temple, mounted the wall and descended into it, and opened its gates, after slaying a multitude of priests. Then Gneus came, and entered into it[l], and greatly admired its beauty and magnificence which he beheld, and was astonished when he saw its riches and the precious stones which were in it: and he forebore to take any thing out of it[m]; and he commanded the

---

[k] The historian Appian states, that Pompey not only captured, but also *destroyed* Jerusalem: he uses the strong expression κατέσκαψεν, he *rased it to its foundations*: but the incorrectness of this is evident. Compare the following note.

[l] Josephus speaks feelingly on this profanation: but he gives Pompey due credit for the forbearance which he shewed, amidst so great temptation to plunder: οὐδένος ἥψατο δι' εὐσέβειαν. We shall see in the next note, that the motives of the Roman general were not rated *quite so high* by one of *his own* countrymen. However, we may hence correct the statements of the later historians, as Dio Cassius, who asserts that on the capture of the temple a general plunder took place, πάντα τὰ χρήματα διηρπάσθη.

[m] It is remarked, that Cicero has praised Pompey for thus respecting the temple and its contents: "At Cneius "Pompeius, captis Hieroso-"lymis victor ex illo fano "nihil attigit. In primis "hoc, ut multa alia, sapi-"enter, quod in tam suspi-"ciosa ac maledica civitate "locum sermoni obtrectato-"rum non reliquerit. Non "enim, credo, religionem, et "Judæorum et hostium, im-"pedimento præstantissimo "Imperatori, sed pudorem, "fuisse." Orat. pro L.

priests to cleanse the house from the slain, and to offer sacrifices according to the ceremonies of their country.

CHAPTER XXXVII.[a]

The account of the appointment of Hyrcanus the son of Alexander to be king of the Jews, and of the return to Rome of the general of the Roman army.

1 HAVING arranged these matters, Pompey appointed Hyrcanus to be king[b]; and carried away
2 his brother Aristobulus in chains: he also ordered that the Jews should have no dominion[c] over those *nations* who had been subdued by their
3 kings before his arrival; and he exacted a tribute from the city of the Holy House; and covenanted with Hyrcanus, that he should receive inauguration
4 from the Romans every year. And he departed[d], taking with him Aristobulus, and two of his sons, and his daughters: and he had a son remaining, named Alexander, whom Pompey could not seize,

Flacco, cap. 28. For my part, I doubt whether this be *praise:* as the orator openly attributes the act, not to principle, but to policy; not to any sense of religion, but solely to motives of private and personal interest.

[a] Compare Joseph. Antiq. XIV. 8. Bell. I. 5.

[b] Josephus only states that he appointed him high priest. In point of fact, the whole power was really lodged in the Roman governor of Cœlo-Syria, Scaurus.

[c] Josephus eloquently laments the evils which the unhappy quarrels of Aristobulus and Hyrcanus had brought and fixed upon their country: its labours wasted—its bounds curtailed—its power diminished—its treasures spoiled—its glory sunk—its sanctuary profaned—its liberty taken away—and itself reduced to the sad condition of a Roman province!

[d] See a summary of the proceedings of Pompey at Jerusalem, as detailed by various heathen (not Jewish) authors, given in Ussher's Annals, at the year B. C. 63.

because he had fled. So Pompey placed in his 5 room in the city of the Holy House, Hyrcanus, and Antipater, and with them his own colleague Scaurus.

CHAPTER XXXVIII.[a]

The history of Alexander the son of Aristobulus.

WHEN Pompey had set out for Rome, Hyr- 1 canus and Antipater marched against the Arabians, to bring them under the dominion of the Romans. To which the Arabians 2 submitted, trusting to their intimacy with Antipater, and paying great regard to his advice; by which acts Antipater designed to reconcile the Romans to him.

B.C. 62.

Therefore when Alexander the son of Aristo- 3 bulus perceived the expedition of Hyrcanus, Antipater, and Scaurus, against the Arabians, and that they had departed to a great distance from the Holy City; he journeyed till he 4 arrived there; and entering into the palace, he brought out thence money for the expence of repairing the city-wall which Pompey had broken down. And he raised for himself an army, and 5 arranged all those matters which he wished, before Hyrcanus and his party should return to the city of the Holy House: and when they returned, 6 he went out to meet them, and engaged them, and put them to flight.

B.C. 58.

[a] Compare Joseph. Antiq. XIV. 9, 10. Bell. I. 6.

CHAPTER XXXIX.[a]

The history of Gabinius and of Alexander the son of Aristobulus.

1 Now Gabinius[b] had gone out from Rome, to dwell in the land of Syria, to take care of
2 it; and it was told him what Alexander the son of Aristobulus had done, by building up that which Pompey had pulled down, and by opposing his successor, and slaying his friends.
3 Wherefore he went straight until he came to Jerusalem; and Hyrcanus and his party joined him.
4 Against whom Alexander went out with ten thousand foot and fifteen hundred horse, and encoun-
5 tered them: and they routed him, and slew a certain number of his friends; and he fled into a certain city in the land of Judah, called Alexandrium[c], in which he fortified himself with his
6 company. And Hyrcanus, and Gabinius, and their forces, marched against him and besieged
7 him. And Alexander went out against them, and engaged them, and slew great numbers of
8 their men. And Marcus[d], who is called Antonius, marched against him, and forced him to flee *again* into Alexandrium.

9 And Alexander's mother went out to Gabinius, deprecating *his anger,* and imploring him to grant
10 her son Alexander his life: to whom Gabinius as-

---

[a] Compare Joseph. Ant. XIV. 10. Bell. I. 6.
[b] He was appointed governor of Syria by the Romans.
[c] Josephus describes this as an elegant fortress built on the summit of a steep hill, near to Coreæ, on the northern border of Judæa. (Antiq. XIV. 6.)
[d] Namely, Mark Antony, the celebrated triumvir.

sented in this point; and Alexander went out to him; and Gabinius put him to death [e]; and thought proper to divide the territories of Judah into five portions. One is, the country of Jerusalem and the parts adjacent; and over this part Hyrcanus was made governor. Another portion is Gadira [f], and the places about it. The third is, Jericho and the plains. The fourth is, Hamath [g] in the land of Judah. And the fifth is, Sephoris [h]. By these means he intended to remove wars and seditions out of the land of Judah; but they were by no means removed.

CHAPTER XL.[a]

The history of the flight of Aristobulus and his son Antigonus from Rome, and their return into the land of Judah: also, an account of the death of Aristobulus.

THEN Aristobulus devised plans, till he had succeeded in escaping from Rome with his son Antigonus, and had arrived in the city of Judah. And when Aristobulus shewed himself in public, a great multitude of men flocked round him; out of whom he selected eight thousand, and marched against Gabinius, and engaged him; and there were slain of the Roman army a very great number: there fell also of his own men seven thou-

B. C. 56.

---

[e] Josephus, at this part of the history, takes no notice of Gabinius putting Alexander to death: and, some chapters later, alludes to the fact of his having been slain by order of *Scipio*.

[f] Or Gadara, a strong town on the eastern side of Jordan, the capital of Peræa.

[g] That is, Amathus, a city on the eastern side of Jordan. (Josephus.)

[h] A large and considerable city, which for some time was considered the capital of Galilee, erected (says Josephus) in a position naturally very strong.

[a] Compare Joseph. Antiq. XIV. 11. Bell. I. 6, 7.

sand, but one thousand escaped; and the enemy's army pursued him; but he and they who were left to him ceased not to resist even till the total 4 destruction of his men; nor was there one left but he alone; and he fought most furiously until he fell overpowered by wounds, and was taken and led to Gabinius; who ordered him to be taken 5 care of until he was healed. Then he sent him in chains to Rome.

[And he remained shut up in prison until the reign of Cæsar; who brought[b] him out of prison, 6 and loaded him with gifts and favours; and giving to him two generals and twelve thousand men, sent him into the land of Judah, [B. C. 49.] to detach the Jews from Pompey's party, and bring them over to obey Cæsar: for Pompey at that time was governor of the land of Egypt.

7 And the report of Aristobulus and his party reached Hyrcanus; who was greatly afraid, and wrote to Antipater to avert his power from him 8 by his customary devices. So Antipater sent some of the chief men of Jerusalem, giving to one of them poison, charging him to administer it 9 craftily to Aristobulus. And they met him in the land of Syria, as though they were ambassadors to him from the Holy City: and he received them joyfully, and they did eat and drink with 10 him. And those men laid plots till they gave him the poison; and he died, and was buried in 11 the land of Syria. Now the time of his reign[c], until he was taken prisoner the first time, was

[b] Compare Joseph. Antiq. XIV. 13.
[c] Compare Josephus: and see Ussher's remark on the passage, in his Annals.

three years and a half; and he was a man of courage, weight, and excellent disposition.]

Now Gabinius had written to the senate, to send away his two sons to their mother, since she had requested it; which they did. But it came to pass, that when Pompey had departed to a great distance from Jerusalem, they broke their engagement of obedience to the Romans: wherefore Gabinius went against them, encountered them, and conquered them, and reduced them again to submission to the Romans.

In the mean time the land of Egypt rebelled against Ptolemy[d], and expelled him from his royal city, refusing to pay tribute to the Romans. Whereupon Ptolemy wrote to Gabinius that he should come and help him against the Egyptians, that he might bring them again into subjection to the Romans. And Gabinius marched out of the country of Syria, and wrote to Hyrcanus to meet him with an army, that they might go to Ptolemy. And Antipater went with a large army to Gabinius, and met him at Damascus, congratulating with him on the victory which he had gained over the Persians[e]: and Gabinius ordered him to hasten to Ptolemy, which he did, and fought against the Egyptians, and slew of them a very great number. Afterwards Gabinius coming up, replaced Ptolemy on his throne, and went back to the Holy City, and renewed Hyrcanus' sovereignty, and returned to Rome.

---

[d] Namely, Ptolemy, surnamed Dionysius Novus. In opposition to him the Egyptians had chosen Archelaus to be their king.

[e] That is, *Parthians*, as before.

CHAPTER XLI.[a]

The history of Crassus.

1 WHEN Gabinius had returned to Rome, the
2 Persians[b] played false to the Romans; and Crassus[c] marched with a large army into Syria, and came to Jerusalem, requiring of the priests that they should deliver to him whatever
3 money there was in the house of God. To whom they made answer, how will this be lawful for you, when Pompey, Gabinius, and others have deemed it unlawful? But he answered, I must
4 do it at all events. And Eleazar the priest said to him, Swear to me that you will not lay your hand upon any thing which belongs to it, and I
5 will give you three hundred minæ of gold. And he sware to him that he would take nothing from the treasure of the house of God, if he would deli-
6 ver to him what he had mentioned. And Eleazar gave him a bar of wrought gold, the upper part of which had been inserted into the wall of the treasury of the temple, upon which were placed every year the old veils of the house, new ones being
7 substituted for them. And the bar weighed three hundred minæ[d] of gold, and it was covered with

---

[a] Compare Joseph. Antiq. XIV. 12.

[b] *Parthians*, as before.

[c] Marcus Licinius Crassus, whose history and fame are well known, after having served under Sylla, and obtained great glory by his timely defeat of Spartacus and the revolted slaves, became consul, censor, triumvir with Cæsar and Pompey, and thus governor of the province of Syria. His subsequent attempts against the Parthians, his defeat and death, are recorded by Plutarch and other writers.

[d] Josephus states here, "the " minæ with us weighs two " pounds and a half:" from whence the immense value of this bar may be understood.

the veils which were accumulated during a long course of years, being known to no one besides Eleazar. Crassus then, having received this bar, broke his word, going back from the agreement made with Eleazar; and he took all the treasures of the temple, and plundered whatever money was therein, to the amount of two thousand talents: for this money had been accumulating from the building of the temple until that time, out of the spoils of the kings of Judah and their offerings, and also from the presents which the kings of the Gentiles[e] had sent; and they were multiplied and increased in the lapse of years; all which he took. Then that *vile* Crassus went off with the money and his army into the country of the Persians; and they defeated him[f] and his army in battle, slaying them in a single day: and the Persian army took as spoil every thing which was in the camp of Crassus.

After this feat, they marched into the country of Syria, which they won, and detached from its submission to the Romans. Which the Romans learning, sent a renowned general named Cassius[g] with a great army: who, arriving in the country of Syria, drove out those of the Persians who were in it. Then proceeding to the Holy City, he delivered Hyrcanus from the war which the Jews were waging against him, reconciling the parties. Afterwards, passing the Euphrates[h], he fought

---

[e] See above, ch. I. 1.

[f] For the miserable end of this expedition against the Parthians, which cost the life of Crassus, and the destruction of his whole army, see the Roman historians.

[g] He was first treasurer to Crassus; after whose death he was made governor of Syria. Subsequently he became conspicuous as one of the murderers of Julius Cæsar.

[h] Ussher remarks, that

B.C. 52.   CHAP. XLII.   379

with the Persians, and brought them back to their
17 subjection to the Romans: he also reduced to submission the two and twenty kings[i] whom Pompey had subdued; and reduced under obedience to the Romans every thing in the countries of the east.

CHAPTER XLII.[a]

The history of Cæsar, king of the Romans.

1 It is reported that there was at Rome a certain woman who was pregnant, who, being near to her delivery, and racked with most vio- 2 lent pains of childbirth, died: but as the child was in motion, the belly of the mother was opened, and it was brought forth thence and lived, and grew, and was named Julius, because he was born in the fifth 3 month; and was called Cæsar[b], because the belly of his mother, from whence he was extracted, was 4 ripped open. (Lat. *cæsa*.) But when the elder *of Rome* sent Pompey into the east, he likewise sent Cæsar into the west, to subdue certain na- 5 tions which had revolted from the Romans. And Cæsar went, and conquered them, and reduced them to obedience to the Romans, and returned to

B. C. 52.

---

there is a mistake in this assertion: as the Roman historians mention indeed the successes of Cassius against the Parthians *in Syria*, but say not a word of his having pursued them back into their own country.

[i] The historian Orosius, after reciting Pompey's exploits in Asia, states; "Hoc "bellum orientis cum viginti "et duobus regibus sese ges- "sisse ipse Pompeius pro "concione narravit." Histor. VI. c. 6.

[a] Compare Joseph. Antiq. XIV. 14, 15. Bell. I. 7.

[b] On this point, which has been contested, see Suidas, in voce Ἰούλιος; and for the various accounts given of the name, consult Hoffmann's lexicon, and the authors there cited.

Rome with great glory: and his fame increased, 6 and his affairs became much renowned, and excessive pride took hold on him; wherefore he requested the Romans to name him king. But the 7 elder and governors answered him, "Truly our "fathers took an oath in the days of Tarquin the "king,—who had taken by force another man's "wife, who laid hands on herself that he might "not enjoy her,—that they would not give the 8 "title of king to any of those who should be "placed at the head of their affairs; on account "of which oath (*said they*) we are not able to gra- "tify you in this particular." Wherefore he 9 stirred up seditions, and waged furious battles at Rome, slaying many people, until he seized on the throne of the Romans, and entitled himself king, putting a diadem on his head. From thence- 10 forth they were called kings of the Romans, from their kingdom: they were also called Cæsars.

When therefore Pompey heard this news of Cæ- 11 sar, and that he had slain the three hundred and twenty[c] governors, he collected his armies and marched into Cappadocia: and Cæsar 12 going to meet him engaged him, conquered[d] and slew him, and gained possession of the whole territory of the Romans. After this, Cæsar went into the 13 province of Syria; whom Mithridates[e] the Armenian met with his army, assuring him that he was come with peaceful designs, and was ready to at-

[c] See above, 2 Macc. viii. 15; also 5 Macc. xii. and xiii.

[d] At the battle of Pharsalia. Shortly afterwards Pompey was treacherously murdered on the coast of Egypt, whither he was fleeing for succour.

[e] Namely, king of Pergamus; not one of the kings of Parthia.

tack whatsoever enemies he should command.
14 *Cæsar* ordered him to depart into Egypt; and Mithridates marched till he came to Ascalon.
15 Now Hyrcanus feared Cæsar very much, because his submission to Pompey, whom Cæsar had
16 slain, was known. Wherefore he despatched hastily Antipater with a brave army to assist Mithridates: and Antipater marched to him, and aided him against a certain one of the cities of
17 Egypt[f], and they took it. But as they departed thence, they found an army of the Jews who dwelled in Egypt, making a stand at the entrance, to prevent Mithridates from entering Egypt.
18 And Antipater produced to them a letter from Hyrcanus, commanding them to desist, and not oppose Mithridates, the friend of Cæsar. And
19 they forbore. But the *others* marched till they came to the city of the then reigning king; who came out to them with all the armies of the Egyptians, and when they engaged with him, he con-
20 quered and routed them; and Mithridates turned his back and fled; whom, when he was surrounded by the Egyptian troops, Antipater saved
21 from death: and Antipater and his men ceased not to resist the Egyptians in battle, whom he routed and conquered, and won the whole country of Egypt.
22 And Mithridates wrote to Cæsar, shewing him what Antipater had done, and what battles he had endured, and what wounds he had received;
23 and that the winning *of the country* was to be ascribed not to him but to Antipater, and that

[f] Namely, Pelusium.
[g] Namely Ptolemy Dionysius II, together with Cleopatra.

he had reduced the Egyptians to obedience unto Cæsar. And when Cæsar had read the letter of Mithridates, he commended Antipater for his exploits, and resolved to advance and exalt him. After these acts, Mithridates and Antipater went to Cæsar, who then was at Damascus; and he obtained from Cæsar whatsoever he liked, and he promised him whatever he wished for.

CHAPTER XLIII.[a]

The account of the coming of Antigonus the son of Aristobulus unto Cæsar, complaining of Antipater who had caused his father's death.

BUT Antigonus the son of Aristobulus came to Cæsar, and related to him the expedition of Aristobulus his father to attack Pompey, and how obedient and obsequious he was to him. Then he told him that Hyrcanus and Antipater had secretly sent a man to his father to destroy him by poison[b], intending (*said he*) to assist Pompey against your friends.

Cæsar therefore sent to Antipater, and questioned him on this matter; to whom Antipater replied; "Certainly I did obey Pompey, because "then he was the ruling person, and conferred "benefits on me; but I did not now fight with "the Egyptians for the sake of Pompey, who is "already dead; nor did I go through difficulties "in defeating them and reducing them to obedi-"ence to Pompey; but I did this out of duty to "Cæsar, and that I might reduce them to obedi-

---

[a] Compare Joseph. Antiq. XIV. 15. Bell. I. 8. is stated above, at chap. xl. 7—10.
[b] According to that which

6 " ence to him." Then Antipater uncovered his head and his hands, and said; " These wounds, " which are on my head and body, testify that " my affection and obedience to Cæsar are greater " than my affection and obedience to Pompey;
7 " for I did not expose myself in the days of Pom- " pey, to the things to which I have exposed my-
8 " self in the days of king Cæsar." And Cæsar said to him, " Peace be to thee, and to all thy " friends, O bravest of the Jews: for thou hast " truly shewn this fortitude, magnanimity, obedi- " ence, and affection towards us."
9 And from that time Cæsar increased in affection towards Antipater, and advanced him above all his friends, and promoted him to be general of his armies, and took him with him into the coun-
10 try of the Persians: and he saw from his bravery and his successful exploits, that he more *and more* excited in him a longing and affection for him:
11 at length he brought him back into the land of Judah, covered with honours and crowned with a post of authority [c].
12 And Cæsar marched to Rome, having settled the affairs of Hyrcanus [d]; who built the walls of the Holy City, and conducted himself towards the
13 people in a most excellent manner: for he was a good man, endued with virtues, of irreproachable life, but his inability in wars was notorious to all men.

[c] It appears that Cæsar confirmed Hyrcanus in the high-priesthood; but committed *really* the chief civil power to the hands of Antipater, creating him procurator or governor of Judæa.

[d] Cæsar ordained that Hyrcanus and his descendants should perpetually retain the principality ($ἐθναρχία$) and high-priesthood of the Jews, according to the ancient usage of the country.

CHAPTER XLIV.[a]

The account of the embassy of Hyrcanus to Cæsar, asking for a renewal of the treaty between them; and of the copy of the treaty which Hyrcanus sent to him.

THEREFORE Hyrcanus sent ambassadors to Cæsar, with a letter concerning a renewal of the treaty which was between him and the Romans. And when Hyrcanus' ambassadors came to Cæsar, he ordered them to be seated in his presence; *an honour* which he had not conferred on any one of the ambassadors of the kings who used to come to him.

Moreover he acted kindly to them, by expediting their business, and ordered an answer to be given to Hyrcanus' letter; to whom also he wrote the treaty, of which the following is a copy.

" From Cæsar, king of kings, to the princes of
" the Romans who are at Tyre and Sidon, peace
" be with you. I give you to know, that a letter
" of Hyrcanus the son of Alexander, both kings
" of the Jews, has been brought to me; at the
" arrival of which I rejoiced, by reason of the
" continued good-will which both he and his peo-

---

[a] Compare Joseph. Antiq. XIV. 16, 17. Josephus, here enumerating the various ordinances, decrees, &c. of the Romans in favour of the Jews, begins by reciting a decree of the senate, differing in almost every particular from this letter of Cæsar. As he states that this transaction took place in the ninth year of Hyrcanus' sovereignty, we ought to assign to it the year 54: but it is clear that the embassy mentioned in the text was subsequent to Cæsar's arrangements in favour of Hyrcanus, related in the preceding chapter. In fact, the letter inserted, as in this passage, by Josephus, belongs to the transactions related in ch. xxii. of this our book.

"ple declare that they have towards me and the
7 " Roman nation. And verily the truth of his
" words I have proved by this; that he formerly
" sent [b] Antipater a captain of the Jews, and their
" cavalry, with Mithridates my friend, whom the
8 " troops of Egypt attacked; and he saved Mithri-
" dates from death, having won for us the coun-
" try of Egypt, and reduced the Egyptians to
" obedience to the Romans: he also marched with
" me into the country of the Persians, serving as
9 " a volunteer. And therefore I order that all the
" inhabitants of the sea-coast, from Gaza as far as
" Sidon, shall pay all the tributes which they owe
" us, every year, to the house of the great God
10 " which is in Jerusalem; except the citizens of
" Sidon; and let these pay to it, according to the
" appointment of their tribute, twenty thousand
" five hundred and fifty vibæ [c] of wheat every
11 " year. I also order, that Laodicea and its pos-
" sessions, and all things which were in the hand
" of the kings of Judah, even to the bank of the
12 " Euphrates; with all those *places* which the As-
" monæans [d] won from the passing over Jordan,—
" be restored to Hyrcanus the son of Alexander

---

[b] See these transactions related above, at ch. xlii. 15—23.

[c] The word which the Latin translator has rendered *viba*, is stated by Meninski to signify a measure containing twenty-two or twenty-four Roman modii. The modius, though familiarly translated a *bushel*, is generally understood to have been equal to one peck and a half of English measure. But Josephus, reciting the same decree, states the appointed quantity to be twenty-six thousand and seventy-five *modii*. [There appears to be a various reading, twenty thousand six hundred and seventy-five.] See edit. Haverk. Ant. XIV. c. 10. §. 6.

[d] Namely, Judas Maccabæus and his successors. For the origin of the name, see the note on book II. ch. ii. 1.

"king of Judah. For all these things his fathers 13
"had won by their sword, but Pompey had un-
"justly taken them away[e] in the time of Aristo-
"bulus: and from this time and for the future 14
"let them belong to Hyrcanus, and to the suc-
"ceeding kings of Judah. And this treaty is for 15
"me, and for every one of the kings of Rome my
"successors: whoever therefore shall break it or
"any part of it, may God destroy him by the
"sword, and may his house and his government
"be made desolate and be cut down! And when 16
"you shall read this my epistle, write it in let-
"ters[f] engraved on tables of brass, in the lan-
"guage of the Romans and in their characters,
"and in the language of the Greeks and in their
"characters: and place the tables in conspicuous 17
"parts of the temples which are at Tyre and Si-
"don; that every person may be able to see them,
"and may understand what I have appointed for
"Hyrcanus and the Jews."

CHAPTER XLV.[a]

The history of Cæsar's death.

THERE were with Cæsar two of Pompey's 1
friends; of whom the one was called Cas-
B.C. 44. sius, and the other Brutus; who laid a
plot to kill Cæsar. For which purpose they con- 2
cealed themselves in the temple[b] at Rome which

---

[e] See above, ch. xxxvii. 2.
[f] Josephus recites this order, but in another place; namely, as given by Antony (for Augustus and himself) after Julius Cæsar's death.
[a] Compare Joseph. Antiq. XIV. 17, 18. Bell. I. 9.
[b] It is known, from the Roman historians, that it was in no temple, but in the senate-house, that Cæsar met his death.

3 he had set apart for himself to pray in. To which therefore when he came, careless, safe, and taking no sort of heed to himself, they rushed upon him,
4 and killed him. And Cassius got possession of the throne[c], and gathered a large army, and transported it beyond the sea; fearing Cæsar's party if he should continue to reside at Rome.
5 And he marched into the land of Asia, and wasted it: from thence he went into the
6 country of Judah: and Antipater wished to attack him; but seeing that his strength was not equal to the task, he made peace with him.
7 And Cassius laid a tribute of seven hundred talents of gold[d] on the land of Judah; and Anti-
8 pater bound himself as surety for the money; and charged his son Herod to raise it on the country of Judah, and to carry it to Cassius: who receiving it marched into the country of Macedonia, and there remained through fear of the Romans.

CHAPTER XLVI.[a]

The history of the death of Antipater.

1 Now the princes of Judah had taken counsel to slay Antipater; and for that purpose had secretly set upon him a man who was called Mal-
2 chiah. And Malchiah made the attempt, but its
3 execution was delayed for a long time. And the report of it reached Antipater, who sought out
4 Malchiah to kill him: but Malchiah cleared himself in the sight of Antipater of the things whereof

[c] This and similar misstatements must be corrected from the Roman historians.
[d] Josephus says, talents of silver: a much more moderate exaction.
[a] Compare Joseph. Antiq. XIV. 19. Bell. I. 9.

he had been accused to him; and sware to him that the report was groundless: and Antipater believed him, putting aside all suspicion from him. But Malchiah, having given a large sum of money 5 to Hyrcanus' cup-bearer, agreed with him to give Antipater poison, while he was on the banqueting couch in the king's presence. And the cup-bearer 6 did this, and king Antipater[b] died on that same day: and the thing was not by the design, nor with the knowledge, of the king. And when An- 7 tipater was dead, Hyrcanus substituted Malchiah in his place.

CHAPTER XLVII.[a]

The history of the death of Malchiah.

Now when Herod the son of Antipater was in- 1 formed that Malchiah had caused his father's death, he thought to rush openly upon Malchiah; but his brother prevented him from doing this, advising that he should be taken off by stratagem. And Herod went to Cassius, 2 and told him what Malchiah had done: to whom *the other* replied, when I am gone to Tyre, and Hyrcanus is with me, and with him Malchiah, *then* rush on him and kill him.

B.C. 42.

When therefore Cassius had gone to Tyre, and 3 Hyrcanus had gone to join him, taking Malchiah

---

[b] I do not remember that this title is given to Antipater in any other passage. Cæsar had made him procurator of Judæa; but though he really had the supreme power, it does not appear that he ever possessed the throne or the name of king. It is said also, in the next verse, that "Hyrcanus substituted Malchiah in his place," evidently implying a subordinate rank.

[a] Compare Joseph. Antiq. XIV. 19, 20. Bell. I. 9.

with him; and they were standing together in Cassius' presence, at a certain feast to which Cas-
4 sius had invited them with all his friends: (now Cassius had given orders to his servants to do
5 whatever Herod should order them:) Herod also was standing with his brother amongst the companions of Hyrcanus, and Herod agreed with some of the servants to kill Malchiah, when a signal
6 should be given by a wink of the eye. When therefore Hyrcanus had eaten and drunken with his friends, they went to sleep in the afternoon:
7 and when they had awaked from sleep, Hyrcanus ordered one to prepare a couch for him in the open air, before the entrance of the banqueting
8 room in which they had slept: and he himself sat down, and commanded Malchiah to sit with him: he also ordered Herod and his brother to be seated:
9 and Cassius' servants stood near Hyrcanus; to whom Herod winked against Malchiah, and they
10 immediately rushed on him and slew him[b]: and Hyrcanus was greatly frightened, and fell into a fit of fainting.

11 But when Cassius' attendants had retired, and the slain Malchiah was carried out, Hyrcanus came to himself again, and asked of Herod the
12 cause of Malchiah's death. And Herod answered; "I am wholly ignorant, nor do I know the "cause of the thing." And Hyrcanus held his peace, and never again asked more of the matter.

13 And Cassius marched into Macedonia, to meet Octavian[c] the son of Cæsar's brother, and An-

---

[b] The circumstances of his death are differently related by Josephus.

[c] Who was afterwards better known by the title of Augustus Cæsar. It is not

tony the general of his army: for they had set out from Rome with a great army in search of Cassius.

CHAPTER XLVIII.[a]

The history of Octavian, (the same is Augustus the son of Cæsar's brother,) and of Antony, general of his army, and of Cassius' death.

WHEN Octavian had marched into Macedonia, Cassius went out to meet him, and engaged with him; and Cassius was put to flight; whom Octavian pursuing, entirely defeated and killed[b]: and Octavian won the kingdom in place of his uncle Cæsar; and he also was surnamed Cæsar, after the name of his uncle.

Now when the death of Cassius became known to Hyrcanus, he sent ambassadors with presents, money, and jewels, to Augustus and Antony: and he wrote to him, asking for a renewal of the treaty which had been *entered into* with Cæsar[c]; and that he would order all the captives of Judah who were in his kingdom, and those who had been made captives in the days of Cassius, to be set free; and that he would permit all the Jews who were in the country of the Greeks, and in the land of Asia, to return into the country of Judah, without requiring any

true that he was the son of Cæsar's *brother:* but his mother Accia was sister of Julius Cæsar; so that in fact he was a nephew, but by the female side.

[a] Compare Joseph. Antiq. XIV. 22, 23. Bell. I. 10.

[b] Namely, at the battle of Philippi, a town of Macedonia, fought in October, B.C. 42.

[c] See above, ch. xliv. 1.

ransom, or redemption, or any obstacle being thrown in the way by any one.

8 So when the ambassadors of Hyrcanus came to Augustus, with their letter and presents, he
9 honoured the ambassadors, and acceded to all things which Hyrcanus had asked; writing to him a letter, of which this is the copy.
10 "From Augustus[d], king of kings, and Antony "his colleague, to Hyrcanus king of Judah;
11 "Health be to you. Your letter has even now "reached us, at which we rejoiced; and we have "sent that which you wished, respecting the "renewal of the treaty, and the writing, to all "our provinces, which extend from the country
12 "of the Indias even to the western ocean. But "that which delayed us from sooner writing to "you concerning the renewal of the treaty was, "our occupation in subduing Cassius, that filthy[e]
13 "tyrant; who, acting wickedly towards Cæsar,
14 "that luminary of the world, slew him. Where- "fore we have contended with him with our "whole strength, until the great and good God "rendered us victorious, and caused him to fall
15 "into our hands; whom we have put to death[f]. "We have also slain Brutus his colleague; and

[d] Josephus states all this to have been done by Antony alone, and in his own name, Cæsar having departed into Gaul or Italy immediately after the battle of Philippi.

[e] The Latin version renders the word by "forni- "carius," literally, a *frequenter of brothels*.

[f] It is related by the Ro- man historians, that neither Cassius nor Brutus fell in battle, nor, strictly speaking, *were put to death* by Octavian: as each of them, feeling that their hopes and prospects were irretrievably destroyed, fell upon his own sword rather than fall into the victor's hands.

"we have delivered the country of Asia out of his hand, after he had laid it waste, and had exterminated its inhabitants. Nor did he adhere to any engagement; nor honour any temple; nor do justice to the oppressed; nor pity a Jew, or any *other* of our subjects: but with his *followers* he wickedly did many evils to all men through oppression and tyranny: wherefore God hath turned their malice *back* on their own heads, delivering them up, with those who were confederate with them. Rejoice now therefore, O king Hyrcanus, and other Jews, and inhabitants of the Holy Region, and priests who are in the temple of Jerusalem: and let them accept the present which we have sent to the most glorious temple, and pray for Augustus ever. We have written also to all our provinces, that there remain in none of them any one of the Jews, be it servant or maid, but that all should be let go, without price and without ransom: and that they should be hindered by no person *from* returning into the land of Judah; and this by command of Augustus, and likewise of Antony his colleague."

Moreover, he wrote[g] to his friends, who are at Tyre and Sidon, and in other places, to restore whatever they had taken out of the land of Judah in the days of that filthy Cassius: and to treat the Jews peaceably, and not to oppose them in any thing, and to do for them whatever Cæsar had decreed in his treaty with them.

---

[g] Josephus, as above, attributes this to Antony, not to Cæsar.

25 Now Antony remained in the country of Syria; and Cleopatra[h] queen of Egypt came to him, 26 whom he took for his wife. She was a wise woman, skilled in magical arts and properties *of things*: so that she enticed him, and got possession of his heart to that degree that he could deny her nothing.

27 At this same time, a hundred men of the chief of the Jews went to Antony[i], and complained of Herod and his brother Phaselus the sons of Anti- 28 pater, saying; They have now gotten every thing belonging to Hyrcanus, and there remains to him nothing of the kingdom except the name; and the concealment of this matter is a proof of the capti- 29 vity of their lord. But when Antony had inquired of Hyrcanus the truth of the things which they had mentioned to him, Hyrcanus declared that they spoke falsely; clearing Herod and his brother from that which they had laid to their 30 charge. And Antony rejoiced at this; for he was greatly inclined towards them, and loved 31 them. Moreover, other persons at another time complained to him of Herod and his brother, 32 when he was at Tyre: but he not only refused to entertain their words, but put to death some of 33 them, and cast the rest into prison; and he advanced the dignity of Herod and his brother, doing them services, and sent them back to Jeru- 34 salem with great honour. But Antony *himself*,

[h] Namely, the fifth (or sixth) princess of that name, the daughter of Ptolemy Auletes: she was the last of the sovereigns of Egypt, Augustus having reduced that country to the condition of a Roman province at her death, B.C. 30.

[i] Who at this time was at Daphne, near Antioch in Syria. (Josephus.)

going into the country of the Persians[k], defeated them, and subdued them, and returned to Rome.

CHAPTER XLIX.[a]

The history of Antigonus the son of Aristobulus, and of his expedition against his uncle Hyrcanus: and of the succour which was obtained from the king of the Persians.

WHEN Augustus and Antony had arrived at Rome, Antigonus went to the king of the Persians[b], and promised him a thousand talents of coined gold, and eight hundred[c] virgins of the daughters of Judah and of its princes, beautiful and wise; if he would send with him a general leading a great army against Jerusalem, and would order him to make him king over Judah, and would take prisoner his uncle Hyrcanus, and kill Herod and his brother. To whom *the king* assenting, sent with him a general with a great army: and they marched until they came into the land of Syria; and they slew a friend of Antony and certain Romans who were dwelling there.

From thence they marched against the Holy City; professing security and peace, and that Antigonus had only come to pray in the sanctuary, and *then would* return to his own friends. And they entered the city; into which when they had gotten, they played foul, and began to kill men, and to plunder the city, according to the orders of the king of Persia to them. And Herod and

---

[k] That is, Parthians, as before.
[a] Compare Joseph. Antiq. XIV. 24, 25. Bell. I. 11.
[b] The Parthians, of whom Orodes was at this time king.
[c] Josephus says, five hundred.

his men ran forward to defend the palace of Hyrcanus: but he sent his brother, and commanded him to guard the way which leads from the walls to the palace. And when he had possessed himself of each position, he chose out some of his men, and marched against the Persians who were in the city; and his brother followed with a certain number of his men; and they slew the greater part of the Persians who were in the city, but the rest fled out of the city.

And when the general of the Persians saw that things had not gone to his mind, he despatched messengers to Herod and his brother, to treat for peace; informing them, that now he was satisfied of their valour and bravery, that they ought to be preferred to Antigonus; and that for that reason he would persuade his troops to aid Hyrcanus and them rather than Antigonus: and this his wish he confirmed by the most solemn oaths, so that Hyrcanus and Phaselus believed him, *but* not Herod. So Hyrcanus and Phaselus, going out to the general of the Persians, signified to him their reliance on him; and he advised them to go to his colleague who was at Damascus; and they went. And when they were come to him, he received them honourably, and made a display of holding them in high esteem, and treated them courteously; although he had secretly given orders that they should be made prisoners. And some of the principal men of the land coming to them, told them of this very design; advising them to flee, with a promise of aiding their escape. But they did not trust these men, fearing lest it were some plot against them; wherefore they stayed. And when night came on, they were seized: Phaselus indeed laid hands on himself; but Hyrcanus was bound in chains, and by order of the general of the Persians his ear was cut off [d], that he might never be high priest *again;* and he sent him to Herak [e], to the king of the Persians; to whom when he came, *the king* ordered his chains to be struck off, and shewed him kindness; and he remained in Herak loaded with honours, until Herod demanded him from the king of the Persians: and when he was sent back to Herod, those things befell him [f] which did befall him.

After this, the general went up with Antigonus into the Holy City: and it was told Herod what had been done to Hyrcanus and Phaselus: wherefore taking his mother Cypris, and his wife Mariamne the daughter of Aristobulus, and her mother Alexandra, he sent them with horses and much baggage to Joseph his brother to mount

---

[d] Josephus adds, that the mutilation of Hyrcanus took place at the suggestion of Antigonus; and his remark is confirmed by an expression occurring at ch. liv. 9. of this book. We know both the object and the ground of this proceeding, from the following express and repeated command of God: "And the "Lord spake unto Moses, "saying, Speak unto Aaron, "saying, Whosoever he be of "thy seed in their genera- "tions that hath any blemish, "let him not approach to of- "fer the bread of his God. "For whatsoever man he be "that hath a blemish, he shall "not approach: no man that "hath a blemish of the seed "of Aaron the priest shall "come nigh to offer the of- "ferings of the Lord made "by fire: he hath a blemish; "he shall not come nigh to "offer the bread of his "God." Lev. xxi. 16. 17. 18. 21.

[e] Josephus does not use this expression; but merely states, that Hyrcanus was sent into the country of the Parthians. Concerning the meaning of the word Herak, see the note on ch. liv. 1. of this book.

[f] See the sequel of his history below, at ch. liv.

22 Sarah [g] : but himself with an army of a thousand men marched slowly, and waited for those of the
23 Persians who might attempt to pursue him. And the general of the Persians pursued him with his army; whom Herod attacked, and conquered, and
24 put to flight. After this, Antigonus' troops also pursued him, and fought with him most fiercely: and these he smote [h], and slew great numbers of
25 them. Then he marched to the mountains of Sarah; and found his brother Josephus, whom he ordered to secure the families in a safe place, and to provide all things which were necessary for
26 them: and he gave them abundance of money, that if need were, they might buy themselves provisions.

[g] This name has occurred frequently in this book, but I do not find it elsewhere: perhaps it may be derived from that part of ancient Idumæa, which in Scripture is called "the mountains of *Seir*." See above, ch. xxi. 29; xxxv. 4. The spot in which Joseph secured the persons entrusted to his charge appears from Josephus (Ant. XIV. 24, 26, 27.) to have been the stronghold of Massada. But this creates some difficulty: for, although we know that Massada was a strong position, and was used as a place of defence by Herod, its situation does not well accord with the statement in the text. Massada is said to have been near to Engaddi, which was not far from Jericho; so that it cannot well be taken for a part of mount Sarah in Idumæa. Consult ch. 26 and 27 of the XIVth book of Josephus' Antiquities; and ch. 11 and 12 of the first book of his Wars; all which passages favour the idea, that Massada was in Idumæa. Salmasius, in his "Exercitationes Plinianæ ad Solini Polyhistor." cap. 35, affords some assistance, by desiring us to remember that the boundary-line between Arabia Petræa (rather Idumæa) and Judæa was not accurately defined; so that places which by one author are assigned to one country, by a second may be referred to the other. Such may be the case with the town in question.

[h] And on the spot where he defeated them, he afterwards, when he came to the throne, erected a castle and palace, bearing the name of Herodium. (Josephus.)

And having left his men with his brother Jose- 27
phus, himself with a few companions went into
Egypt, that he might take ship and proceed to
the country of the Romans. Cleopatra entertained 28
him courteously, and requested him to take the
command of her armies and the management of
all her affairs; to whom he notified that it was
quite necessary for him to go to Rome. And she 29
gave him money and ships: and he went till he
reached Rome, and abode with Antony, and told
him what Antigonus had done, and what he had
committed against Hyrcanus and his brother, by
help of the king of the Persians: and Antony 30
rode with him to Augustus and to the senate, and
told them the selfsame thing.

CHAPTER L.[a]

The history of Herod when the Romans appointed him king over the Jews, and his departure from Rome with an army to fight against the Holy House.

AUGUSTUS and the senate, informed of what 1
Antigonus had done, with one consent appointed
Herod king over the Jews; commanding him to 2
put a golden diadem on his head, and to mount a
horse, and that it should be proclaimed by trumpets preceding him, "Herod is king over the Jews
" and the holy city Jerusalem:" which was done.
And returning to Augustus, he rode, and Augus- 3
tus, and Antony; and they went to Antony's
house, who had invited the senate and all the citizens of Rome to a banquet which he had prepared.
And they did eat and drink, and rejoiced over 4

---

[a] Compare Josephus, Ant. XIV. 26, 27. Bell. I. 11, 12.

B.C. 40.   CHAP. L.   399

Herod with great joy, making with him a treaty engraven in tables of brass; and it was placed in
5 the temples. And they inscribed that day as the first of Herod's reign, and from that time it was taken for an æra, by which times are counted.
6 After these things, Antony and Herod departed by sea with a great and abundant army: and when they came to Antioch, they divided their
7 forces: and Antony took a part, and led it into the country of the Persians which is Herak[b] and the parts adjacent: and Herod, taking another
8 part, went straight till he came to Ptolemais. So Antigonus, hearing that Antony had made an expedition into the country of the Persians, and that Herod had reached Ptolemais, marched out from the Holy House to the mountain Sarah[c], to take Josephus, Herod's brother, and those who were
9 with him. Whom he assaulted, and besieged; and having cut off a canal, intercepted the water which flowed down to them: so that thirst prevailed *among them*, and their affairs were reduced
10 to great straits. Wherefore Josephus determined to flee; and the families had deliberated upon surrendering themselves to Antigonus, if Josephus
11 should flee. But God sent to them an abundant rain, which filled all their cisterns and vessels: wherefore their hearts were encouraged, and their
12 condition was improved; and Josephus continued to repulse Antony[d] and his men from the strong

[b] See the note on ch. liv. 1.
[c] See above, at ch. xlix. 21. 24, and the note. Josephus states the place to be Massada.
[d] This obviously is a mistake for *Antigonus*: Antony, as we have read at ver. 7, had led his troops into Babylonia at this time, where we find him employed at ch. lii. 1—3.

hold, nor could *the latter* gain any advantage over him. But Herod marched straight to the mountain Sarah, to bring back his brother, and the families, and the men who were with him, to Jerusalem. And he found Antigonus besieging his brother; upon whom he made a sudden attack; and Josephus and his men came out to them, and the greater part of Antigonus' army was destroyed, and he fled into Jerusalem.

Whom Herod pursued with a great army of Jews, who had come to him from every quarter, when they found that he had returned; and he was well supplied with assistance, so that he stood in less need of the army of the Romans. When therefore Herod had reached the Holy City, Antigonus shut the gates in his face; and fought against him; and sent much money to the chiefs of the army of the Romans, requesting them not to assist Herod: which they did[e] *for him*. Wherefore the war lasted a long time between Antigonus and Herod, neither of them prevailing over his fellow [i. e. antagonist].

CHAPTER LI.[a]

The history of the magnanimity of certain of Herod's men, and of their bravery.

Now thieves, and they who were longing for the property of others, had multiplied during the time of Antigonus; betaking themselves to some caves in the mountains, to which there was no approach except for one man

---

[e] It appears that Silo, a Roman general, was bribed, and exerted himself in defence of Antigonus' interests.

[a] Compare Josephus, Ant. XIV. 27. Bell. I. 12.

at a time, through certain places fitted for the
3 purpose by them, and known to them alone: and
even though others should know them, they could
not go up to the cave; because that a man was
ever ready at the mouth, who, with a very little
trouble, could easily repel a person who was
4 climbing up. And now some of these men had
gotten to themselves in that cave abundance of
arms, provisions, and drink, and all those things
5 which they needed; together with all the spoils
which they had gained by attacking those whom
they met, and that which they had taken by right
or wrong.

6 When therefore Herod had learnt their proceedings, and found that their matters were likely to cause delay[b]; also that men could not at present mount up to them by ladders, nor in fact
7 climb up in any way; he made use of great wooden chests fitted and joined together, and filled them with men, (adding food and water,) bearing
8 very long hooked spears: and those chests he ordered to be let down from the summit of the mountains, at the middle of which the caves were, until they were placed opposite to their mouths:
9 and when they were opposite to these, *he desired that his men* should attack them in close fight with swords, and from a distance should drag
10 them out with those spears. And the chests were
11 made, and filled with men. And when some of them were let down, and were opposite to the mouths of those caves, no information having

[b] In other words, that in all probability their marauding system would not easily be put a stop to, from the difficulty of coming at their retreats.

been given to the persons living there; one of the men who were in the chests rushed into the caves, followed by his companions; and they killed the 12 robbers who were in them, together with their followers, and threw them down into the valleys below; all the men whom Herod had sent, emulating these *first*. And in this exploit, their cou- 13 rage, bravery, and boldness was so conspicuous, that the like of it was never seen: and they wholly rooted out the robbers from all those parts.

CHAPTER LII.[a]

An account of Antony's return from the country of the Persians after killing the king of the Persians, and his meeting with Herod.

THEN Antony, after leaving Herod[b], marched 1 from Antioch into the country of the Persians, and fought with the king of the Persians, overcame, slew him, and won *his land;* and having 2 reduced the Persians to obedience to the Romans, he turned aside to the Euphrates[c].

And when his fame was told to Herod, he set 3 out to congratulate with him on his victory; and to request him to come with him into the Holy Country. And he found a very large multitude 4 collected[d], wishing to approach Antony; to which many bodies of Arabians had opposed themselves, preventing it from coming to Antony's presence. And Herod marched against the Arabians, and 5

[a] Compare Joseph. Antiq. XIV. 27. Bell. I. 13.
[b] See above, ch. 1. 7. The great defeat, however, was given to the Parthians, not by Antony, but by Ventidius his lieutenant.
[c] On the banks of which river he laid siege to, and subsequently took, the important city of Samosata.
[d] In the neighbourhood of Antioch. (Josephus.)

slew them, opening a passage for all who wished
6 to approach Antony. And this was reported to Antony, before that Herod arrived: whereupon he sent him a golden diadem, and a great many horses.

7 But when Herod came, Antony received him courteously, praising him for his exploits against the Arabians: and he attached to him Sosius the general of his army, with a large force, ordering him to go with him to the city of the Holy House:
8 giving him also letters to all the country of Syria, which is from Damascus even to the Euphrates, and from the Euphrates to the country of Ar-
9 menia; saying to them, "Augustus, king of kings, "and Antony his colleague, and the Roman se- "nate, have now appointed Herod king over the "Jews; and they desire you to lead forth all "your men of war with Herod to assist him: if "therefore you act contrary to this, you must go "to war with us."

10 Then Antony marched to the sea-coast, and thence into Egypt: but Herod, and Sosius with his
11 army, commanded the forces of Syria. But when Herod drew nigh to Damascus, he found that his brother Josephus had gone out from the Holy House with an army of Romans, to besiege
12 Jericho and to cut down its corn: against whom came forth Pappus the general of Antigonus' forces, and slew of them thirty thousand[e], having
13 also slain Josephus Herod's brother: and when his head was presented to Antigonus, Pheroras

---

[e] Probably there is an error in the number. Josephus relates that six cohorts, that is, about *three* thousand men, were slain.

his brother bought it for five hundred talents[f], and buried it in the sepulchre of his fathers: and *he heard* also that Antigonus and Pappus were advancing against him with a large army. Which Herod having fully ascertained, determined to make an onset on Antigonus, and to crush him unexpectedly: and he agreed with Sosius that he should take twelve thousand Romans and twenty thousand Jews, and march against Antigonus, but that the other should slowly follow his footsteps with the remainder of the army.

And Herod marched with his troops in a body, and met with Antigonus in the mountainous parts of Galilee: and they fought with him from midday even until night. Then the army was dispersed; and Herod with some of his men passed the night in a certain house, and the house fell upon them; but they all escaped[g] from the ruin with their lives, without a bone of any one of them being broken.

Shortly afterwards Herod hastened to fight with Antigonus, and there was a very great battle between them, and Antigonus fled into the Holy House; Pappus *meanwhile* resisting bravely, and continuing the fight, for he was high-spirited and very brave. And the greater part of Antigonus' army was slain on that day; Pappus also was killed, whose head Pheroras cut off, and they

---

[f] Truly a large sum to be given for such an object. Josephus, with greater probability of being right, states *fifty*.

[g] Josephus, who frequently in his works manifests a strong partiality for Herod, adduces this occurrence for a proof how much he was beloved by God, whose providence preserved his life in so extraordinary a manner.

carried it to Herod[h], who ordered it to be buried.

21 When therefore none remained of Antigonus' army, except prisoners or runaways, Herod gave orders to his men to take rest, and to eat and
22 drink. But he himself went to a certain bath which was in the next town, and went into the
23 bath unarmed. Now there lay hidden[i] in the bath three strong and brave men, holding in their hands drawn swords: who, when they saw him come into the bath, and unarmed, made all haste to go out one after the other, being afraid of him; and so he escaped.

24 After this came Sosius; and they marched together to the city of the Holy House, which they surrounded with a trench; and fierce battles took
25 place between them and Antigonus: and great numbers of Sosius' men were slain, Antigonus frequently overcoming them; but he could not put them to flight, by reason of their firmness
26 and endurance in bearing *his assaults*. Then Herod prevailed against Antigonus; and Antigonus fled, and entering the city shut the gates against Herod, and Herod besieged him a long time.

27 But on a certain night the guards of the gate fell asleep: which some of Herod's men discovering, twenty of them ran, and taking ladders placed them against the wall, and climbing

[h] Or rather, Herod cut off the head, and sent it to Pheroras.

[i] It appears from Josephus that they had not gone thither for the purpose of attacking Herod; but that they had chanced to resort to the bath as a place of concealment; and upon the unexpected appearance of Herod with his attendant, were too happy to escape with their lives.

up killed the guards. And Herod with his men 28 hastened to the gate of the city which was opposite to them, and burst it in, and entered the city. Which the Romans taking, began to slaughter 29 the citizens; at which Herod being troubled said to Sosius, "If you shall destroy *all* my people, "over whom will you appoint me king?" and So- 30 sius ordered proclamation to be made that the sword should be stayed; nor was any person slain after the proclamation. But Sosius' cap- 31 tains, eager for prey, ran to plunder the house of God: but Herod standing at the gate, holding a drawn sword in his hand, prevented them; and sent to Sosius to restrain his men, promising them money. And Sosius ordered proclamation 32 to be made to his men to abstain from plunder, and they abstained. And they sought Antigonus and found him, and Antigonus was taken prisoner.

After these things, Sosius betook himself into 33 Egypt to his colleague Antony, carrying with him Antigonus in chains. But Herod sent to 34 Antony a very great and fair present, requesting him to slay Antigonus; and Antony slew him[k]: and this was in the third year of the reign of Herod, which also was the third year of Antigonus.

CHAPTER LIII.[a]

The history of Herod after the death of Antigonus.

WHEN Herod was certified of the death of An- 1

---

[k] Thus terminated the government of the Asmonæan princes, in the hundred and twenty-sixth year from its first establishment under Judas Maccabæus. See some remarks on Antony's putting to death the king, given by Josephus out of Strabo.

[a] Compare Joseph. Antiq. XV. 1. Bell. I. 13.

tigonus, he considered himself secure that no one of the royal Asmonæan family would contend with
2 him: wherefore he employed himself in advancing the dignities, in kindnesses and promotions, of those who were well inclined to him and
3 obeyed his will. He also exerted himself in destroying those persons, together with their families, and in plundering their cattle and their goods, who had opposed him, furnishing aid against him.
4 And he oppressed persons, taking away their property, and despoiling all those who had shaken off obedience to the Jews; and slew those who re-
5 sisted him, and plundered their goods. Also he made an agreement with all who were obedient to
6 him, that they should pay him money. He also stationed *guards* at the gates of the Holy House, who might search those who went out, and take whatever gold or silver they should find on any
7 one, and bring it to him. He also ordered the coffins of the dead to be searched; and whatever money any person might endeavour to carry out
8 by stratagem, *the same* to be taken. And he heaped together so much *money* as none of the kings of the second house had amassed.

CHAPTER LIV.[a]

The history of Hyrcanus the son of Alexander, the uncle of Antigonus, and of his return into Jerusalem at the request of Herod, and of the death to which he put him.

1 HYRCANUS, after that the king of the Persians had set him at liberty[b], remained in Herakin[c], in

[a] Compare Joseph. Antiq. XV. 1, 2, 9.
[b] See the preceding part of this narrative above, at ch. xlix. 17, 18.
[c] Josephus *in loco* reads

a most respectable condition and great honour: wherefore Herod was afraid lest any thing might induce the king of the Persians to appoint him king[d], and send him into the land of Judah. Wherefore wishing to set his mind at rest, he laid plots for this business; and sent to the king of the Persians a very great present, and a letter; in which he made mention of Hyrcanus' deserts and kind deeds towards him; and how he had gone to Rome on account of what Antigonus his brother's son had done to him; and that having now attained the throne, and his affairs being in order, he wished to reward him in a proper manner for the benefits which he had conferred.

So the king of the Persians sent a messenger to Hyrcanus, saying; "If you wish to return into "the land of Judah, return: but I warn you to "beware of Herod; and I distinctly inform you, "that he does not seek for you to do you any "good, but his design is to render himself secure, "as there is none remaining whom he fears, ex- "cept you: wherefore take heed of him most dili- "gently, and be not led into a snare." The Jews of Babylon also came to him, and said to him the like words. Again they say to him, "You now "are an old man, and not fit to discharge the "office of high priest, because of the stain which "your nephew[e] inflicted on you: but Herod is a

---

Babylon. In fact Yerak, or Irak, the Arabian name for the district or country of Babylonia, is retained to the present day. See above, ch. xlix. 17, 18. 1. 7.

[d] Although the loss of his ear disqualified Hyrcanus from the office of high priest, yet the crafty Herod knew that this was no obstacle to his reappearing among his countrymen in the capacity of their monarch.

[e] See the account of this transaction at ch. xlix. 16,

"bad man, and a shedder of blood; and he re-
"calls you only because he fears you; and you
"do not want for any thing among us, and you
"are with us in that station in which you ought
11 "to be. And your family there is in the best
"condition; wherefore remain with us, and do not
"aid your enemy against yourself."

12 But Hyrcanus acceded not to their words; nor listened to the advice of one who advised him
13 well. And he set out and journeyed till he came into the Holy City, for the very great longing which he had towards the house of God, his family, and his country.

14 And when he had come near to the city, Herod met him, shewing such honour and magnificence, that Hyrcanus was deceived, and trusted in him.

15 And Herod in the public assembly, and before his own friends, used to call him "Father:" but nevertheless he ceased not to devise plots in his heart, only so that they should not be imputed to
16 him. Wherefore Alexandra and Mariamne her daughter go to Hyrcanus, putting him in fear of Herod, and counselling him to take care of him-
17 self; but neither to them did he attend, although they repeated this to him again and again, advising him to flee to some one of the kings of the
18 Arabians: yet he attended not to all these things, until they drove him to it by repeated warnings and alarmings.

19 Then therefore he wrote to that king[f] of Ara-

of this book, and read the note there.

[f] Namely, Malchus. See above, ch. xlix. 20, and the corresponding part in Josephus. It is to be observed, that Josephus places the present transaction somewhat later in the history, viz. after Herod had heard of the de-

bia; and having sent for a certain man, (whose brother[g] Herod had slain, and had confiscated his goods, and had visited him with many evils,) he told him that he wished to impart to him a certain secret, adjuring him not to tell it to any one; and giving him money and the letter to the king 20 of the Arabians, communicated to him what he requested in the letter. So the messenger, having 21 received the letter, thought that he should obtain a high post with Herod, and should remove from himself the evil which he was continually fearing at his hands, if he communicated the matter to Herod; and that this would be more profitable to 22 him than the keeping of Hyrcanus' secret: since in the other case he was not safe, and sure that the thing would not be told to Herod at some time or other, and thus would be the cause of his destruction. He therefore carried the letter to 23 Herod, and unfolded to him the whole business: who said to him, Carry the letter, as it is, to the king of the Arabians, and bring me back his answer, that I may know it: tell me also the place 24 where the men will be, whom the king of the Arabians will send, that Hyrcanus may go back with them.

So the messenger went, and carried Hyrcanus' 25 letter to the king of the Arabians; who rejoiced, and sent some of his men; ordering them to go 26

---

feat of Antony at Actium, and had become apprehensive of the reception which he might meet with from Augustus; i.e. in the year B.C. 30, which indeed appears nearly to agree with the statement made in the last verse of this chapter, that Hyrcanus had reigned forty years.

[g] Josephus names him Dositheus, and his brother Josephus.

to a certain place near to the Holy City, and there to wait until Hyrcanus should come to them; and then to attend Hyrcanus till they brought him to
27 his presence. He wrote likewise to Hyrcanus an answer to his letter, and sent it by the messenger.
28 So the men proceeded with the messenger to the appointed place, and there waited: but the messenger carried the letter to Herod, who learned its contents: he told him also the place of the men, to whom Herod sent persons to take them.
29 Afterwards, having sent for seventy old men of the elders of the Jews, and having sent also for Hyrcanus; when he came, he said to him, Is there any interchange of letters between you and
30 the king of the Arabians? and Hyrcanus said, No. Then he said to him, Did you send that you
31 might flee to him? and he said, No. And Herod ordered his messenger to come forward, and the Arabians, and the horses; he also brought out
32 the answer to his letter, and it was read. Then he commanded Hyrcanus' head to be stricken off[h]; and his head was stricken off, and no one dared to utter a word for him.

---

[h] Josephus, agreeing in these particulars, informs us that he took his account from the "Commentaries, or Acts, "of Herod himself," other authors relating them in a different manner. There is reason to believe that these *Acts* were written by a personal friend of Herod, Nicolaus Damascenus, who is mentioned by Josephus, Ant. XIV. 2; XVI. 15, 16, 17; XVII. 7. From the accounts of him which remain to us, it appears that Nicolaus was intimate with Augustus; and in fact that it was he who succeeded in procuring for Herod a favourable reception by the Roman court, at a most critical juncture. He wrote several works; as, "A History of "Augustus:" "A History "of the World:" a large volume of "Assyrian History:" "A Collection of strange "Customs," &c. See Photii

Now Hyrcanus had delivered Herod[i] from the death which was justly awarded him in the assembly of judgment, commanding the assembly to be deferred till the morrow, *and* sending away Herod that same night. Whence he was destined to become his murderer, regardless of his services to him and to his father. Hyrcanus was put to death when he was eighty years old, and he reigned forty years: nor was there any one of the kings of the Asmonæan race of a more praiseworthy conduct[k], or more honourable way of life.

33
34
35

CHAPTER LV.[a]

The history of Aristobulus the son of Hyrcanus.

ARISTOBULUS the son of Hyrcanus[b] was of such beauty of form, and exquisite figure and understanding, that his equal was not known. His sister Mariamne also, the wife of Herod, was like to him in beauty; and Herod was wonderfully attached to her. But Herod was averse to appoint Aristobulus high priest in the place of his

B.C. 36.

1
2
3

Bibliothec. cod. CLXXXIX. Montacutii Apparatum 5 ad Origines Ecclesiast. p. 169. (ed. 1635), Valesii Excerpta Peiresc. 4to. 1634, where are considerable fragments of his writings: Fabricii Biblioth. Græc. edit. Harles. III. p. 500: and especially, Grotii Epistol. ad Gallos, p. 249—320. edit. 1648. 12mo.

[i] See Joseph. Ant. XIV. 9.

[k] Josephus, although in general a favourer of Herod, cannot here refrain from bearing testimony to the respectable character of Hyrcanus, and to the shameful usage which he met with at the hands of Herod, whose very best friend and benefactor he in truth had been.

[a] Compare Josephus, Ant. XV. 2, 3.

[b] This is an error: Aristobulus and Mariamne were the children, not of Hyrcanus, but of Alexander son of Aristobulus the brother of Hyrcanus, by Alexandra daughter of Hyrcanus. See the Genealogical Table subjoined to the introduction to this volume.

father; lest the Jews, being attached to him through their affection to his father, should at 4 some future time make him king. Wherefore he appointed some one of the number of common priests[c], who was not of the family of the Asmonæans, to be high priest.

5 At which Alexandra the mother of Aristobulus being vexed, wrote to Cleopatra; requesting to have a letter from Antony to Herod, that he should remove the priest whom he had elevated, and appoint her son Aristobulus high priest in 6 his stead. And Cleopatra granted this; and requested Antony to write a letter to Herod on this subject, and to send it by some chief man of his 7 servants. So Antony wrote a letter, and sent it by his servant Gellius: and Gellius coming to 8 Herod, delivered to him Antony's letter. But Herod forbore to do that which Antony had written *to order*, asserting that it was not the custom among the Jews to depose any priest from his station.

9 Now it happened that Gellius saw Aristobulus, and was greatly struck with the beauty of his form and the perfection of his carriage, which he 10 saw. Wherefore he painted a picture of his likeness, and sent it to Antony, writing beneath the picture to this effect; that no man had begotten Aristobulus, but that an angel cohabiting with 11 Alexandra, begat him on her. Therefore when the picture reached Antony, he was seized with a

---

[c] Josephus states, that he sent to Babylon for one of the obscure Jews residing there, whose name was Ananelus. Ant. XV. 2. Yet afterwards he describes him as being τοῦ ἀρχιερατικοῦ γένους. (See XV. 3.)

most vehement desire to see Aristobulus. And he 12 wrote a letter to Herod, reminding him how he had appointed him king, and had assisted him against his enemies, recounting his kindnesses towards him: adding a request, that he would send 13 Aristobulus to him; and he threatened him in this business for the words[c] which he had sent back.

But when Antony's epistle was brought to Herod, he refused to send Aristobulus, knowing what Antony designed; and on that account he disdained to do it: and he hastily deposed [d] the high priest whom he had appointed, establishing Aristobulus in his place. 14

And *then* he wrote to Antony, informing him 15 that he had already executed that which he had formerly written to him, about the placing Aristobulus in his father's post, before his *last* letter arrived: which business he had *to that time* delayed, because it was necessary to debate the matter with the priests and Jews, after an interval of some days, as the thing was unusual; but it having passed according to his wish, he had immediately appointed him. But now that he was appointed, it was not lawful for him to go out of Jerusalem; as he was not king, but a priest at- 16 17

---

[c] Or the sense may be, "he threatened him repeatedly if he should not comply with his desires in this matter."

[d] Josephus complains, that in this Herod acted contrary to the law; which declared that a person once appointed high priest could not be removed from his office. He states that the first instance of this being done was that of Antiochus Epiphanes, who through bribery consented to depose Jason, and substituted his brother Menelaus (or Onias). See the account of that transaction above, at 3 Macc. iv. 23, 24.

18 tached to the service of the temple: and as often as he wished to compel him to go out, the Jews refused, and would not allow him, even if he
19 should slay the greater part of them. Therefore when Herod's letter reached Antony, he desisted from asking for Aristobulus; and Aristobulus was made high priest.
20 Then came on the feast of tabernacles; and men, assembled before the house of God, beheld Aristobulus clothed in the sacerdotal robes standing at the altar, and they heard him blessing
21 them: and he pleased men so much, that they exhibited their affection towards him in a very
22 marked manner. Which Herod being fully informed of, was much grieved; and feared lest, when Aristobulus' party gained strength, he should demand from him the kingdom, if his life should be prolonged: wherefore he began to plot his death.
23 Now it was customary for the kings to go out, after the feast of tabernacles, to some pleasure-residences at Jericho which former
24 kings had made: and there are many gardens adjoining each other, in which were wide and deep fish-ponds, to which they had conducted streams of water, and had erected fair buildings in those gardens: they also had built in Jericho fair palaces and handsome edifices.
25 Now the author of the book[e] relates, that bal-

---

[e] Who is the author alluded to? [See the same expression occurring before, at ch. xxv. 5, and below, at ch. lix. 96.] Josephus in various passages mentions the balsam-trees; as at Antiq. IV. 5; VIII. 6: where he states that they were first brought into Judæa by the queen of Saba, who presented them to Solomon: and IX. 1. Again

sam-trees grew abundantly in Jericho; and that they were *found* no where else but there; and that many kings had carried them thence into their own country, but none grew, except those

at XV. 4, he says, Φέρει δ' ἡ χώρα τὸ βάλσαμον, ὃ τιμώτατον τῶν ἐκεῖ, καὶ παρὰ μόνοις φύεται. But Josephus is not " the " author" of this book. Several heathen authors relate the fact of the balsam being thought peculiar to Judæa; but I have not discovered what early writer it is that has recorded the experiment of transplanting, and the failure of the original trees, mentioned in the text.

Diodorus Siculus (speaking of the balsam) says, οὐδαμοῦ μὲν τῆς ἄλλης οἰκουμένης εὑρισκομένου τοῦ φυτοῦ τούτου. Biblioth. II. 48. and XIX. 9. (ed. Wesseling.) But we must remember that Diodorus Siculus assigns the lake Asphaltites and its coasts, not to the Jews, but to the Nabathæan Arabians; which circumstance perhaps may help to reconcile the seemingly conflicting accounts of different historians; some of whom confine the plant to Judæa, while others assert its native place to be Arabia.

Pliny states, " Omnibus " odoribus præfertur balsam" um, uni terrarum Judææ " concessum.—Quondam in " duobus tantum hortis, utro" que regio, altero jugerum " xx non amplius, altero pau" ciorum. Ostendere arbus" culam hanc urbi Impera" tores Vespasiani; clarumque

" dictu, a Pompeio magno in " triumpho arbores quoque " duximus. Servit nunc hæc " et tributa pendit cum sua " gente." Hist. Nat. XII. 54. Again; " Fastidit balsamum " alibi nasci." Id. XVI. 39. Justin reports to the same effect.—It is proved, that the Romans, after their conquest of Judæa, enlarged the plantations of balsam at Jericho; so that the produce became greater, and the article itself less costly. It is perhaps almost needless to observe, that the " vineyards of Engaddi," mentioned in the Song of Solomon, are the groves of balsam, which were in that neighbourhood. Historians have said, that some of the trees were carried from Judæa into Egypt by Cleopatra, in the days of Herod: but this is contested in a note to Haverkamp's Josephus, vol. II. p. 66. See the fullest details on this subject in Salmasii Exercitationes Plinianæ in Solini Polyhistorem, cap. 35. p. 418— 430. edit. Traject. 1689: also in the notes on Theophrasti Hist. Plant. IX. 6. edit. Stapel, fol. 1644.

Some Arabian authors relate, that the balsam-tree had been carried by the Saracens to Matarea, (the ancient Heliopolis,) but that the plants had continually failed there.

26 which were carried into Egypt; and that they did not fail in Jericho until after the destruction of the second House; but then they withered away, and never sprouted forth again.

27 So Herod went out to Jericho in quest of plea-
28 sure, and Aristobulus followed him. And when they came to Jericho, Herod commanded some of his servants to go down into the fish-ponds, and play as was customary: and that if Aristobulus should come down to them, they should play with
29 him for some time, and then drown him. But Herod sat in a banqueting-room which he had prepared for himself to sit in: and Herod sent for Aristobulus, and made him sit by his side: also the chief of his attendants and of his friends sat
30 in his presence: and he commanded eatables and drink to be brought; and they did eat and drink: and the attendants hastened down to the waters
31 according to custom, and sported. And Aristobulus greatly wished to go down with them into the water, the wine now mastering them, and
32 asked leave of Herod to do so: who replied, This neither befits you nor any one like you: and when he was urgent, he admonished him and forbade him: but when Aristobulus repeated his request to him, he said to him, Do as you please.
33 And then Herod, rising up went to a certain pa-
34 lace that he might go to sleep there. And Aristobulus went down to the waters, and played for a long time with the attendants: who, when they perceived that being now weary and tired out he wished to go up, held him under water, killed him, and carried him out dead.

And there was a great tumult of the people, 35 and cry, and a lamentation was set up. And He- 36 rod running up, came out to see what had happened: who, when he saw Aristobulus dead, bewailed him, and wept over him very tenderly with a most vehement flood of tears. Then he ordered 37 him to be borne into the Holy City, and accompanied him until he came into the city, and compelled the people to attend his funeral, and there was no point of the very highest honour which he omitted to pay him. And he died when a 38 youth of sixteen years of age, and his high-priesthood continued only for a few days.

On which account enmity grew up between his 39 mother Alexandra and her daughter Mariamne Herod's wife, and the mother and sister of Herod[f]. And the execrations and revilings which Mari- 40 amne heaped upon them were known; and although these reached Herod, yet he did not forbid her nor reprove her, through his great affection for her: he feared also, lest she should ima- 41 gine in her mind that he was well inclined towards the others: from hence these doings lasted long between these women. And Herod's sister, 42 who was endued with the greatest malice, and consummate artifice, began to plot against Mariamne: but Mariamne was religious, upright, 43 modest, and virtuous: but she was a little tinged with haughtiness, pride, and hatred towards her husband.

[f] Namely, Cypris his mother, who was mentioned above, at ch. xlix. 20; and Salome his sister.

CHAPTER LVI.[a]

The history of Antony, and of his expedition against Augustus, and of the aid which he asked from Herod. And an account of the earthquake which occurred in the land of Judah, and of the battle which took place between them and the Arabians.

1 CLEOPATRA, the queen of Egypt, was the wife of Antony: and she discovered such methods of adorning and painting herself, by which women are wont to allure men, as no other woman
2 in the world had found out: so that, while she was a woman advanced in age, she seemed as a little unmarried girl, and even more delicate and
3 more fair. Antony also found in her those methods of beauty, and those means of creating pleasure, which he had never found in the vast number of women whom he had enjoyed. Wherefore she so completely gained possession of Antony's heart, that no room was left in it for affec-
4 tion to any other person. She therefore persuaded him to discomfit certain kings who were subject to the Romans, from her own private considerations; and he obeyed her in this, putting to death certain kings[b] at her instance; and some he left alive by her orders, making them servants and slaves to her.
5 And this was told to Augustus; who wrote to him, abominating such conduct, and desiring him
6 not to be guilty of the like again. And Antony told Cleopatra what Augustus had written to

---

[a] Compare Joseph. Antiq. XV. 6, 7, 8. Bell. I. 14.
[b] As Lysanias, and Artabazes, &c.; the account of which proceedings may be seen in Josephus.

to him; and she advised him to revolt from Augustus, and shewed him that the thing was very easy.

To whose opinion he assenting, openly played 7 false with Augustus; and gathered an army and supplies, that he might go by sea to Antioch, and thence might march by land to meet Augustus wheresoever he might chance to find him. He sent also for Herod, that he 8 might accompany him. And Herod went to him with a most powerful army and most complete supplies. And when he had come to him, 9 Antony said to him; Right reason advises us to make an expedition against the Arabians, and to engage with them: for we are by no means secure that they may not make an incursion upon the Jews and the land of Egypt, so soon as we shall have turned our backs.

And Antony departed by sea: but Herod 10 made an inroad upon the Arabians: and Cleopatra sent a general named Athenio with a great army, to assist Herod in subduing the Arabians: and she commanded him to place Herod and his 11 men in the first rank[c], and to make agreement with the king of the Arabians, that they together should enclose Herod and cut his men to pieces. To this she was led by a desire of obtaining pos- 12 session of all which Herod was worth: Alex- 13 andra also some time previously had requested her to induce Antony to put Herod to death;

---

[c] Even thus, at an earlier period of Jewish history, had the same iniquitous command been given: "Set ye Uriah "in the forefront of the hot- "test battle, and retire ye "from him, that he may be "smitten and die!"

which indeed she had done, but Antony refused
to commit this act. To this was added the circumstance, that Cleopatra had formerly longed for Herod, and had at some time desired intercourse with him; but he restrained himself, for he was chaste. And these were the causes which had induced her to this line of conduct. So Athenio coming to Herod, according to the command of Cleopatra, sent to make agreement with the king of the Arabians, that he might surround him. And when Herod and his Arabians met and encountered, Athenio and his men attacked Herod, who was intercepted between the two armies, and the battle grew fierce against him both before and behind. But Herod seeing what had happened, collected his men, and fought most vigorously until they were beyond the reach of both armies, after the greatest exertion; and he returned into the Holy House.

And there happened a great earthquake in the land of Judah, such as had not occurred since the time of king Harbah[d], in which a great number of men and of animals was destroyed. And this alarmed Herod much, and caused him great fear, and broke down his spirit. He therefore took counsel with the elders of Judah about making an agreement with all nations round about them; designing peace, and tranquillity, and the removal of wars and bloodshed. He sent also ambassadors on these matters to the *surrounding* nations, all of whom embraced the peace to which he had

---

[d] Probably by this name is meant *Uzziah* king of Judah, in whose days we learn from Scripture that a violent earthquake took place. See Amos, i. 1. and Zechariah, xiv. 5.

invited them, except the king of the Arabians; who ordered the ambassadors whom Herod had sent to him to be put to death; for he supposed that Herod had done this because his men had been destroyed in the earthquake, and therefore, being weakened, he had turned himself to making peace. Wherefore he resolved to go to war with Herod; and having collected a large and well-provided army, he marched against him.

And this was told to Herod; and he was much vexed, for two reasons: one, on account of the slaughter of his ambassadors, an act which none of the kings had hitherto committed; another, because he had dared to attack him, imagining in his mind his weakness and want of troops. But he wished to shew him that the matter was otherwise: that all, to whom he had sent ambassadors, to treat of peace, might know that he had not done this through any fear or weakness, but from a wish of that which was kind and good; that no one might dare make attempts against the Jews, or imagine in his mind that they were weak. Besides, he wished to take vengeance on the king of the Arabians for his ambassadors: on these accounts he determined in all haste to march against him.

Therefore he collected troops from the land of Judah, and said to them: "You are aware of the "slaughter of our ambassadors perpetrated by "that Arab; an act which no king hitherto has "committed: for he thinks that we have been "weakened and have become powerless; and he "has dared to provoke us, and thinks that he "shall obtain all his desires over us: nor will he

28 " cease from warring on us continually. Where-
" fore you must struggle against difficulties, that
" you may shew forth your bravery, and may
" subdue your enemies, and bear off their spoils:
29 " although fortune may at one time shew herself
" favourable, at another time adverse to us, ac-
" cording to the custom and usual vicissitudes of
30 " this world. In truth, you must immediately
" undertake an expedition, to take vengeance on
" those oppressors, and to curb the audacity of
31 " all who hold you in little esteem. But if you
" shall say, this earthquake has disheartened us,
" and has destroyed great numbers of us; you
" know full well, that it has destroyed none of
32 " the fighting men[e], but certain others. Nor
" ought we to think it at all unreasonable, that it
" has destroyed the worst among our nation, but
" has left the best to survive. It is also un-
" doubted, that this has improved your spirits
33 " and your inward feelings. But the duty of him,
" whom God has saved from destruction, and has
" preserved from ruin, requires that he should
" obey Him, and should do what is good and
34 " right. And truly no obedience is more honour-
" able or glorious, than to seek redress for the
" oppressed on the oppressor; and to subdue the
" enemies of God and his religion and nation, by
" aiding those who shew obedience and attention
35 " to Him. Nor is it unknown to you, what befell
" us lately with those Arabs, when they had sur-

[e] Josephus remarks, that about ten (in another place he says *thirty*) thousand persons perished in this earthquake, principally from the houses having fallen upon them; but that the soldiers, being abroad and under tents, escaped free from every harm.

"rounded us with Athenio[f]; and how the great "and good God helped us against them, and "delivered us from them. Therefore fear God, 36 "following your ancient custom, and the laudable "custom of your forefathers; and prepare your-"selves against this enemy before he makes ready "against you, and be beforehand with him before "he anticipates you: and God will supply you "with aid and succour against your enemy."

So when the men had heard the address of He- 37 rod, they replied, that they were ready to undertake the expedition, and would make no delay. And he returned thanks to God and to them for it, 38 and ordered many sacrifices to be offered: he also ordered an army to be raised; and a great multitude was gathered from the tribe of Judah and Benjamin. And Herod marching against the king of 39 the Arabians, encountered him; and the battle grew fierce between them, five thousand of the Arabians being slain. There was again a battle, 40 and four thousand of the Arabians were killed: wherefore the Arabians returned to their camp, and remained there; and Herod could do nothing against them, for the place was fortified; but he remained with his army, besieging them in the same place, and not allowing them to go out. And they remained five days in this condition; 41 and a most violent thirst came upon them; they sent therefore ambassadors to Herod with a most valuable present, asking for a truce, and liberty to draw water to drink: but he did not listen to them, but continued in the same furious hostility.

[f] See above, verses 10, 15, 16.

42 The Arabians then said therefore, Let us go out against this nation; for it is better for us to con-
43 quer or die, than to perish from thirst. And they went out against them; and Herod's party overcame them, and slew nine thousand of them; and Herod with his men pursued the Arabians as they fled, slaying great numbers of them; and he
44 besieged their cities and took them. Wherefore they sued for their lives, promising obedience; to which he agreeing, retired from them, and returned into the Holy House.
45 Now the Arabians mentioned in this book are the Arabians who dwelled from the country of Sarah as far as to Hegiaz[g] and the adjacent parts; and they were of great renown and large numbers.

CHAPTER LVII.[a]

The history of Antony's battle with Augustus, and of the death of Antony, and of Herod's going to Augustus.

1 WHEN Antony had marched out of Egypt into the country of the Romans, and had encountered Augustus[b], most severe battles

B.C. 31.

[g] This name is still preserved in Arabia; a large and important district, extending down the shore of the Red sea, and embracing the cities of Mecca and Medina, still bears the appellation of Hedjaz. It is likely that formerly there was a chief town, bearing nearly the same name.

[a] Compare Joseph. Antiq. XV, 9, 10. Bell. I. 15.

[b] Namely at Actium, a town on the sea-coast of Epirus, which was at this time part of the Roman dominions, where his fortunes were fatally shattered: but it is not true that he fell in battle, or at Actium. Antony lived till the next year, and had retired into Egypt: when, after fruitless attempts at a reconciliation with his rival, he once more resolved to try the chances of war, and made ready for battle at Alexandria: but fortune again proved adverse to him; and on hearing a (false) report of

took place between them, in which victory sided with Augustus, and Antony fell in battle; and 2 Augustus got possession of his camp and all which was in it. After this done, he proceeded to Rhodes, that taking ship there he might pass into Egypt.

And tidings were brought to Herod, and he was 3 very much concerned at the death of Antony; and he feared Augustus most exceedingly; and he resolved to go to him, to salute him and congratulate with him. Wherefore he 4 sent his mother and sister with his brother, to a strong hold[c] which he had in mount Sarah: he sent also his wife Mariamne and her mother Alexandra to Alexandrium[d], under the care of Josephus a Tyrian[e]; adjuring him to kill his wife and her mother, so soon as his death should be reported to him.

After this, he went to Augustus with a very 5 valuable present. Now Augustus had already de- 6 termined to put Herod to death; because he had been the friend and supporter of Antony, and because he had formerly deliberated[f] upon marching

B.C. 30.

Cleopatra's death, in despair he fell on his own sword.

[c] Namely Massada, mentioned above, in the notes on ch. xlix. 20, and l. 8. as a place made use of by Herod for the same purpose on an occasion somewhat similar.

[d] Which see described above, at ch. xxxix. 5.

[e] Josephus reads, "to Jo-"seph his steward, and Soe-"mus an Ituræan." (Compare ch. lviii. 1.) In another place he calls him "the "husband of his sister Sa-"lome," agreeably to our author: see below, ch. lviii. 1.

[f] See the preceding chapter, ver. 8, 9. Herod, however, appears even in this instance not to have forgotten his usual crafty foresight: and in dividing the duties of the campaign with Antony, managed so as to avoid coming into direct collision with Augustus, and to employ himself rather in subduing the Arabians; that if at a future

7 with Antony to attack him. When therefore Herod's arrival was notified to Augustus, he ordered him into his presence, in his royal habit which he had on; except the diadem, for this he had
8 ordered to be laid aside from his head. Who, when he was in his presence, having laid aside his diadem as Augustus had commanded, said:
9 " O king, perhaps on account of my love towards " Antony you have been thus violently angry with " me, that you have put off the diadem from my
10 " head; or was it from some other cause? Since, " if you are wroth with me by reason of my ad-" herence to Antony, truly, I say, I adhered to " him because he deserved well of me, and placed " upon my head that diadem which you have
11 " taken off. And indeed he had requested my as-" sistance against you, which I gave him; even " as he also many times gave his assistance to me:
12 " but it was not my lot to be present at the battle " which he fought with you, nor have I drawn " my sword[g] against you, nor fought; the cause " of which was, my being engaged in subduing
13 " the Arabians[h]. But I never failed supplying " him with aid of men and arms and provisions, " as his friendship and his good deeds to me re-" quired. And in truth I am sorry that I left " him; lest men should conceive that I deserted " my friend when he was in need of my help.
14 " Certainly, if I had been with him, I would have

time the sun of Antony should set before the power and influence of his aspiring rival, the door of reconciliation might not be irretrievably closed against him.

[g] See the preceding note.
[h] According to an arrangement made with Antony, as related above, at ch. lvi. 9—1.

"helped him with all my might; and would have
"encouraged him if he had been fearful, and
"would have strengthened him if he had been
"weakened, and would have lifted him up if he
"had fallen, until God should have ruled matters
"as He pleased. And this truly would have been 15
"less grievous to me, than that it should be ima-
"gined that I had failed a man who had implored
"my aid, and thus it should come to pass that
"my friendship should be little esteemed. In my 16
"opinion indeed he fell through his own bad po-
"licy, by yielding to that enchantress Cleopatra;
"whom I had advised him to slay, and thus to
"remove her malice from him; but he did not
"assent. But now, if you have removed from 17
"my head the diadem, certainly you shall not re-
"move from me my understanding and my cou-
"rage; and whatever I am, I will be a friend to
"my friends and an enemy to my enemies."

Augustus replied to him, "Antony indeed we 18
"have overcome by our troops; but you we will
"master by alluring you to us; and will take
"care, by our good offices towards you, that your
"affection to us shall be doubled, because you are
"worthy of this. And as Antony played false by 19
"the advice of Cleopatra, by the same reason he
"behaved ungratefully towards us; returning for
"our kindnesses evils, and for our favours rebel-
"lion. But we are glad of the war which you 20
"have waged with the Arabians, who are our
"enemies: for whoever is your enemy, is ours
"also; and whoever pays you obedience, pays it
"to us likewise."

Then Augustus ordered the golden diadem to 21

be placed on Herod's head, and as many provinces to be added to him[h] as he already had.

22 And Herod accompanied Augustus into Egypt; and all the things which Antony had destined for Cleopatra were surrendered to him. And Augustus departed to Rome: but Herod returned into the Holy City.

CHAPTER LVIII.[a]

The history of the murder which Herod committed on his wife Mariamne.

1 Now Josephus[b], the husband of Herod's sister, had revealed to Mariamne that Herod had ordered him to put her and her mother to death, as soon as he himself should perish in his 2 going up to Augustus. And she already had a dislike of Herod, since the time when he killed her father and brother; and to this no little addition of hatred was made, when she was informed of the orders which he had given against her.

3 Therefore when Herod arrived out of Egypt, he found her totally overcome by hatred towards him: at which being greatly troubled, he tried to 4 reconcile her to him by all possible methods. But his sister came on a certain day, after some quarrels which had taken place between her and Ma-

---

[h] Augustus not only restored those portions of Judæa which Antony had taken away and given to Cleopatra, but likewise enlarged Herod's dominion by the gift of many other towns and districts, which the reader may see enumerated in Josephus.

[a] Compare Josephus, Ant. XV. 11. Bell. I. 17.

[b] The person who was left in charge of Mariamne and her mother, as related above, at ch. lvii. 4; and see the note there.

riamne, and said to him, Certainly Joseph my husband has gone aside with Mariamne. But Herod paid no attention to her words, knowing how pure and chaste Mariamne was. After this, Herod went to see Mariamne on the night which followed that day, and behaved kindly and affectionately towards her, recounting his love for her, saying much upon this head: to whom she said, "Did you ever see a man love another, and order "him to be put to death? and is he a hater un- "less he shews such *proofs?*" Then Herod perceived that Josephus had discovered to Mariamne the secret which he had entrusted to him; and *believed* that he would not have done that, unless she had given herself up to him: and he believed that which his sister had told him on this subject; and immediately departing from Mariamne, he hated and detested her.

Which his sister learning, went to the cupbearer, and giving him money, delivered to him some poison, and said; Carry this to the king, and say to him, Mariamne the king's wife gave me this poison, and this money, commanding that it might be mixed in the king's drink. This the cupbearer did. And the king seeing the poison, doubted not of the truth of the thing: whereupon he gives orders to behead Josephus his brother-in-law immediately; and also orders Mariamne to be put in chains, until the seventy elders should be present, and should pass a due sentence upon her.

So Herod's sister feared[c], lest what she had

---

[c] It is observable, that this account of Mariamne's condemnation and death differs in some few circumstances from that which is given by Josephus.

done should be discovered, and she herself should perish, if Mariamne were set free: so she said to him, O king, if you put off Mariamne's death till to-morrow, you will not be at all able to effect it:
13 for as soon as it shall become known that you wish to kill her, the whole house of her father will come, and all their servants and neighbours, and will interpose; and you will not be able to
14 obtain her death until after great tumults. And
15 Herod said, Do as it seems *best* to you. And Herod's sister sent in all haste a man to bring out Mariamne to the place of slaughter, setting upon her her maids, and other women, to insult her[d], and upbraid her with all manner of indecency:
16 but she answered nothing to any of them, nor even moved her head[e] in the least: nor was her colour changed by all this treatment, nor did any fear or confusion appear in her, nor was her gait
17 altered; but with her wonted manner she proceeded to the place whither she was led to be slain; and bending her knees, she held out her
18 neck voluntarily: and departed this life, renowned for religion and chastity, marked by no crime, branded with no guilt; howbeit she was not wholly free from haughtiness, according to the

[d] It deserves remark, that the author of this book takes no notice whatsoever of the story which appears in Josephus, of Alexandra joining with the wicked Salome and her creatures, in their indecent revilings of her own daughter Mariamne. In truth, such an act would have been not only most unworthy of a mother, but also unlike the straight-forward conduct of that spirited, but unfortunate queen.

[e] I am not satisfied as to the correctness of this rendering: Gabriel's Latin has " apicem protulit;" and the French version is here too loose to afford any certain information. Perhaps the sense may be, " she did not utter a " single syllable, or letter."

habit of her family. And of this not the least cause was the obsequious attention and affection of Herod towards her, by reason of the elegance of her form; from whence she suspected no change in him towards her.

Now Herod had begotten of her two sons[f], namely, Alexander and Aristobulus; who, when their mother was slain, were living at Rome; for he had sent them thither, to learn the literature and language of the Romans. Afterwards, Herod repented that he had killed his wife; and he was affected with grief to that degree on account of her death, that by it he contracted a disease, of which he had nearly died.

Mariamne being dead, her mother Alexandra laid plans to put Herod to death; which coming to his knowledge, he made away with her.

B.C. 28.

CHAPTER LIX.[a]

The history of the coming of the two sons of Herod, Alexander and Aristobulus, as soon as they heard that their mother had been put to death by Herod.

WHEN news was brought to Alexander and Aristobulus of the murder committed on their mother by Herod, they were overcome by excessive grief; and departing from Rome[b] they came into the Holy City, paying no

B.C. 16.

---

[f] Josephus informs us that she bare him *three* sons, but that the youngest of them died while pursuing his studies at Rome.

[a] Compare Joseph. Antiq. XVI. 1, 2, 6, 7, 8, 11, 12, 16, 17. Bell. I. 17.

[b] From the text of this verse it would appear that the brothers quitted Rome *immediately* after hearing of their mother's death: but from Josephus we collect that

respect to their father Herod as they had formerly been wont to do, through the hatred of him which they felt in their minds on account of their mo-
3 ther's death. Now Alexander had married the daughter of king Archelaus[c]: and Aristobulus had married the daughter of Herod's sister[d].
4 Therefore when Herod perceived that they paid him no respect, he saw that he was hated by them, and he avoided them: and this did not escape the observation of the young men, and of his family.
5 Now king Herod had married a wife before Mariamne, by name Dosithea[e], by whom
6 he had a son named Antipater. When therefore Herod was assured respecting his two sons, as was observed above, he brought his wife Dosithea to his palace, and attached to himself his son Antipater, committing to him all his business; and he appointed him by will his successor.
7 And that Antipater persecuted his brothers Alexander and Aristobulus, designing to procure peace to himself while his father lived, that after his
8 death he might have no rival. Wherefore he said to his father, " In truth my brothers are " seeking an inheritance[f] because of the family of " their mother, because it is more noble than the " family of my mother; and therefore they have " a better right than I have to the fortune of

they did not return until several years after; namely, in the year B.C. 16.
[c] He was king of Cappadocia. (Josephus.)
[d] Namely, Bernice, daughter of Joseph and Salome.
[e] Josephus calls her *Doris*.
[f] That is, they are devising means of securing to themselves the succession to the throne, which they know you have destined for me.

"which the king has judged me worthy: for this "cause they are striving to put you to death, and "me also they will slay soon after." And this he frequently repeated to Herod, sending also secretly to him persons to insinuate to him things which might produce in him a greater hatred towards them.

In the mean time Herod goes to Rome to Augustus, taking with him his son Alexander. And when he had come into Augustus' presence, Herod complained to him of his son, requesting that he would reprove him. But Alexander said; "Indeed I do not deny my "anguish on account of the murder of my mother "without any fault; for even brute beasts them- "selves shew affection to their mothers much "better than men, and love them *more*: but any "design of parricide I utterly deny, and I clear "myself of it before God: for I am possessed of "the same feelings toward my father as toward "my mother: nor am I that sort of man as to "bring upon me guilt for crime towards my "parent, and more especially eternal torments." Alexander then wept with bitter and most vehement weeping; and Augustus pitied him, and all the chiefs of the Romans, who were standing near, wept *also*. Then Augustus asked Herod to take back his sons into his former kindness and intimacy: and he desired Alexander to kiss his father's feet, who did so. He also ordered Herod to embrace and kiss him, and Herod obeyed him.

Afterwards Augustus ordered a magnificent present for Herod, and it was carried to him: and after passing some days with him, Herod

returned to the Holy House; and calling to him
18 the elders of Judah, he said: "Know ye that
"Antipater is my eldest son and firstborn, but
"his mother is of an ignoble family: but the
"mother of Alexander and Aristobulus my sons
"is of the family of the high priests and kings.
19 "Moreover, God hath enlarged my kingdom, and
"hath extended my power; and therefore it
"seems good to me to appoint these my three
"sons to equal authority; so that Antipater shall
"have no command over his brothers, nor shall
20 "his brothers have command over him. Obey
"therefore all three, O ye assembly of men, nor
"interfere in any thing which their minds may
"be able to agree on; nor propose any thing
"which may produce misleadings and disagree-
21 "ment among them. And do not drink with
"them, nor talk too much with them. For from
"thence it will come to pass, that some one of
"them may unguardedly utter to you the designs
22 "which he has against his brother: upon which,
"that you may conciliate them to you, will follow
"your agreements with every one of them, accord-
"ing to what seems good to him; and you will
"bring them to destruction, and yourselves will
23 "be destroyed also. It is your parts indeed, my
"sons, to be obedient to God, and to me; that
"you may live long, and that your affairs may
"prosper." Soon afterwards he embraced and
kissed them, and commanded the people to retire.

---

g That is, by which means you will be led to become partisans of one individual or the other, from motives of personal interest, instead of remaining faithful counsellors and supporters of their united authority.

But that which Herod did came to no happy result, nor were the hearts of his sons united in agreement. For Antipater wanted every thing to be put into his hands, as his father had formerly appointed: and to his brothers it did not seem at all fair that he should be thought equal to them. Now Antipater was endued with perseverance, and all bad and feigned friendship; but not so his two brothers: Antipater therefore set spies on his brothers, who should bring him tidings of them: he also planted others who should carry false reports of them to Pilate[h]. But when Antipater was in presence of the king, and heard any one relating such things of his brothers, he repelled the charge from them, declaring that the authors were unworthy of credit, and entreating the king not to believe the reports. Which Antipater did, that he might not inspire the king with any doubt or suspicion[i] of himself. From hence the king entertained no doubt that he was well-inclined towards his brothers, and wished them no harm.

Which when Antipater found out, he bent to his purpose Pheroras his uncle, and his aunt, (for these were at enmity with his brothers on their mother's account,) offering Pheroras a most valuable present, requesting him to inform the king

---

[h] This manifestly is a mistake of the author or copier, for *Herod*. Pilate does not appear in Jewish history till more than thirty years had elapsed after this transaction; namely, in the reign of Tiberius Cæsar. See Luke iii. 1.

[i] The reader will have remarked the just retaliation upon Herod by his crafty son; who now practises against his own father, and with equal success, that system of duplicity and false accusation which Herod and his father Antipater had ever employed for their own advancement.

that Alexander and Aristobulus had laid a plan
30 to murder the king. (Now Herod was well inclined towards Pheroras his brother, and attended to whatever he said; inasmuch as he paid every year to him a large sum out of the provinces which he governed on the bank of the
31 Euphrates.) And this Pheroras did. Afterwards Antipater went to Herod, and said to him; " O " king, in truth my brothers have laid a plot to
32 " destroy me." Antipater moreover gave money to the king's three eunuchs, that they should say, " Alexander has given us money, that he might " make a wicked use of us, and that we might " slay thee: and when we shrank from it, he " threatened us with death."
33 And the king was wroth with Alexander, and ordered him to be put in chains: and he seized and put to the torture all the servants of Alexander, till they should confess what they knew about
34 Alexander's plot for murdering him. And many of these, though they died under the torture, never told a falsehood respecting Alexander: but some of them, being unable to endure the violence of the torment, devised falsehoods through a desire
35 of liberating themselves; asserting that Alexander and Aristobulus had planned to attack the king, and slay him, and flee to Rome; and having received an army from Augustus, to march against the Holy House, to slay their brother Antipater, and to seize on the throne of Judæa.
36 And the king commanded Aristobulus to be seized and put in chains: and he was bound, and was placed with his brother.

But when news of Alexander was brought to his father-in-law Archelaus[k], he went to Herod, pretending to be in a great fury against Alexander: as if, on hearing a report of the *intended* parricide, he had come on purpose to see whether his daughter, the wife of Alexander, was privy to the business, and had not revealed it to him, that he might put her to death: but that, if she was not privy to any thing of the kind, he might separate her from Alexander, and take her to his own home.

Now this Archelaus was a prudent, wise, and eloquent man. And when Herod had heard his words, and was satisfied of his prudence and honesty, he wonderfully got possession of his heart; and he trusted himself to him, and relied on him without the slightest hesitation. Archelaus therefore, finding Herod's inclination towards him, after a long intimacy, said to him one day when they had retired together; " Truly, O king, by reflect-
" ing on your affairs I have found, that you being
" now in advanced age are much in want of re-
" pose of mind, and to have solace in your sons;
" whereas on the contrary you have derived from
" them grief and anxiety. Moreover I have
" thought respecting these your two sons, and I
" do not find that you have been deficient in de-
" serving well of them; for you have promoted
" them, and made them kings, and have left un-
" done nothing, which might drive them wickedly
" to *contrive* your death, nor have they any cause
" for *entering on* this business. But perhaps this

[k] The king of Cappadocia, as mentioned above, at verse 3.

"has come from *some* malicious person, who is "desiring evil against you and them, or who "through envy or enmity has induced you to ab-
44 "hor them. If therefore he has gained influence "over you, who are an old man, endued with "knowledge, information, and experience, chang- "ing you from paternal mildness to cruelty and
45 "fury against your children; how much easier "could he have wrought on them, who are young, "inexperienced, and unguarded, and with no "knowledge of men and their guiles, so that he "has gained from them that which he wished in
46 "this matter. Consider therefore your affairs, "O king; and do not give ear to the words of "informers, nor do any thing hastily against your "children; and enquire who that is who has been "contriving evil against you and them."

47 And the king replied to him; "Indeed the "thing is as you have mentioned: I wish that I "knew who has induced them to *do* this." Archelaus answered, "This is your brother Phero- "ras." The king replied, "It may be so."

48 After this, the king became greatly changed in his behaviour towards Pheroras: which Pheroras perceiving, was afraid of him; and coming to
49 Archelaus, said to him; "I perceive how that "the king is changed towards me; wherefore I "intreat you to reconcile his mind to me, remov- "ing the feelings which he cherishes in his heart
50 "against me." To whom Archelaus replied; "I "will do it indeed, if you will promise to disclose "to the king the truth concerning the plots which "you have laid against Alexander and Aristobu- "lus." And to this he assented.

And after a few days, Archelaus said to the 51 king; "O king, truly a man's relatives are to "him as his own limbs: and as it is good for a "man, if any one of his limbs becomes affected by "some disease which befalls it, to restore it by "medicines, even although it may cause him "pain; and it is not good to cut it off, lest the 52 "pain should be increased, the body be weak- "ened, and the limbs should fail; and thus from "the loss of that limb, he should feel the want of "many conveniences: but let him endure the 53 "pains of the medical treatment, that the limb "may become better, and may be healed, and his "body may return to its former perfectness and "strength. So is it meet for a man, so often as 54 "any one of his relatives is altered towards him, "from any abominable cause whatsoever, to re- "concile him to himself; alluring him to civility 55 "and friendship, admitting his excuses, and dis- "missing the charges against him: and that he "do not put him hastily to death, nor remove "him too long away from his presence. For the 56 "relatives of a man are his supporters and assist- "ants, and in them consists his honour and glory; "and through them he obtains that which other- "wise he would not be able to obtain. Pheroras 57 "truly is the king's brother, and the son of his "father and of his mother: and he confesses his "fault, entreating the king to spare him, and to "dismiss *from his mind* his error." And the king replied, " This I will do." And he ordered Phe- 58 roras to come before him; who, when he was in the presence, said to him; " I have sinned now " in the sight of the great and good God, and to "the king, devising mischiefs, and *plans* which might injure the affairs of the king and his sons, by lying falsehoods. But that which induced me to act thus was, that the king took away from me a certain woman, my concubine, and separated her and me." The king said to Archelaus, "I have now pardoned Pheroras, as you requested me: for I find that you have cured the disease which was in our affairs by your soothing methods, even as an ingenious physician heals the corruptions of a sick body. Wherefore I entreat you to pardon Alexander, reconciling your daughter to her husband; for I regard her as my daughter, since I know that she is more prudent than he, and that she turns him aside from many things by her prudence and her exhortations. Wherefore I pray you not to separate them and destroy him: for he agrees with her, and obtains many advantages from her guidance." But Archelaus answered, "My daughter is the king's handmaid: but him my soul hath lately detested, by reason of his evil design. Let the king therefore permit me to separate him from my daughter, whom the king may unite to whomsoever of his servants he pleases." To whom the king replied; "Do not go beyond my request; and let your daughter remain with him, and do not contradict me." And Archelaus said; "Surely I will do it; and will not contradict the king in any thing which he shall enjoin me."

Soon afterwards, Herod orders Alexander and Aristobulus to be loosed from their chains, and to come before him: who, when they were in his presence, prostrated themselves before him, confessing their faults, excusing themselves, and begging for pardon and forgiveness. And he commanded them to stand up, and causing them to come near him, he kissed them, and ordered them to depart to their own homes, and to return the next day. And they came to eating and drinking with him, and he reinstated them in a place of greater honour. And to Archelaus he gave seventy talents and a golden couch, enjoining likewise all the chief men of his friends to offer valuable presents to Archelaus: and they did so. This being accomplished, Archelaus departed from the city of the Holy House to his own country; whom Herod accompanied, and at length, having taken leave of him, returned to the Holy House.

Nevertheless, Antipater did not leave off his plots against his brothers, that he might make them odious. Now it happened that a certain man[b] came to Herod, having some valuable and handsome articles, with which kings are usually won; these he presented to the king, who, taking them from him, repaid him for them; and the man obtained a very high place in his affections, and having been taken into his retinue, enjoyed his confidence: this man was named Eurycles. When therefore Antipater perceived that this man had wholly engrossed his father's favour, he offered him money, requesting that he would

---

[b] Josephus informs us that he was a Lacedæmonian, by name Eurycles, of a sordid and treacherous disposition; so much so, that when he returned to his own country, after having kindled fatal discord in Herod's family, the Lacedæmonians banished him from the realm.

dexterously insinuate to Herod, and maintain that his two sons Alexander and Aristobulus were planning to murder him; which the man pro-
73 mised him to do. He soon afterwards went to Alexander, and became intimate and familiar with him to that degree, that he was known to be in his friendship, and it was made known to the
74 king that he was intimate with him. After this, he went aside with the king, and said to him; " Certainly you have this right over me, O king, " that nothing ought to prevent me from giving " you good advice: and in truth I have a matter " which the king ought to know, and which I
75 " ought to unfold to you." The king said to him, " What have you?" The man answered him, " I heard Alexander saying, 'Truly God hath " deferred vengeance on my father for the death " of my mother, of my grandfather, and of my " relatives, without any crime, that it may take " place by my hand: and I hope that I shall take
76 " vengeance for them upon him.' And now he " has agreed with some chiefs to attack you, and " he wished to implicate me in the plans which " he had formed: but I held it to be a crime, on " account of the king's acts of kindness towards
77 " me, and his liberality. But my intention is to " admonish him well, and to report this to him, " for he has *both* eyes and understanding."
78 And when the king had heard these words, he by no means set them at nought, but speedily be-
79 gan to make enquiry as to their truth: but he found out nothing on which he could rely, except a letter forged in the name of Alexander and Ari-

stobulus to the governor of a certain town[c]. And there was in the letter, "We wish to kill our fa-"ther, and to flee to you; wherefore prepare us "a place wherein we may remain until the people "assemble round us, and our affairs are settled." And this indeed was confirmed to the king, and appeared probable: wherefore he seized the governor of that city and put him to the torture, that he might confess what was inserted into *that* letter. Which this man denied, clearing himself from the charge: nor was any thing proved against them in this matter, or in any thing else which the informer had charged upon them. But *Herod* ordered them to be seized and bound with chains and fetters. Then he went to Tyre[d], and from Tyre to Cæsarea, carrying them with him in chains. And all the captains and all the soldiers pitied them: but no one interceded for them with the king, lest he should admit that to be true of himself which the informer had asserted.

Now there was in the army a certain old warrior[e] who had a son in the service of Alexander. When therefore the old man saw the wretched condition of Herod's two sons, he pitied their change of fortune marvellously, and cried out with as loud a voice as he was able, "Pity is "gone; goodness and piety have vanished away;

---

[c] Of Alexandrium. (Josephus.)

[d] Josephus relates that Herod brought his sons to a public mock trial *at Berytus*, himself accusing them in most violent language, and allowing no defence to be made. Of course the unhappy youths were condemned. He *then* carried them off to Tyre and Cæsarea.

[e] Josephus records his name, which was Tero (or Tiro).

86 " truth is removed out of the world." Then he said to the king, " O thou merciless to thy chil-
" dren, enemy of thy friends, and friend to thy
" enemies, receiving the words of informers and
87 " of persons who wish no good to thee!" And the enemies of Alexander and Aristobulus ran up to him, and reproved him, and said to the king;
" O king, it is not love towards you and towards
" your sons which has induced this man to speak
88 " thus; but he has wished to babble out the hatred
" which he bare in his heart towards you, and to
" speak ill of your counsel and administration, as
89 " *being* a faithful adviser. And indeed some ob-
" servers have informed us of him, that he had
" already covenanted with the king's barber, to
" slay him with the razor while he was shaving
90 " him." And the king ordered the old man, and his son, and the barber, to be seized; and the old man and the barber to be scourged with rods till they should confess. And they were beaten with rods most cruelly, and were subjected to various kinds of tortures; but they confessed nothing of those
91 things which they had not done. When therefore the son of the old man saw the sad condition of his father, and the state to which he had come, he pitied him, and thought that he would be liberated, if he himself should confess that which was laid to his father, after receiving from the king a pro-
92 mise for his life. Wherefore he said to the king;
" O king, give me security for my father and my-
" self, that I may tell you that which you are
" seeking." And the king said, " You may have
93 " this." To whom he said; " Alexander had al-
" ready agreed with my father that he should kill

"you: but my father agreed with the barber, as "has been told you."

Then the king commanded that old man and his son to be slain, and the barber. He likewise ordered both his sons Alexander and Aristobulus to be taken to Sebaste, and there to be slain and fixed on a gibbet: and they were taken, killed, and fixed on a gibbet.

Now Alexander left two sons who survived him, namely, Tyrcanes and Alexander, by the daughter of king Archelaus: and Aristobulus left three sons, namely, Aristobulus, Agrippa, and Herod. But the history of Herod's son Antipater has already been described[f] in our former accounts.

[f] What are the "former accounts" here spoken of, it is not easy to determine. The subsequent history of Antipater must be sought in the 17th book of the Antiquities of Josephus. In truth, the conclusion of this tragedy, is quite in keeping with the former melancholy scenes of it: Antipater becoming at last afraid of his father, whose ferocious and indiscriminate massacres he had not only witnessed, but had abetted for some time past, seeks means to destroy him by poison: but Herod detecting the plot, although tormented by a complication of diseases, and almost at death's door, summons his last energies to order Antipater to be slain, which is instantly done. He himself follows his son to the grave within five days, one year after the birth of our Saviour Jesus Christ.

END OF BOOK V.

# INDEX.

A.

AARON, II. vii. 14. IV. vii. 10, 11.
Abel, IV. xviii. 13.
Abominations, (i. e. idols,) I. ii. 18. vi. 7.
——— of desolation, II. i. 54.
Abraham, I. vi. 3. II. ii. 52. xii. 21. III. i. 2. IV. vi. 14, 19. vii. 17. ix. 21. xiii. 14. xv. 1, 24. xvi. 18, 22. xvii. 6. xviii. 1, 20, 22.
Absalom, II. xi. 70. III. xi. 17.
Abubus, (the son of,) II. xvi. 11, 15.
Accaron, II. x. 89.
Acche, (Ptolemais,) V. xxviii. 2.
Accos, II. viii. 17.
Acrabattine, II. v. 3.
Adar, (the month,) II. vii. 43, 49. III. xv. 36.
Adasa, II. vii. 40, 45.
Adida, in Sephela, II. xii. 38. xiii. 13.
Adora, II. xiii. 20.
Æmilius, (Paulus,) V. xii. 5.
Æra, of the Seleucidæ, II. i. 10, note.
——— of Simon the high priest, II. xiii. 42. xiv. 27.
——— of Herod's reign, V. l. 5.
Affection (natural) of birds, IV. xiv. 13. and of bees, ver. 17.
Africa, V. xii. 2, 12, &c. to 26.
Africans, V. xii. 25.
Agrippa, son of Aristobulus Herod's son, V. lix. 95.
Alcimus, II. vii. 5, 9, 12, 20, 21, 23, 25. ix. 1, 54—57.

III. xiv. 2, 13, 26. V. iii. 6. xvi. 3, 12.
Alema, II. v. 26.
Alexander, of Macedon, II. i. 1, 7.
Alexander Balas, II. x. 1, 4, 47—51, 58, 59, 68, 88. ii. 1, 2, 8, 9, 12, 14—17, 39.
Alexander Jannæus, son of J. Hyrcanus, V. xxvi. 1—4. xxvii. 2. His history, xxviii. 1, &c. xxix. 1, &c. His death, xxx. 1, &c. xxxi. 8. xxxii. 1, 4. xxxv. 3, 4, 27. xxxvi. 31.
Alexander, son of Aristobulus the second, V. xxxvii. 4. xxxviii. 3. xxxix. 1—10.
Alexander, son of Herod, V. lviii. 20. lix. 1, 3, 7, 11, 12, 15, 16, 18, 29, 32—35, 37, 38, 50, 61, 65, 72, 73, 75, 79, 85, 87, 93—95.
Alexander, son of Alexander Herod's son, V. lix. 95.
Alexandra, (I.) wife of Alexander Jannæus, V. xxx. 3, 15. Her history, xxxi. 1, &c. xxxii. 2. Her death, xxxiii. 1, &c. xxxiv. 1—3.
Alexandra, (II.) daughter of Hyrcanus, wife of Alexander, and mother of Mariamne, V. xlix. 20. liv. 16. lv. 5, 11, 39. lvi. 13. lvii. 4. Her death, lviii. 22.
Alexandria, I. ii. 30. iii. 1, 21.
Alexandrium, a fortress, V. xxxix. 5, 8. lvii. 4.
Amathis, (or Hamath,) II. xii. 25.
Ammon, (children of,) II. v. 6.

INDEX.

Ammon, (country of,) V. xxix. 19.
Ammonites, III. iv. 26. v. 7.
Ananias, Azarias, and Misael, II. ii. 59. (IV. xiii. 9. xvi. 3.) IV. xvi. 19. xviii. 14.
Andronicus, III. iv. 31, 32, 34, 38. v. 23.
Angels, V. x. 17.
Annibal, V. xii. 2, 4, 6, &c. to 26.
Antigonus, (I.) son of Hyrcanus, V. xxiii. 4. xxvi. 1. His history and death, xxvii. 2, &c.
Antigonus, (II.) son of Aristobulus, V. xl. 1. xlii. 1. xlix. 1, 5, 10, 19, 23, 28. l. 1, &c. li. 1. lii. 12—33. He is slain, 34. liii. 1, 4.
Antioch, Antiochia, near Daphne, II. iii. 37. iv. 35. vi. 63. xi. 13, 44, 56. III. iv. 9, 33. v. 21. viii. 35. xi. 36. xiii. 23, 26. xiv. 27. V. xiii. 3. xvi. 2. xxix. 16. l. 6. lii. 1. lvi. 7.
Antiochians, III. iv. 19.
Antiochis, III. iv. 30.
Antiochus III. (the Great,) I. i. 1, 2, 5, 12, note. II. i. 10. viii. 6.
Antiochus IV. (Epiphanes,) II. i. 10, 16, 20, 41. iii. 27. vi. 1, 16, 55. x. 1. III. i. 14, 15. ii. 20. iv. 7, 21, 37. v. 1, 5, 17, 21. vii. 24. ix. 1—28. Is tormented and dies, x. 13. xiv. 2. IV. iv. 15, 16. v. 1, 5. x. 15. xvii. 22. xviii. 5. V. iii. 1, 8, 9, 13. v. 5, 31, 38, 45, 52, 54. vi. 2, 20. vii. 10, 12, 17. viii. 1, 7. ix. 2. x. 3. xv. 1. xvi. 19.
Antiochus V. (Eupator,) II. iii. 33. vi. 15, 17, 55. vii. 2. III. ii. 20. ix. 25. x. 10, 13. xi. 22, 27. xiii. 1, 3, 4. V. xiii. 2. xv. 1, 12.

Antiochus VI. (Theos.) II. xi. 39, 40, 54, 57. xii. 39. Is slain by Tryphon, xiii. 31.
Antiochus VII. (Sidetes, or Pius,) II. xv. 1, 2, 10, 11, 13, 25. His letter to Simon, xiv. 2, &c. V. xix. 3, 6, 7. Attacks Hyrcanus, V. xxi. 1, &c. He is slain, xxi. 24.
Antiochus IX. (Cyzicenus,) V. xxiii. 6.
Antipater, the son of Jason, II. xii. 16. xiv. 22, 24.
Antipater, father of Herod, his history, V. xxxv. 1, &c. xxxvi. 1, &c. xxxvii. 5. xxxviii. 1—3. xl. 7, 8, 18. xlii. 16—25. xliii. 2—11. xliv. 7. xlv. 6, 7. His death, xlvi. 1, &c.
Antipater, son of Herod, V. lix. 5, 7, 18, 19, 24—32, 35, 69, 72, 96.
Antonius, (Marcus,) V. xxxix. 8. xlvii. 13. xlviii. 3, 11, 23 —35. xlix. 1, &c. l. 3, &c. lii. 1, &c. lv. 5—19. lvi. 1, &c. His battle with Augustus, and death, lvii. 1, &c.
Aphærema, II. xi. 34.
Apollonius, son of Thraseas, II. iii. 10, 12. III. iii. 5, 7. iv. 4. v. 24.
Apollonius, governor of Cœlosyria, II. x. 69, 74, 77, 79. IV. iv. 2, 4, &c.
Apollonius, son of Menestheus, III. iv. 21.
Apollonius, son of Gennæus, III. xii. 2.
Apollophanes, III. x. 37.
'Αποστολαὶ, its meaning. Note on III. i. 2.
Arabia, II. xi. 16. III. xii. 11.
Arabians, II. v. 39. xi. 16, 39. xii. 31. III. v. 8. xii. 10. V. xxviii. 28. xxix. 19. xxxvi. 9. xxxviii. 1—3. lii. 4, 5, 7. liv. 17—20, 23—25, 29—31. lvi. 9—11, 15, 16, 21, 25,

INDEX.

26, 35, 39—42, 45. lvii. 12, 20.
Aradus, II. xv. 23.
Arbattis, II. v. 23.
Arbela, II. ix. 2.
Archelaus, V. lix. 3, 37, 39, 40, 47—51, 60, 63, 64, 67, 68, 95.
——— Aretas, III. v. 8. See *Hartas*.
Appearances, (preternatural,) see *Visions*.
Areus, or Arius, king of Sparta, II. xii. 7, 19, 20.
Ariarathes, II. xv. 22.
Aristobulus, III. i. 10.
Aristobulus, son of J. Hyrcanus, V. xxiii. 4. xxvi. 1, 2. His history and death, xxvii. 1, &c.
Aristobulus, son of Alexander Jannæus, V. xxxi. 6. xxxii. 3. xxxiii. 2, 5, 7. is appointed king, xxxiv. 1, &c. xxxv. 5, &c. xxxvi. 3, &c. xxxvii. 1, 4. escapes from Rome, V. xl. 1, &c. xliii. 1. xliv. 13.
Aristobulus, son of Hyrcanus the second, V. lv. 1, &c. is drowned by Herod's orders, 34, 38.
Aristobulus, son of Herod, V. lviii. 20. lix. 1, 3, 7, 18, 29, 35, 36, 50, 65, 72, 79, 87, 94, 95.
Aristobulus, son of Aristobulus, Herod's son, V. lix. 95.
Armenia, Armenians, V. xxxvi. 1, 2. lii. 8.
Arsaces, (Mithridates,) II. xiv. 2, 3. xv. 22.
Arsinoe, I. i. 2, 5.
Ascalon, II. x. 86. xi. 60. xii. 33. V. xlii. 14.
Asdrubal, V. xii. 15.
Ashes, a tower full of, III. xiii. 5, and note.
Asia, I. iii. 14. II. viii. 6. xi. 13. xii. 39. xiii. 32. III. iii. 3. x. 24. IV. iii. 21. V. xlv. 5. xlviii. 7, 16.

Asmonæans, whence derived. Note on II. ii. 1. V. xliv. 12. liii. 1. liv. 35. lv. 4.
Asphar, the pool, II. ix. 33.
Assidæans, (or Hasdanim,) II. ii. 42. vii. 13. III. xiv. 6.
Assyria, I. vi. 5. II. vii. 41. IV. xiii. 9.
Atargatis, III. xii. 26. and note.
Athenio, V. lvi. 10, 15, 16, 35.
Athenobius, II. xv. 28, 32, 36.
Athens, III. vi. 1, and note. ix. 15.
Attalus, II. xv. 22.
Augustus, (see *Octavian*,) V. xlviii. 3, &c. xlix. 1, 29. l. 1, 3. lii. 9. lvi. 5—7. Conquers Antony, lvii. 1, &c. Receives Herod into favour, lvii. 18—22. lviii. 1. lix. 11, 15—17, 35.
Azarias, one of Judas' captains, II. v. 18, 56, 60.
Azotus, (or Ashdod,) II. iv. 15. v. 68. x. 77, 78, 83, 84. xi. 4. xiv. 34. xvi. 10. V. xvii. 12.
Azotus, (mount,) II. ix. 15. V. xvii. 12.

B.

Babylon, I. vi. 6. vi. 4. III. viii. 20. V. xxxv. 1. liv. 8.
Bacchides, II. vii. 8, 12, 19, 20. ix. 1, 11, 12, 14, 25, 26, 29, 32, 34, 43, 47, 49, 50, 57, 58, 63, 68. III. viii. 30. V. xvii. 1—12. xviii. 1 —8.
Bacchus, I. ii. 29. III. vi. 7. xiv. 33.
Bacenor, III. xii. 35.
Bæan, (children of,) II. v. 4.
Balsam-trees, V. lv. 25.
Barber, (Herod's,) V. lix. 89—94.
Bascama, II. xiii. 23.
Bath, Herod in danger in one, V. lii. 22.
Bathzacharias, II. vi. 32, 33.
Beasts, i. e. (elephants,) I. v.

G g

29, 31, 47. vi. 16. II. vi. 35, 36, 37, 43. III. xv. 20, 21.
Beersheba, V. xviii. 4.
Benjamin, (tribe of,) III. iii. 4. V. ii. 11. lvi. 38.
Berœa, II. ix. 4. III. xiii. 4.
Beth-basi, II. ix. 62, 64.
Beth-Dagon, II. x. 83.
Beth-el II. ix. 50.
Beth-horon, II. iii. 16. 24. vii. 39. ix. 50.
Beth-ner, V. xi. 3, 9. xv. 3.
Bethsan, II. v. 52. xii. 40, 41.
Bethsura, II. iv. 29, 61. vi. 7, 26, 31, 49, 50. ix. 52. x. 14. xi. 65. xiv. 7, 33. III. xi. 5. xiii. 19, 22.
Bezeth, II. vii. 19.
Blood, innocent avenged, V. xxvii. 20—29.
Bosor, II. v. 26, 28, 36.
Bosora, II. v. 26.
Brutus (L. Junius), V. xlv. 1. xlviii. 16.
Burying-place: the meaning of πολυάνδριον. Note on III. ix. 4.

C.

Caddis, son of Mattathias, II. ii. 2.
Cades in Galilee, II. xi. 63, 73.
Cæsar, Julius, V. xl. 5, 6. his history, xli. 1, &c. xliii. 1, &c. xliv. 1, &c. his death, xlv. 1, &c. xlvii. 13. xlviii. 4, 14.
Cæsarea, V. lix. 83.
Cain, IV. xviii. 13.
Caleb, II. ii. 56.
Callisthenes, III. viii. 33.
Calphi, II. xi. 70.
Capharsalama, II. vii. 31.
Caphenatha, II. xii. 37.
Cappadocia, V. xlii. 11.
Captivity, the third, V. ix. 5, and note.
Caria, II. xv. 23.
Carnaim, II. v. 26, 43, 44.
Carnion, III. xii. 21, 26.
Carthage, V. xii. 2, 18, 19.

Casleu, the month, II. i. 54. iv. 52, 59. III. i. 9, 18. x. 5. V. ix. 6.
Casphon, II. v. 26, 36.
Caspis, III. xii. 13.
Cassius, V. xli. 14. xlv. 1, &c. xlvii, 2, &c. xlviii. 1, &c.
Catapeltæ, (instruments of torture,) IV. ix. 26. x. 7. xi. 22. xviii. 20.
Cedron, II. xv. 39, 41. xvi. 9.
Cendebæus, II. xv. 38, 40. xvi. 1, 4, 8, 9.
Chæreas, III. x. 32, 37.
Chalisam, V. x. 21.
Chanaan, II. ix. 37.
Characa, III. xii. 17.
Chelcias, V. xxiv. 2.
Chettiim, the land of, II. i. 1.
Cilicia, II. xi. 14. III. iv. 36. IV. iv. 2.
Citims, II. viii. 5.
City of the Holy House, V. xxi. 1. xxiii. 5. xxvii. 3. xxviii. 23, 34. 37. xxx. 8. xxxv. 33. xxxvi. 6, 37, 38. xxxvii. 3, 5. xxxviii. 5. lii. 7. 24. lix. 68.
City of the House of God, V. xxi. 10.
City of Judah, V. xl. 1.
Cleopatra, daughter of Ptolemy Philometor, II. x. 57, 58.
Cleopatra, wife of Ptolemy Physcon, and mother of Ptolemy Lathyrus, V. xxiv. 1— 4. xxviii. 2, 15, 26, 27.
Cleopatra, daughter of Ptolemy Auletes, V. xlviii. 26. xlix. 27. lv. 5, 6. her character, lvi. 1, &c. lvii. 16, 19, 22.
Cloistered court, I. v. 23, and note.
Cnidus, II. xv. 23.
Cœlosyria, I. iii. 15. III. iii. 5, 8. iv. 4. viii. 8. x. 11.
Coin. Leave given to Simon to coin money, II. xv. 6, and note.

Collector, (Apollonius the king's,) II. i. 29.
Constantius Chlorus, I. vii. 11. note.
Corinthians, Apocryphal Epistle to, I. vi. 8, note.
Cos, II. xv. 23.
Country of the Holy House, (i. e. Judæa,) V. viii. 1.
Crassus, V. xli. 2, &c.
Crates, governor of Cyprus, III. iv. 29.
Crete, II. x. 67.
Crown-taxes, II. x. 29. xi. 34. xiii. 39.
Cynæus, V. xxii. 7.
Cyprians, III. iv. 29.
Cypris, Herod's mother, V. xlix. 20.
Cyprus, II. xv. 23. III. x. 13. xii. 2. V. xxiv. 4. xxviii. 27.
Cyrene, II. xv. 23.

D.

Dagon, (or Docus,) a castle, V. xx. 6, 7.
Dagon, the temple of, II. x. 84. xi. 4.
Damascus, II. xi. 62. xii. 32. V. xxxvi. 2, 3, 10, 26, 27, 34. xl. 18. xlii. 25. xlix. 12. liii. 8.
Daniel the prophet, I. vi. 7. II. ii. 60. IV. xvi. 3, 19. xviii. 14. V. xii. 1.
Daphne, III. iv. 33.
Darius (i. e. Arius) king of Sparta, II. xii. 7, and note.
Dathan and Abiram, IV. ii. 17.
Dathema, II. v. 9.
David, II. ii. 57. iv. 30. IV. iii. 7, 8. xviii. 16. his sons, V. xxi. 17.
David, city of, II. i. 33. ii. 31. vii. 32. xiv. 36.
Dedication, V. x. 1.
Delos, II. xv. 23.
Demetrius I. (Soter,) II. vii. 1, 4. viii. 31. ix. 1. x. 2, 3, 15, 22, 25, 48—52. III. xiv. 1, 4, 5, 11. V. xv. 11. xvi. 2, 5. xix. 3.
Demetrius II. (Nicator,) II. x. 67, 69. xi. 9, 12, 19, 30, 32, 38—42, 52, 55, 63. xii. 24. 34. xiii. 34—36. is captured by Arsaces, xiv. 1—3. xv. 22. III. i. 7, 14.
Demetrius III. V. xxix. 6—15.
Demophon, III. xii. 2.
Denarius, the Roman coin, V. ii. 13.
Dessau, III. xiv. 16.
Diogenes, V. xxxii. 1.
Dioscorinthius, the month, III. xi. 21, see note.
Discus, the game of, III, iv. 14.
Docus, II. xvi. 15.
Dora, II. xv. 11, 13.
Dorymenes, II. iii. 38. III. iv. 45.
Dositheus, one of Judas' captains, III. xii. 19, 24, 35.
Dositheus, son of Drimulus, I. i. 4.
Dosithea, Herod's wife, V. lix. 5, 6.
Drachmæ of silver, I. iii. 28. III. iv. 19. x. 20. xii. 43.

E.

Earthquake in Judæa, V. lvi. 18—21, 31.
East, men of the, V. x. 4.
Ecbatana, III. ix. 3.
Egypt, I. ii. 25. iii. 20. iv. 18. vi. 4. vii. 1. II. i. 16, 17, 18, 19, 20, &c. &c. xi. 13, 59. III. i. 1, 10. v. 1, 8, 11. ix. 29. IV. iv. 22. V. ii. 1, 4, 11, 14. xii. 24. xxiii. 8. xxiv. 2. xxviii. 27. xxxi. 1. xl. 6, 15, xlii. 14, 16, 17, 21. xliv. 7, 8. xlviii. 26. xlix. 26. lii. 10, 33. lv. 25. lvi. 9. lvii. 1, 2, 22. lviii. 3.
Egyptians, V. ii. 1. xxiii. 2, 10. xxiv. 2. xl. 16, 19. xlii. 19—23. xliii. 4. xliv. 8.

INDEX.

Elder, (i. e. chief of the Roman senate,) V. xii. 10. xiii. 1, 5. xxii. 1, 3. xxxvi. 23. xlii. 4.
Elders, of Jerusalem, I. i. 23, 25. V. xv. 4. xxxiv. 8. xxxvi. 27. liv. 29. lvi. 19. lviii. 11. lix. 17.
Eleasa, (a place,) II. ix. 5.
Eleazar, a priest, I. vi. 1, 16.
Eleazar Avaran, son of Mattathias, II. ii. 5. vi. 43. V. xv. 8.
Eleazar, (the martyr,) III. vi. 18—31. IV. i. 8. v. 4, 14. vi. 1, 4, 12, 13. vii. 1, 5, 9, 11. ix. 5. xvi. 14. xvii. 13. V. ii. 4, 9, 10. iv. 1, 2, 4, 7, 13. vii. 34.
Eleazar, reads the holy book, III. viii. 23.
Eleazar (another) a priest, V. xli. 4, 6, 7, 8.
Elephants, I. v. 1, 2, 4, 10, 20, 23, 38, 42, 45, 48. vi. 21. II. vi. 34, 35, 46. viii. 6. xi. 56. III. xi. 4. xiii. 15. xiv. 12. V. viii. 7. xi. 2. xv. 2, 5, 7, 9.
'Ελέπολις, an engine of war, II. xiii. 43, note.
Eleutherus, the river, II. xi. 7. xii. 30.
Elias, (Elijah,) II. ii. 58.
Elul, the month, II. xiv. 27.
Elymais, II. vi. 1.
Emmaus, II. iii. 40, 57. ix. 50.
'Εμπαιγμὸς, its meaning, note on III. vii. 7.
Engine of war, ('Ελέπολις,) II. xiii. 43, and note.
Enrol, I. iv. 14.
Enrolment, I. iv. 17.
Ephron, II. v. 46. III. xii. 27.
Epiphanes, or Epimanes, note on II. i. 10.
Epiphanius, (Antiochus Epiphanes,) V. xi. 1.
Epiphi, a month, I. vi. 38.
Esaias, the prophet, IV. xviii. 15.

Esau, children of, II. v. 3, 65.
Eumenes, II. viii. 8.
Eunuchs, V. lix. 32.
Eupator, (Antiochus,) II. vi. 17. III. ii. 20. V. viii. 18. xi. 1, 2. xvi. 1.
Euphrates, II. iii. 32, 37. V. xli. 16. xliv. 11. lii. 2, 8. lix. 30.
Eupolemus, II. viii. 17. III. iv. 11.
Eurycles, V. lix. 71.
Exercise, a place of, II. i. 14. III. iv. 10, 12, 14.
Ezechias (Hezekiah) king of Judah, III. xv. 22. V. xvi. 22.
Ezechiel, the prophet, IV. xviii. 18.
Ezra the priest, V. xxxv. 1.

F.

Fælix, left as governor of Jerusalem by Antiochus Epiphanes, V. iii. 14, and note. iv. 1, 5, 13. v. 54. vi. 7, 10, 19. vii. 8, 33, 34.
Fast, a solemn, V. xxiii. 3.
Feast, of the Dedication of the temple after its profanation by Antiochus, II. iv. 52—59. V. ix. 6.
—— of Tabernacles, III. i. 9. x. 6. V. xx. 17. xxi. 11. xxviii. 34. lv. 20, 23.
—— of Pentecost, or weeks, III. xii. 31, 32.
—— of Purim, or Mardocheus' day, note at III. xv. 36.
—— of the Jews on their deliverance from the elephants, I. vi. 31, &c. vii. 19.
—— of Bacchus, III. vi. 7.
—— of the new altar, V. ix. 6.
—— of joy on Nicanor's death, III. xv. 36. V. xvi. 26.
Fire (holy) kindled in the temple, III. i. 18—22. V. ix. 4, 5.
—— from heaven, III. ii. 10.

INDEX.

G.

Gabatha, V. xxxii. 3.
Gabinius, V. xxxvi. 43, 44. xxxix. 1, 6, 9, 10. xl. 2, 20. xli. 1, 3.
Gadira, V. xxxix. 12.
Galaad, (Gilead,) II. v. 9, 17, 20, 25, 27, 36, 45, 55. xiii. 22.
Galatians, II. viii. 2, and note. III. viii. 20.
Galgala, II. ix. 2.
Galilæans, V. x. 11.
Galilee, II. v. 14, 15, 17, 20, 21, 23, 55. x. 30. xi. 63. xii. 47, 49. V. x. 7, 9. xxviii. 16. lii. 17.
Game, (Olympic,) III. iv. 18. IV. vi. 9.
Garizim, III. v. 23. vi. 2.
Gaza, II. xi. 61, 62. xiii. 43. V. x. 21—23. xx. 4, 5. xxviii. 28—33. its temple destroyed and the city plundered, V. xxviii. 33. xliv. 9.
Gazara, II. iv. 15. vii. 45. ix. 52. xiii. (43?) 53. xiv. 7, 34. xv. 28, 35. xvi. 19, 21. III. x. 32.
Gellius, V. lv. 7, 9.
Genesar, the water of, II. xi. 67.
Gentiles, II. ii. 12, 48. iii. 10. iv. 60. v. 15. vi. 53. III. vi. 4. xi. 2, 24. IV. xviii. 6, 20. V. i. 1. xi. 10. xli. 10.
Gerrhenians, III. xiii. 24.
Giants, I. ii. 4. V. v. 42.
Giares, (i. e. Gilead,) V. x. 5.
Gilead, see *Galaad*.
Gneus, (i. e. Pompey,) his history, V. xxxvi. 1, &c.
Gorgias, II. iv. 1, 5, 18. v. 59. III. viii. 9. x. 14. xii. 32, 35, 36, 37. V. vii. 18, 31, 32. ix. 1. x. 1, 2, 3, 11. xiv. 4, 5.
Gortyna, II. xv. 23.
Governments, the three, II. x. 30, 38. xi. 28, 34.
Governments, the four, II. xi. 57.
Governors, (i. e. the Roman senate,) V. xiii. 1, 5. xxii. 1. xxxvi. 23. xlii. 7, 11.
Grecian, II. vi. 2. viii. 9, 18. III. vi. 8. IV. vi. 9. viii. 10. V. i. 1.
Greece, II. i. 1.
Greek, III. iv. 10. (language,) V. xliv. 16.
Greeks, I. iii. 8. II. i. 10. III. iv. 36. vi. 9. V. xiii. 3. xlviii. 7.
Gymnasium, IV. iv. 20.

H.

Halepus, V. xxi. 25. xxxvi. 2.
Halicarnassus, II. xv. 23.
Hamath, (or Hemath, or Amathis, or Hames,) V. xxviii. 37. xxxvi. 2. xxxix. 12.
Hananias, V. xxiv. 2.
Harbak, king of Judah, V. lvi. 18. See the note.
Hartas, (i. e. Aretas,) V. xxviii. 28, and note, 36. xxxii. 6. xxxv. 20, and note, 35. xxxvi. 6, 9.
Hasdanim, (Assidæans,) the sect described, V. xxv. 5, and note. (xxxii. 12.)
Hebrews, III. vii. 31. xi. 13. xv. 37. IV. iv. 11. v. 2, 4. viii. 3. ix. 18. xvii. 9. V. iii. 9. viii. 11. xxix. 7.
Hebrew tongue, IV. xii. 6. xvi. 14.
Hebron, II. v. 65.
Hegiaz, V. lvi. 45.
Heliodorus, III. iii. 7, 8, 13, 23, 25, 27, 31—33, 35, 37, 40. iv. 1. v. 18. V. i. 2, 3, 7, 14, 16, 18, 19.
Herak, (in Persia,) V. xlix. 17, 18. l. 7. liv. 1.
Hercules, III. iv. 19, 20.
Hermo, I. v. 1, 4, 10, 18, 23, 26, 29, 30, 33, 37.

Herod the Great, son of Antipater, V. xxxv. 3. xlv. 8. xlvi. 1, &c. xlviii. 28, 30, 32, 34. xlix. 2, &c. is appointed king by the Romans, l. 1, &c. he destroys the thieves, li. 1, &c. lii. 1, &c. he takes Jerusalem, 27—32. liii. 1, &c. liv. 2, &c. he destroys Aristobulus, lv. 1, &c. beats the Arabians, lvi. 23—45. goes to Augustus, lvii. 3, &c. puts Mariamne to death, lviii. 1, &c. suspects his sons Aristobulus and Alexander, and slays them, lix. 1, &c.
Herod, son of Aristobulus, Herod's son, V. lix. 95.
Hieronymus, III. xii. 2.
High priest, must not be mutilated in body, V. xlix. 16, 19. liv. 9.
Hippodrome, I. iv. 11. v. 46. vi. 16.
Holy City, I. vi. 5. V. i. 1. xvi. 17. xx. 18. xxi. 26. xxxiv. 7. xxxv. 31. xxxvi. 9, 19, 25. xxxviii. 3. xl. 20. xliii. 12. xlix. 5, 19. l. 2, 16. liv. 13, 26. lv. 37. lvii. 22.
Holy House, V. xx. 7. xxiii. 3. xxxvi. 34. lii. 11, 19. liii. 6. lvi. 17, 44. lix. 17, 35, 68. See note at V. xx. 7.
Holy Land, V. vii. 35. xvi. 7. xlviii. 20. lii. 3.
Holy place, I. i. 10. iii. 17. III. ii. 18. IV. iv. 9.
House (a) falls upon Herod, V. lii. 18.
House of the sanctuary, V. viii. 16.
House (the) i. e. the temple, V. i. 2, &c. &c. xxi. &c. xxxvi. 52. xli. 6. lv. 26.
House of sanctification, I. ii. 18.
House of God, V. i. 1, 7. vii. 21. ix. 7. xi. 7. xvi. 16, 17. xxvii. 4. xxxiv. 9, 10. xli. 2, 5. xliv. 9. lii. 31. liv. 13. lv 20.
Houses of abomination, I. ii. 18.
Hyrcanus, grandson of Tobias, III. iii. 11.
Hyrcanus, a man from whom John Hyrcanus obtained his surname, V. xx. 1—3.
Hyrcanus, John, son of Simon, his history, V. xx. 1, &c. xxi. 1, &c. xxii. 1, &c. he styles himself king, V. xxii. 8. xxiii. 1, &c. his death, xxvi. 1, &c. xxviii. 3. xxxi. 1, 2. xxxii. 4. Hyrcanus, son of Alexander Jannæus, V. xxxi. 6. xxxiii. 6, 7. is appointed high priest under his brother Aristobulus, xxxiv. 1, &c. xxxv. 5, &c. xxxvi. 3, &c. is appointed king by Pompey, xxxvii. 1, &c. xxxviii. 1, &c. xxxix. 3, 6, 11. xl. 7, 17, 20. xli. 15. xlii. 15, 18. xliii. 2, 12. xliv. 1, &c. xlvi. 7. xlvii. 3. xlviii. 3, 9—11, 20, 29, 30. xlix. 2, 7, 10—12. he is mutilated, xlix. 16, 19. he returns to Jerusalem, and is put to death by Herod, liv. 1—35.

I. J.

Jacob, I. vi. 3, 13. II. i. 28. iii. 7, 45. v. 2. III. i. 2. IV. ii. 19. vii. 17. xiii. 14. xvi. 22.
Jambri, children of, II. ix. 36.
Jamnia, II. iv. 15. x. 69. xv. 40.
Jamnites, III. xii. 8, 9. xii. 40.
Jason, son of Eleazar, II. viii. 17.
Jason of Cyrene, III. ii. 23.
Jason, the high priest, III. i. 7. iv. 7, 13, 19, 22—26. v. 5, 6. IV. iv. 16.
Jazer, II. v. 8.
Idols, (a city of two,) V. vii. 32.
Idumæa, II. iv. 15, 29, 61. v.

3. vi. 31. III. xii. 32. V. xiv. 4. xxi. 29.
Idumæans, III. x. 15, 16. V. x. 1. receive circumcision, xxi. 30. xxxv. 3, 4.
Jeremiah, the prophet, III. ii. 1, 5, 7. xv. 14, 15.
Jericho, II. ix. 50. xvi. 11, 14. III. xii. 15. V. xxxix. 12. lii. 11. lv. 23—28.
Jerusalem, I. i. 9. iii. 16. II. i. 14, 20, 38, &c. &c. V. xxviii. 17, &c. &c.
Jesus, (i. e. Joshua,) II. ii. 55.
Jezabel, mount, V. xxi. 28.
Jewish, I. vii. 10. IV. iv. 19. V. xi. 17.
Jewish sects, V. xxv. 1, &c. xxviii. 1, &c.
Jewish women and children slain by Lythras, V. xxviii. 25.
Jews, I. i. 8. ii. 28. iii. 3, &c. &c. V. vii. 19, &c.
Images of himself made by Antiochus Epiphanes, and ordered to be worshipped, V. iii. 4, 5, 14.
India, II. viii. 8.
Indian, ruler of the elephant, II. vi. 37.
Indias, the country of, V. xlviii. 12.
Joannan, II. ii. 2. he is called *Joseph* at III. viii. 22.
Joarib, or Jarib, II. ii. 1. xiv. 29.
John, son of Simeon, and father of Mattathias, II. ii. 1. V. vi. 1.
John, son of Accos, II. viii. 17. III. iv. 11.
John, Maccabæus, II. ix. 35, 36, 38.
John, or Jochanan, (Hyrcanus,) son of Simon, II. xiii. 53. xvi. 1, 2, 9, 19, 21, 23. his history, V. xx. 1, &c. See *Hyrcanus.*

John, (sent ambassador to Lysias,) III. xi. 17.
Jonas, the prophet, I. vi. 8.
Jonathan, the son of Saul, II. iv. 30.
Jonathan Maccabæus, II. ii. 5. v. 17, 55. ix. 19, 28. takes the government on him, II. ix. 31, 33—73. x. 3—18. puts on the high priest's robe, 21, 46, 74, &c. xi. 5—7, 20—23, 28—30, &c. xii. 1, 3, &c. he is taken, 48. and slain, xiii. 23. III. viii. 22. xii. 5, &c. &c. V. xvii. 3. his history, V. xviii. 1—8.
Jonathan, the son of Absalom, II. xiii. 11.
Jonathan, contemporary with Nehemiah, III. i. 23.
Joppe, II. x. 75, 76. xi. 6. xii. 33. xiii. 11. xiv. 5, 34. xv. 28, 35. III. iv. 21. xii. 3, 6.
Jordan, the marsh of, II. ix. 42.
Joseph, the patriarch, II. ii. 53. IV. ii. 2. xviii. 13.
Joseph, son of Zacharias, II. v. 18, 56, 60.
Joseph (Johannan) Maccabæus, III. viii. 22. x. 19.
Joseph, son of Antipater, V. xxxv. 3. xlix. 20, 24, 26. l. 8—14. he is slain, lii. 11, 12.
Josephus, a Tyrian, Herod's brother-in-law, V. lvii. 4. lviii. 1, 4, 8, 11.
Joshua, the son of Nun, III. xii. 15.
Isaac, the patriarch, III. i. 2. IV. vii. 17. xiii. 10, 14. xvi. 18, 22. xviii. 13.
Israel, I. ii. 6, 10, 16. vi. 4, 9. II. i. 20, 25, 36, 53, &c. &c. IV. xvii. 21.
Israelites, II. i. 43. iii. 46. v. 9. vii. 23. IV. xviii. 1.
Ituræa, note on V. xxvii. 30.
Judæa, I. v. 43. II. iii. 34. v. 18, 60. vi. 12, 48. vii. 24,

46. ix. 50. x. 38, 45. xi. 20, 28, 34. xii. 35. xiv. 33. xv. 30, 39—41. III. i. 1, 10. v. 14. x. 24. xi. 5. xiii. 1, 13. xiv. 12, 14. V. iii. 6.

Judæa divided into five portions by Gabinius, V. xxxix. 10—12.

Judah, land of, II. i. 29, 44, 51, &c. &c. V. xi. &c. &c.
—— towns of, V. xxxii. 9, 11.
—— tribe of, V. ii. 11. lvi. 38.

Judaism, III. ii. 21. xiv. 38.

Judas Maccabæus, II. ii. 4. iii. 1, &c. viii. 20. is killed, II. ix. 18. III. ii. 19. v. 27. viii. 1, 12. xii. 5, &c. xiii. 1, &c. xiv. 1, &c. his battles, V. vi. 1—19. viii. 1. x. 1, &c. xi. 1, &c. xiii. 1, &c. xiv. 1, &c. xv. 1, &c. xvi. 1, &c. his death, xvii. 1, &c.

Judas, the son of Calphi, II. xi. 70.

Judas, son of Simon Maccabæus, II. xvi. 2, 9, 14.

Judas, III. i. 10. ii. 14.

Julius, V. xlii. 2.

Jupiter, III. vi. 2, and note.

Ivy-leaf, I. ii. 29. III. vi. 7.

K.

Καθάρσιον (αἷμα), note on IV. vi. 24.

Kingdom of the Greeks, (i. e. æra of the Seleucidæ,) II. i. 10.

Kings of the second house, V. liii. 8.

L.

Lacedæmonians, II. xii. 2, 5, 6, 21. xiv. 20, 23. xv. 23. III. v. 9.

Lalis, V. xvii. 2.

Land of the sanctuary, (i. e. Judæa,) V. x. 35.

Laodicea, V. xliv. 11.

Lasthenes, II. xi. 31, 32.

Law of Moses, its great power, IV. ii. 5, &c. v. 16, &c.

"Law (the) and the Prophets," IV. xviii. 12.

Levi the patriarch, IV. ii. 19.

Lucius, Roman consul, II. xv. 16.

Lycia, II. xv. 23.

Lydda, II. xi. 34.

Lydia, II. viii. 8.

Lysias, II. iii. 32. 38. iv. 26, 28, 34, 35. vi. 6, 17, 55. vii. 2. III. x. 11. xi. 1, 12, 15, 16, 22, 35. xii. 1, 27. xiii. 2, 4. xiv. 1. V. vii. 12, 18, 36. viii. 2. xi. 2, 4, 6, 7, 14, 17. xv. 3, 12. xvi. 2.

Lysimachus, III. iv. 29, 39—41.

Lythras, (i. e. Ptolemy Lathyrus,) V. xxiii. 8. his history, V. xxiv. 1, &c. xxviii. 2.

M.

Maccabæus, (Judas,) II. ii. 4, 66. iii. 1. v. 34. III. viii. 5, 16. x. 1, 16, 19, 21, 25, 30, 33, 35. xi. 6, 7, 15. xiv. 27, 30. xv. 7, 21.

Maccabees, the sepulchre of, II. xiii. 27—30.

Macedon, or Macedonia, V. i. 2, 17. ii. 1. iii. 1. v. 54. x. 4. xvi. 1. xxix. 6. xlv. 8. xlvii. 13. xlviii. 1.

Macedonians, III. viii. 20. V. x. 7, 9, 11. xvii. 1. xxiii. 2. xxix. 7, 8, 10.

Machmas, (Michmash,) II. ix. 73.

Maked, II. v. 26, 36.

Malchiah, V. xlvi. 1—7. his death, xlvii. 1, &c.

Mallos, III. iv. 30.

Manlius, (Titus,) III. xi. 34.

Marcus, (Mark Antony,) V. xxxix. 8.

Mardocheus' day, III. xv. 36.

Mariamne, V. xlix. 20. liv. 16.

lv. 2, 39, 40, 42, 43. lvii. 4, is entrapped by Salome, and put to death by Herod, lviii. 1—17. her character, 18—22. lix. 5.
Marisa, III. xii. 35.
Martyrdom of seven brethren, III. vii. 1, &c. IV. viii. 4, &c.
Maseloth, II. ix. 2.
Maspha, II. iii. 46. v. 35.
Mattathias, II. ii. 1, 14, 16, 17, 19, 24, 27, 39, 45, 49. xiv. 29. V. vi. 1—19. vii. 1, &c. xvii. 15.
Mattathias, one of Judas' and Jonathan's captains, II. xi. 70. iii. 14, 19.
Mattathias, son of Simon Maccabæus, II. xvi. 14.
Medaba, II. ix. 36.
Medes, II. i. 1.
Media, II. vi. 56. viii. 8. xiv. 2.
Memmius, (Quintus,) III. xi. 34.
Menelaus, III. iv. 23—50. v. 5, 15, 23. xi. 29, 32. xiii. 3. is put to death, xiii. 7. V. iii. 6. xv. 14.
Menestheus, III. iv. 21.
Μεριδάρχης, its meaning. Note on II. x. 65.
Mina, of gold or silver, I. i. 5. and note, II. xiv. 24. xv. 18. V. xli. 4.
Mingling with the Gentiles, III. xiv. 3, 38.
Misael, (one of the three children,) IV. xvi. 3, 19. xviii. 14.
Mithridates, V. xlii. 13—25. xliv. 6.
Moab, the country of, V. xxix. 19.
Modin, II. ii. 1, 15, 23, 70. ix. 19. xiii. 25, 30. xvi. 4. III. xiii. 14.
Moses, III. i. 29. ii. 4, 8, 10, 11. vii. 6, 30. IV. ii. 17. ix. 2. xvii. 18. xviii. 19.

Mother (the) of the seven brethren; her trials, and fortitude, IV. xiv. 9, &c. xv. *passim*. her death and eulogy, ch. xvii.—her address, ch. xviii. and V. ch. v.
Mountain of the house, II. iv. 46.
Mounts for shot, II. vi. 20, 51.
Myndus, II. xv. 23.

N.

Nabathites, or Nabathæans, II. v. 25. ix. 35.
Nadabatha, II. ix. 37.
Nanæa, III. i. 13, 15.
Nasor, the plain of, II. xi. 67.
Nazarites, II. iii. 49.
Neapolis, (i. e. Sichem,) V. xxi. 27.
Neemias, III. i. 18—36. ii. 13.
Nepthai, Nepthar, III. i. 36.
Nicanor, II. vii. 26, &c. to 47. viii. 1. III. viii. 9—24. ix. 3. xii. 2. xiv. 12—39. his death, xv. 1—37. V. vii. 18—36. ix. 1. xvi. 6—24.
Nicomedes, V. xxxvi. 10, 20, 26.
Nicolaus Damascenus. Note on V. liv. 32.
Nile, the river, V. ii. 14.
Noah, his ark, IV. xv. 26.
Nomades of Arabia, III. xii. 11.
Numenius, son of Antiochus, II. xii. 16. xiv. 22. xv. 15.

O.

Ocean, the western, V. xlviii. 12.
Octavian, (i. e. Augustus Cæsar,) V. xlvii. 13. his history, xlviii. 1, &c.
Odollam, III. xii. 38.
Odonarces, II. ix. 66.
Olympius, (Jupiter,) III. vi. 2.
Onias II, (high priest,) II. xii. 7, 8, 19, 20.
Onias III, (high priest,) III. iii.

458 INDEX.

1, 5, 31, 33, 35. iv. 1, 4, 7, 33. is slain, 34, 36, 38. appears to Judas, III. xv. 12, 14. IV. iv. 1, 13, 16. V. i. 6, 13—16.
Orthosias, II. xv. 37.

P.

Pachon, a month, I. vj. 38.
Pamphylia, II. xv. 23.
Panthers, (in cruelty,) IV. ix. 28.
Paper and pens, I. iv. 20.
Pappus, V. lii. 12, 14, 19. he is killed, 20.
Patroclus, III. viii. 9.
Pentecost, III. xii. 32. V. xxi. 23.
Persepolis, III. ix. 2.
Perseus, king of Macedon, II. viii. 5.
Persia, Persians, II. i. 1. iii. 31. vi. 1, 5, 56. III. i. 13, 19, 20, 33. ix. 1, 21. IV. xviii. 7. V. iii. 3. vii. 11, 13, 17. viii. 1.
Persia, (i. e. Parthia,) II. xiv. 2. V. xxi. 19, 20, 21, 23, 24, xlix. 6. see note at V. xxi. 19.
Persians, (Parthians,) V. xl. 18. xli. 1, 11, 12, 14. xliii. 9. xliv. 8. xlviii. 35. xlix. 1, &c. l. 7. lii. 1, 2. liv. 1.
Πέτασος, introduced by Antiochus Epiphanes, III. iv. 12.
Petra. Note at V. xxxv. 20.
Phalaris, I. v. 20, 42.
Pharaoh, I. ii. 6. vi. 4. II. iv. 9.
Pharathoni, II. ix. 50.
Pharisees, V. xxv. 1, &c. xxvi. 7. their quarrels, xxviii. 1, &c. xxx. 4, 10, 13. xxxi. 1, &c. xxxii. 1, &c. xxxiii. 4, &c. xxxiv. 4.
Phaselis, II. xv. 23.
Phaselus, son of Antipater, V. xxxv. 3. xlviii. 28. xlix. 11, 12, 16, 19.
Phasiron, children of, II. ix. 66.

Pheroras, son of Antipater, V. xxxv. 3. lii. 13, 20. lix. 29, 30, 47, 48, 57, 58, 60.
Philip, father of Alexander the Great, II. i. 1. vi. 2.
Philip of Macedon, II. viii. 5.
Philip, foster brother of Antiochus Epiphanes, II. vi. 14, 55, 63. III. v. 22. vi. 11. viii. 8. ix. 29. xiii. 23. V. xv. 11.
Philistines, II. iii. 41. and note. iv. 30. v. 66, 68. IV. iii. 8. V. vii. 19. xxix. 19.
Philometor, (Ptolemy,) III. x. 13.
Phineas, II. ii. 26, 54. IV. xviii. 14.
Phœnice, I. iii. 15. III. iii. 5, 8. iv. 4, 22. viii. 8. x. 11. IV. iv. 2.
Phrygian, III. v. 22.
Phylarches, III. viii. 32.
Pictures, (idolatrous,) note on II. iii. 48.
Pilate, V. lix. 25. see the note.
Poetry, Greek, I. v. 31. vi. 2, &c. (notes.)
Πολυάνδριον, its signification. Note on III. ix. 4.
Pompey, (see also Gnæus,) V. xxxvi. 10, &c. xxxvii. 1, &c. xxxviii. 1, &c. xxxix. 2. xl. 6, 13. xli. 3, 17. xlii. 4, 11, 15. xliii. 1, &c. xliv. 13. xlv. 1.
Posidonius. III. xiv. 19.
Principle, its definition, IV. i. 15.
Prophet, (one expected,) II. iv. 46. ix. 27. xiv. 41.
Ptolemais, the rose-bearing, I. vii. 17.
Ptolemais, (in Phœnicia,) II. v. 15, 22, 55. x. 1, 39, 56—60. xi. 22, 24. xii. 45, 48. xiii. 12, 24, 25. V. xxviii. 2, 5, 9. l. 8.
Ptolemy I, (Lagus,) note at I. iii. 21. vi. 25.

Ptolemy II, (Philadelphus,) obtains a translation of the Hebrew scriptures, V. ii.
Ptolemy IV, (Philopator, or Eupator,) I. i. 1, 3, 4, 7. iii. 11, 12. vii. 1.
Ptolemy VI, (Philometor,) II. i. 18. x. 51, 55, 57. xi. 3, 8, 13, 15—18. III. iv. 2. ix. 29. x. 13. IV. iv. 22. V. iii. 2. x. 3—33.
Ptolemy VII, (Euergetes II, or Physcon,) III. i. 10.
Ptolemy XIII, (Dionysius Novus,) V. xl. 15—20.
Ptolemy, the son of Abubus, II. xvi. 11, 16, 18, 21. V. xix. 9. xx. 4—10.
Ptolemy, Macron, son of Dorymenes, II. iii. 38. III. iv. 45, 46. vi. 8. viii. 8. x. 12. V. vii. 18, 31, 32. ix. 1. xiv. 1, 3.

R.

Ragaba, V. xxx. 2.
Ramathem, II. xi. 34.
Raphia, I. i. 2.
Raphon, II. v. 37.
Region of the Holy House, V. xi. 9.
Register, I. ii. 29. iv. 15. vi. 34, 38.
Registry, I. ii. 28, 29, 32. vii. 22. *inventory*
Rhazis, III. xiv. 37. (V. xvi. 18.)
Rhodocus, III. xiii. 21.
Rhodus, II. xv. 23. V. lvii. 2.
Romans, the language of, V. xliv. 16.
Romans, II. viii. 1, 21—29. xi. 4, 16. xiv. 40. xv. 16. III. viii. 10, 36. xi. 34. account of their power, V. xii. 1—26. their treaty with Judas, II. viii. V. 13. xvi. 2, 7. xxi. 32, 33. their letter to Hyrcanus, V. xxii. 1, &c. xxxvi. 1, &c. xxxvii. 3. xxxviii. 1, 2.
xl. 2, 13—16. xli. 13—17. xlii. 4, &c. xliv. 1, 4, 6, 8. xlv. 8. xlix. 5, 26. l. 15, 16. lii. 2, 11, 16, 29. lvi. 4. lvii. 1. lviii. 20.
Rome, II. vii. 1. viii. 17, 19. xi. 1, 3. xiv. 16, 24. xv. 15. III. iv. 11. V. xii. 7, 15, 17, 22. xxxvi. 23. xxxviii. 1. xxxix. 1. xl. 5, 20. xli. 1. xlii. 1, &c. xliii. 12. xliv. 15. xlv. 2, 4. xlvii. 13. xlviii. 35. xlix. 1, 27, 28. l. 3. liv. 4. lvii. 22. lviii. 20. lix. 35.

S.

Sabat, the month, II. xvi. 14.
Sabbatical year, IV. ii. 8.
Sadoc, V. xxv. 23.
Sadducees, V. xxv. 3, 7, &c. xxix. 1, &c. xxxi. 4, 7. xxxii. 1, &c. xxxiii. 2, &c.
Samaria, II. iii. 10. v. 66. x. 30, 38. xi. 28, 34. III. xv. 1. V. xxi. 27.
Samaritans, V. xxi. 28. xxiii. 1, 4, 8, 10.
Samos, II. xv. 23.
Sampsames, II. xv. 23, and note.
Sanballat, V. xxi. 28.
Sanctuary, II. i. 21, 36, 37, 39, 45, 46. ii. 7, 12. iii. 45, 51, 58, 59. iv. 36, 38, 41, 43, 48. vi. 7, 18, 26, 51. x. 39, 44. xiv. 15, 29, 31, 36, 42, 48. xv. 7. III. ii. 17. xv. 17. V. vii. 3. viii. 16. ix. 3. xxvii. 6. xlix. 5.
Sarah, (mount,) V. x. 1. xiv. 4. xxi. 29. xxix. 19. xxxv. 4. xlix. 20, 24. l. 8, 13. liv. 45. lvii. 4.
Saramel, II. xiv. 28, and note.
Scaurus, V. xxxvi. 3. xxxvii. 5. xxxviii. 3.
Schedia, a seaport, I. iv. 11.
Scipio, V. xii. 10, 11, 14, 18, 19, 23, 24, 26.

Scorpions, engines of war, II. vi. 51.
Scythian barbarity, I. vii. 5.
Scythians, III. iv. 47.
Scythopolis, (Bethsan,) III. xii. 29.
Scythopolitans, III. xii. 30.
Sebaste, V. xvi. 13. xxi. 28. xxiii. 1, 6, 7, 11. lix. 94.
Sects, Jewish, V. xxv. 1, &c.
Seleucia, II. xi. 8.
Seleucus I, (Nicanor,) IV. iii. 21.
Seleucus IV, (Philopator,) II. vii. 1. III. iii. 3. iv. 7. v. 18. IV. iv. 3, 4, 13, 15. V. i. 2, 17.
Senate, (Roman,) II. viii. 19, 22. xii. 3. note on II. viii. 15. V. xii. 10. xl. 12. xlix. 29. l. i. 3. lii. 9.
Senate-house, (Roman,) II. viii. 15.
Seniors, I. i. 23.
Sennacherim, I. vi. 5. III. viii. 19. xv. 22. V. xvi. 21.
Sephela, II. xii. 38.
Sephoris, V. xxxix. 12.
Sepulchre of the Maccabees, II. xiii. 27—30. V. xvii. 15.
Seron, II. iii. 13, 23. V. vii. 8.
Serpent, seducer, IV. xviii. 10, and note.
Seven brethren martyred, III. vii. IV. viii—xii. V. v.
Shadrach, &c. I. vi. 6, note.
Shekels of silver, II. x. 40, 42.
Shield of gold, II. xiv. 24. xv. 18, 20.
Shields of brass, V. xxviii. 18.
Sichemites, IV. ii. 19.
Sicyon, II. xv. 23.
Side, II. xv. 23.
Sidon, II. v. 15. V. x. 7. xxviii. 4, 10, 12, 14. xliv. 4, 9, 17. xlviii. 24.
Simalcue, II. xi. 39.
Simeon, the patriarch, IV. ii. 19.
Simon II, high priest, I. ii. 1.

Simon Maccabæus, II. ii. 3, 65. v. 17, 20, 21. ix. 19, 33, 62, 65, 67. x. 74, 82. xi. 59, 64, 65. xii. 33, 38. he succeeds Jonathan as leader of the Jews, xiii. 1, &c. &c. recovers the tower in Jerusalem, xiii. 49—52. the decree of the Jews concerning him, xiv. 27—49. has permission to coin money, xv. 6, 24, 26, 32, 33, 36. is entrapped and slain by Ptolemy, xvi. 1, 2, 13, &c. III. viii. 22. x. 19, 20. xiv. 17. V. x. 9—11, 17, 3. xviii. 4, 6, 8. his history, V. xix. 1, &c.
Simon, governor of the temple, III. iii. 4. iv. 1, 3, 4. iv. 23. IV. iv. 1, 4. V. iii. 6.
Sinful nation, denoting the Gentiles, note on II. i. 34.
Sion, or Zion, (mount,) II. iv. 37, 60. v. 54. vi. 48, 62. x. 11. xiv. 27.
Sirens, their melodies, IV. xv. 19.
Sodomites, I. ii. 5.
Solomon, III. ii. 8, 10, 12. IV. xviii. 17.
Sosipater, III. xii. 19, 24.
Sosius, V. lii. 7, 10, 16, 24, 25, 29—33.
Sostratus, III. iv. 27, 29.
Spain, II. viii. 3.
Sparta, II. xiv. 16.
Swans, their musical notes, IV. xv. 19.
Syria, Syrians, II. iii. 13, 41. vii. 39. xi. 2, 60. IV. iv. 2. V. ii. 11. v. 54. vii. 19. xxi. 25. xxxvi. 2, 7. xxxix. 1. xl. 9, 10, 17. xli. 2, 13, 14. xlii. 13. xlviii. 26. xlix. 4. lii. 8, 10.
Syrian tongue, III. xv. 36.

T.

Table (a splendid gold) pre-

sented by Ptolemy Philadelphus to the temple at Jerusalem, V. ii. 14, &c.
Talents, of silver, gold, &c. II. xi. 28. xiii. 16. xv. 31, 35. III. iii. 11. iv. 24. v. 21. IV. iv. 17. V. xxi. 15. xxxvi. 10. xli. 8. xlv. 7. xlix. 1. lii. 13. lix. 67.
Taphon, II. ix. 50.
Tarquin, king of Rome, V. xlii. 7.
Tarsus, III. iv. 30.
Temple of Jerusalem, I. i. 10. v. 43, &c. &c. profaned by Antiochus, II. i. 54, &c. recovered and purified by Judas Maccabæus, iv. 43, &c. III. x. 1, &c. V. xvi. 17. xxi. 13. xxxvi. 42, 49, 50, is entered by Pompey, xxxvi. 51, 52. xli. 6—9. xlviii. 20, 21. lv. 17.
——— the liberties of, II. x. 43.
Thamnatha, II. ix. 50.
Thecoe, wilderness of, II. ix. 33.
Theodotus of Ætolia, I. i. 3, and note.
Theodotus, one of Judas' captains, III. xiv. 19.
Thieves destroyed by Herod, V. li. 1, &c.
Thracia, III. xii. 35.
Tigranes, see *Tyrcanes*.
Timotheus, II. v. 6, 11, 34, 37, 40. III. viii. 30, 32. ix. 3. x. 24, 32, 37. xii. 2, 10, 18, 21, 24.
Tobie, the places of, II. v. 13.
Torah, the religion of, V. xxi. 29.
Torture, various instruments of, IV. viii. 14, &c.
Tower (the) in Jerusalem, II. i. 33—36. vi. 18, 24, 26. ix. 53. x. 6, 9, 32. xi. 20—22, 41. xii. 36. xiii. is recovered by Simon, xiii. 49—52. xiv. 7, 36. xv. 28. III. xv. 31, 35.
Towers, on the elephants. Note on II. vi. 37.
Treasury of Jerusalem, II. xiv. 49. III. iii. 6, 24, 28, v. 18. IV. iv. 3. V. i. 1, 2, 16. viii. 15. xxi. 17. xli. 6.
Treaty, between Judas and the Romans, II. viii. V. xiii.
Treaty, between Judas and Antiochus Eupator, V. xv. 2, 12.
Tripolis, III. xiv. 1.
Tryphon, II. xi. 39, 54, 56. xii. 39, 42, 49. xiii. 1, 12, 14, 19—24. seizes the throne, xiii. 31, 34. is attacked by Antiochus, xv. 10, 25, 37, 39.
Tubieni, III. xii. 17.
Tyrcanes, king of Armenia, V. xxxvi. 1.
Tyrcanes, son of Alexander, Herod's son, V. lix. 95.
Tyre, } II. v. 15. III. iv. 18,
Tyrus, } 32, 44, 49. V. x. 7. xxviii. 4, 37. xliv. 4, 17. xlvii. 2. xlviii. 24, 32. lix. 83.
——— the ladder of, II. xi. 59, and note.

V.

Varro, a Roman consul, V. xii. 5, 7.
Venusia, V. xii. 7.
Viceroy, V. v. 34.
Vineyard of gold, presented to Pompey by Aristobulus, V. xxxvi. 10, 23.
Visions, or apparitions. *viz.*
——— of a horse and rider, scourging Heliodorus, III. iii. 24, &c. 33, &c. V. i. 8, &c.
——— of troops of horsemen in the air, III. v. 2, &c. V. iii. 7.

Visions, of Onias and Jeremiah appearing to Judas, III. xv. 12—14.
――― of an armed warrior on horseback, III. xi. 8. V. xi. 10.
――― of five mounted warriors, III. x. 29, 30. V. x. 16.
――― of angels riding on horses, and terrifying Apollonius, IV. iv. 10, &c.

W.

West, the land of the, V. x. 3.

X.

Xanthicus, the month, III. xi. 30, 33, 38.

Z.

Zabadæans, II. xii. 31.
Zabdiel, the Arabian, II. xi. 17.
Zacchæus, III. x. 19.
Zambri, son of Salom, II. ii. 26.
Zion, see *Sion*.